The Marches

ALSO BY RORY STEWART

Non-Fiction

The Places In Between
Occupational Hazards: My Time Governing in Iraq

As co-author

Can Intervention Work? (with Gerald Knaus)

The Marches

Border Walks with My Father

RORY STEWART

JONATHAN CAPE
LONDON

1 3 5 7 9 10 8 6 4 2

Jonathan Cape, an imprint of Vintage Publishing,
20 Vauxhall Bridge Road,
London SW1V 2SA

Jonathan Cape is part of the Penguin Random House group of companies whose addresses can be found at global.penguinrandomhouse.com

First published by Jonathan Cape in 2016

penguin.co.uk/vintage

A CIP catalogue record for this book is available from the British Library

ISBN 9780224097680

Typeset in India by Thomson Digital Pvt Ltd, Noida, Delhi

Printed and bound in Great Britain by Clays Ltd, St Ives PLC

To my mother

List of Maps

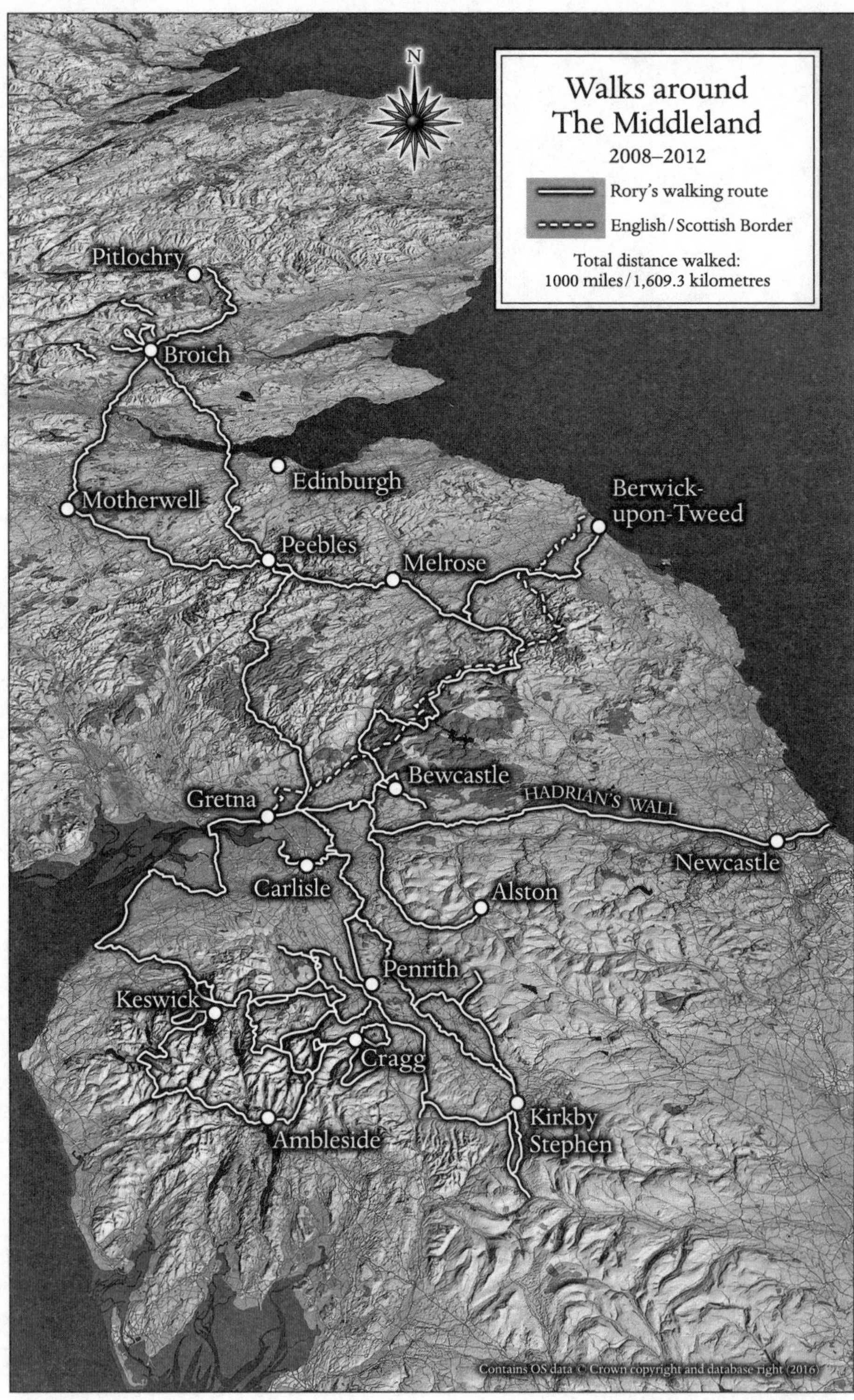

N
Walks around
The Middleland
2008–2012
Rory's walking route
English/Scottish Border
Total distance walked:
1000 miles/1,609.3 kilometres
Pitlochry
Broich
Edinburgh
Motherwell
Berwick-
upon-Tweed
Peebles
Melrose
Bewcastle
HADRIAN'S WALL
Gretna
Newcastle
Carlisle
Alston
Penrith
Keswick
Cragg
Kirkby
Stephen
Ambleside
Contains OS data © Crown copyright and database right (2016)

The Marches

BOOK ONE

The wall

Preface

I was five years old and it was just before six in the morning. I walked into my parents' room and poked the shape on the right-hand side of the bed. My father's head emerged. He rolled himself upright, retied his checked sarong, pushed his white hair flat on his head and led me back out of the bedroom. Once we had dressed, we marched to Hyde Park for fencing practice. Then we marched back to the house and laid out toy soldiers on the floor to re-enact the Battle of Waterloo. The front line was the Highland Division. (We had painted the feathers on their bearskins red, and their kilts green and black, to show that they were the Black Watch.) Behind them were the redcoats of the English line. Our Dutch, Hanoverian and Prussian allies were not represented.

Then we had a shower. I admired the gash on the outside of his right thigh. It had once been almost six inches long and an inch deep, cut open by shrapnel from a German shell. He thought it was a mortar shell. An expert on the Black Watch's role in the Battle of Rauray in 1944 thought it was more likely to have been a shell fired by an MK IV or a StuG III assault gun. Thirty-four years after the battle, it was just the right size into which to fit my index finger.

Best was the sound when he held me against his chest and sang. He had what he called 'a British baritone'. In the shower, we sang, 'With cat-like tread, upon the prey we steal. No sound at all. We never speak a word. A fly's footfall would be distinctly heard.' Or arpeggios and scales.

With my ears to his chest, I could hear his voice and a slight vibrato echoing through his broad ribcage. His accent was stronger when he sang, as though his training in music as a seventeen year old had trapped, for posterity, the Scottish accent of his youth.

Ho rrro the nut-brrrown maiden
Ho rrro the nut-brrrown maiden

Ho rrro, rrro, maiden
Forrr she's the girrrl forrr me.

This evening, he was home early, and had gone to the drawing room to have a drink with my mother. This meant I could show him my plane. I had folded a piece of A4 paper in half, turned the corners in to make an arrow-head, flattened the edges for wings and placed it for the first time on a landing strip – two felt-tip lines on a cardboard box. I did not normally spend much time in the drawing room. As my father said, 'Not fun for the adults, not fun for the children. Not the right room.' So I entered politely.

My father, who was talking to my mother, smiled, put down his whisky carefully to avoid marking the table, and received the plane. 'How's the little flower?' he asked, kissing me on the head. But when he dropped the plane back into the cardboard box, it was clear from the position into which it fell that he had ignored my new runway. I was frustrated.

Leaving again, I drew red, white and blue RAF badges on the wings, twisted up the flaps, drew circles down the centre of the box to re-emphasise the runway and returned to the drawing room. My father looked at the plane again very briefly, smiled and gave it back.

This time, I left the drawing room, closed the door and wrote a note which said, 'Because you would not look at my plane and runway, I am running away.' I placed the note outside the door, with the plane neatly on its track, and went downstairs. When I heard my parents' footsteps on the landing, I hid behind the curtains in the dining room.

Through a gap, I saw them coming down, heading for the front door. In my father's right hand was the note and the cardboard box. He held my mother's hand with his left. He was not paying attention to my creation – in fact he had tipped the box, so that the plane had slid sideways once more.

I saw from his face how frightened he was. I realised how easily I could hurt him. I never wanted to see him like that again.

I

Thirty-three years later, in 2011, my father and I decided to march the length of Hadrian's Wall together. I thought this walk would allow us to explore and answer questions about Scottish nationalism, Rome, frontiers and empires. He probably thought it was a good opportunity to spend some time with his son. My father, who was eighty-nine, travelled down from our house in Scotland. I came across from my cottage in English Cumbria.

We were to meet in a B&B at Newcastle – the east end of the wall. He was out when I arrived. I found his Black Watch tie – its knot left intact 'to save time' – on the back of a chair. On the desk was a vigorously underlined guidebook to the wall. One saucer on the bedside table contained two used teabags; the other had been turned into a palette. Thick whorls of black and red paint lay around the rim. He had put his brushes in glasses lifted from the bathroom. Each was now stained by an inch of purple water.

On a bath-towel, he had laid a roundel of Boursin cheese. The blade of his wooden-handled penknife was buried in the cheese. And beside it on the bed lay a sheet of A4 printer paper, crinkled with wet paint. The image he had painted on the paper was presumably supposed to be his lurcher Torquil. The door opened slowly behind me. A deep bass-baritone voice said, 'Hello, darling.' He hugged me, and because this man, once six foot tall, was now only five foot six, I kissed him on the forehead. Pointing to the dog in the picture, he added, 'The only thing I've got right about him is that he's black.'

We had spent much time together in hotel bedrooms. In a hotel in Austria, when I was six, he had tried to teach me three proofs of the existence of God, which he had just read in a paperback introduction to philosophy: he favoured Aquinas. I went to boarding school when I was eight and then we often met at weekends in the bedroom of his B&B in

Oxford. Our diet by then had ceased to be chocolate milk and became instead tropical fruit juice, oatcakes, pâté and Boursin.

It was on that bed in his Oxford B&B that he encouraged me to paint a heroic picture of Magellan being clubbed by a giant Polynesian on a beach. It was there that he encouraged me to sing Gilbert and Sullivan until I was polished enough to get the part of Koko in the school *Mikado*. And it was there that we worked on an essay on the Battle of Culloden; and there too that he listened while I played the bagpipe chanter.

In a hotel bedroom in Taiwan, when I was fifteen, he watched me study Chinese qigong. He preferred more direct self-defence, usually beginning with a knee to the groin, and another knee to the chin, but he patiently admired my attempts at breathing exercises.

Now, though, I had to write an article for my local newspaper about the community hospital. I perched on my bed, grimacing and tapping at the keyboard, and he, politely, returned to his painting. After an hour or so, he looked up and, seeing me still at work, said he was going to bed. I could see he would have liked to chat. As I continued to work, I was vaguely aware of his familiar movements in and out of the bathroom.

The checked Malay sarong he wore to sleep looked like a cotton tartan kilt, reaching to his ankles. He got into bed, propped up three pillows behind his head, picked up his book on Hadrian's Wall and was snoring within three minutes. I finished work at two in the morning. I woke late, long after he had breakfasted, and spent twenty minutes removing the paint from the landlady's saucers and mugs. Deep purple streams ran down the sink, staining the enamel. I used half a loo roll mopping it up.

Before we left, I found a frayed Black Watch tartan scarf, wrapped it round his neck and tucked it into the front of his olive-green cashmere greatcoat. His pale skin – which he called 'my Highland skin' – was almost translucent beneath his soft white hair.

Finally, I handed him some black ski mittens. He rejected them in favour of a pair of fingerless gloves which he had bought in China. They were almost certainly lined with cat fur.

2

My father generally referred to himself as a Highlander. He often talked about his 'thin Highland blood' and his 'Highland skin' which burned easily. He also said he was as 'sensitive as a Highland shepherd'. As a child, reflecting on this phrase, I imagined him and other shepherds weeping over their flocks.

Being a literal-minded person, I tried to investigate my father's identity as a Highlander in blood and soil: I made him take a DNA test. He obligingly spat into a test tube and I sent it to a laboratory – an act of curiosity costing an expensive £200. Six weeks later, we were informed that the trunk of our paternal ancestor was called R-P312-4, L21, M529 or S145.

This DNA strand had apparently emerged in Western Europe during the Old Stone Age, 7,000 years ago. In May 2012, the same strand was found in two Bronze Age skeletons in Germany. But his particular variant of the strand was concentrated in Scotland, and to a lesser extent Ireland. The genetic testing company therefore argued that it was an old Scottish strain: that my father's ancient paternal ancestor had lived in what is now Scotland for at least 3,000 years. (The company was Scottish.) For reasons less obvious to me, they said this meant he was a 'Pict'. But because the strand also existed in Ireland, my father said it showed that he was 'really Irish'.

Of course, it didn't mean very much. His patrilineal DNA was only a sliver of his total genetic make-up. All that this showed was that his – my – father's father's father's line, the line that had called themselves, at least for the last few hundred years, 'Stewart', had possibly been in Scotland a few thousand years ago. They may well have left the country and returned again (some 'Stewarts' were certainly in Brittany a thousand years ago). And it didn't say anything about the millions of his other ancestors who were alive at that time.

Next, I turned to ancestry.com, a genealogy site with the addictive tricks of a video game. Whenever I refreshed the page, the crisp boxes of our family tree sprouted delicate green leaves, trembling seductively. The program had created a hyperlink between each leaf, and a database of census records, certificates and family trees. I clicked for hours on one after another, without ever beginning to exhaust the leaves, amassing fifth cousins and maternal great-great-uncles, each with their own hyperlinks to further trees. I eventually collected 5,735 of these people. My father was little help in filling in the family tree. Although he liked to talk to me about 'taking pride in the past', this did not extend to his own ancestry. He could not remember his great-grandparents' names. He had once suggested our family were Stewarts of Appin, who left the West Highlands 'after the disaster of Culloden'. But despite staying up, night after night, till three in the morning, clicking on leaf after leaf and peering at hundreds of separate parish records, I never found a link to Culloden.

Often ancestry.com led me to images of birth and death certificates. His great-great-grandfather's death certificate had a crossed-out scrawl by the coroner: 'suicide by hanging' had been replaced with 'suicide by cutting his throat with a razor in the street, 11 a.m., aged 71'. I could only guess at how the coroner could make such a mistake. Mostly the activity was sterile because all I was doing was establishing a name, a date and a kinship tie. And although my father sat patiently looking at the computer screen while I clicked on sprouting leaves, occasionally throwing out a comment ('That is Aunt Petruchia I think'; 'Ah yes, Grandfather Cuba'), he had very little to say about any of these people.

My research confirmed, however, that my father Brian was the son of Redvers son of George son of Alexander son of Alexander son of Charles son of David son of David son of David. And that all these men, my Stewart ancestors, were in the same town doing the same things in the same square mile, right from their first appearance on the first charred half-page of the earliest parish records. And all his father's father's ancestors, his father's mother's ancestors and his mother's father's ancestors were born, lived and had died, for at least two centuries, in one tiny geographical area – limited to just three parishes of the county of Forfarshire in Scotland.

This is where my father and his brother – a year apart in age – were brought up. Neither boy crossed the border into England until they were seventeen. And when the war came, they both, like their father and grandfather before them, joined their local regiment, the Royal Highland Regiment, the Black Watch. There was no record of a single one of his ancestors on any side coming from England.

Nineteenth-century Scotland was one of the most mobile societies on earth. By the beginning of the nineteenth century the majority of the people in the central belt of Scotland did not live in the place where they had been born. Between 1831 and 1931, 2 million Scots moved abroad – equal to the total population of Scotland at the start of that period. My father's ancestors were the exceptions. Which may be why my father said ancestry was 'pretty boring stuff'.

As Stewarts, they defined themselves as Highlanders. But they had all lived – as he continued to live – right on the Highland Line, on the border between Highland and Lowland Scotland.

3

The front of my father's house looked over a flat ten-acre field. To the right stood a cedar of Lebanon and a copper beech, the latter twice the height of the house. When my grandfather first came here there had been another half-mile of fields, mostly belonging to the house, and then the Highlands. Now to the north was a skateboard park, to our north-east was a landfill site, and to our north-west, beyond the gasworks, the old gathering ground for the Crieff Highland Games was designated for a future Tesco's supermarket. Only to our west was the view still unbroken, rising past the woods to the 3,000-feet heather-topped mountains above Loch Turret.

We kept a Highland cow in the field. The calf feed was stored in a large metal dustbin. My father passed me a plastic cup; I tipped the feed into my hand. Mairi shoved her wet pink freckled nose against my forearm. Her long tongue twisted into my palm. I then pushed her huge horns out of the way, and wiped the spittle off onto her matted ginger hair. She was fourteen. Her calves had been taken to market years ago. It took her nearly ten minutes to walk the length of the field. Every summer she was joined by forty Aberdeen Angus bullocks. Every autumn they left, and she stayed. I could feel her horns splintering with age when I stroked them. No real farmer would keep an animal even half so long.

Just beyond my father's fences, and the suburbs of Crieff, lay the starkest geological division in Britain. Four hundred million years ago, two continents – once 4,500 miles apart – had collided. A little later, two further plates had struck, slipped and sheared, driving tight ripples diagonally across Scotland. The older schists and slates of rock to the north-west rose to form the Grampian Mountains. This chain – 200 million years older than anything in southern Scotland or England – was the beginning of the Highlands. At its foot to the south was the rift valley of red sandstone, once an ocean, in which our fields stood – a separate geology that stretched a hundred miles long and fifty miles south, forming a separate culture.

This lowland soil was rich: seven feet of loam on a free-draining sandstone base. Our land could grow barley and potatoes and some of the tallest evergreens in Britain. On the Highland hills above, there were neither crops nor trees. Bare rock jutted above patches of thin acidic soil. Deep peat – supporting anaemic shoots of sphagnum moss – lay among cold streams, inedible rushes and long heather. Mairi could be supported on a single acre in front of our house. Two miles away, in the Highlands, she would need ten acres, and even she – a tough native cow – would struggle to survive.

The different geologies, altitudes, climates and soils once fostered quite different human societies. It was not simply a division between Lowland agriculturalists who planted crops, and Highlanders herding animals and hunting deer. Every aspect of daily subsistence differed. To survive in the Highlands was a terrible discipline: rocks needed to be dug out from the soil and laid in drystone walls; the ground had to be improved – limed, or drained – and the reeds burned back for manure, and cut year after year. It was hardly worth planting crops: they could fail three years out of four. A bad winter – we had one near us in 1946 – could lay six feet of snow for three months, and kill all the stock. In other parts of the world, Rwanda for example, the cattle-keepers were traditionally wealthier than the crop-planters. Here it was the other way round. The Highland pastoralists were very poor.

Contemporary historians question whether these different soils had always coincided with a recognised border between two different economic systems, social structures and languages. It was certainly true, however, that by the sixteenth century the Highland side wore tartan plaids around their waist and shoulders, had bagpipes and lived in clan structures – in our area under a Stewart, MacGregor, Maclaren, Moray, Drummond or Campbell chief – and the Lowland side did none of these things. In fact they dressed and lived in a culture not very different from that of northern England.

As late as 1800 everyone on the flat land around our house in Crieff spoke English. But two miles away, behind the first hill in Monzie, or

N
HIGHLAND SCOTLAND
GAELIC SPEAKING
Metamorphic Rocks
KIRRIEMUIR
Old Red Sandstone
Campbell
Moray
Maclaren
Stewart
BROICH
Drummond
Graham
Drummond
GRAHAM'S DYKE
ANTONINE WALL
LOWLAND SCOTLAND
ENGLISH SPEAKING
PICTE'S WALL
HADRIAN'S WALL
NORTHERN ENGLAND
The Highland Line
c. AD 1500
The Highland Boundary Fault
The Highland linguistic line
Skye to Crieff drover's road
Moray
Highland clan name
Gask Ridge Roman fortifications
English/Scottish Border
0
50 miles
0
50 kilometres
Contains OS data © Crown copyright and database right (2016)

in Comrie, almost everyone spoke Gaelic. The poet Hugh MacDiarmid might talk of the Highlands in terms of:

> blaeberries
> With bright green leaves and leaves already turned scarlet
> Hiding ripe blue berries; and amongst the sage-green leaves
> Of the bog-myrtle the golden flowers of the tormentil shining.

But in Monzie they were more likely to have said:

> *Monainn mhaotha ina mongaibh*
> *Uisge uar ina haibhnibh*
> *Dioghlaim chorcra ar a cairrgibh.*

In the seventeenth century, the Highlanders would gather their black cattle in the far north and drive them south. The drovers would stop in Crieff, the frontier edge and beginnings of the richer land, to sell and then return home. They called our valley a' Ghalldachd, 'the place of the foreigner'. Ten thousand highland cattle had bellowed and jostled on market day in the fields in front of our house. Every year, Highlanders quarrelled with the townsfolk – or were accused of stealing. Some would be hanged on the gallows at the end of our drive. The first thing Highlanders would do, when coming down the drove roads into the Lowlands, would be to doff their bonnets to what they called 'the kind gallows of Crieff'. The Highlanders had burned the town in 1715. And when Bonnie Prince Charlie led his Highland army back through Crieff in 1746, their first thought was to give it 'a good burning again'. We lived a hundred miles north of the modern English–Scottish border, on the Highland Line – the division between what foreigners today might associate largely with England, and the culture that they might associate with Scotland.

4

My father taught me as a child to read the Highland landscape in terms of clans and warfare. The Sma' Glen, five miles from our house, was where he had been taken by his parents when he was a child in the 1930s. He took me there too, and taught me to hide in that heather to ambush Romans, English redcoats and Campbells. I sometimes wanted to be Roman but never a Campbell. I learned that loose stones in rings hinted at where the 'shielings', or huts for summer pasture, had lain. I learned that the grass plateau below was one of Agricola's camps, and that my father had helped to excavate it sixty years earlier.

By the time I was fifteen, I knew that this was Moray land, and that over the next watershed ran a chain of Campbells – from tiny septs such as Campbell of Shean through to the vast estates of Breadalbane, running from Loch Tay to Argyll and the sea. South-west were Drummonds and then the patchwork of the Balquhidder valleys – Stewarts at Ardvorlich; MacGregors and Maclarens beyond. The histories of these families were preserved in the place-names. Thus you could stand on Creagan an Lochain and see Lochan na Mna – named after the woman that the MacGregors drove mad. You could see the island from which the MacDonald raiders had crossed, the shallow graves where they were placed when executed and the spot where Ardvorlich's corpse was hidden from his enemies.

Much later, in Afghanistan, when I crossed watersheds and found that every valley contained almost a separate nation, I – like an embarrassing number of Scottish travellers before me – was reminded of the Highlands. In Afghanistan almost everyone within a village was descended from a common ancestor, while DNA studies confirmed that a staggering 25,000 people today with our common surname, Stewart, were descended from a man called Sir John Stewart of Bonkhill who lived in the 1200s. Perhaps like Afghans, Highlanders in a single clan had once physically resembled each other. At least, the clan name Cameron echoes the Gaelic

Cam Sron, 'bent nose'. I imagined the Highlanders focused on their own valley, talking incessantly about what had happened on the surrounding ridges – stories not unlike those told in rural Afghanistan, of an ambush, lost animal or saint. Stories from two years ago, or from a deep mythical past: local stories linked to the local rocks.

My much older friend, the Black Watch colonel David Rose, told me that the valley that ran beneath his cottage had once been the territory of the McGruders. The mouth of the valley was called Blarinroar, which meant 'the place of the bloody battle'. And the first field, below the pines, was called 'the field of the weeping', because that is where the women met the survivors who had escaped from the horror of Culloden.

It was not clear how long the McGruders had been in Glenartney. Perhaps – like the Maclarens in Balquhidder – for 1,500 years; perhaps longer. There seemed to have been very little difference between their eighteenth-century huts and those of the pre-Roman period. The Highlanders had sat, ate and slept on the damp earth, gently smoked by the guttering fire, before venturing back out into the sleet and the fog to care for the animals.

5

Our house sat below this bearpit of Highland warfare, in fields where archaeologists had found Iron Age roundhouses, pit-burials, graves, standing stones and Neolithic processional ways. A cairn, or mound of stones, twelve yards in diameter, once stood on the edge of our front field. When it was finally opened in 1860, it was discovered to contain partially cremated human bones and a pot, perhaps dating to the late Stone Age. Each pebble, rock and boulder that covered the crypt had passed through a human hand. Each stone had been hefted, the shape felt, and softly laid or flung from a woman's palm, a child's fingertips or the cracked and blackened hand of a man. The position of each stone, and the way it had chipped against other stones, clattering down the pile, was the result of the exact velocity, angle and spin of a throw that came from a particular whim to pitch it up or down, 6,000 years ago: the contour of the cairn was the sum of 100,000 human actions.

And it was on this cairn – with who knows what understanding of the monument – that the medieval lords of the valley held their court. The surrounding estate, called Broich for the cliff on which the houses sat, had been given by Robert the Bruce to a chieftain of the Drummond clan, as a reward for his part in the Battle of Bannockburn in 1314. In 1745, his thirteen-times great-grandson 'came out' in support of Bonnie Prince Charlie's rebellion, and after defeat Broich was confiscated in retribution and sold to his neighbours, the McLaurins.

In 1856, McLaurin's great-grandson and heir, Alexander, became a district officer in the North-West Frontier Province of India, having taken the medals in Sanskrit and Persian at the Indian Civil Service School. He married the sister-in-law of Sir Richmond Shakespear, who had defended Herat against Russian attack and ridden into Khiva to liberate white slaves.

Alexander's career, however, was less Kiplingesque than his brother-in-law's. He became the Director General of the Indian Post Office. And his last act before retirement was to award a generous ten-year government postal contract to a friend, who then gave him a seat on his company board. Alexander used his new wealth to build a new wing at Broich. (My father later tore it down. Not because of the corruption – although he didn't like that either – but because of the dry rot.) Broich was then passed between different Highland families in Calcutta, from the McLaurin-Monteaths to the Murrays and from them to my father's branch of the Stewarts.

6

My father had originally had no intention of following his father into the Empire. Instead he wanted to be an aeronautical engineer with Rolls-Royce. The war, however, made him a soldier. He had joined the Royal

Highland Regiment, the Black Watch, in 1941 without completing his degree, and marched, with the pleats of his kilt swinging behind him, through training camps, barracks and garrison towns in Shropshire, Warwickshire, Wales and Ireland. His brother took his Black Watch kilt to fight in North Africa. My father landed on the Normandy beaches with the regimental red hackle on his Highland bonnet.

At the end of the war, he answered an advertisement in the *Army Gazette* and became a Malayan civil servant. Although he had loved the army, and continued to think like a soldier, he had not considered making it a career. Much later in life, he wondered why he had not stayed in the army, and had no answer.

As a young civil servant, my father was sent to learn Cantonese, Malay and Hokkien. He got the highest marks ever awarded to a Malayan service cadet in the Cantonese language exams. But joining almost a century after Alexander Monteath had taken the medals in the Persian and Sanskrit exams, my father sensed that colonial officers were no longer figures of admiration among his fellow Scots, but instead ones of derision. 'They seemed to think,' he said, 'that all we did was lounge under the palm trees, drinking gin and tonic, before asking the gardener to hose down his daughter . . .'

In 1946, he had met his first wife – 'a young Grace Kelly' – and married her against the rules. After he was posted to Malacca as Secretary of Chinese Affairs, they lived in a one-bedroom bungalow, which became the home of my two half-sisters, Annie and Heather. His salary did not stretch to a car. He established a routine of being at his desk, with his bacon and egg sandwich, at six in the morning, so that he had cleared all his paperwork before his colleagues appeared at eight. He forced himself to improve his Hokkien by taking extra classes. He combined his job as Secretary of Chinese Affairs with being superintendent of Education. He worked so hard he collapsed, and the doctors sent him to hospital for two weeks. 'The problem was,' he reflected, 'that I wasn't having a proper breakfast. I never had that problem again.' He loved the Chinese pork buns and the glimpses of the jungle.

He had inherited a nonsensical job as 'protector of virtue', a role dreamt up to prevent human trafficking in the 1930s, but he decided to expand it. He built affordable public housing for slum dwellers, only to find that within a week they had sold off their new homes and returned to the slum. His schools were more successful. 'They were cheap and cheerful, darling, a hundred pounds each, with wire-mesh windows, and an asbestos roof, painted red, to try to blend in with Malacca tiles, and erected in record time.'

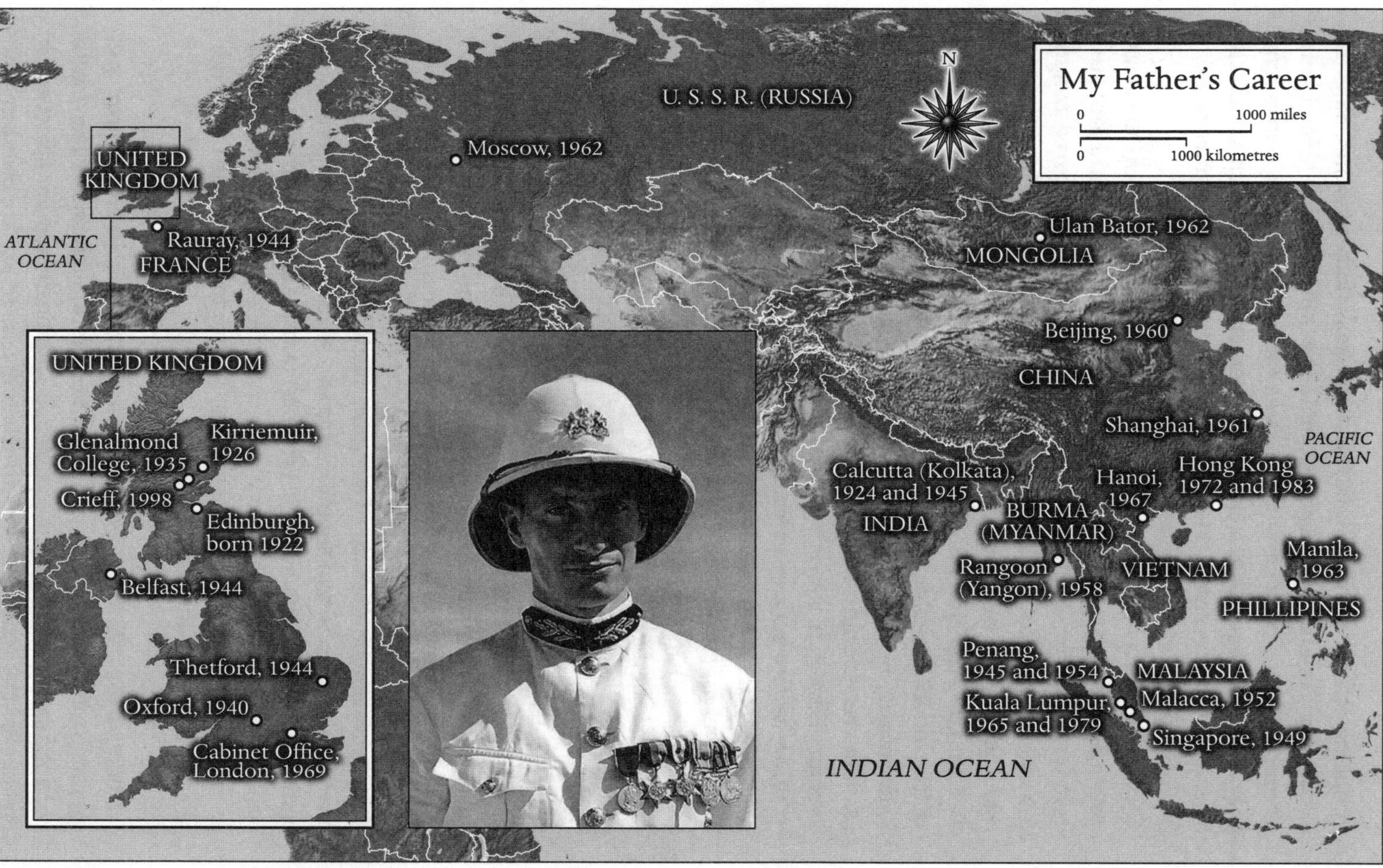
My Father's Career
0
1000 miles
0
1000 kilometres
N
U. S. S. R. (RUSSIA)
Moscow, 1962
UNITED KINGDOM
Rauray, 1944
FRANCE
ATLANTIC OCEAN
UNITED KINGDOM
Glenalmond College, 1935
Kirriemuir, 1926
Crieff, 1998
Edinburgh, born 1922
Belfast, 1944
Thetford, 1944
Oxford, 1940
Cabinet Office, London, 1969
Ulan Bator, 1962
MONGOLIA
Beijing, 1960
CHINA
Shanghai, 1961
PACIFIC OCEAN
Calcutta (Kolkata), 1924 and 1945
INDIA
BURMA (MYANMAR)
Hanoi, 1967
Hong Kong 1972 and 1983
Rangoon (Yangon), 1958
VIETNAM
Manila, 1963
PHILLIPINES
Penang, 1945 and 1954
MALAYSIA
Kuala Lumpur, 1965 and 1979
Malacca, 1952
Singapore, 1949
INDIAN OCEAN

But this was the era of the Malayan Emergency. Increasingly, he focused on winning the Malayan Chinese community away from the Chinese-led communist insurgency. He pioneered a new strategy called the 'white area policy' – where regulations were relaxed for communities that proved their loyalty to the government. He became close to General Templar, the new High Commissioner and Commander-in-Chief.

When he got a car, he drove into the middle of the terrorist-held areas with a loaded pistol on the dashboard. (His predecessor had been shot dead on the same road.) He created an entire Chinese police battalion to fight the insurgency. No one had managed this before, and his superiors could never work out how he had succeeded. ('The answer, of course, was that I had convinced the Chinese business community to double their salaries, under the table.')

In Penang, he dealt with a rioting crowd of students by firing tear gas into the schools. ('I was known as the butcher of Penang,' he said. I assumed this was a joke.)

When Malaya became independent in 1957, he joined the British secret service. He spent the next twenty years mostly working 'under diplomatic cover' out of embassies in Asia. In Burma, he specialised in the hill tribes of the Shan States. In Beijing and as Consul General in Shanghai, he tracked the beginnings of the Cultural Revolution. In Malaysia, he focused on the '*confrontasi*', the covert fight against Indonesia in the Borneo jungle.

In Manila, he chased a kidnapper through Zambuanga, carrying a bag of gold with which to pay the ransom, and a gun, in case things didn't go to plan. As the British representative to North Vietnam during the Vietnam War he was bombed by the Americans. As the secretary of the Joint Intelligence Committee he fought for more direct and provocative assessments in the face of what he called 'Civil Service-ese'. And as director of Technical and Support Services – 'Q' in James Bond terms – he commissioned gadgets that delighted him but which, he conceded, often took years to develop and rarely worked. After he retired from government service, he commanded a police force of 2,000 in Malaysia, and then spent fifteen years in business in China.

I belonged to the later period of my father's life. He had met my mother in Malaysia in the mid-1960s. He was already fifty when I was born in 1973, and my half-sisters, Annie and Heather, were twenty-one and twenty-two. He was fifty-four when my sister, Fiona, was born with Down's syndrome. I went to his university – Oxford – briefly served in his regiment, the Black Watch, and then, like him, joined the Foreign Office. My first posting was in Indonesia in 1997. My father, who was then seventy-five, was living in Hong Kong.

He sent me a forty-foot-long shipping container of family furniture to fit into the small bungalow in a side-street behind the embassy in Jakarta. It included a grandfather clock with a picture of Bonnie Prince Charlie and Flora MacDonald on its face. His own father had taken it to Calcutta, and it had been shipped, with some damage to its pulley system, through Penang, Rangoon, Peking, Shanghai, Manila, Kuala Lumpur, Hong Kong, London and back to Hong Kong. I propped it up on a back wall and laid the lead weights in the bottom of the case, because I couldn't trust the mechanism. Then I began to try to fit the sideboard, the dining table and the Chinese lamps into the sitting room. And wondered where we would be able to dance.

7

Wherever he was posted in the world, my father introduced Scottish dancing. He had begun to drill me as a five year old, to make sure my pas-de-basque (he pronounced it 'paddy-bar') was correct. In Kuala Lumpur, he had introduced me to the sword dance. He had taken a wave-bladed kris from the wall and his ceremonial sword from the umbrella stand, and crossed them on the floor. In time to the music, I was taught to stretch my foot across the blades, and then to jump back and forth, avoiding the sharp edges. My father was very proud of his dancing. He had been officer commanding Scottish dancing in his battalion of the Black Watch. His travelling steps, and heel-heel toe-toe, and the position of his foot on his calf, were impressively exact.

The Black Watch kilt he wore at that time was his father's. He thought his father had worn it in Mesopotamia during the First World War. His favourite kilt jacket, however, was made by Wong Kee, a Chinese tailor in Malacca, for a Scottish dance in 1947. (The buttons were made from

Malaccan silver.) The kilt he gave me had been made for his brother by the regimental tailor of the Calcutta Scottish in 1928. He organised reel parties in Burma, Malaysia, Beijing, Shanghai, Vietnam and Hong Kong, and taught the bewildered guests to dance by barking and clapping, 'One, two, three – come on, you're behind – one, TWO, three – that's right – and on – turn, two, three – turn, two, three.'

His favourite story involved the Russian consul in Shanghai in 1962. The consul, a KGB officer and firm Communist, asked him (my father always performed the line in a strong Russian accent), 'In your country, Brian, are these the dances of the aristocracy or the peasantry?' My father replied in a Scottish accent, 'In my country, Consul General, we have no classes.' I found the story confusing. I was not quite sure what my father actually made of the Scottish class system.

As a teenager, I travelled a long way to attend dances in the Highlands. I came to recognise men less by their faces than by their sporrans. Duncan had a badger-head sporran, Charles a white-tasselled, goat-hair sporran, mounted in silver. Mine for a time was a moth-eaten otter. I could tell you which man liked to spin a double in eightsome, or could dance a foursome, yet I didn't know their names. I learned that a very beautiful girl who wore a red top over a silk Fraser tartan skirt could be trusted always to meet her partner's left palm at speed in the Reel of the 51st – and that another in a blue silk dress would fall if turned too fast.

In village halls, on lawns, in marquees, at birthday parties, at weddings and at Hogmanay, the first sensation was of tartan: thrown over women, men and furniture. The second sensation was the reel music from a fiddle, or an accordion, or a stereo carried down from a teenager's bedroom.

Imagine the Reel of the 51st (Aberdonian). A long line of men faces a long line of women. As the music starts, every second person steps into the centre, the rest forming a corridor of hands, whose function is to be spun. The rules of the dance were, I later learned, strictly codified by the Royal Scottish Country Dance Society, but that was not how we danced it. What mattered was that the boundary lines stayed firm, and that you ended up back in line at the end of a bar. You ran into the centre of the line, perhaps bumping hips in a sweaty Scottish version of flamenco, spun your partner two or even four times in the centre, and then released them into the waiting hands on the side rows, who flung them back into the centre again.

Most waiting couples were doubling – whooping, leaning, twirling, swaying – their sporrans and kilts rising, taffeta spinning, long hair flying. You tried to adjust, slightly, to whether you were facing a grandmother or a six year old, because both could be in the line, but it was essentially a dance for the fast of feet. The old men bellowed, 'You're behind the beat,' and the visitors from England fell over, and no one, except the very youngest and the very oldest, performed the steps correctly. Sometimes I danced till four in the morning, and finished with breakfast. More often I danced till shortly after midnight, and drove home shivering slightly in my father's 1947 Malacca kilt jacket, my bare knees against the gearstick. Almost the only working tape in the car for many years was a recording of the Scottish nationalist poet Hugh MacDiarmid reading:

It's guid to see her lie
Sae snod an' cool,
A 'lust o' lovin' by –
Wheesht, wheesht, ye fule!

I had learned some of the tunes when I was taught to play the bagpipes, but I hardly understood the music: I did not even grasp that the Hamilton House was a strathspey. I knew that the Reel of the 51st had been invented by the Black Watch and the other Highland regiments in a German prisoner-of-war camp during the Second World War, and was therefore designed initially for male dancers. I imagined the other dances were very ancient, when in reality what seemed an unbroken tradition from the Highland clans were dances mostly influenced by the French court and codified in the nineteenth century. But my ignorance did not stop me feeling that these dances made us Scottish.

There was very little time between dances – hardly enough to find a drink for your last partner and track down your next one – and we danced every one. The girls smiled at me as we turned, but we hardly spoke. Years passed, hands clasped, caught, spun, but there was much I never learned about the other dancers – their disappointments, their jobs outside Perthshire, their lives away from the sprung dance floor. I grew to like the people I danced with very much, felt they were almost family, and day-dreamed about marrying them. Later I went to their weddings and their babies' christenings. Few would have ever seen me except in a kilt.

My father often went home early from the dances. He did not dance the way that other people danced. He would join in the eightsome and the Dashing White Sergeant. He might try the Duke of Perth. But soon he would become frustrated. He wanted to teach, and give orders in the dance, but the dances were moving too quickly for him, and he himself, particularly as he got older, was the person turning the wrong way, or setting out of time with the rest of the dancers. He would roar his disapproval, throw his hands in the air and step out of the set, leaving his partner – who initially would have been reassured to have this distinguished, confident, beautifully dressed partner, with his long sporran and silver-buckled shoes – marooned.

He liked to say that our neighbours, and the modern officers of the Black Watch – and indeed me – were all sloppy with our steps, and wild, and that we danced complicated dances he did not like. Sometimes he wondered whether it was the contrast between Angus and Perthshire, or whether it was the army. At any rate, he wanted to teach Highland dancing and to host dances, but he did not like dancing with our neighbours. And in the real world this type of dancing was done by very few Scots at all.

8

My father was the seventh consecutive generation – Monteaths, Murrays, Stewarts – to have worked in Asia and then returned to Broich in retirement. Like every predecessor, he had found that the grounds had been neglected by the previous, ageing, generation and dedicated himself to improvements. When he was eighty, he discovered how easy it was to hire a miniature digger for a week. Suddenly projects which would have taken him three days with pick and spade could be accomplished in minutes.

Aerial photography would reveal that my father dug small rectangular pits, round holes, sinuous shallow-scraped lines and a curving ditch half a mile long. Closer investigation by future archaeologists would struggle to establish a reliable sequence of construction. Lines of posts were inserted, then removed, then reinstated. A ditch would be filled in four years after it had been dug, or one shallow-scraped line would be abandoned and another created a few yards away.

My father justified his earthworks in different words – as ponds, ditches, dykes, raised hedges, screens, defences, mounds, trenches, tracks, drives and roads. His favourite earthworks were the large pond and the concealed sheep fence (or, as he would call them, the lochan and the ha-ha). But in the end, his diggings seemed to be about either altering the view, or controlling access.

The view was altered in one way only, to ensure we saw as much as possible of the Highlands and as little as possible of Crieff and its encroaching suburbs.

At the north-east edge of the field, he cut through dense bushes of broom and made a long earth track, which he said would be suitable for an electric wheelchair. But instead of buying a wheelchair he invested in a quad bike with a spider's mask painted on the front.

His most important earthworks were the territorial boundaries, separating two pieces of ground. They were designed to make sure that something – sheep or humans, deer or water – stayed in a particular space and did not wander, possibly destructively, into a neighbouring location.

Behind the beech and holly hedge, which he had planted on the western 'march' or boundary, he had laid a line of barbed wire. The hedge was ten foot high. If you managed to cross it, and the barbed wire, you would fall into a ditch four feet deep and four feet wide. On the far side was a further beech hedge, 'cut' with holly, twelve feet high. And beyond that another fence. Five times, at least, he had built and taken down different designs of plain wire, barbed wire, drystone wall, cemented wall and electric fences. He referred to these borders as 'tank-traps'.

My father's works were in a long tradition. Over a hundred other earthworks (and another hundred monuments and archaeological finds) had been identified by archaeologists within a mile of our front door. They spread in a blue rash across the website of the Scottish Royal Commission for Ancient and Historical Monuments. The earthworks, ditches and mounds had been discovered through aerial photography. They hinted at a landscape some 3,000 to 5,000 years old, a time when some of my father's ancestors may have settled here.

What an archaeologist had named an 'earthwork' seemed to depend largely on whether it looked like a circle, a rectangle, a sequence of small holes or a sequence of square pits. By their logic it seemed my father's own style of digging might be classified as 'pit-circle'.

The ancient foundations and ditches were invisible to the naked eye. I knew them only as patches of green turf, across which the swifts dived or the roe deer scattered. But once I had studied the aerial photographs I began to sense in them the imaginations of forgotten cultures. My father had been delighted to read that the maternal DNA of a teacher living in the Cheddar Gorge in 1997 established him as the direct descendant of a 9,000-year-old skeleton found two miles from his house. Walking over the sites, amidst the cries from the skateboard park, I remembered the screams of unattended childbirth coming from a round hut in Irian Jaya and lasting a day and a night. Maybe one of these shallow mounds or ditches could – if I was attentive enough – reveal something of the mind of our Neolithic ancestors.

I thought of how the communities which had once lived in the fields in front of our house had changed their identities and languages. If my father's family had lived here in such a hut on the frontier between the Highlands and the Lowlands 2,000 years ago, they might have called themselves members of the Venicones tribe; 400 years later the descendants of the Venicones began to call themselves Picts. Then, 600 years later, their descendants would have ceased to speak Pictish and adopted Northumbrian as their tongue; a century later, they were perhaps speaking Norse, and a century after that, Scottish Gaelic. Eventually Gaelic too would be forgotten in favour of English. And they, like my father, would come to call themselves simply 'Scots'.

The language, culture and nationhood – the sense of ethnicity – in a single family, stuck in a single valley, could change again and again. My father's ancestors might have been, like some Stewarts, immigrants from Brittany, who reimagined themselves as indigenous Scots. Or they might have been actually genetically descended from late Iron Age communities in Scotland, but have claimed at different times to be the children of immigrants from Angeln in northern Germany, from Norway, from Ireland, from Brittany, from Normandy – eventually believing these stories, without moving an inch, and with very little change in the shape of their huts or the character of their possessions. (Scholars say something of this sort happened, for example, among communities in northern England who called themselves 'Anglo-Saxon' and spoke English but who were in fact genetically descended from Welsh-speaking Celts.) As the millennia passed, the landscape and the traces of ancestors' houses would have been soaked with contradictory claims about who they – who we – 'really' were. The myths passed on by fathers are fragile, and sometimes unreliable.

In a single sunny afternoon, my father and his yellow digger were able to create structures larger than these monuments of our ancestors. He and thousands of others, with perhaps more practical projects in mind, would soon make it very difficult to distinguish the ancient from the modern. And within the next generation, the structure of the fragile soil would be so densely tattooed with interwoven ditches as to be indecipherable by even the most scrupulous archaeologist. I was still, however, living in the moment between the invention of the plane – which has allowed the prehistoric earthworks to be seen – and the moment when the growing squadrons of mechanical diggers would obliterate them entirely. It was still possible to make some sense of what once surrounded the house.

Many of the ancient earthworks were simply straightforward ways of preventing livestock from getting out or damaging plantings. Others – the rectangles – probably marked the boundaries between the living and the dead, defining the edges of places where bodies were left exposed to the elements, or were buried, cremated in pots, or interred as skeletons, with or without possessions, in different-shaped 'barrows'. Some of the earthworks were near standing stones – great granite blocks, seven feet high and twelve feet in diameter.

But some of these earthworks may have acted not as field fences or property lines or sacred enclosures, but instead as that abstraction of all abstractions: a political boundary – because a border, the edge of a nation, had been placed here, shadowing the division between Lowlands and Highlands.

9

One afternoon, soon after I had returned from my walk across Afghanistan, my father and I were walking with a friend, Roderick, around the edge of our grounds. We walked slowly, to look at the fourteen lime trees and discuss pleaching them; and to see the copse of deodar cedar, planted in memory of our trip together to Simla. We passed my father's new Chinese pagoda (he had made it from six doors which he had bought at B&Q, painted blood red and arranged on a concrete plinth). Then we went on to inspect the hundred rhododendrons that we had planted above Mairi the Highland cow's field. In the role of a retired officer and diplomat, my father seemed to be enjoying not just what he cheerfully called 'the comedy', but even perhaps the dignity of life in the country.

We had been walking for about twenty minutes, and I was a little ahead of him, when I suddenly heard him angrily shout 'Hey!' He was addressing a man who was halfway over one of our fences. A girl, who was with the man, stood to one side.

'I don't mind you coming onto my land,' barked my father, 'but don't pull down my fences.'

The man turned full on to my father. He was about eighteen, I guessed, with a shaven head and a sheet-white face.

'Fuck you,' he shouted, towering over my father. His face was contorted and he was trembling. 'Do you want to fight me? Do you want to fucking fight me? I'll take you . . .'

As I ran back, I could see my father standing his ground, leaning on his walking stick – but there was uncertainty flickering through his eyes, as though this time he had picked a fight he could not win.

I had just walked across Asia, where respect for the aged has a religious importance. I could never have imagined an eighteen-year-old man in Pakistan thinking it appropriate to publicly challenge an eighty-five year old to a fight. I had a strong instinct about how an Afghan would respond to this kind of threat to his father, and I was very angry. I shouted at the man, and then Roderick wrapped his arms around me and pulled me back. The young man's girlfriend grabbed the man. He tore away from her and shouted at my father again. 'Fuck you, rich man. You think you can talk to me like that because you shit money.' He turned his back on my father, and mimed dropping his trousers. 'Shitting money,' he shouted. 'I'm coming back for you.'

I wanted to hit him. Roderick was saying in my ear, 'Leave it. Leave it. Leave it. Don't push it, or he'll come back.' He added, with a confident prediction which still confuses me, 'And burn your sheds.'

We walked back to the house. My father, and the land, seemed different. No longer were they courtly, dignified, nestled deep within the traditions of Scotland; instead, in this young Scot's eyes, they were, apparently, despicable.

10

In retirement, it seemed at times that my father was protesting his Scottishness too much. It was not just that he wore tartan trews every day. The lurcher, spreadeagled on the tartan blanket on his bed, was called Torquil; there were oatcakes, a Jacobite history and a Gaelic dictionary next to the whisky on his desk. Every morning he ate porridge, and twice a week haggis. In the corner of the room stood what he called a 'squeezebox': it was his instrument of choice, now that his fingers no longer allowed him to play the fiddle.

At other times, however, it was not quite clear how seriously he took his Scottish identity. Because he often asked me to read Rabbie Burns for guests, I assumed until I was forty that he had a deep affinity for the national bard. We even had a small marble bust of Burns mounted on a bookcase. Finally, one evening, I asked him what he thought of Burns. 'Nothing much,' he replied. 'I just enjoy the dialect.' He also enjoyed mounting half-academic assaults on Scottish heroes. My Stewart, or Stuart, or Steuart, neighbours kept pictures of the Prince in their houses, and relics too: locks of hair, and small lockets with pictures of Flora MacDonald. Some even held their wine glasses over the water glass for the royal toast, to show that the toast was not simply to 'the King' but to the 'King over the water'. But when my father went off with his kinsmen on the Stewart Society pilgrimage to see Bonnie Prince Charlie's tomb in Rome, he spent the trip saying, 'Useless man. Didn't stand a chance. No strategy. Poltroon.'

When he found himself in a room full of clan chiefs, he liked to say, 'No one here is Scottish, you know.' And when they objected, he would continue, 'The Drummonds are Hungarians, the Frasers and the Lindsays and the Gordons are Norman French. And the Stewarts are originally from Brittany.'

There were a dozen different tartans on his trews, and on the furniture and cushions. His day trews were ancient hunting Stewart; his day kilt, modern hunting Stewart; his waistcoat and evening trews, Stuart of Bute;

there were Royal Stewarts, and Stewarts of Appin and Black Stewarts among the cushions on the Black Watch armchairs. He was certain, however, that the associations of any of these tartans with the Stewart clan was only a nineteenth-century invention of Sir Walter Scott's.

His favourite kilt was a red one that he wore with lace at his neck and a midnight blue velvet jacket. It looked a little bit like Stuart of Bute but was in fact some form of Macfarquhar, a clan with whom we had absolutely no connection. He had bought it for £10 in a charity shop in Crieff.

II

In 2009, after a dozen years abroad – working in Indonesia and the Balkans, walking across Iran, Afghanistan, Pakistan, India and Nepal, working in Iraq and Afghanistan, and finally teaching in the United States – I decided to come home to Britain and stand for Parliament. But since there was no vacancy in my home seat in Perthshire (and no chance of being elected there), I chose to stand elsewhere. I was eventually elected as an MP for Penrith and the Border. This constituency had historically been part of an independent nation, and then part of Scotland, but was now in modern England, and included half the English–Scottish border. A year later, the Scottish National Party won a majority in the Scottish Parliament and announced they would hold a referendum on Scotland's independence. Just over 4 million of the 61 million people in the United Kingdom were told they could decide whether the island of Britain should be split into two. My father, mother and sister were allowed to vote in the referendum because they lived on the Scottish side of the border. Because I lived on the English side, I was not.

Of course, I had a personal stake in this. If Scotland separated, I would still have a constituency, but I would no longer have a country to represent. Although my father was Scottish, my mother was English. My family home was in Scotland, my constituency in England. So I was, for that reason and others, a Unionist.

I assumed the whole debate about national independence would rest on questions of Scottish ethnicity, history and soil. I was ready to challenge claims that there was some separate 'Scottish' genetic identity, and to argue that many things which were blamed on the English – from the Jacobite rebellion to the Highland Clearances – were really conflicts between fellow Scots. But such issues of blood and soil hardly featured at all in the nationalist debate. No one on either side attempted to revive – or define – a sense of British identity. I found almost no opportunity to emphasise how much my constituency of Cumbria had in common with Scotland, linguistically, historically and culturally. To my surprise, the artificial border that divides Scotland from England, first sketched by a Roman emperor on open ground in AD 122, seemed to be regarded as something 'natural'. Scotland and England were treated as though they were simple, straightforward and unchanging entities.

My father, like me, had never felt that by studying in England, or later living in London, that he had moved 'abroad'. The institutions which we had joined, the army and the Foreign Office, did not feel to him, or to me, English or Scottish, but instead British. But, unlike me, his vision of the United Kingdom owed almost nothing to the institution of a common parliament. He tended to agree with most people in Britain that an MP was somewhere between a disappointment and an outrage. He regretted my decision to stand for office instead of staying at Harvard. I overheard him say, 'I can't understand how he puts up with it – a terrible life – paper-shuffling, speeches, committees.' To me he said, 'I'd be tempted to just leave that talking shop, and move back to America. I'm not quite sure whether Britain's got the energy any more.'

And yet, despite all this pessimistic talk, Britain – the whole of Britain – remained the purpose and meaning of my father's world. His theme was almost always Britain, whether deploying Scottish regiments on the nursery floor or discussing Scots' roles in defining policy in the Foreign Office. He insisted that his ancestors had also been conscious of Britain – not in exactly the same way, in every generation, but that there was a family resemblance in how they linked their Scottish-British identities, references, practices and institutions. But what exactly was this Stewart idea of Britain?

This was more difficult to say – in part perhaps because when I finally pressed him hard on these issues, he was already in his late eighties. If I asked him about his ideas for British politics, he often drew from his experience in Malaya, suggesting that I work to build affordable housing along the lines of the housing he had built in Malacca. When he spoke about contemporary politics, he spoke about terrorism, wars or defence cuts. He did not talk about poverty or equality; most of his domestic designs had a military flavour. He wanted to create a part-time, reserve police force in Britain, establish a new anti-terrorism unit and reintroduce national service. He often complained that Britain was 'not a democracy', but I never heard him define democracy, and it seemed unlikely that he would have actually liked such a thing, if it had existed. Nevertheless, he insisted that as 'public servants' we were both serving Britain.

★

'What did you mean by serving Britain?' I asked him over a cup of tea in his bedroom. (He drank from a plastic thermos mug – the mixture being half tea and half milk with three lumps of sugar.)

'It was pretty straightforward,' he said. 'I joined the army, then the Colonial Service, then the Foreign Office.'

'Serving the British people?'

'I felt I was serving the Queen, not the man in the street. Not sure what the man in the street was thinking about, but don't think he was thinking of me. For the rest of my life even as a businessman I thought I was serving the Queen – jobs, exporting, serving the Queen. A cheerful way to go through life. No questions. The good of Britain is a very amorphous concept – but I could believe I was doing good for Britain – making friends.'

'But what *is* the Queen?'

'I never ask that question.' He laughed. 'She represents her country. Does her best.'

12

My father felt that his forefathers would not have wanted Scotland to separate from the rest of Britain. 'When it suited us, we could claim England as part of our own country.' They could spend part of their life living in England. They could find Cumbria more homely than Scotland but the Highlands more invigorating than Devon, appreciate the architecture of Edinburgh but find London the greater city, and feel it was their capital. His family had always claimed Shakespeare and Dickens as part of their national culture.

My father feared that Scottish independence would give competition between Scots and English a different context and tone; that we could no longer love the Highlands and London as aspects of a single country; that when we faced threats or challenges beyond our shores, we would no longer respond as a single force.

I knew some English people who felt about Scotland as he felt about England. My neighbour in Cumbria, for example, called himself an English nationalist. He expressed contempt for the bagpipes, the Scottish rugby team and Scottish politicians. But he still felt an ownership of marching Scottish regiments, Eric Liddell's triumph in *Chariots of Fire*, David Livingstone and David Stirling, the founder of the SAS. So each could feel an outsider in some part of our own country, and could be challenged by the pride of our fellow nations.

But in my father's mind the Scots still remained different from the English. His ancestors, he thought, would have agreed with him that Scots were more energetic, more egalitarian, and were tougher soldiers. Above all, 'the English are boring'.

His Scottishness relied on the existence of the English. When English visitors stayed, there was more haggis and there were more Arbroath smokies (a salty fish with a leathery brown skin over an oily grey interior). It was only with the English that we got his half-remembered version of the Selkirk grace:

> Some hae meat and cannae eat
> And some can eat and hae nae meat
> But we hae meat and we can eat
> And so the Lord be Thank'it.

I sensed he would have no fun being Scottish if he didn't have the English to annoy.

Many Scots had long despised my father's kind of Scottishness. The poet Hugh MacDiarmid, for example, dissected almost every element of such an identity. He attacked the war dead, the 'lairds', and the Scots who had prospered in government in London and India. He had no sympathy for the doggerel of William McGonagall, which my father loved, and despised the music-hall comedian Harry Lauder, whose songs my father sang. MacDiarmid did not seem to like people who could make fun of their own Scottish identity.

Others saw my father's culture as politics. When Tom Nairn, the most articulate intellectual advocate of Scottish independence of the next generation, wrote from his post at Melbourne University about what he hated about Britain, he described it as 'a new style of colony – the sergeant major and cheerleader of American-led globalisation', and the Scots as 'fleas upon the Washington organ-grinder's despicable monkey'. Nairn attacked the Scots' 'cultural over-compensation and romantic chest-beating, to efface or embellish powerlessness; [and] over-effusive loyalty to a distant cause and metropolis, welcomed and yet somehow never welcomed enough'. His entire critique seemed a caricature of my father's personality and diplomatic career.

13

In 2011, I had taken my father to Burma and Vietnam. Because he was eighty-eight, he thought that our two-week holiday in Vietnam and Burma might be the last time he left Scotland. 'You got me just in time,' he said. He had often taken me with him as a child. But he had soon discovered that I could remember almost nothing about these trips. Sometimes, I could not even remember that we had been there. One of his favourite stories was of asking me – aged perhaps seven – why he bothered taking me to all these amazing places. I had, he claimed, replied very solemnly, 'Well, Daddy, I'm sure you enjoyed it at the time.'

I was certain, however, that I had never been to either Burma or Vietnam. He hadn't been back to Burma in fifty years, or Vietnam in forty. I hoped our 2011 visit would weave his reflections on the Vietnam War into my reflections on Iraq and Afghanistan. And I hoped to collect – there, directly on the ground – clues to things which had eluded me about his past in those countries.

For example, I knew only two things about his time in Burma. First, that he had imported a canoe – bought in the Army and Navy Stores – and tried to assemble it in his very hot garage, cooling himself down with bottles of beer. He had got fantastically drunk, without being aware of it, and hardly made it to his bed. Second, that a colonel in the Kachin Rifles had given him a honey-bear. 'Every day, the honey-bear climbed up a tree. Every evening, when I came back from work, your sisters would say,' (here he assumed a falsetto), '"Daddy, Daddy, the honey-bear has climbed up the tree." And I had to climb up with a baby-bottle to tempt it down.'

So, in Rangoon, I set up a tape-recorder, and asked him question after question. For three hours one evening he told a story – punctuated by such long pauses that I thought he was falling asleep – about a day when he had been stuck in a traffic jam in the jungle. The point of the story seemed to be that he had eventually encouraged a truck-driver to pull off the road to let the cars through. I could not understand what it revealed about him or about Burma.

One day we found his old house. A green bungalow, completely unchanged, on the airport road by the Inya Lake. The new owners let us in. I waited for the memories to come bubbling to the surface, after fifty years of submersion.

'Is this the house?' I asked.

'Yes, this is it,' he said.

'Are you sure?'

'Yes, absolutely.'

'Has it changed?' I asked.

'Not at all.'

'Does it bring back any memories?'

There was a long pause.

'That,' my father said with delight, 'is the stump of the tree that the honey-bear used to climb. Every evening when I came back from work, the girls . . .'

'Yes, Daddy. Shall we look at the house?'

We walked in.

'That's right.'

'Any changes?'

'No,' he said decisively. 'Bedrooms on the left, kitchen on the right, dining room here.'

'Aha. Any memories?'

'Not particularly,' he said cheerfully.

'Did you have parties here?'

'Yes.'

'Do you remember your cook?' I asked.

'Yes.'

'What was he like?'

'He was a Mugh from Chittagong,' my father replied.

He walked outside again. 'I can't believe it – it is exactly the stump – the very stump.' I peered at the blackened wood, a foot off the ground. 'He climbed up from there – the honey-bear. It's amazing. "Daddy, Daddy, the honey-bear is stuck up the tree" and I had to climb up and bring it down.'

I should have remembered that he was well trained in resistance to interrogation.

14

The first time my father and I visited Hadrian's Wall I had expected the Great Wall of China.

He and I had already been to the Great Wall half a dozen times in the early 1980s, walking west along the top of the section nearest to Beijing. (He was then working in China.) At first it appeared as tall and neat as in any *National Geographic* film. Then, further west, the wall began to shrink, the stones to crumble and subside, and finally the ruins were lost beneath gravel and sand. We saw Mongolian families in great felt coats, their flocks searching for tufts of desiccated grass in the grey soil. I recited for my father Ezra Pound's poem on the Chinese frontier guard, which I had learned at school:

> By the North Gate, the wind blows full of sand,
> Lonely from the beginning of time until now!
> Trees fall, the grass goes yellow with autumn.
> I climb the towers and towers
>   to watch out the barbarous land.

My father tried different Chinese dialects on the dromedary driver to bargain for square Ch'ing dynasty coins. (He gave the coins as Christmas presents.) We ate sugar fritters which we'd bought from street stalls.

Hadrian's Wall must have felt once a bit like the Great Wall. The late-sixteenth-century traveller William Camden, for example, found it still ten feet high and surrounded by unfamiliar people:

> Verily I have seene the tract of it over the high pitches and steepe descents of hilles, wonderfully rising and falling [and – to turn to modern English] you may see as it were the ancient Nomads, a martial kind of men who, from the month of April into August, lie out scattering and summering (as they term it) with their cattle. I could not with safety take the full survey of [the Roman fort at Housesteads] for the rank robbers thereabout.

In Camden's day, grass mounds cushioned the sharp edges of limestone altars, and peat lay in hypocaust foundations. Visitors could scratch moss from the stones to reveal inscriptions which gave hints of Roman units drawn from Syria, or the report of the death of a Dacian baby. At the cavalry fort Chesters, near Hexham, a statue of the god of the Tyne was half visible, his bearded head sticking out of the turf.

But in 1745, the invasion from Scotland led by Bonnie Prince Charlie convinced the government to upgrade its military infrastructure. So General Wade demolished part of the wall and used the rubble to construct a new military road. It was designed – like the Roman road that lay buried beneath it – to allow soldiers to march rapidly between Carlisle and Newcastle. Then entrepreneurs began to use the wall as a source of limestone, saving them the costs of quarrying.

So when Walter Scott saw Hadrian's Wall, in 1800, the central section had largely vanished. But it remained a fine ruin for a Romantic writer. Miniature plants still nestled in the masonry – some of them perhaps introduced to Britain by the Romans. Scott walked along the wall, wrote poems about it and proposed to his wife on it. He saw the wall as a symbol of empire, romance and decay; of the evolution of botany and heraldry. It was a symbol of nationhood, a figure of love, the source of a flower given to his lover:

> Take these flowers which, purple waving,
> On the ruin'd rampart grew,
> Where, the sons of freedom braving,

Rome's imperial standards flew.
Warriors from the breach of danger
Pluck no longer laurels there;
They but yield the passing stranger
Wild-flower wreaths for Beauty's hair.

By 1985, however, when I first saw Hadrian's Wall with my father, the ruins had been tidied up and the vegetation had been removed from the crevices. The fort at Housesteads now consisted of one-foot-high walls, arranged in squares and rectangles, like the lines of a playing field for a game whose rules were forgotten. The Ministry of Public Building and Works and the Department of the Environment (I did not then understand any distinction between such bodies) had torn out the plants. The varying tints of the Roman mortar – each shade a mark of different periods of Roman building and restoration – had been replaced with homogenous grey modern cement. And the statues, altars and military equipment which had once lain scattered across the sites had been dug up, cleaned and placed in museum storage vaults in Newcastle and London.

The robbers whom Camden had feared had long gone, and so had most of the shepherds. The only human presence consisted of tourists in anoraks and a ticket-seller at the gate. Amidst the stubby plans of the fort buildings, filled with a thin surface of gravel, one plastic sign caught my eye. It stood beside a stone bench with holes in the seat, and depicted a row of Roman legionaries, chatting and laughing with their britches around their ankles, one waving, on a stick, the sponge with which he had cleaned his bottom. Further west, there was no sign of the wall. (Later I learned that this was not because it was not there; in fact, archaeologists had uncovered an impressive section of red sandstone wall, five courses high, but – being more interested in preserving the site for future scholars than in engaging contemporary visitors – had reburied it.)

Our walk along Hadrian's Wall in 1985 was the culmination of a two-week school holiday that began in China. The previous week, my father and I had been in Macau. There he had 'trotted' with me – a sort of stiff-legged jog he had learned as an army cadet – through a tropical thunderstorm. I had never seen so much water come down so fast. We took shelter in a casino, and he led me – aged twelve – to the roulette wheels. I did not understand his explanation of his gambling system, but he won, and so did I.

Then we had crossed the border into China proper. In Canton, we followed a thin man who was offering antiquities for sale. He led us down a lane, glancing from side to side, muttering about police spies, to a narrow alley where he sold us, for illegal foreign exchange certificates, a rose-pink Kang Hsi bowl, thin as glass. (When we returned to the hotel, and examined it in the bright light of our hotel room lamp, my father proclaimed with delight that the pot was a fake. He suggested we should both go into the fake antique business; the secret of success, he said, was to mutter about police spies.)

Next, we had taken the train to Beijing and hired bicycles. When we were cycling past the Temple of Heaven, a vast limousine had drawn up alongside us, and the Indonesian Foreign Minister had stuck his head out of the window and shouted, 'Brian.' The minister invited us back to his hotel, where I sat and listened to him lecture my father on his recent discussion with Saddam Hussein about Saddam's ambition to create a new caliphate in the Middle East.

But we did not gamble, meet smugglers or uncover international secrets during the following week's trip to Hadrian's Wall. My father had produced a voluble commentary on each lion and dragon in the avenue of mythical animals outside the Ming Tombs, but he had nothing to say about the Roman fort. Instead, he recalled a trip he had once taken with his father when he had been my age. 'We went to the beach at Skye. It rained all the time. Poor man. Didn't know his sons, thought he would take them on holiday, but we were just fed up. Not a great success.'

★

My father was then the most punctual, efficient and focused person I knew. Far more than any teacher. At home, he watched every movement to make sure that no one was carrying too much on a tray, that no cup was put down on a wooden surface without a coaster. Whenever anyone poured from a teapot, he would say 'Archimedes!', by which he meant that the law of leverage increased the chance of the lid of the teapot falling off.

If we ever had to go somewhere as a family – to church on Sunday, for example – my father would bark, long before the departure time, 'Too much initiative', 'Too many chiefs and not enough Indians', 'Come on, everyone', eventually striding out to the car so that he could be 'five minutes before parade'. He gave directions in the style of a rally-car navigator: '300 yards, 200 yards, hard left', and if my mother in her panic still tried to turn right, he would bark, 'Left – army left.' He always had a map. He never spilt anything. He never lost anything. He never forgot anything, because he had 'drills'.

But that day, when I was twelve, I discovered that he had left five shirts behind in the B&B on Hadrian's Wall.

15

Twenty-six years later, I was thirty-eight, he was eighty-nine and he had only brought one spare shirt to the B&B. We walked out together, in our standard uniforms. I was in my worn black down jacket with a pack on my back, and carrying a 'dang', an absurdly large Punjabi stick with a metal tip and head that I had had with me as I walked through Asia more than a decade earlier. I worried the dang would get me arrested in the centre of Newcastle, but I was addicted to swinging it as I walked, and to rubbing with my right thumb a tiny pockmark in the wood. My father was in his tartan trews and tam-o'-shanter cap. It took me time to arrange the latest Chinese hearing aid, which relied on a microphone hung on his neck. I felt I needed to check and change the batteries. It was difficult to guess from his responses whether he was listening.

Arm in arm, we walked slowly along a four-lane highway edged with squat Victorian terraces. Black solar panels glittered on slate roofs. A line of dock-buildings on our right allowed glimpses of the River Tyne. And then, between the terrace and a dockyard, we reached a noticeboard which proclaimed that we had reached the beginning of Hadrian's Wall. The illustration on the board, clearly by the same artist who had drawn the latrine we had seen twenty-six years earlier, showed sailing ships in the river, native huts in the fields, and in the foreground Roman cavalry clattering along a curving mud path towards red-tiled gates. In the picture the sun was shining, the light was clear – almost Mediterranean.

This day, the light was paler. My father muttered that seventy years earlier he had spent six years of his life with 400 men who had been born within four miles of this place. Many of his fellow soldiers had been coal miners. The shafts in which they had worked still ran beneath our feet. Ten thousand other men had worked in the adjoining shipyards of Wallsend. 'But I had no ship-workers,' said my father. 'They must have been a protected profession.'

It was a battalion of the Royal Highland Regiment, the Black Watch. But his soldiers had Newcastle accents, and they would have called themselves Geordies. The commanding officer was a solicitor from Durham.

'So it wasn't a very Scottish battalion?' I suggested.

'Well, many of them were originally from Scottish families who had moved to England during the Industrial Revolution,' he replied.

'But that was two generations earlier . . .'

'I don't care. They were proud to be Scottish. We had joined a Highland regiment, wore Black Watch kilts, and marched to battle to the sound of pipes. When they got their steps wrong they had to buy me – The Officer In Charge of Scottish Dancing – a shot of whisky. I got a lot of free drinks. Although,' he conceded, 'the regular Black Watch officers liked to pretend we never existed.'

He said that he and his Geordie anti-tank platoon had destroyed sixteen Panzer tanks in a day. All of his platoon had been either killed or wounded. And they had won a 'battle honour' for the regimental flag. Yet the Tyneside Scottish were not mentioned in the Black Watch regimental museum. Until very recently, my father had gone every year to Newcastle to meet the other survivors of the battle. They were now all dead.

The terraces we could see ran behind the remains of what had once been his soldiers' houses. In the 1970s most of the occupants had been relocated to a new estate, and the housing had been flattened. The Vickers tank and artillery factories went. In front of us – stretching over 4,000 feet of river frontage – were the old shipyards which once had built the *Mauretania*. It crossed the Atlantic in four and a half days in 1909. But in 2006, the Swan Hunter shipyard folded, and in 2007 the bright blue and orange cranes and floating docks were moved to a 300-acre site in Dabhol in western India.

The local council had tried to use the remains of this Roman fort to revive the post-industrial city. They did it through a seven-year paid-work archaeological excavation programme, which used unemployed labour to dig fifteen feet or more below the level of the Victorian houses. The Roman fort at which we were looking was, they boasted, 'the most excavated fort in Britain'. But the finds were disappointing – no great artistic treasures, no previously unknown gods or touching inscriptions to the dead: nothing that really changed our view of Roman Britain. Presumably the Victorian builders had removed or destroyed most of what was left of the Romans when they laid out the terraces; and now the council had in turn removed the terraces. So if there were only disappointing, scattered signs of the Romans, there were no signs at all of the thousands of homes which had belonged to the men with whom my father had served.

The floor plan of the Roman cavalry dormitories was marked out in stone, on a large gravel site, set back from the remains of the deserted shipyard. The old Swan Hunter offices had been converted into a museum (a stone Roman lavatory seat sat alongside part of the Edwardian state-room fittings of the *Mauretania*). A medieval copy of an ancient manuscript suggested the Romans called this place 'Segedunum', which the curators translated as 'the strong fort', although this seemed to me a somewhat improbable title for one in a line of fourteen almost identical forts along the wall.

Why would visitors come to such a place? When the *Mauretania* was launched in 1906, my father's father, then in his twenties, living in a British culture which celebrated the Empire and the military, might have seen in this fort flattering reflections of his own values. My father didn't.

'I'm not sure I get much out of this. And I'm pretty sure that my soldiers wouldn't have found it very exciting either.'

The council marketed it all as 'a mighty frontier system' devised by 'one of the most powerful empires the world has ever seen'.

'Doesn't look very mighty to me,' said my father, prodding a line of stones, one foot high, with his foot.

A replica of a Roman bathhouse had been built in one corner of the fort. This appealed to him more. In the central hall – painted with hurried images of dolphins – was a raised fountain. The basic plan was recognisable from the house in which I had lived for three years in Afghanistan. Here, as in Kabul, you passed through a changing room and a cold room into heated chambers, on a raised hypocaust floor. This was billed as a working replica, so that it would still have been possible to see the steam, and hear the jokes and grunts of half-naked figures pushing sweat from their eyes, and moving carefully over the wet floor from the *frigidarium* to the *calidarium*. In the damp cold of Tyneside it seemed indecently luxurious. It did not so much show the connection between Newcastle and the Roman past, as emphasise how little link remained.

We left Segedunum and set off west along a busy road, which our map suggested marked the line of wall. I took my father's arm. I liked holding his arm. But his wrists were thinner and sharper than I remembered. He leaned hard. We found a small section of wall in a narrow strip of park between a major road and an old railway line. Like the bathhouse it had been reconstructed in the 1990s: it was seven battlements long and fifteen feet high. In front of it, archaeologists had found a twelve-foot ditch of sharpened stakes.

My father had been reading a book that described Hadrian's Wall as 'a permeable trading frontier'. 'Doesn't look very permeable to me,' he observed. 'Did you need a *laissez-passer* to leave?'

'We don't know.'

'You don't know anything about dictatorial regimes. They care deeply about whether you go out. There must have been some documentation.'

I had expected my father to see the wall, as almost everyone else did, as a way of keeping the barbarians out. Instead – perhaps because he had been a Cold War intelligence officer – he saw it as a structure built to keep the Romans in, a bureaucratic edifice of paranoia and surveillance. In Hadrian's Wall he saw Berlin.

16

We had talked – because we had once done this in Iran – of his walking with me along Hadrian's Wall for the first hour, or the first three miles, of every day. And he had not objected, perhaps because he had not wanted to disappoint me. But Iran had been ten years earlier. We had never walked more than half a mile at a time recently – slowly round the circuit of his mini-park at home. And it was already clear from our slow shuffle that morning that this was about the limit of what he could do as an eighty-nine year old.

I left him at the reconstructed section of the wall and told him to take a car and meet me in the Great North Museum. I set off on an abandoned railway track, a short distance south of the original line of the wall, which was now buried under tarmacked roads and the back gardens of terraced houses. An hour later I was coming onto a road above the Newcastle dockyard gates, dark in the shadow of half-abandoned administrative buildings, when I spied a familiar figure in a tam-o'-shanter at the top of the street. My father had persuaded the car to drop him, and come to intercept me.

I wasn't on the Hadrian's Wall path, and this hadn't been part of our plan. I asked, a little crossly, why he had thought he could find me. 'Don't you worry about that,' he replied, 'I knew you'd be here.' Instead of being touched by the initiative and energy he had put into ambushing me, I was simply worried that he might have got lost. For most of our slow walk, arm in arm, up the street, I grumbled about the risks of us heading off in different directions. Then we reached the waiting car, where he left me again, and where I again quickened my pace.

My solo walk now led along the Newcastle quays. The derelict Victorian docks and warehouses had been converted into executive apartments and restaurants. Two giant Pyrenean mountain dogs, the size of small ponies, newly blow-dried, occupied the centre of the street, admired by a circle of young Persian-Bahrainis wearing huge sunglasses. One petted the nearest dog, another jumped in terror whenever they looked up, and a third posed for photographs. ('Seventy-four kilos,' she giggled, 'that is my weight.')

I stopped for an espresso from a van parked on the quayside. My father had described his three years of living alongside Geordies in terms of small men in khaki battledress. The Geordies I passed now wore espadrilles and Uggs, velour tracksuits and paisley shirts, or carried Prada handbags and macaroons in pink-striped bags. Until the Newcastle factory had closed, the barista who served me had been a lathe-operator building precision machinery for Siemens.

Across the river and downstream, nearer the estuary, at South Shields, the Industrial Revolution had turned a fishing village into a city and the council, anxious for more housing, had decided to build terraces over yet another Roman fort. Into these terraces in 1875 went Scottish immigrant families, and a thousand Yemeni sailors who had settled here to work the coastal and Baltic trade. (Some of their descendants still live in South Shields.) The terraces had been named Aurelian Road, Valerian Road and Claudius Close. (It was a relief to find that the pub near the Hadrian Primary School had chosen a non-Roman theme: the Lookout, with a picture of a sailor.)

During the Second World War, the factories and shipyards had been hit with German incendiary bombs and parachute mines. (A single bomb in the market square killed forty people.) A memorial to the dead had been built and then, quite recently, demolished. The coal and the shipyards had gone, and South Shields now had the highest unemployment rate in mainland Britain.

But here too the council hoped that ancient Rome might offer employment and regeneration. Like Wallsend, South Shields removed its Victorian housing and re-exposed its fort. Here too they had left a large open area of gravel, scattered with low stone foundations, and cartoon illustrations on noticeboards. Photographs in a small exhibition hall showed the excavation – women in drainpipe jeans and bearded men in singlets and micro-shorts in a deep pit surrounded by housing terraces. A display case held five small chunks of grey and scratched plaster, 1,800 years old, on which you could still see the confident line of a green leaf, the bottom quarter of a red flower, and what seemed to be the edge of some golden fruit – peaches perhaps.

South Shields had opted to reconstruct not the fort bathhouse but the prefect's or commanding officer's residence, a suite of fine painted rooms, halls and drawing rooms, finishing with an underfloor-heated winter dining room. But the Roman military engineer had also insisted on maximising the space in the fort, so the courtyard ended abruptly in a cement wall, which left little light and no view; and the prefect shared another wall with the soldiers' barrack block, so that I guessed he would have heard the soldiers snoring from his own bedroom.

These excavations had been more rewarding than those at Wallsend. They suggested that South Shields was more diverse and cosmopolitan in the Roman period than it had been at any time until the arrival of the Yemenis. One tombstone from AD 350, for example, commemorated a British woman with a flat, vacant face who had married a merchant from Palmyra in the eastern desert of Syria, now in danger of becoming the western frontier of a new Islamist state. There was also a funerary relief commissioned by a Spanish cavalryman for his slave, Victor, a Moor from North Africa. It depicted Victor as a Roman in a toga, waited on in the afterlife by his own miniature barbarian slave. The Roman name for this fort was Arbeia, which perhaps came from El-beyt Arabeia, meaning 'the house of the Arabs' in Aramaic. And a Roman list of units, preserved in Ravenna, said that the fort was garrisoned by a thousand *barcariorum Tigrisiensium* – 'Tigris bargemen' from Iraq.

17

I found my father in the Great North Museum, as promised. I was excited by the day's discoveries and listed – loudly so he would be sure to hear – all the parallels I had seen between the life lived by the Romans here and my year in Iraq on that other Roman frontier – the Tigris. I explained how my office in Amara had been as cramped as that of the Roman prefect in South Shields. And how not only our weapons and ammunition but also all our hamburgers, cheesecakes and acid-coloured powdered juices had been imported by plane from the United States to Kuwait, and then by convoy to the town. A 250-pound 'contracting officer' from Arkansas had sat with us, in an air-conditioned office, recording in triplicate, for Halliburton, the purchase of every plastic chair. We flew in our own drinking water, because we did not trust the local water.

In 2,000 years' time, archaeologists in Iraq will be able to excavate the landing strips, the generator platforms, the rows of tents, the dining halls and tank parks – structures indistinguishable from the bases we built a thousand miles away in Afghanistan, or indeed in the Balkans a decade earlier. And among them, they will find vast pits filled with American cake wrappers and plastic water bottles.

'The Roman forts, Daddy, were built to an almost identical design in Iraq, through Libya, to Britain. As soon as he marched into the camp, a legionary would know immediately where the paymaster's office was. And a vast system of contractors supported their lives. The Roman prefect here imported shoes from Provence, fish paste from Spain, olive oil from Libya, coin for salaries from Rome, and ceramic dinnerware from factories in Gaul. And they threw away so much: one and a half million Roman nails hidden in a pit in a single abandoned legionary fortress in Scotland.'

My camp in Iraq, I continued, had been manned by the King's Own Scottish Borderers – a British regiment recruited from the Scottish side

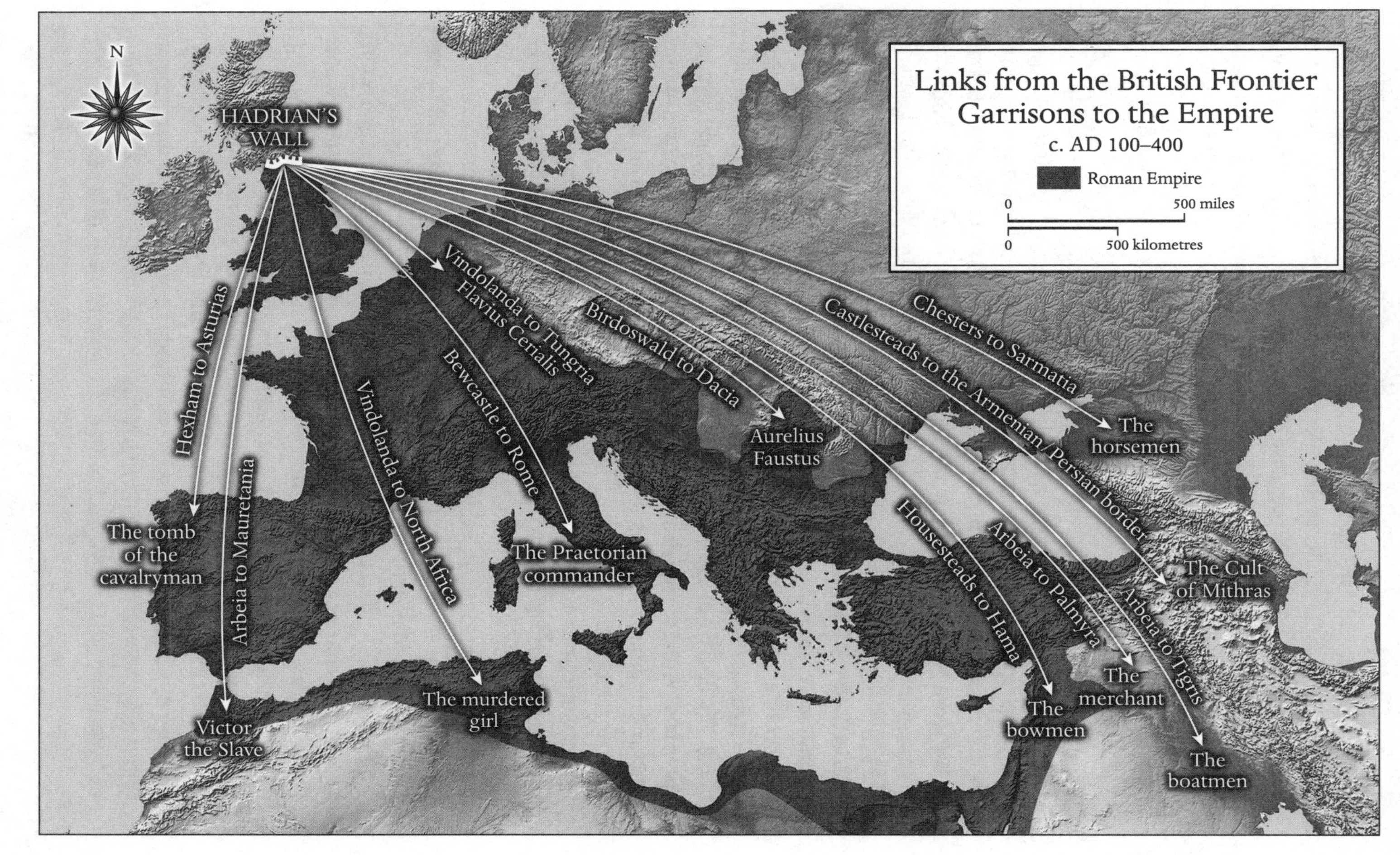
Links from the British Frontier Garrisons to the Empire
c. AD 100–400
Roman Empire
0
500 miles
0
500 kilometres
N
HADRIAN'S WALL
Hexham to Asturias
The tomb of the cavalryman
Arbeia to Mauretania
Victor the Slave
Vindolanda to North Africa
The murdered girl
Bewcastle to Rome
The Praetorian commander
Vindolanda to Tungria
Flavius Cerialis
Birdoswald to Dacia
Aurelius Faustus
Chesters to Sarmatia
The horsemen
Castlesteads to the Armenian/Persian border
The Cult of Mithras
Housesteads to Hama
The bowmen
Arbeia to Palmyra
The merchant
Arbeia to Tigris
The boatmen

of the border, but whose headquarters was on the English side of the border. The coalition included nations that had been enemies sixty years before. The next base to our east was manned by Italian soldiers from Naples, who had imported heavy full-sized espresso machines and built pizza ovens. And further east the Japanese soldiers were constructing Japanese baths in the compound at Samawah.

'There seem to have been different languages, cultures and faces too in almost every fort along the wall,' I said to my father. 'There were a fair number of tribes from what we would now call Belgium and Holland but there were also Hungarians, Aramaic-speaking Iraqis, and 5,000 Sarmatians, who were nomadic horsemen from Central Asia. All of them had been enemies of Rome. And in one of the camps there were Africans who left behind their own ethnic cooking pot – a clay tagine.'

My office in Amara had once been the Iraqi governor's house. It overlooked the Tigris. Every sunset I watched the silhouettes of figures poling or rowing their slender boats, and then casting their nets over the bronze waters of the river. Some preferred to use car batteries to electrocute the fish. But I could not speak to the Tigris boatmen: I was divided from them by a line of razor wire. I felt closer to the sparrows. Amidst the drab bare mudflats, which had emerged when Saddam drained the marshes, tiny brown birds, clustered in hundreds on a dusty bush.

I explained all this to my father. 'Quite right, darling,' he said. I wasn't sure how much he had taken in. He had often complained that no one had been able to engage with his own experience of empire. 'If you haven't experienced something, you can't understand it.'

I asked him how he thought my experience in Iraq compared to his experience in Malaya.

'Completely different. You had bags of money, we had none; your system was chaos, we had a proper administration.' Nevertheless, when I was in Iraq, he had given me confident advice. I had called him, for example, when a large crowd was demonstrating outside our gates.

'Very straightforward, darling,' he had said down the satellite phone. 'Shoot the ringleaders, and impose a twenty-four-hour curfew.' Not only did the colonel and I not consider shooting the ringleaders, we did not even know how to impose a twenty-four-hour curfew. So, as my father had predicted, the crowd had looted the government offices.

18

After we had shared a sandwich in the museum café, I went to look at some Roman inscriptions and he headed for the museum shop, where, ignoring the books on the Romans, he bought one on the birds of Northumberland. When I had finished reading the inscriptions ('I think you like museums more than me, darling'), he was in the café again, copying images of birds into his notebook. We parted, to meet again that evening. 'Be sure to remember and tell me exactly what you see,' he said.

Leaving Newcastle, walking west along the line of the wall, my boots hammered hard over mini roundabouts. Blonde women in new black trouser-suits, smoking outside a hair salon and a Polish grocery store, glanced at my stained blue trousers and pack. After a couple of hours on a busy road, I glimpsed a field of maize through a gap in a hedge, and then I was back in a town, looking through picture windows at porcelain decorations and wing-backed armchairs. Cul-de-sacs had swallowed a village green.

Then crescents gave way to patches of forestry and high hedges, until, at the first hill, I left the last houses behind, and found an even, satisfying stride. The rocks beneath my feet were 200 million years younger than the rocks that surrounded my father's house in the Highlands, but they were harder and older than the rocks of southern England. The wet cold ground on either side reflected an area which had up to two hours less sunshine a day, and much more rain than southern England.

I had entered a terrain stretching to the west coast of Cumbria, and deep into what is now Scotland, which had its own distinctive buildings and patterns of settlement long before the Romans came to Britain. By the first century BC when communities in the Scottish Highlands had been experimenting with stone buildings and producing impressive ceramics, and the communities in southern England were creating a culture based on large hill forts and coinage, this region, stretching from coast to coast across the modern Borders, had avoided ceramics, coins or grand forts. It was instead an area defined by a scattering of small farmsteads in circular compounds – settlements in which it had been difficult to detect any great inequalities of wealth or power. And after the Romans departed, the whole zone had again become a place of independent, now largely forgotten, kingdoms and cultures, belonging to neither England nor Scotland.

My father called this land, through which the wall ran – and which he believed belonged particularly to us as hybrid-Scot-Britons struggling with debates over Scottish independence – 'the Middleland'. And I was hoping that, by walking along it, we could begin to bring the Middleland back to life.

An hour later, I reached the first section of Hadrian's Wall. I had seen many pictures of the wall curving sinuously and steeply along a precipitate ridge in evening light. But this section in a flat field to my left turned out to be two feet high, 'capped' with a surface of modern cement. It looked as though it could have been made quite recently as a bench, or the foundation of a shed. I ran my fingers over the diagonal marks made by a Roman quarryman's chisel on the square dark masonry. The wall-stub ended after six feet and there was no clue to its onward course through the cow-trampled ground. I sat on the stones, drank some water and then continued west through a farm gate and back onto the road. After a few minutes I came across another rectangle of stone, then again nothing: the wall stopped and started like a message in Morse.

A dozen people walked past me in waterproof trousers and jackets – moving fast in the other direction on the path towards Newcastle. For them the wall had apparently become a racetrack for sponsored charity walks – the toughest, they explained, could do the eighty-one miles in twenty-four hours. Five hours into the walk, after more short sections of stone (and more information boards: 'Here the gauge of the wall changes from 10 to 8 Roman feet'), I arrived at a small metal sign indicating the site of another fort. Beyond, in a patch of uneven pasture, a flock of thick-necked, flat-faced Texel sheep inspected the ground almost as closely as an archaeologist. The map revealed a handful of isolated farms ahead.

Eighteen hundred years earlier I would have already walked past three forts, eleven mile-castles and twenty-two turrets containing thousands of armed men. This place – rural Northumberland – now has one of the smallest populations and lowest levels of immigration in Britain. But from about AD 122 to AD 400, this particular empty field would have been the home of 500 men from a Frisian regiment, originally raised in Northern Holland. Two forts further on there was a unit of Syrian cavalry, whose altar to a Syrian god survived. Almost none of the first generation of these men would have been able to speak the local British language. And whatever their origins, they had adopted many Roman customs such as eating olives and fish paste (imported through the Newcastle and South Shields docks) – customs which were as alien to the local British population as heated bathhouses. The only 'British' civilians then recorded inside the wall were slaves.

19

My father had chosen a corner-table for our dinner that night, so I could speak more loudly and he could hear. He didn't want to discuss the Romans. He wanted to quiz me about my new job as a politician. He had always enjoyed trying to help me in my career. When I was sent to Jakarta for my first diplomatic posting, he arrived only two days after me, and began with 'sorting out my house'. Half an hour after dropping his bags in my hall, he set off on a recce ('time spent in reconnaissance is seldom wasted'). He returned in a motorised rickshaw with two bamboo plants, two hibiscus and two bougainvilleas. 'I've found you the metal-workers' street and the toyshops – though they are pretty useless – and I think I know where we can get you a machete fitted with a handle.'

The next day he tracked down Khotib, a Javanese man who had worked for us when I was a child in London. I had grown up admiring Khotib's biceps, his somersaults into swimming pools and his ability to shoot rabbits in Scotland with a piece of lead piping converted into a blowpipe. Khotib had since retired to a village twenty miles outside Jakarta. Together he and my father began constructing an aviary in my garden – twenty feet long and ten feet wide.

They acquired a chameleon, an iguana, three parrots, and a sulphur-crested cockatoo, who sat on my shoulder and nibbled my ear. 'A pity,' said my father, 'that you couldn't have a honey-bear.'

But most of his focus in Jakarta had been on advising me how to succeed as a diplomat. He convinced me first to adopt his 'Peking system', which involved breakfasting with an Indonesian-language teacher every morning, so that we could read the Indonesian-language newspapers together. Next, he recommended his 'Malacca system', which required clearing all my telegrams before the other officials got into work, so that I could be in a 'state of grace' for whatever happened over the course of the day.

His 'Burma system' suited me particularly well. His first ambassador in Rangoon had said, 'I don't want you in the embassy, Brian, I want you out in the country.' I, therefore, was in the office as little as possible, made friends with as many Indonesians as I could and did not spend my time with what he called 'the boring Europeans'. Such systems were reinforced by mottos, ranging from 'a good staff officer always carries a pen', through 'better to seek forgiveness than permission' to 'always make love to the ambassador's wife'. (I interpreted this last instruction to mean one should charm her.)

Beneath these models and a hundred anecdotes lay his basic assumption that the existing government system was useless, and would try to frustrate any plan for reform, but that 'Stewart' could always outwit the bureaucrats, and get things done. An anecdote from 1941 ran, 'On my first day, when I was taking my platoon for a run, a soldier said to me, "I only run in jail," so guess where I sent him?' An anecdote from 1968 ran, 'When I joined the Joint Intelligence Committee they were all drafting by committee, so I thought, "I'll fix you," and the next meeting when they turned up, I said, "Right, gentlemen, would one of you like to take on the job of drafting future reports? . . . I thought not," and that was that – from then onwards it was Stewart's reports. And this was 1962: 'I thought it best no one knew I was going to Mongolia, because the Foreign Office would have objected. I just rediscovered my report in the Public Record Office; someone has scribbled on the top, "Who is this officer? Who gave him permission to go?"'

When I moved from Jakarta to Montenegro in 1999, my father came out to see me again. In my overheated hotel room he encouraged me in the doctrine of 'fait accompli'. 'The more people you ask, the more likely they are to say no. Tell them as little as possible.' He composed a telegram with me to send to head office on a Friday evening, just as everyone was leaving for the weekend, informing them that I would be attempting a one-man recce of a war criminal's house, 'unless I hear to the contrary by Sunday morning'.

20

When I complained the next morning on Hadrian's Wall about all the people walking the wall for charity, without looking at the forts, my father reminded me that he had walked the wall to raise money for a Down's syndrome charity ten years earlier, taking our giant Scottish mastiff, Morag, with him. He had skipped sections even then. Unspoken was the thought that if he had found the journey too much when he was only seventy-eight, then this was perhaps not the most sensible idea for a joint holiday. After breakfast, he did not offer to walk even the first couple of hundred yards with me. Instead, we arranged to meet for lunch, by the bus stop at Chesters.

I walked on alone, passing what was marked on my map as the junction of two main Roman roads – Stanegate and Dere Street – probably marked originally by a Roman triumphal arch. It was now a roundabout, connecting two A roads and fronted by a closed pub. An hour later I clambered over a fence to inspect a deep, broad ditch with high grass mounds on either side, running straight across a field. As I walked further away from Newcastle, fields of crops had given way to fields full of dairy cows, then, as the grass became less good, suckler cows had replaced dairy cows, and now, with land ever rougher and more sour, I could see more Swaledale sheep and fewer cows. A farmer raced up on a quad bike – the first farmer I had seen in two days of walking. His family had been farmers, apparently with land on either side of the wall, for more generations than he knew. 'Hundreds of years, I'd say.' His sheep were moving up and down the slopes of the ditch, searching for sweet grass among the rushes and thistles.

'I've always wondered what this ditch is,' he said. 'Someone said they thought it was an Iron Age fortification built long before the Romans came.'

'I don't think so,' I said, 'it's a Roman *vallum* – a ditch to protect the back of the wall – built at the same time as the wall.'

'Thanks. I always wondered,' he said, and rode off. He did not seem particularly keen to learn more about this monument in his family's field.

My father had asked me to be very precise about my arrival time for our lunch by the bus stop at Chesters. It was difficult to select an exact time as it was a twelve-mile walk, so I was pleased that by keeping up a good pace through the rain, I arrived to the minute. My father was nowhere to be seen. I spent half an hour pacing the fort and the back roads, trying to work out where he had got to. I had given him very clear instructions. Why had no one seen him at the fort? An eighty-nine year old in tartan trews is easy to describe, and just as difficult to forget. When he finally came stumping into sight along the road from the bridge, sweating under his tam-o'-shanter, I was angry. I explained my anger to myself largely as worry – worry that he had got lost, or fallen, or worse. It transpired that he had arrived early and gone for a pint in the pub.

But it was something else too. There was a frustration at wasting time we could have spent together. There was the slight weariness of having hurried the last seven miles to make sure I wasn't late. And then there was having been told off so often as a child for not being at a rendezvous 'five minutes before parade', and then the emotion – he would have called it *Schadenfreude* – of discovering this living embodiment of the virtues of military punctuality and efficiency in the wrong place at the appointed time.

We didn't really stop arguing, apologise and kiss until we got to the fort gate. Then, a little crestfallen, we traipsed around the remains of the bathhouse. It was identical to the bathhouse at Segedunum, to the metre, it seemed.

The statues which had been found in the fort had been moved to a museum. I wished they, or at least replicas of them, had been left in place. I would have liked to see the statue of the bearded god of the Tyne still lying in the bathhouse, and to have seen the altars as they had been found, crowded in the garrison treasury, rather than packed in museum cases or hidden in basements in Newcastle. In the museum itself, my father seemed struck not by the objects themselves, but by how poorly they had been presented – how small the print was on the information boards, the lack of detail. It was, he said, 'boring'.

21

That night my father and I had dinner in an Indian restaurant in a market town. I glanced around at two bearded men in rugby shirts sharing two bottles of wine; and a young man, who was staring hard at his credit card while his girlfriend was in the bathroom. Among the yoghurt- and cream-based curries on the menu was a lot of fish. The photo of the half-open door of a Bengali shrine suggested that the owners were from Sylhet. The curries were freshly made.

'It's difficult to get Bengali fish,' said the chef. 'Sometimes there is catfish and dogfish in the Newcastle market, but we have so many thousand fish in Bangladesh and if they come to England at all, they come frozen and in too much bulk.'

'Do you offer fresh fish of the day?' I asked.

'I am aware of a restaurant in Wales that offers fresh fish.'

I was surprised he knew this. Wales was 300 miles away.

'We all know each other in this business,' he explained. 'One of us may be in Wales, and another in Hexham, but we all grew up a maximum of ten miles apart in Bangladesh. If I don't know someone my father will. He came here in the 1950s. It was tough then: there were only men, and they all lived together, they did not speak good English, and they did not understand where they were. When I first suggested to my father that I should look for an opportunity in the countryside, he told me off. He was only comfortable being in Newcastle. But I pressed on – we are all now looking for opportunities in towns and villages.'

'Do you live here?'

'No, we all live in Newcastle. When it is all over tonight, we will pack up, get in a ten-seater bus, put on the music, and play tabla and sing Bengali songs.' He mimed hitting the drums. It seemed too picturesque to quite be true. But then, perhaps the same could be said for my father on his bagpipe chanter. When I probed a bit more, the chef explained that he was a 'personal friend' of Alan Shearer and the Newcastle football team and that Prince Harry had eaten in his restaurant ('paid with a note with his mother's head on it'). The chef's brother was thinking of running to be a Member of Parliament.

When I stood up to leave, he asked me where I lived.

'Penrith,' I replied. 'Near Carlisle.' He did not seem to have heard of it. I added, 'The other end of Hadrian's Wall . . .'

He laughed. 'Hadrian's Wall?' he said with delight. 'You've heard of Hadrian's Wall?'

22

As we finished dinner, my father said, 'Right, that's that. Now tell me what is happening in the nuthouse.' It was two years since I had put myself forward to become a parliamentary candidate for Penrith and the Border through an open primary – a new system where everyone in the constituency, regardless of their party, could vote to choose the Conservative candidate. It was then ten years since I had walked across Afghanistan, and seven years since I had worked in Iraq – a place where my father had not been able to visit me and help. But my father had 'deployed' for the primary. He turned his B&B room in Penrith into 'HQ'. There he carefully read through my leaflets ('I'd emphasise "public service" – your life and your father's life have been dedicated to "public service" – that sort of thing'). He had made me practise my speech on him three times in the bedroom – loud enough for him, which meant that the neighbouring rooms were hearing most of it too. And, perhaps because he could not hear all of it, he focused on my posture and expressions more than the words: 'That's right, darling, a few more smiles – look up – speak clearly – enjoy yourself. Faster and funnier.'

The primary took place in the auction mart. We candidates stood in the cattle ring. The voters sat on the cold concrete seats above us and shouted questions from all sides. The convenor sat in the place of the auctioneer. My father was not in the ring because he was a Scottish, not an English, visitor. Instead, he sat outside on a plastic chair, in his tam-o'-shanter and tartan trews, his shoulders hunched in his grey tweed jacket.

One of the other candidates – a lady who, like my other five opponents, had stood in many selections for other constituencies – had been to commiserate with him in advance. 'Rory won't make it this time – but perhaps in five years' time.' 'We shall see, my friend, we shall see,' he scowled. He shook his shoulders, peered at the ground and tapped his feet up and down to keep warm, humming the regimental quick marches 'Black Bear' and 'Hielan' Laddie'.

I didn't think it had gone very well – though I had managed to speak clearly, look up and occasionally smile, as he suggested. I apologised for taking up his time and suggested we should probably drive home to Broich. 'Don't worry about that, darling,' he'd said, 'we shall see.' When the news came that the audience had voted for me to be their candidate, he muttered to the lady candidate, 'You didn't know my son, madam.' When the general election came six months later, he 'deployed' to Penrith again, standing in the centre of the high street with a rosette on his lapel and Torquil the lurcher at his feet, to 'warm up' passers-by. And he was with me in the counting hall, after a night without sleep, when I heard that I had been elected to Parliament.

But he had not been with me, when, three days after the election, I travelled down from Penrith to the House of Commons, and found myself at the base of a broad staircase. My heels sounded too loud on the marble steps. When I opened a great oak door, by pressing the brass grille on the gothic glass, I recoiled in the face of a sudden procession of the serjeants-at-arms, men and women marching like clockwork toys in black frogged tailcoats, black knickerbockers and black stockings, hands on their swords.

At the door of the chamber I encountered for the first time the stale smell of coffee-charged, hot bodies on overfilled leather cushions. I was not sure when to enter, when to stand or when to sit. The new MPs packed the chamber so tight that I could only find a place on the steps halfway up the aisle, and I could not ask a question unless I had a seat.

After a month or so, I was elected to the Foreign Affairs Committee. Often, just as we were questioning a witness, a bell would ring, like in a school. Far from our committee room, in the chamber, whips cried out a ritual phrase, the Speaker echoed them and posed his own question, the chamber responded, 'aye' and 'no', the Speaker shouted 'Division', and men in black tailcoats bellowed into antique telephones, like captains on a First World War liner, 'Clear the lobbies.'

We and the other 650 MPs rushed from our desks or meetings, flooded from six doors into two lobbies – which were as confusing and intimidating as a first visit to the Marrakesh bazaar. For eight minutes, sometimes as often as seven times a day, groups formed and dissolved in motion, with a crackle of enmities, generosity, disappointments and jokes. But what did any of this mean? Did my committee forensically challenge civil servants on the details of their administration? Was a question in the chamber a genuine question? Was a vote a choice, in the sense of a rational act preceded by deliberation? Was Parliament a daily check on the executive?

If I worried too much about these matters I would be accused of taking it all too seriously. But if I implied that these things were meaningless, colleagues would insist we were there to hold the government to account. Thus we were trained to be neither entirely literal, nor entirely cynical. Whenever I was about to conclude that Parliament was a theatrical sideshow, or an instrument of an elective dictatorship, it would show its power. It rebelled and forced the government to hold a referendum on Europe, it destroyed the government's proposal to abolish the House of Lords, and it prevented the government's intervention in Syria. In these brief moments, once or twice a year, Members of Parliament threw the system into disarray, destroyed the work of hundreds of civil servants, humiliated the government, attracted the fury and contempt of the party managers, and destroyed the promotion prospects of another dozen MPs, who had ceased to be ministerial potential and had become 'rebels'. I began to think of Parliament as though it was an elderly Alsatian: generally placid by the fire, but just occasionally, if someone stepped on its tail, waking in a wild fury of barking, and then just as suddenly curling up to go back to sleep.

Sometimes I felt that we could contribute far more in the outside world, and that it was a waste of all our talents. Often I was aware that the issues we were discussing were unbelievably important, and we were hardly qualified to decide on them. Sometimes I believed that Parliament didn't deserve us, and sometimes that we didn't deserve to be in Parliament. In short, in this world of endless corridors and hurrying men with giant gold watch chains, we felt like Alice in Wonderland, sometimes too large, and sometimes too small.

I tried to explain all this to my father. Perhaps I told him more about his government than he was comfortable hearing. He watched me on television in debates. He emailed enthusiastically when he saw me speaking. But his hearing was now so bad that he could not have made out much of these debates, and I doubted he would have wanted to. He praised me for 'leading and winning' the campaign to force the government to spend 2 per cent of GDP on defence. Yet I knew few of my colleagues would have seen me as the leader of that campaign, that those in government who associated me with it at all held it against me, and that 2 per cent might not quite mean 2 per cent. And despite his praise, I guessed that my father would not have been surprised to learn any of this.

Over supper that night, he said, 'I think you should give up on the parliamentary whips and become "District Commissioner for Cumbria Rural".'

'And what should I do then?'

'Organise everyone into a voluntary body – a sort of national service – do projects up and down the constituency, then all over rural Britain. Show them how to get things done.'

'And how about the long term, what comes after that?' I asked.

'Wake everyone up. Sort out the police.'

But I was still looking for a grander political manifesto, some new future. 'What do you think I should be trying to achieve for the British people?'

'Give them a sense of pride and purpose,' he suggested.

I wouldn't let the subject go. 'But I think I'm looking for something bigger than that. I mean, what do you think we should be trying to make Britain look like in fifty years' time?'

'That's beyond me, my darling. I'm afraid I can't help you there.' So I moved the conversation on to something more immediate and personal in my career.

A few months earlier, I had joined ninety-two other MPs and voted against the government's proposal to abolish the House of Lords. I felt that the constitution existed to protect the people against Parliament, and thus Parliament should not be able to use a simple majority vote to reconfigure its second chamber. In every other country, I said in my speech (limited to four minutes by the Commons clock), constitutional law was different from normal law – you needed some special procedure, such as a referendum, if you wanted to change the constitution. I felt the same should be true in Britain.

The whips were angry, the Prime Minister and the Chancellor were disappointed, and many of my colleagues were infuriated with our group of rebels. These constitutional changes had been linked to redrawing the electoral boundaries in our party's favour. They felt that our rebellion had forfeited our chances in the next election. That didn't prove to be

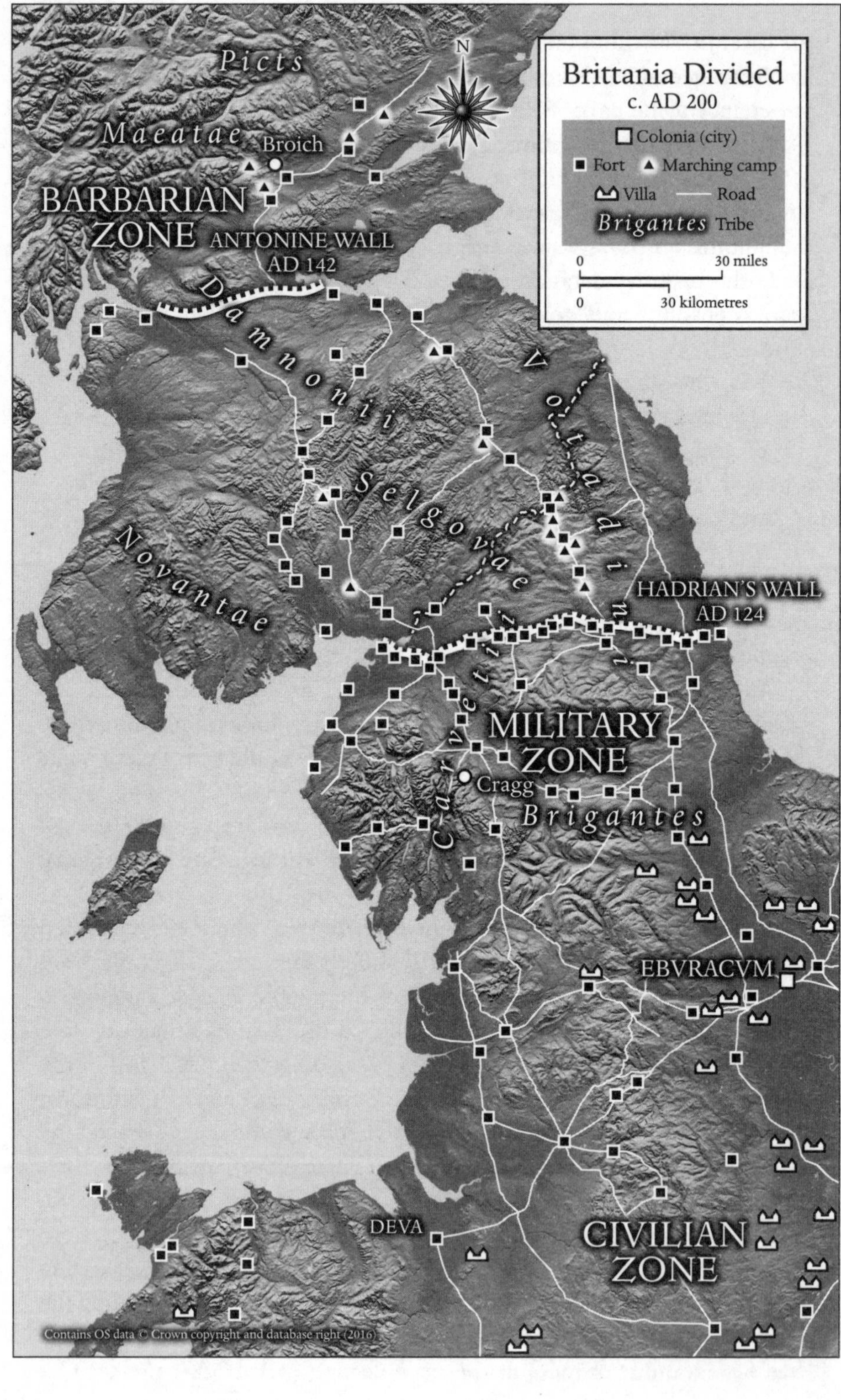

Brittania Divided
c. AD 200
Colonia (city)
Fort
Marching camp
Villa
Road
Brigantes Tribe
0
30 miles
0
30 kilometres
N
Picts
Maeatae
Broich
BARBARIAN ZONE
ANTONINE WALL AD 142
Damnonii
Votadini
Selgovae
Novantae
HADRIAN'S WALL AD 124
Carvetii
MILITARY ZONE
Cragg
Brigantes
EBVRACVM
DEVA
CIVILIAN ZONE
Contains OS data © Crown copyright and database right (2016)

the case. But as the months went on, I began to realise that the threats had been genuine – by rebelling I had forfeited for the next five years any chance to be part of the government.

Five years was a long time. I wanted to debate my decision, this 'sacrifice' which felt so significant to me, with my father, but he wouldn't engage in the topic. I suspected that he did not understand why I had thought this vote was so important, and that, in my place, he would have made the contrary decision, and tried his best to become a minister as soon as possible, and 'get things done'.

23

After another five miles of walking the next morning, from Newcastle towards my new Cumbrian constituency, the wall still stood no higher than the drystone field walls. The next mile-castle was a low square of masonry, projecting south of the wall, on a patch of unruly grass. I half remembered that the most detailed guidebook recorded that on this site something like three leather boots, one dice and the coins of four different emperors had been found; that it had been constructed by the fourth cohort of the second legion; that the line of the wall had been moved, a gate had been opened, and then walled up.

On a steep slope, where the wall ran over fell, through ghylls and becks shadowed by birch, a flock of horned Swaledale ewes trotted past, followed by a barking collie. The dog chased the sheep over the parapet, rounded the birch thicket and drove them back out of the old barbarian lands again, making the sheep leap, shove and roll over the wall stones.

This landscape had been farmed before the Romans came – pollen samples from the deep peat showed that the local population had cleared the forests in the early Iron Age, pastured livestock on the land and even planted crops in the thin soil. Aerial photographs picked up the lines of Iron Age ploughs, running diagonally under the wall.

But the Romans had driven the farmers from the land, and from their houses, turning the fields into a military camp. The area in which I was standing had become a military road, running between the wall and the great *vallum* ditch. The area I was looking at, just north of the wall, had become a killing zone, protected by ditches, mounds and sharpened stakes. In the thousands of square miles of territory behind me, not a single villa had been found. The area was governed by military not civilian rulers. And even behind the wall, the few villages were only extensions of Roman camps, and the scattered roundhouses of the local population seemed to contain hardly so much as a Roman pot.

Civilian life flourished south of the Humber. There, in the richer soil of lowland England, Rome produced a simulacrum of Mediterranean urban civilisation. There, over a thousand villas had been excavated – one with a mosaic floor of over a million separate tiles, another with great silver trays, embossed and decorated with dancing beauties. Meanwhile, the land around my father's house, north of the military frontier – the Highlands of Scotland – became an excluded land, defined by its resistance to Rome, a place outside the Empire – a place of freedom; a place of barbarians.

Hadrian's biographer claimed the wall was built to 'divide' the country in two, and separate Romans and barbarians. But it would be more accurate to say that it created the categories of Roman and barbarians in Britain, where they had not existed before. And it split the land in three parts: civilian Rome in the south, a barbarian land in the north, and a frontier Middleland in between.

Three hundred years later, when the Romans left, the distinction between Romans and barbarians seemed at first to fade. Wall stones were used to build churches and monasteries. Farmers moved back into the wall-corridor with their livestock, using the lime-mortared masonry as a drystone field boundary to pen their sheep and cows and protect their pasture. Then, in 1080 and 1092, the sons of William the Conqueror turned the Roman wall forts at Luguvalium and Pons Aelius – or, as they called them, Carlisle and Newcastle – into castles, and made the wall the border again.

Today, at this point, the wall no longer even marked the edge of the farmer's field, let alone a nation. On the ridge line, I could see an old farmer calling his dog, the straight line of his crook extended beneath his still hands. A dozen sheep broke loose, and jumped the wall again.

★

At lunch on the third day, I asked my father, 'Do you think that you felt proud of the British Empire in the way in which Romans felt proud of the Roman Empire?'

'Well, it is very difficult to answer that kind of question,' he said. 'We were imperialists, no doubt. I was very proud of the Empire. Even my aunties in Kirriemuir liked the idea of "the Empire on which the sun never sets".'

'And was it a Scottish empire?' I asked.

'Absolutely. Our heroes were Scots connected to Empire: that chieftain, for example, not Lord Lovat – the other one – Maclean. Fitzroy Maclean. We Scots dominated almost half the Diplomatic List – and we were the best soldiers in the army. And so on. But we didn't want to be a separate Scotland – we'd have thought it was boring – we wanted to be part of a British Empire.'

He talked about humming bagpipe tunes to keep his spirits up under bombardment in Hanoi. (His windows were blown out and his neighbours were killed.) He had poured whisky into the soup at every lunch in Vietnam to keep other ambassadors onside. And everywhere he was the Scot. 'Ah yes,' a Malay said once, 'you were the Scottish Chinese Affairs officer.'

I remembered – although he did not mention it then – that when he was the Consul General in Shanghai, his best friend, a woman called Nien Cheng, had called him her 'Scottish diplomat'. He had begged her to leave with him, but she had stayed, and had been sent to jail for a decade. She had been tortured, and her daughter had been killed because she was accused of having a relationship with an English spy.

24

I explained to my father that, as I walked west, I had come across more evidence of a unit called the *Cohors Prima Aelia Dacorum* – the First Aelian Cohort of the Dacians – a unit from what is now Romania. 'They grew up in a civilisation that nestled between the Black Sea and the Central

Asian steppe. Their capital city had a sundial 120 feet long, used for intricate astronomical calculations.'

'Not much hope for a sundial on the wall, darling,' he said. 'They must have found it pretty dreich. What did these people look like?'

I thought my father was missing the point. That he didn't realise how very little we would ever know about the units on Hadrian's Wall. It was a miracle that we even knew the Dacian cohort had been there. How could he expect us to know what the Dacians looked like?

But it turned out that it was me who wasn't trying hard enough. I discovered that there was a statue of a Dacian in the attic of the Vatican in Rome. And that I could show it to my father on Google Images. It depicted a man with hair to his shoulders, a beard down to his chest, tight moccasins knotted halfway up his calves, and his chest pushing forward from a fur-lined cloak. There were also Dacians on Trajan's Column in tight trousers and rearing felt hats. I pointed out an image of their king Decibalus cutting his own throat with their traditional weapon: a *falx*, or sickle. 'A Roman historian recorded that they had red hair and startling blue eyes.'

'That's more like it, darling,' he said. 'A bit of colour.'

I showed him the Dacians' Draco banner – half snake-head, half wolf-head, made from a metal tube, which howled as the wind moved through it. I explained that they may have had a wolf totem. None of this was mentioned in the museum of their main fort, at least as far as we could see. I guessed that the curator was suspicious of defining ethnic groups. Most archaeologists like to emphasise that the Roman auxiliary regiments soon began to recruit people born in Britain, even if they continued to be called 'Scythian' or 'Spanish'. It is a romantic mistake, they feel, to see the wall as a collection of exotic ethnic camps, flamboyantly proclaiming alien identities in the Northumbrian landscape. The Dacians, they feel, were 'Dacian only in name'.

'Academics have no understanding of military matters!' my father observed with relish. I was – as usual – not quite sure whether he had heard what I had said.

'That's not quite it. It's more their thoughts on ethnicity. I imagine the curator knows a lot about military theory.'

'Ah, yes, theory!'

'And practice too,' I said impatiently. 'The point is how little any of us can really know about the past from digging up the ground under our feet.'

'Hmm.'

The *Cohors Prima Aelia Dacorum* was stationed on the wall for perhaps 275 years. Longer, I pointed out to my father, than the entire existence of the Black Watch. Its culture would have changed dramatically over the centuries. We know that soldiers who at first were not allowed to marry, were able to; that families settled in the forts; that uniforms and military equipment changed; and we know something of the different skirmishes and prolonged periods of peace, which must have defined each particular generation of soldiers in the Dacian cohort. And this evidence of change would have encouraged archaeologists to be even more sceptical about defining a 'Dacian regimental culture'.

But as my father retorted, 'You and I know from personal experience that a regiment like the Black Watch can change its purpose, its uniform, its rules and its campaigns, without losing a jot of identity or national feeling. Remember we were originally established in the early eighteenth century as a police force for the Highlands, with clan chieftains serving as company commanders. Then we became a regular infantry unit, the 42nd regiment of the British Army, sent to fight across the Empire.'

My great-grandfather had been the first generation to exchange a scarlet jacket for a khaki coat. My grandfather went to war in his kilt. My father did not. He was reduced to a tiny scrap of tartan on his sleeve, and a red hackle. None of the weaponry my father used was still in service by the time I joined. Soldiers' accommodation improved, families played a more prominent role in life. By the time that I joined, the battalion had not fought since the Korean War – two full generations without seeing artillery fired in anger. In the following decade the regiment had campaigned in the Balkans, Iraq and Afghanistan, and then, through a merger, found itself with commanding officers from completely different regiments. Through design or neglect, they broke most of the links with the old regimental family.

But it was almost impossible to understand – unless you've experienced it – how conservative a regiment could remain through all this historical change. The Black Watch had not changed the colour of its tartan, or its red hackle, in its entire existence of 250 years. I was only the fourth generation of my family in the Black Watch, but there were officers whose connections went back much further. And at the time when I joined in 1991 the regiment continued to recruit 92 per cent of its soldiers from the three counties of Perthshire, Angus and Fife in Scotland.

How much of this would be apparent to a future archaeologist, peering at fragments, accidentally preserved for 2,000 years, in the foundations of the barracks? It was not only that no trace would have remained of the tradition – preserved for at least a century – that officers drank chilled kümmel, and that it was a forbidden, fineable offence to scoop the Stilton rather than cut it. Nothing in what remained of the regimental headquarters would have recorded the sound of bagpipes striking up to announce a dawn attack, or the tune (still less the 250-year-old joke) with which we were woken every morning:

> O hey! Johnnie Cope, are ye waukin' yet?
> Or are your drums a-beating yet?
> If ye were waukin' I wad wait,
> Tae gang tae the coals in the morning.

All this made my father feel that the *Cohors Dacorum* might have remained 'Dacian' in character for longer than the archaeologists believed. And, to my delight, some surviving masonry seemed to confirm this. Above the granary at Birdoswald, for example, carved in the Cumbrian sandstone, was a perfect image of the Dacian fighting sickle, the *falx*, commemorating the building's construction between AD 205 and 208, almost a century after the Dacian wars. A tomb inscription in Romania shows that although twenty years later many of the soldiers in the unit on the wall may already have been ethnically 'British', their commander Aurelius Faustus had still retired as a veteran to Dacia. And outside the fort was a tombstone, for a baby who had been named Decibalus – eighty years after the last Dacian king called Decibalus used the *falx* to kill himself when resisting the Romans.

'So what language did these Dacians speak?' asked my father.

'As usual we don't really know. There's a lot of talk about it being a dialect of Indo-European – which means not very much; about it being related to Thracian – but we only know about thirty words of Thracian. There are theories about it being related to Scythian or Armenian, but I don't think that means much more than they came from near the Black Sea –'

'So who are the Dacians now?' interrupted my father.

'No one. First, the Romans killed many of the Dacians in their homeland – this Dacian cohort in Britain was partly a way of removing potential resistance fighters – and then, after they had made peace with the Romans they were overrun by Visigoths and Ostrogoths . . .'

'. . . And every other kind of Goth,' he added, quoting Asterix.

'And their language, their dress, their religion seem to have faded over time. Then their entire nation vanished. Some of the strongest traces of the Dacians are here, 4,000 miles from their homeland.'

Perhaps, I reflected, the best way to understand how a regiment could have remained 'Dacian' in spirit long after it had ceased to be 'Dacian' in practice was to look at my father's wartime battalion, the Tyneside Scottish. Some future archaeologist would be tempted to emphasise that even those of his soldiers with Scottish ancestry had mostly been living for three generations on Tyneside, and spoke with Geordie accents; that the regiment had no organic historical connection to the Black Watch, and no regular Black Watch officers; and had been raised in Newcastle, a hundred miles south of the regimental recruiting grounds. The archaeologist could easily make them seem 'Highland Scottish' and 'Black Watch' only in name.

But through talking to my father, I knew how carefully the Tyneside Scottish wore their red hackles and Black Watch kilts, or practised their reeling on a Thursday night. How they attacked with the pipers playing 'Hielan' Laddie' and felt on the battlefield that they were fighting and dying in a regimental tradition. How whatever the reality of where people were born, or stationed, or served, the name and traditions of their regiment might still make this a set of soldiers with a shared imagination, another *Cohors Dacorum*, a *cohort*, of Black Watch Highlanders.

25

Decibalus, the seven-month-old child with a Dacian name, had been buried and commemorated with his ten-year-old brother at the Dacian fort on the wall. And it struck me that their father, a Roman officer, Dacian in imagination, Mediterranean in culture, and who knows what in ethnicity, had cherished them and buried them, 4,000 miles from the Dacian heroes after which they were named. But when I tried to understand Roman families, bringing up children in Britain, I found only fragments – a scrap of a child's exercise book, copying out lines of Virgil, for example, or an invitation sent by the wife of a Tungrian prefect, probably born in what is now Holland, to a fellow officer's wife in Carlisle in AD 70:

> You are warmly invited to my birthday party on the 11th of September – do come – you'll really make the day much more fun – and regards to Cerialis – from Aelius and from the little one.

In Carlisle there was a Roman tombstone, dedicated to Vacia, aged three. The Northumbrian peat had also preserved a play-horse on wheels, a toddler's shoes – small enough to sit in the palm of an adult hand – and, fittingly for a child of a Roman soldier, a wooden toy sword. It was not much, but enough perhaps to question whether the Romans were really as unsentimental about their children as the stern, unbending marble statues of imperial heroes might suggest.

★

Although I was born in Hong Kong and brought up in Malaysia, I did not feel I had been brought up as a child of the British Empire. My father's time in the Malayan Colonial Service was over before I was born. The pictures of him in his white uniform, with his pith helmet and ceremonial sword, seemed to resemble to the last detail the Sargent portrait of Sir Frank Swettenham in 1904, which was also on the dust jacket of a book in our house. So it surprises me, writing this, to realise that when we returned to Malaysia from London in 1979 (he had by then left 'the office' and become the director of the Rubbers Growers' Association) it was still only just over twenty years since independence.

In Malaysia, we continued to spend the first three hours of each day together, but the context had changed. Now we began the day not fencing, but with a swim in the pool. First, both of us turned somersaults, blowing bubbles underwater. And he would throw coins for me to collect. Then he would hold his breath. A friend of his, a former commanding officer of an SAS battalion, had come to visit and demonstrated how to extend our time underwater. So my father would stand by the side of the pool, sucking in short breaths – 'Hyperventilating, darling' – and then sink down to the bottom, while I counted above him.

After two minutes, seeing this immobile form still lying underwater, his white hair standing horribly upwards, I would become worried and eventually dive in, and try clumsily to push this drowning flesh out of the water. He would resist, waving his arms, only to finally emerge grinning. He could do about three and a half minutes at that point.

If it was not a school day he put on reel music – not I think on his great brass-horned gramophone, but on a small cassette player. And I put on my batik shorts and shirt. (My father had designed a patent 'Stewart' batik for the household, with a white background and a blue Black Watch thistle.) 'One-two-three-one-two-three – higher, neater – that's right – in front – behind – one-two-three-one-two-three.' He was concerned that my calves, like his, were not shapely enough for Highland stockings, so he also taught me an exercise to flesh them out. We stood side by side with our toes on a step, standing on tiptoe and lowering ourselves down again.

If it was a Sunday we drove in his new silver Toyota, with a leather cover on the steering wheel, playing Clarke's 'Trumpet Voluntary', to a street stall where we ordered *te tarik* – condensed milk and tea, poured together into a glass from a great height to make a pink bubbling sweetness – and *roti chani* – thin sheets of unleavened bread. He ate them with curry, and I dipped them in sugar. We returned with packs of Chinese pork buns for my mother.

Sunday afternoons were my least favourite time, because this was when he tried to teach me the recorder. Generally, he let me follow my inclinations. He once asked me, for example, why I wouldn't join him in building models. (It never gave me the joy I experienced building my plastic, machine-made Lego castle.) And I, aged four, had apparently said, 'You can't have everything, Daddy.' This delighted him.

He hadn't fought me when I complained about my Chinese teacher, an elderly lady who fed me sugared rose-hip tea while I sat on a cold marble and black-wood stool. He said that he would take me to China to try to convince me to keep up the lessons, but if I still didn't want to learn Chinese after that trip I could give it up. We went in 1980, just as the country was 'opening up'. I rode a dromedary for the first time on the Great Wall. I was taken down into the excavations of the Terracotta Army, where one of the archaeologists allowed me to pull out a terracotta arm. We were not allowed to take photographs of the digs. My father did so by concealing his camera in a special compartment in his shoulder bag and photographing them in the same way that he recorded Chinese submarine bases. I remembered the scene by opening and closing my eyes repeatedly. I still have the image in my mind. But I was determined throughout the trip that I would not change my mind about learning Chinese. So with my first footstep onto the tarmac back at Kuala Lumpur airport, I announced that I was giving up Chinese. He accepted this defeat without murmur. But music was a different matter.

He and his brother had sung in choirs and played in orchestras and quartets all their lives. They had written long letters to each other about different Italian recordings of Beethoven. They sang Schubert lieder to their mother. I, however, was not musical. This my father could not accept. It was a fundamental article of his philosophy that everyone was musical, just as 'everyone can paint'. It was just a question of application. 'Every Victorian lady could paint a watercolour,' he insisted. 'Now, darling, it is true you may not be quite like me with music, but with a little effort . . .'

So we would begin with me blowing nervously into the recorder – reading the music, note by note, in a stumbling fashion – while he tried to keep time.

Once he slapped me during recorder practice. It was a single slap and he never did it again in my life. I don't even remember where exactly he slapped me – my wrist? My back? But the shock of that moment stayed with me. And it changed my relationship with my father. I felt that in addition to protecting him, I had also to protect the world from him.

My favourite days were Saturdays. We would collect our bacon and egg sandwiches from the dark kitchen and drive into the jungle before the sun rose. Then we would walk for an hour through the red mud. Since I was barefoot, I could feel the mud between my toes, and see the leeches as soon as they fixed on my ankles: he believed in burning them off with a match. I had a special technique of sword-dancing between the jungle twigs, which I thought made me a more silent walker. I thought I was very good at imitating the call of the white-handed gibbons.

When we reached a river, my father unpacked the bundle which he carried on his back. It consisted of bamboo sticks and inner tubes which he lashed together. Then we took a break to unwrap the foil from the sandwiches. The egg was somehow always still runny. We didn't carry water – I think because he claimed Lawrence of Arabia had gone three days without it. And then we clambered onto his tubes and bamboo and floated downstream.

26

Three days after leaving Newcastle I reached the fort of Housesteads, paid homage to the cartoon of the legionaries with their trousers round their ankles, and, because I was getting bored of the slow trudge, ran across the hill to the adjacent fort of Vindolanda. I came through a quarry, across a road, down into a ditch and over a fence into the side of the fort. I found my father again in the museum shop. It was only much later when I found, in a box at Broich, a photo which he had taken of me astride a catapult, next to the reconstructed wall, that I realised that we had also visited Vindolanda together twenty-nine years earlier. Much of the site was unchanged, but neither of us recognised the place. He said he'd prefer to sit in the café, and he would give the fort and the museum exhibition a miss.

I went to look for the director, Andrew Birley, whose grandfather had bought the fort at auction in the 1920s, and then dedicated his family's life to restoring it. There had been a break for almost fifteen years when the government tried to prevent them from excavating. Something about this family's energy and attitude appeared to have riled the heritage establishment. People, who I thought would have liked the fort, affected to think it was 'overdone' and groaned when I praised it. But I enjoyed the fact that the Birleys had relied for decades on teams of volunteers – hundreds of people camping over the summer – often the Birleys' students, many of whom had since become professors. Andrew's grandfather had been a professor at Newcastle University. And they were a northern family rooted to this soil and this project.

In books and photographs, Andrew's father, uncle and grandfather seemed donnish, pipe-smoking figures. His grandfather's desk, preserved in the museum at Vindolanda, surrounded by sepia photographs of men in tweed, reinforced this image. But Andrew had a close-shaven head and broad shoulders and wore jeans and a climbing jacket. His accent seemed to me less don or even Northern: more Essex. But he had decided to become the third generation in a row to dedicate itself to the site. It had taken them eighty years, he calculated, to excavate about 20 per cent of the fort. At this rate, I worried, they would be excavating for longer than the fort itself had been occupied.

One of the most controversial aspects of Vindolanda was that the Birleys had reconstructed a section of the wall. This was the wall in front of which I had been photographed by my father in 1985. It stood just over fifteen feet high. Below the battlements was a projecting sill. Andrew suggested that this made it more difficult to climb. I tried, by throwing a rope over the battlements. He was wrong. The sill was a very useful footrest for pushing over the battlements. It took about twenty seconds to climb the wall. I wondered whether the sill had been damp-coursing.

The most famous discovery of the Birleys was that the peat of the fort had preserved a pile of discarded Roman correspondence. It was written on thin wooden tablets, in ink which could be revealed only under ultraviolet light. Informed guesswork seemed to underlie every act of deciphering. The tablets were a tiny fraction of those that must have once existed – and they had lain on a rubbish pile, intended to be destroyed. The Birleys had, however, established that the tablets included orders for fish paste, to be imported from the Mediterranean (I had seen one of the factories, now revealed twenty feet underground in Barcelona). You could read about centurions setting off south to pick up more supplies, negotiating with contractors for transport; and civilian traders, enraged with military brutality. There were leave tickets, and muster rolls, showing soldiers going back and forth to London, or on temporary postings to neighbouring bases, or to the governor's staff. This small fort alone generated thousands of documents a month: a tiny glimpse of the millions of documents that must have passed back over centuries to the provincial headquarters and to Rome.

In the museum there was also a collection of Samian pottery – beautiful red ware imported to this remote heather-rich valley from a ceramics factory in what is now central France – almost as though a contemporary officer had brought his family dinner service to a forward operating base in Afghanistan.

They had also excavated a human skull, which appeared to have been stuck on a spike at the fort gate. Analysis of the teeth suggested that the individual was a native Briton, originally from what is now the English–Scottish border. Roman burial practices were highly regulated: bodies were permitted to be buried only outside settlements. But at Vindolanda bodies had been thrown in the fort ditch.

They had also found the skeleton of a child, whose tooth enamel revealed that she had moved to Britain from North Africa or Southern Europe when she was eight. Less than two years after her arrival in Britain, her hands had been tied, and she had been murdered and then buried in a hastily dug shallow grave beneath the flagstones of the cramped dormitory of a unit of Gaulish legionaries.

27

Eighty of the letters in the Vindolanda archive were written by the prefect of the fort in about AD 100. On the surface, he might have seemed a classic Roman officer and a gentleman. He had a Roman name – Flavius Cerialis – he lived in fine Roman apartments, dining on imported Roman delicacies, and quoted Virgil. He was also, from the perspective of his soldiers, a man of the upper classes, worth at least 400,000 sesterces, or 500 times their salary. Back home on the Continent he almost certainly had a country estate and a villa.

But he was not a tribune in one of the great legions, he was a prefect of an auxiliary unit. He was not from the senatorial class. He could never be a praetor or quaestor in Rome. Ethnically, he was a Tungrian from Belgium. His father probably spoke a Germanic language, not Latin, and ruled – as a minor clan chieftain – from a wooden hall. And although he was an officer of Rome, his father may have fought against Rome. From a distance, from the perspective of a local Briton, looking at the prefect on his horse, or even from the perspective of his own soldiers, Flavius Cerialis might have appeared the quintessence of a Roman gentleman. But in Rome he might not quite have fitted in.

★

'Ah, the laird returns,' said my father when I reappeared in the Vindolanda coffee shop. He often referred to me, because he had given the house to me when his father died, as 'the laird' of Broich. In his many emails (he sent upwards of forty thousand words to me in a month) he often wrote about us both as though we were little more than entries in *Who's Who*. He often described himself as though he were a cliché of the British establishment: a public-school- and Oxford-educated Black Watch officer, colonial administrator and diplomat, who finally retired to his father's small estate in Perthshire. Strangers sometimes perceived him as the very model of an old-fashioned Highland officer.

But none of this was quite as it appeared. For a start he often insisted he was Irish, that he had the charm and luck of the Irish. I had long found this difficult to understand. My ancestry.com research had confirmed that all my father's father's ancestors were clearly in Scotland on the Highland Line since the parish records began. 'It was my mother's side,' he said. Yet the same sprouting hyperlinked leaves also showed that his mother was descended from two sea captains, both born in Dundee in the late eighteenth century.

Then one night, at two in the morning, I found the connection. In 1890 my grandmother's Scottish Presbyterian engineer father, the descendant of the ships' captains, had fallen for an Irish Catholic and married her. The census database revealed that she worked in a jute mill not far from his house in Dundee. I traced her birthplace back to an overcrowded Perth tenement block called 'the Meat Vennel', where her mother had died in childbirth after bleeding for many hours without a medical attendant to help. In the marriage certificate the father of the girl – my great-great-grandfather – was described as a 'jobbing gardener'. His name was Reilly or Riley; the spelling hardly mattered, since he and his wife had signed their names with crosses.

Different classes, different religions. Accounts of Catholic–Protestant, Irish–Scottish relations in Dundee in 1890 suggest it can't have been an easy marriage for the couple. They had brought their children up, educating them privately as Episcopalians, and then moved to Cuba, perhaps to get away from the complications. My grandmother, the embodiment of propriety in her long snakeskin Ferragamo shoes, had not told my father any of this detail. No photographs of her parents survived, and although my father was thirty-three when his grandfather died he never met him. But she had given her mother's mother's Irish family name to her first son, and an Irish king's name to my father, her second son. And she had told him he was Irish. Which was why he had focused on an Irish strand in his DNA test. And which was ultimately what led my father to say, if pushed, that it was not just the English but the Scots too who were boring.

So my father was not quite Scottish in the way he appeared, and his Oxford education was not quite what it appeared either. He had arrived on his scholarship to Oxford at the beginning of the war, and, knowing he was going off to fight, had not attended lectures. His leisure time had not been spent in aristocratic dining clubs, but on performances of Gilbert and Sullivan and Mozart operas in the playhouse. He left Oxford to join the army without completing his degree, and unlike many others, he did not return to complete it after the war. So he never felt that he was fully educated.

He had never been a regular Black Watch officer. Instead he had an emergency war commission in a battalion which was only very recently affiliated with the Black Watch – the territorial unit from Newcastle 'led by a Durham solicitor'. And, later, when he joined the Foreign Office, the diplomats made it clear that they had little time for ex-colonial civil servants like him, and even less time for spies.

My father still respected the tone of *Who's Who* entries. His own was a masterpiece of condensed self-assertion ('Hobbies: ski-ing, orientalia particularly chinoiserie'). He went to school and Oxford and regimental and office and club reunions. He wrote a book about the Black Watch, one about Malaya and one about the secret service. He wore a Black Watch tie, and a Special Forces Club tie. He was proud of his medals – which he carefully arranged between his father's, his mother's, his brother's and his grandfather's medals and mine. But when I mentioned that I had met a man who had served with him on the Joint Intelligence Committee, and that the man had said that my father 'didn't really fit in', my father had barked in triumph: 'I'm glad I didn't fit in.'

28

Five miles before Housesteads, the wall left the flat ground and began to climb along the edge of a cliff. Now I could see much more clearly the sour, wet soil, scattered with reeds, that stretched from the wall to the Scottish border. Much of this land would once have been scattered with Iron Age houses. I had found it tempting, when pounding along the ground, spinning a staff as though it were an Iron Age spear, to imagine native chariots racing wildly over the hilltops. But the British-Celts had not built in mortared stone, and their wooden huts and thatched roofs had rotted away. There was nothing to see in the landscape to reflect the culture that emerged in the two millennia between the erection of the Neolithic standing stones and Hadrian's Wall.

Then for more than 300 years of occupation the Romans had slept with British slaves and prostitutes, and established colonies for the families of retired legionaries in Lincoln, Colchester, Gloucester and York. But new DNA analysis suggested that the modern British population has very little Roman blood, whereas perhaps half the population are descendants of the pre-Roman British-Celtic population. Our landscape was dominated by the buildings of the Romans to whom we were not related, while the dwelling houses of our 'ancestors' had vanished. My meagre understanding of these ancestors came only slowly – through reading typewritten reports by archaeologists, zooming in to aerial photographs, and comparing archaeological excavations conducted miles, and decades, apart.

I only felt I was beginning to grasp something of their life when later I visited a reconstructed Iron Age hut in southern England. It was a cold, rain-drenched afternoon – the leaves yellowing, but not yet fallen. At the front entrance a woman was milking a goat, watched by two teenagers in bright anoraks, and by a black mongrel with a red bandanna round its neck. I offered to help her with the milking, but she insisted that goats would only tolerate someone they knew well. Behind her ran a low fence of woven wicker, and beyond it five huts with conical grass roofs twenty to thirty feet high.

She and her husband and a group of friends had reconstructed these buildings in the last decade by taking the excavation reports of actual Iron Age sites and exactly replicating their details and dimensions on this empty field by the A3. At one site, for example, they had found small rectangular holes in the earth, about a foot deep and an inch wide, arranged in a rough overlapping circle, about fifty feet in diameter. The archaeologists had concluded that this had been the oak wall of the house. So the reconstructors had driven oak planks, of exactly the right dimensions, in precisely the same position, and then attempted to lay a straw roof over the walls.

Previously everyone had imagined Iron Age houses with low, almost flat roofs. But when they tried a shallow roof, the water collected and rotted the thatch. When they tried a steeper pitch, the water came down too fast, close to the mud and plank walls, and rotted the foundations. They discovered that ten degrees was the optimum angle to balance durability and water flow. And this created an astonishing piece of architecture. Inside, you could look up at a ceiling that rose steeply up to a conical peak, twenty feet high at the apex. The diameter of the round room, faithfully replicated from the original site, was ten times the size of the Papuan grass hut in which I had sat, and far larger than the tent of a nomad chief, or the main room of a very substantial leader's house in central Afghanistan. It was a place where I guessed fifty men could sleep.

I spent the next four hours sitting by the fire in the centre of the hut. The reconstruction team had concluded that there had been no chimney-hole, because a chimney made the fire rise too fiercely and could set the thatch alight. Visitors, like me, unaccustomed to the room, coughed and wept continually, and humiliatingly tried to keep our heads close to the earth floor to breathe. Locals, who were used to it, could sit upright. You would have to smoke an immense number of cigarettes to do the same damage to your lungs. In Papua, where there were also no chimneys, almost everyone had respiratory problems. This was one of many reasons why twenty-six year olds looked fifty. I washed my hair four times when I got home. The smell lasted three weeks.

I had, I think, imagined that the Romans would simply have pitied their British subjects, registering with contempt the absence of sanitation, mortared stone, flooring and bathing. But now I realised that British culture, rather than being merely contemptible, might also have been intimidating. I imagined a Roman prefect like Flavius Cerialis walking under the human skulls at the entrance to the compound, past the chariots (with their delicate bronze tracery) and over – in the case of the Iron Age site at Danebury – a central pit filled with the corpses of executed men, before crossing the dark threshold, and seeing with weeping eyes through the smoke of this vast high-roofed hall the erect figure of the chief, tattooed and iron-clad.

29

Over lunch in the coffee shop at Vindolanda, my father had brought up the subject of Islamist terrorism. He presented me with a note that he had written while I was walking:

> It really is time that we shaped up and fought terrorism, not merely wailed after each incident. I have no feeling for this living behind a beech hedge in Bonnie Perthshire, but I am incensed by the sympathy for the terrorists 'wee Ahmed was such a lovely lad', etc. Part of the problem is the spreading disease of political correctness, which seems to trump common sense. The Muslim community must come off the fence, and lend a hand. They are not entitled to live in our country and muck up our civilisation and turn a blind eye to the rotten bits of Muslim society. Is there no one we can appoint to rally good Muslims and take the fight to the enemy?

I found it uncomfortable reading this. I tried to give my father the benefit of the doubt and disentangle his wisdom from his prejudice. He looked at me. 'Sorry, rant over . . .' he said, and stopped. But a few minutes later, he was encouraging me to write about Abu Musab al-Zarqawi, the al-Qaeda in Iraq leader, calling him 'some bastard Jordanian who thrives on cruelty'.

Partly to change the subject, I showed him a picture of a tombstone of a Roman soldier, which I had seen by the steep stone monastic staircase of Hexham Abbey. He was twenty-six when he died; not an officer, but a non-commissioned cavalryman. Someone who cared for him had commissioned a megalith nine feet tall, carved with a picture of him on a leaping horse.

The Roman soldier's face was worn into anonymity, little more than a suggestion of eyebrows and a nose. He had settled his crescent standard firm by his waist, as his horse reached skyward. The double fan of feathers above his helmet reared beyond the frame of the monument. Focused on that jump, and his neat pony gathered beneath his knees, he hardly seemed to notice how his fine leather boot kicked the bare bottom of a man kneeling beneath his horse's belly.

The crouching nude beneath him held a naked sword. His head was circled by a shock of upright hair and a stiff beard; the nose was flat; the eyes slits: the features of an ape. His head was stretched back so that at first it looked like an agony of prostration, but it was at an angle far beyond any anatomical possibility. He had been decapitated and was cradling in his arms his grimacing bearded head. He was us – a Briton – a naked barbarian, kicked aside by the leaping hooves of Rome.

The Roman Empire had not been racist. First Italians, then Gauls, grandsons of the enemies of Caesar, were admitted to the Senate; the emperor Hadrian was a Spaniard; the emperor Septimus Severus, who repaired the wall, was a Libyan. The tribal towns of Rome were administered by local native people and they, and later everyone in the empire, were given full Roman citizenship. But somehow this colour blindness, this national and religious tolerance, did not quite extend to the Roman treatment of the natives of Britain. There were no senators or provincial governors or legionary commanders who were ethnically British. The idea of a British poet was a well-known joke. Roman writers described British culture with something approaching disgust. Herodian writes:

> Because the greater part of the body is naked they do not mind the mud. They are unfamiliar with the use of clothing, but decorate their waists and necks with iron . . . They tattoo their bodies with various patterns and with pictures of all kinds of animals.

And whereas the Romans were generally tolerant towards other religions, quick to worship local gods and endow local temples, they seem to have hated the Druids, the British priests. In fact they set out to kill all of them and destroy their sacred groves, on the grounds, it seems, that the British worshipped a fanatical insurgent religion with disgusting rites – a threat to civilisation.

The Roman occupation of Britain had often been considerably more brutal than that of the US–British coalition in Afghanistan. More than ten thousand Britons were killed, for example, in retribution for Boadicea's rebellion. And the Romans appear to have invested little time in trying to learn local languages like my father – still less in dressing like locals in the fashion of Scottish officers on the North-West Frontier.

'But the Romans,' I said to my father, 'still seemed much more interested than American and British commentators today in describing how their enemies lived, and much better at imagining why their enemies might consider their cause to be just.' Tacitus, for example, a prominent Roman politician, did not describe Rome's enemies as my father sometimes described Islamist insurgents, as 'cowardly' or 'pure evil'. Instead Tacitus found the British – notwithstanding their 'fanatical religion', nudity and muddy legs – engaging, dignified and often admirable. He did not seem to feel threatened by their attitudes or their religious beliefs. He did not even seem to resent their massacres of Roman soldiers and citizens and still less to see these conflicts as an existential threat to Roman civilisation. Instead, he was interested in seeing Roman soldiers through the insurgents' eyes.

The climax of Tacitus' *Agricola*, written in AD 90, comes in the final battle with the British leader Caratacus. Tacitus constructed a speech for the insurgent, praising British courage and love of freedom, and attacking Roman imperial hypocrisy. Most famously, he makes the insurgent say of his own father-in-law's Roman army, 'The Romans create a desert, and call it peace.'

★

My father, who was so hostile to the terrorists he read about in the comfort of Perthshire, had taken a very different attitude to the terrorists he had fought in Malaya. He had told me that he was shocked by the racism of the Scottish planters in Penang, and had broken their apartheid ban on Malay Chinese and Indian members in their club. He spoke three Chinese languages fluently, and seemed to have made closer Chinese friends than British ones, while fighting a mostly Chinese-led insurgency.

He took peculiar delight in remembering the night raids he mounted against insurgents, ambushing bandits, 'threatening hooligans and gangsters in Penang', and firing tear gas at students. And he was dismissive about the British MPs at the time who had complained about abuses of the human rights of the terrorists and criticised the interrogation techniques used by the soldiers. But he never seemed to take personally the fact that the Communist insurgents in Malaya had been trying to kill him – and indeed had succeeded in killing his predecessor. In fact he saw their point: 'It was not difficult to empathise with the communities who disliked us. The farmers were displeased to be taken off their land, subject to curfew, food regulation . . .'

He defended the Malayan Chinese community against his superiors' demands that they should 'come off the fence'. He explained to the centre that 'community leaders' would not be able to play a major public role in fighting Chinese Communism and still retain the support of their communities.

As for the terrorists themselves, he did not describe them then as 'evil' but as 'ill-fed, unpaid, poorly clad, short of medical supplies, and out of touch'. His instinct was to try to win the communities over by pushing through projects in education and social housing, and he had lifted all the 'Emergency restrictions' in his district of Malacca 'in exchange for good behaviour', infuriating many of his superiors who thought he was compromising with the terrorists, and endangering lives.

30

Much later, I was given the chance to see the whole zone of the Roman frontier from the air. I flew with David Wooliscroft, an archaeologist with a full white beard – more Santa Claus than Hemingway. We took off from a Second World War air force strip that lay beside the Roman camp at Castlesteads, which had once housed an altar to an Iranian god. In the 1950s and 1960s, the airstrip had been used to train foreign airmen – Iranian pilots had shivered, and prayed, in Nissen huts on the edge of the airfield through Cumbrian winters. Some had married Cumbrian women.

I sat in the back, wedged behind David. He seemed uncomfortable. 'I have vertigo – it's ridiculous, I know,' he chuckled, 'but once we are high enough it hardly seems to matter any more.' And it was true. When we levelled out at 1,000 feet, he opened the window and stuck his head into the cold air.

In the clear morning light, we could see the breadth of Britain, from the Solway tides to the smoke of Tyneside. We floated over the wrinkled backs of the Cheviots and the sharper ridge of the Pennines, over reservoirs, forestry plantations and farm sheds. Patches of densely grazed green gave way to the sere, washed-out khaki of the moorland; yellow and chocolate lines, formed of peat hags or burnt heather, snaked across fells and fields; pines sprouted from glacial debris in the Bewcastle wastes.

The plane took us quickly along the lines of a Roman ditch, of the turf wall, then the stone wall, and then the Stanegate road. It took only three minutes to reach the next Roman fort; following the lines relentlessly, across the Irthing River, and along the course in the field at Willowford.

'I have gone to Scotland because that is where the funding is,' said David, 'but Hadrian's Wall has always been my first love.'

'Why?' I asked.

'The engineering. I still remember when I first saw it age eleven and thinking an empire that can do this . . .'

'But why was it built? Why all this effort? Why exactly here?' I asked.

Instead of answering, he spoke about the engineering of the wall. He had studied Roman surveying techniques using laser-measurement, magnetometry and aerial photography. 'My laser measurements show that the Roman distances between separate forts were off by only 0.1 per cent – I am still not sure whether they or my measurements were inaccurate.'

'But why did they build the wall in the first place?' I asked.

He did not answer the question; instead he pointed out of the window at a bonfire by the Roman fort at Bewcastle, twenty miles away. He had discovered that the smoke could not be seen from the next existing fort – he had had to calculate the locations of two additional signal stations to make the system work, and to his delight, his prediction had been confirmed by excavations. It seemed to suggest that the Bewcastle fort had been built – from the point of view of signalling at least – in the wrong place. But David marvelled at the efficiency of the system. 'Once the signalling was properly established,' he said, 'a Roman could get a message from Carlisle to York within a couple of minutes.'

But why was the wall here? Despite the immense scale of the project, the Roman writers hardly referred to it. The Colosseum appeared in hundreds of separate sources, but Hadrian's decision to build the wall seemed to be mentioned only twice, in references which were tautologous. Hadrian's biographer, for example, says Hadrian built a wall *'ut barbaros Romanusque divideret'* – and although I once wasted an hour pondering the meaning and even etymology of these words, hoping this might reveal whether the Romans felt Hadrian had split – in exactly two – an island that was intrinsically one, it basically meant little more than what it seemed to mean: 'to divide the Romans and the barbarians'. No text contradicted the basic view, popular since at least the sixth century, that Hadrian had intended the wall as the frontier of an empire, to rigidly divide and protect Roman civilisation from a barbarian threat.

David, however, disagreed with this view, as did almost every specialist on Hadrian's Wall in the last forty years. They were determined to understate the significance of the wall. The wall could never, they argued, have been intended to divide communities; the wall was porous; it was not the frontier of the empire, and the very distinction between Romans and barbarians was misleading.

Insofar as the wall had a point at all, these academics seemed to feel it was designed first as some kind of obstacle to cattle-raiding, and as a customs post which became, secondarily, a useful place in which to house soldiers and keep them busy (repairing the wall). And with these strikingly modest claims for the wall came a series of other claims: that the wall was a meeting place, a zone of cultural exchange and encounter rather than a military barrier.

Most archaeologists emphasised that borders were artificial; but they also liked to believe, as did David Wooliscroft, that Hadrian's Wall followed a 'natural frontier' in the landscape. On the one hand they wanted to minimise cultural difference (insisting, for example, that the garrisons on the wall were 'really British' despite their exotic Roman names); but they also wanted to present the wall as a creative encounter of different cultures – what one scholar called a *'metissage'*.

These conclusions had made their way into the guidebooks and noticeboards in every fort museum. And for the public, the wall had begun to feel exactly the opposite of what it had seemed for Kipling. The great stone blocks began to seem fungible and porous: 'ideological' not objective.

Such views, radical in the 1980s, are now conventional. By 2007, the Scottish history examiners insisted in their marking guidelines that the wall was only a 'base for patrols and for the army, to stop small-scale raids, slow down big raids, stop smuggling, and keep the troops busy building and repairing it . . . There is no debate', insisted the examiners, 'about the purposes of the wall: all historians/archaeologists agree.'

31

If my father had still been able to climb the wall, he would, I suspected, have seen very little on the ground that seemed to match these academic accounts. And, of course, nothing was more likely to make my father suspicious or belligerent than the hint of academic consensus. If historians had recently agreed that James IV had trained pikemen for the Battle of Flodden, he would set out to prove they knew nothing about military training; if they referred to 'command and control' at Agincourt, he would point out how impossible it would have been for the officers to control anything once the fighting began. 'They can always be relied upon to miss the point', to overlook 'glimpses of the blindingly obvious'. He felt that the only valuable history came from lived experience.

I lowered myself down cliffs beneath the wall, resting on small ledges of bright turf forty feet above the gully. I clambered up the cliff, wrapping my hand around the trunks of mountain rowan. (On this poor soil the old trunks were hardly two inches in diameter.) I walked along the top of the wall, turned around and walked back; leapt over it, jumped from it, ran on it, hopped on it, sat on it, and lay on my stomach, looking over the parapet.

Mostly, however, I stood in the rain beside the wall with my boots slowly absorbing the water, my hands stuck deeper into my down jacket and waterproof shell, chewing on power bars that I hated – and stared at the wall stones. Every half an hour or so, figures would come up the path towards me – a Chinese couple who seemed to be on honeymoon, a park ranger, three teenagers on a school challenge – but the rain was too heavy for them to stop long.

I noticed that although each stone of the wall was a similar size – about two house bricks – they were not cut with precision. The edges were rough and broken, the stone pockmarked and scratched. The blocks bulged as though swollen by the incessant rain. In some sections they were light pink, in others they darkened from grey to black. I could not quite believe that I could repeatedly touch the stones and feel the roughness beneath my palms.

None of what I saw on the ground corresponded with what David had told me in the air. When walking, I saw the wall as a deeply artificial line, only sometimes placed on a natural barrier, and running for most of its length through flat fields over the broad Northumberland trough. It looked like the straight lines drawn across flat ground by colonial officers in Africa. Other Roman frontiers might have shadowed pre-existing tribal boundaries, but I kept finding examples where Hadrian's Wall tore straight through them.

Above all, walking along the wall made me feel how extravagant and excessive this construction had been. There was no other stone monument on this scale in Europe. The wall had taken 20,000 men more than a decade to build. None of the legionaries had ever been asked to build anything like it before: bisecting a country from sea to sea with 20 million cut stones. The German and African frontiers were turf. This required more stone and labour than the Pyramids.

My walk was helping me to imagine it, stone by stone, stretching fifteen feet high, entire and intact, from coast to coast, running straight up hillsides, down gullies and over cold rivers. Every 300 yards I had passed the remains of a watchtower, every mile a castle, every seven miles a fort, that could contain up to 1,000 men.

I spent an hour trying to run back and forth across the wall, sprinting over the ditch and mounds of the north side, climbing over the wall itself, then tackling the southern ditch and mounds. I tried to imagine what it would have been like when the mounds were ten feet high and the ditches fifteen feet deep and filled with stakes and thorns. Or when a military road ran in the broad passage between the wall and the back *vallum* ditch – with couriers galloping, officers cantering, cavalry trotting, and the auxiliaries marching at a regulation four miles an hour in a packed and clattering column. I saw how the sheer stone face of the wall had then completely concealed the final obstacle course of the *vallum*.

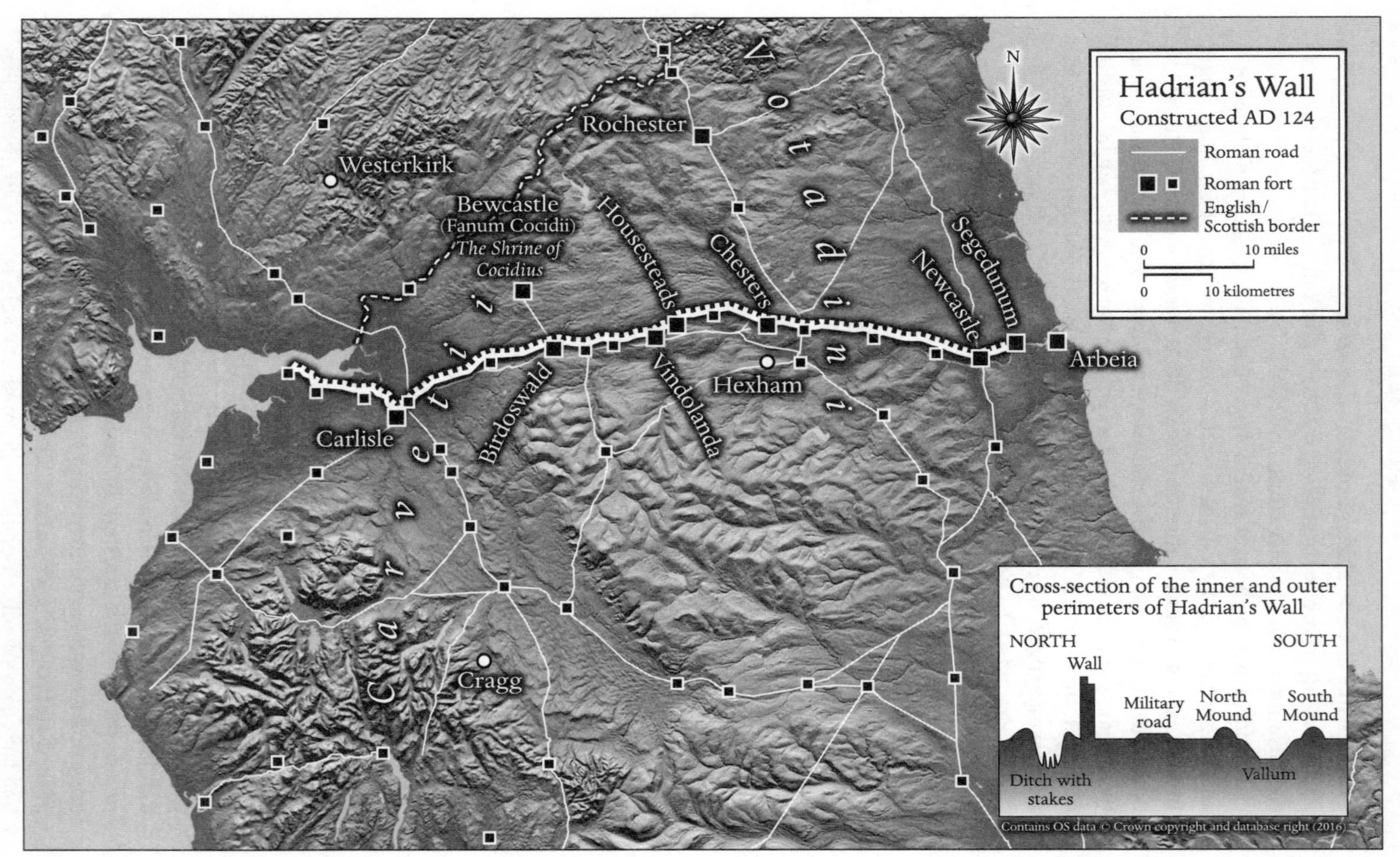
Hadrian's Wall
Constructed AD 124
Roman road
Roman fort
English/
Scottish border
0
10 miles
0
10 kilometres
N
Votadini
Carvetii
Rochester
Westerkirk
Bewcastle
(Fanum Cocidii)
The Shrine of
Cocidius
Housesteads
Chesters
Newcastle
Segedunum
Arbeia
Hexham
Vindolanda
Birdoswald
Carlisle
Cragg
Cross-section of the inner and outer
perimeters of Hadrian's Wall
NORTH
SOUTH
Wall
Military
road
North
Mound
South
Mound
Ditch with
stakes
Vallum
Contains OS data © Crown copyright and database right (2016)

I ran up and down a dozen times, as fast as I could, as though I were a Briton trying to break through from the barbarian lands.

This monstrous military camp, half a mile wide and eighty miles long, could not, I felt, have conceivably been intended simply, as the Scottish examiners claimed, as a 'base for patrols' and to stop smuggling. North Britain exported little more than dogs, furs and slaves, and, it seemed, until they were hunted to extinction, an occasional Caledonian bear. Could such trade, and the activities of cattle-rustlers, ever have been economically significant enough to justify an investment of this scale and permanence? Would not a deep ditch have sufficed?

32

And then there were the many outpost forts built north and south of the wall. One of the northern outposts was now occupied by my friend and constituent Moira's brother Malcolm. So, with her encouragement, I interrupted the walk to visit him. He picked me up at the point at which I had stopped walking, and drove me to his farm.

I hadn't quite believed Malcolm's claim that his farm had been a Roman fort, until I saw the great masonry blocks beneath the barn and bungalow. The fort, Bremenium, was almost twenty miles, or a hard day's march, north of the wall, and more than eight miles from the nearest fort to the south. It looked down onto the long narrow valley of Redesdale. You could see almost everything in the valley from the fort: sheep, cars, people, moving over the natural gap in the Cheviot range which now formed the Scottish border.

There seemed to be little record of the mid-nineteenth-century excavations of this particular fort, and there had been no significant investigation of the site for eighty years. Archaeologists had, however, concluded that the platform, which stood above the great masonry blocks at the gate, had been constructed as an artillery platform for an *onager*: a Roman catapult, which could fling an eight-pound rock or an exploding jar 500 yards down into the valley to hit a column of marching men, or support Roman soldiers on the ground.

'Eight-pounders?' said my father, when I told him later. 'Wah! We only had six-pounders.'

Research on this aspect of the wall was not confined to post-colonial analysis of *metissage*. I found online a thirty-page paper from Louisiana State University establishing a 'torque calculation' for an *onager*. The string of numbers and operations suggested the immense patience invested in the slenderest details of Roman archaeology – expressed in language that no Roman artilleryman would recognise: $3.62\text{kg}^{\star}(2.44\text{m})^{2\star}437\text{rad}/\text{s}^2 + 10.86\text{kg}^{\star}(1.22\text{m})^{2\star}437\text{rad}/\text{s}^2 + (3.62\text{kg}^{\star}(2.44\text{m}) + 10.86\text{kg}^{\star}(1.22\text{m}))^{\star}9.81\text{m}/\text{s}^2$.

Malcolm was getting frustrated with the fort under his farm; heritage legislation prevented him from building on it, and from working the land around it. Moira, his sister, who farmed dairy cows in the remains of a First World War munitions depot, was luckier. No one prevented her reusing her military bunkers as cattle sheds.

After tea, he took me over the back of the hill to show me the military firing range at Otterburn. My father had spent weeks training there in the Second World War. ('Cold – very cold – but not as cold as Thetford.') Here artillery still flung shells into sheep pasture. There were craters everywhere. The farmers made a decent living receiving compensation for sheep which, they claimed, had been killed by the shells.

Now the soldiers were training for a different type of war. He told me that on the facing hill the Ministry of Defence had built an entire Afghan village, manned with real Afghans. They pretended to be corrupt police chiefs, angry mullahs and manipulative village headmen in order to prepare British soldiers for fighting in Afghanistan.

★

Martin, Malcolm's neighbour, was a wiry, shy, dark-haired man, the son of a sheep farmer and fox hunter, with a gentle Northumbrian accent. Martin explained he had commanded the Fusiliers in a forward operating base beyond Nadi Ali in Helmand in 2009. Like Malcolm's Roman fort, his base had only been resupplied with difficulty.

'It was on a rocky outcrop looking over a valley bottom,' he said, 'quite a spectacular panorama. You could see the day-to-day life of the entire population down below you. It was quite a lonely existence.'

The coincidence of his home being by a Roman frontier fort, and part of his career being in an Afghan fort, seemed very neat.

I asked him what an Afghan farmer would have felt about him and his men, because I was interested in an occupier's sense of the mindset of the occupied. But, as with my father, his statements about war did not quite answer my questions. He spoke with his own specialised vocabulary, in phrases which I guessed he would still be using as a ninety-year-old veteran. My father said things like 'I am proud to represent my regiment, the Black Watch, remembering the bravery and tenacity with which the Jocks of my anti-tank platoon fought. I remember with pride the sterling performance of the young soldiers we trained, as well as mourning my closest friends who gave their lives for freedom.'

Martin's jargon was different. He said, 'They'd have seen one of the best-equipped armed forces in the world, weapons at every corner, antennae everywhere, helicopters dropping off supplies every other day perhaps, be it ammunition, water. They'd see a lot of coming and going, and then quite often periods of activity. And as for the farmers next to our base: the first thing they would know that something was happening on the other side of the valley was when we started firing in support of troops on the ground.'

I asked him what his soldiers made of the Afghans.

'They would see a culture that was at least 100 or 150 years . . . I hesitate to say the word 'backward' but . . . less developed than what they'd come from.'

Three years later this forward operating base would be captured by the Taliban.

33

The fundamental fact – which historians seemed to resist, and which the Romans too perhaps resisted – was that the very existence of the wall and its forts signified failure.

Initially, Roman commanders seem to have regarded Britain as a single island whose natural boundaries were the sea. And they had intended to conquer it all. On the face of it, this did not seem an unrealistic task for an empire that had already conquered 2 million square miles of territory, and defeated the successors of Alexander the Great. The Roman general Agricola had argued that conquering the whole island was strategically essential, because it was prohibitively expensive to man an extended frontier, and Rome would only be safe when it had 'banished liberty from the sight of the Britons'. To leave a 'barbarian' space beyond a frontier would be to create – in our modern jargon – 'safe havens for insurgents' and 'rogue states'.

Agricola therefore fought his way right up to the Gask Ridge on the Highland Line, beside our house in Scotland, and the forts he built there seem to have been intended only as a temporary frontier, before pressing further north. My father had excavated one of these Agricolan forts as a schoolboy in the 1930s.

'I remember looking miserably at ramparts and walls, never found a damn thing, except for the marks of the wood in the ground. Apparently when the earth was discoloured it was a sign that there had been a wooden post. But the posts had gone, so there were just dark pits of earth.' He thought his most exciting personal discovery was a kitchen area. But then again seventy-five years later he saw some photographs of bread ovens in the fort 'taken by my brother's friend, Enslie-Smith – a more serious chap than me'. Perhaps, he now thought, it was Enslie-Smith who had found the kitchen. 'It was a long time ago. All I remember thinking was that the signal station – if that was what it was – must have been a very uncomfortable place for a soldier: no view up the valley, and easily cut off from the fort if there was an attack.'

Agricola's legionaries who had built this fort on the Gask Ridge frontier had still been serving when the decision was made in about AD 80 to dismantle the fort, abandon the ground to the enemy, and fall back more than a hundred miles to the line of what would become, forty years later, Hadrian's Wall. Some of the legionaries who built Hadrian's Wall would still have been serving in AD 140 when the emperor Antoninus Pius decided to abandon the wall and advance north again, to build a new wall along the line of the firths of Clyde and Forth. Ten years later, that wall too had been abandoned, and the soldiers were drawn back to Hadrian's Wall.

In AD 220, a century after Hadrian, the emperor Septimus Severus felt that the reason why the North remained unconquered was that the tactics had been too soft. So he ordered his soldiers to invade the North again, killing everybody they met – 'include', he said, quoting Homer, 'the unborn in their mothers' wombs'. But genocide didn't work either. Within two years, the army had fallen back again to the line of Hadrian's Wall.

Governors and generals were changed every three years, which must have encouraged each new man to blame their predecessors for the mess, and to launch a dozen contradictory strategies – co-option, conquest, withdrawal, indirect rule, containment, expansion to a new line of control, maintenance of forward operating bases, punitive raids – while always insisting that all would have been well if only they had been given sufficient troops, money and time to finish the job.

Egypt, a much wealthier and more populated Roman province, had needed only one legion to control it. The Romans struggled to hold Britain with three legions, and a total of almost 50,000 men – the equivalent proportionately of the British and Americans keeping half a million troops in Afghanistan – and they maintained this presence for 300 years. And even this remarkable commitment was not sufficient for them to pacify the North, or create in the South local state structures that could survive their departure.

Historians of Rome and modern Iraq always seem to agree with the generals that there was nothing intrinsically impossible about these interventions. The problem lay with resources or the details of the implementation – and the answer was generally a 'surge'. Analysts of Afghanistan argue that the problem was that there had only been one soldier for every forty members of the adult population, while, as the Rand Corporation had 'established', the real ratio should have been one to twenty. And in Roman Britain, where there was one Roman soldier for every twenty adults, historians argue that the ratio should have been closer to one for every fifteen – that the problems would have been solved if there had been four Roman legions, rather than three.

I told my father over coffee in Vindolanda that I thought this was, in our shared vocabulary, 'nutty'. I felt that if the tens of thousands of troops in Roman Britain – or in Vietnam, Iraq or Afghanistan – had not been sufficient, then no number would have been; that the problem was simply that the occupier lacked the knowledge, the legitimacy or the power to ever shape such a society in the way that it wished.

I assumed he would agree with me on all of this. My father had been a fierce critic of the Vietnam War. His first-hand experience of the situation on the ground had shown him that, despite the 'establishment wisdom', intervention was going to be a failure. (And he was proud that Lyndon Johnson had read his telegram suggesting that the Americans had no chance of victory after the Tet Offensive.) He often insisted that interventions and occupations where the occupier was not the colonial power were likely to be amateur affairs, doomed to failure. He could explain clearly why an Afghan counter-insurgency would not work. 'In Malaya, the committee was run by me, a British police chief and a British colonel. We didn't have to deal with the equivalent of an Afghan government. We *were* the government.'

34

I had learned from him. The time I had spent in villages on my walk across Afghanistan had shown me why I felt the Afghan intervention would be a failure. Now I wanted to combine our experiences and challenge the 'establishment wisdom' about the Roman intervention and Hadrian's Wall. I suggested we could make a radio programme about our reflections on empire and Hadrian's Wall. 'Good idea,' he said.

For a start, I suggested, we could both explain how impossible it was to win an argument with 'the establishment'. If a senator in Rome had tried to criticise the venture in Britain, a Roman general would just have replied that the politician did not appreciate the real situation on the ground – how backward Britannia had been before the intervention; or how many recent improvements there had been in health care and education, roads and sewerage systems. If the senator had tried to emphasise the threat posed by insurgents based beyond the wall, he would have been told how much improvement was being made in 'capacity-building' and local 'governance', and in the training of auxiliary troops.

I increasingly understood as a politician how the problem of acknowledging failure in an intervention was not simply a problem of knowledge. The commitments that had already been made to allies and to voters, the millions that had been spent and the thousands of lives that had been lost prevented any questions about whether the whole venture made sense. And if there was a surreal gap between the rhetoric of the 'strategies' and the reality, it was because these strategies were not actually a realistic programme to improve conditions abroad, but instead mostly soothing words for people at home.

So perhaps, I suggested, it was a mistake to take the Roman strategy too literally – to ask how the wall was really supposed to function, or what exactly prevented the Romans from pacifying the North or creating a sustainable state across the island. For there to be a wall, it was enough that someone in the capital had proposed one.

I doubted that there was any answer to the questions which academics had debated, such as why eighty gates had been placed in the wall (did this mean it was never intended as a defensive line?); and why the material of the wall had changed from turf to stone, and from one width to another. Why should there be a rational explanation? Was it not equally likely that someone had been confused by an imperial instruction, or was following an inappropriate model from elsewhere?

'Perhaps the narrower-gauge wall had simply been the whim of some earlier version of you, Daddy, deciding that your superiors were wrong, presenting them with a "fait accompli" and getting on with it.'

I sometimes suspected, although I did not say this, that the emperor Hadrian would no more have been able to produce a more coherent and satisfactory account of his wall than my father could for the endlessly drawn and redrawn earthworks in his garden.

I suggested that perhaps we could focus on the bureaucratic wrangling within governments. Tacitus, for example, had insisted forty years before the wall was built that frontiers should naturally be on mountains and rivers, that Britain should have no frontier, but, if it were forced to have one, it should be on the Firth of Forth. And this disagreement about the position of the frontier clearly continued decades after the wall had been built.

But within a century, none of this mattered. For the wall, whatever it was not, was at least a magnet for money and promotion. Senators, tax farmers, grain producers in Libya, olive-oil farmers in Spain, sword manufacturers in Germany all sold their products to the garrisons on the wall. Generals needed it as a place where they could fight and win battle honours. If not here, then somewhere had to be a frontier, because an empire needed adversaries, and a civilisation needed barbarians.

So, while archaeologists seemed to want to insist there was a rational, practical purpose to the wall, which could be read from its architectural design, I sensed absurdity. The wall was cripplingly expensive to build and maintain. It failed to prevent the incursions from the North, that devastated the economy and society of southern Britain. Over the course of the occupation, tens of thousands of Romans and hundreds of thousands of Britons were killed and indigenous cultures were smashed for ever. And in the end nothing sustainable was left behind when the Romans departed. This astonishing feat of engineering, the origin of the idea of England and Scotland, this cherished monument running from coast to coast, was a surreal tragedy.

'Wow,' he said when he had heard all of this. 'Powerful stuff. Well done.' I waited. But he said nothing more.

★

At the end of the meal, I tried to start the conversation again – this time by asking him questions, rather than talking at him. I asked him what he made of Roman counter-insurgency tactics, and how they compared to his in Malaya? Could the Romans have won in north Britain? I reminded him that in a letter found in the wet peat of Vindolanda, one of the commanders referred dismissively to 'the Brituncult' or 'nasty little Britons'. How did this compare to British attitudes to colonial populations?

'Not my subject,' he said.

My father was usually energised by the follies of government, and even had his own jargon – 'group-think' and 'mirror-imaging' – for their mistakes. But he had never, I realised, really enjoyed my suggestion that there was always something inherently surreal in military adventures. I had encouraged him to read *Catch-22* because everything in the book reminded me of my time in Iraq and Afghanistan – and it was set exactly during his years in the army. But he could see no point in the book at all.

He had indeed served as a colonial officer, and in Vietnam, fought a counter-insurgency campaign and loyally read all that I had written. But where I saw impossible choices, or surreal paradoxes in our very presence, he saw simply tactical errors – or, as he would say, 'uselessness' and 'nuttiness'.

And he did not like my suggestion – in either Afghanistan or Roman Britain – that generals could be at least as responsible as the politicians in encouraging an irresponsible strategy. 'The answer is almost always that there should be less political control of the military, not more,' he said. This tied in with his broader views on life. Although he had devoted a lot of time to writing a critique of the intelligence errors that preceded the invasion of Iraq, and believed that the intelligence services had 'sexed' up their reporting to suit their political masters, he remained instinctively on their side. Nor did he like criticism of the United States.

What, I persisted, did he make of the evidence of the Romans clearing the entire population from north of the wall to create empty land? Wasn't this like the early policies of the Malayan Emergency, where he had cleared the Chinese population from the villages and relocated them to houses in fenced compounds, so that they could be prevented from providing assistance to the insurgents?

Again, he simply replied, 'Not my subject.'

I wondered whether his reluctance to engage with my criticism of the Roman Empire was that it came too close to a criticism of the British Empire, but perhaps he simply felt that he did not know enough about Rome, and was exhausted by my questions.

Or were my analogies just not that interesting? I thought that Roman Britain was a profound and powerful symbol for our age, and that what I was saying was very important, because I felt that such flimsy arguments had dragged us into the terrible humiliations of Iraq and Afghanistan. But Iraq had ended, and Afghanistan was ending, and it must all have seemed, even for people like my father, yesterday's news. It was 2011. A theory which had seemed recently so compelling had become obscure, cranky and irrelevant: a worldview no one wished to acknowledge or claim any more. Iraq and Afghanistan, even more than Rome, seemed ancient history.

35

Walking onwards, along the stretch of the wall beyond Vindolanda, and approaching Cumbria, I tried to stop thinking about the Romans and to think more about what the native landscape had been like before the

Roman invasion. It was raining continuously now. When I stopped to eat a sandwich, my fingers were cold and the bread was soon soaked. The rain glinted from the knapped edge of the wall stones and dripped through the crevices in the mortar. Only occasionally a break in the clouds allowed me to see the wet clay soil beyond the wall, littered with boulders left by the retreating ice, and fringed by distant ridges.

These empty fellsides had once been dotted with the circular fields and wooden homesteads of the 'native' population, soot-blackened and snow-rotted under russet thatch. The conical roofs must once have nestled between the hollows and drumlin mounds, the colour of the walls blending into the shades of the heather, reed and alder. Only the seeping grey smoke, and the lake of black manure on the unpaved forecourts – churned by cattle, pigs and bare human feet – would have stood out from the muted colours of the vegetation.

And then suddenly, in AD 122, out of this land of sere scrub and curved buildings, a rigid masonry structure had risen, fifteen feet high. It would have concealed the familiar view behind it, and at eighty-two miles long, it would have seemed to be without beginning or end. From then on, while everything on my right would have been wet, sour ground, crags and moss, and scrub trees, and a glimpse of further ridges: a place of occasional pasture, roamed by deer and wolves, on my left there would have been no view, no natural thing, nothing except a wall almost three times the height of a man.

It must have been like staring at the perimeter wall of a vast compound. Every mile that I walked made it seem more prodigiously incomprehensible. At one spot, I saw two different sets of foundations for the wall, and two routes for the Roman road, as though the lines had been redrawn repeatedly in the flat fields. Elsewhere the wall ran diagonally over the top of the plough lines of an Iron Age field. The men and women who had cleared, drained and ploughed this bleak soil had been swallowed in a military enclosure. Their hut would have been demolished, the family moved, and their large field split between two different nations.

I reached sections where the grey stone of the wall became black granite and then a red sandstone, but the shape and size of the blocks of masonry never changed. In places, the wall was white with lime (whether once painted on, or simply leaking from poorly applied mortar, was unclear). I realised how ugly it had been: a vast industrial intrusion, artificial, straight, undecorated, windowless, like the wall of an eighty-mile-long Victorian factory shed, cutting off the view.

After the wall was built, the Iron Age Carvetii people could no longer have visited the shrine of their god Cocidius north of the wall, nor could the Votadini have come from the North to visit their tribal settlement at Corbridge. Free movement was prohibited for 300 years. (Regulations of the Roman frontier in Germany suggest that they might have been able to cross only if they came unarmed, in groups of two, with a permit.)

For an Iron Age traveller, the wall continued unbroken for four full days of walking. Inspect every yard of the foundations of the wall and you could never find a gap. A Pict must have been tempted to imagine that great delights lay on the other side of the wall, but, in reality, if he had made it over the fifteen-foot mounds, the ditches, past the sharpened stakes, and climbed the masonry face of the wall, without being killed by the soldiers stationed every 300 yards, he would not have seen paradise. Nor would he have seen the villas which appeared so suddenly and dramatically on the inner side of the Roman timber wall in Germany.

Instead, he would have seen almost identical ground extending for another twenty miles, without a city or a garden: the same sour earth, the same wet moss, the same crags, and, in the distance, only the thin soil of the Lake District hills. A little more worked, ploughed and cultivated, but by no means a different country. The single soil of a single island had been severed by a vast military structure, manned by 15,000 men, for 300 years.

36

My father seemed genuinely to want to support local native traditions. He was far closer to the locals in Malaya than to the British, so that I grew up partly with the family of a man who was from the Iban, traditionally a headhunting tribe in Sarawak. (The man was later a government minister.) And although my father took over as chieftain of the local St Andrew's society and presided, in a kilt, over their dances and Burns Night suppers, he did so, it seemed, largely because he enjoyed showing Scottish culture to foreigners, and packed his chieftain's table with Malays not Scots.

When he felt that there weren't enough local traditions, he invented some. First, in Malacca, he got prisoners to make Chinese puppet dolls of the kung-fu hero Monkey (the shopkeepers refused to sell them). Then he invented a Malaccan tradition of making model boats, to submit to a national craft competition. Finally, he created an entire water festival in Penang, with dragon boats. He was delighted to see when he returned to Penang forty years later great flotillas of gilded dragon boats, fighting their way through the surf, to the sound of giant drums. The Malaysian tourist board had made his invented festival into a vast annual event, and promoted it as an 'ancient tradition'.

Two hundred years earlier, the British government had done much the same in the Highlands. By 1746, Scottish clan society was essentially finished. The glens were beginning to empty. People were abandoning Gaelic for English. By 1770, Dr Johnson struggled, in even the most remote parts of the Highlands, to find anyone who still wore a tartan plaid. 'I have seen only one gentleman completely clothed in the ancient habit, and by him it was worn only occasionally and wantonly.'

The British government, worried by Jacobite rebellions, Highland violence and Scottish separatism, had initially believed that the key was to wipe out all the remaining Highland traditions by banning the kilt, bagpipes and the carrying of traditional weapons. But then other officials argued that the way to win back the loyalty of the Highlanders was to do the reverse, and instead invest in their traditions.

This is why a Highland regiment was formed, and equipped with kilts in a government tartan, when every other infantry regiment in the British Army wore red coats and white britches. Instead of flutes, they were allowed to carry bagpipes. While everyone else in the Highlands was forced to disarm, they were allowed to carry swords: basket-hilted 'claymores' of an antique design. They were the only regiment taught to dance Scottish reels, and their soldiers were made to perform public sword dances. This regiment was the Black Watch.

★

Seven miles north of Hadrian's Wall, I climbed onto a broad, roughly hexagonal mound, the base of a Roman fort, now occupied by a farm, a church, a rectory and a medieval castle, all presumably built in part with stones from the fort. The ground around was a savannah of scrub and reeds with surprisingly few houses or signs of pasture. In the distance, the Cheviot ridge marked the modern Scottish border. Here a sandstone altar had been uncovered, on which was carved, *'To the divine god, Cocidius, Quintus Peltrasius Maximus, tribune, former cornicularius in the Praetorian Guard, most prominent man, willingly and deservedly fulfilled his vow.'* Quintus, a senior officer in the most elite unit in the empire, would once have stood, I realised, where I was standing, performing the appropriate ritual, his head covered in linen, pouring the libation of oil, blinking perhaps in the Cumbrian rain, and sacrificing an animal. And he had made this dedication not to a Roman but to a local British god.

This god Cocidius clearly mattered. Whereas other Roman forts had landscape names – the watercourse, the hillside, the peak, the glen – this fort was simply called 'the shrine of Cocidius'. And the fort had been sited in a very unmilitary location: the surrounding, undulating ground would have concealed any enemy forces; and it was positioned seven miles from the wall and the nearest reinforcements. As a result the Romans had had to build the bathhouse inside the fort walls for protection, create an awkward signalling system, relying on two even more isolated towers, and man it with one of only two specialised double-strength units in the island of Britain. There was no obvious strategic justification for the fort's location. No major route continued beyond it.

So the most plausible justification for this exposed site was that the Romans had wanted – whatever the risk and expense – to occupy the pre-existing local shrine of Cocidius, a god who appeared on one silver plaque as a tiny pot-bellied figure with no neck, goggling eyes and bandy legs, supporting an oversized lance; and on another plaque with two thin horns, like a cockroach in battledress.

But what exactly was the native religious tradition of Cocidius which the Romans found at the shrine when they arrived? There is no sign that the British had had their own temple here. There is no evidence that they had had altars. And there is no hint that the British had depicted their gods in human form until the Roman plaques of Cocidius were cast. In fact, the British worship here probably relied on Druids whom the Romans had outlawed and then exterminated.

So, although at first I had seen the praetorian tribune's altar as evidence of a Roman's awe in the face of an ancient local religious power, I now began to wonder whether it had not been more of a public relations exercise. Perhaps exactly the kind of 'hearts and minds' initiative that my father had backed during the Malayan Emergency, or that the British government had backed in the Highlands – an attempt to win back the support of the local population by demonstrating respect for local culture and religion. Perhaps, in particular, it was a gesture to the Carvetii tribe, who had been angered that their shrine had been marooned north of the wall. Perhaps the commissioning and dedication of the altar was not an act of lonely piety by the praetorian officer, but part of the standard duty and tour of inspection – a performance for the natives, before the long ride back to Carlisle.

37

Shortly after my visit to the fort at Bewcastle, I proposed to my father than we should abandon the walk and drive home. And, slightly to my disappointment, he did not argue. Instead, he suggested we drive back to Crieff through Carlisle and Westerkirk. In the car he showed me some more notes he had been compiling while I had been walking. They were not about Hadrian's Wall. They were his new version of *You Know More Chinese Than You Think*.

My father's Chinese remained very good. At the age of ninety he could still read about 5,000 separate characters. And his musical ear had allowed him to catch exactly the nine separate tones used in Cantonese.

He loved to sing them to me, 'Pín . . . pîn . . . pǐn . . . pīn . . . pi̱n . . . pȉn . . . pi̱n . . . pìn . . . pík . . . pɛ̄:k . . . pìk,' while holding up his right hand like a conductor. With a loving pause between each, he went crisply and precisely from dark flat (陰平) to dark rising (陰上), dark departing (陰去), light flat (陽平), light rising (陽上), light departing (陽去), upper dark entering (上陰入) and lower dark entering (下陰入) to light entering. And then off again with another consonant: 'Tín . . . tîn . . . . tǐn . . . tīn . . . ti̱n . . . tȉn . . . ti̱n . . . tìn . . . tík . . . tɛ̄:k . . . tìk.'

And it allowed him, somewhat showily, to be able to recite Tang dynasty poetry in Cantonese, catching ancient Chinese tones, which were not present in modern Mandarin. But typically, he had also decided that there weren't nine tones, and that he could get away with using only six.

In the last ten years of his working life in China, his hearing – damaged by his time firing anti-tank guns in the Black Watch – was beginning to go entirely. He could not hear anything in the higher register: the soprano line in an opera, or most female voices. It became more and more difficult for him to differentiate Chinese tones. He therefore increasingly bluffed his way, and answered what he guessed someone had asked him rather than what they had actually said, so that it was difficult to differentiate him – a deaf person who spoke beautiful Chinese – from someone who could not understand Chinese at all.

When he retired he focused on the written rather than the spoken language, and in particular on a book he had been planning for thirty years, *You Know More Chinese Than You Think*. He had planned other similar books on Vietnamese, Malay and Filipino. They were based on his assumption that people who say they cannot speak other people's languages – like those who say they can't sing or paint – are simply not trying hard enough. Chinese was easy, he thought. It was simply that all Chinese teachers were 'idiots' (he pronounced this word in what he thought was the French fashion: 'eed-ee-o').

The key was to see that a Chinese character is a picture, and teach the easiest pictures first. So if you looked at the character for 'tree', you could see the trunk and branches; and in the character for 'water' the three streams; the legs in '*ren*', the character for man; and the outstretched arms of a big man for '*da*', meaning big. '*An*', the character for 'peace', was a picture of a woman under a roof – a peaceful image; while 'discord' was a picture of two women under a roof.

But his Chinese friends were displeased with his approach. ('The problem with the Chinese,' he said, 'is they have never had to learn their language as a second language – they just learned these characters by rote – they have no idea how to make it easy for a foreigner.') Academics seemed to think that his suggestion that Chinese characters were pictographs 'naive'. In their view a 'character' represented at best a word and in many cases only a syllable, and sometimes only part of a syllable. The marks on the paper recorded a word, just as an English word did, it was misleading to see them as pictures. And they particularly disliked his claim that Chinese was easy to learn because 'it has no grammar'. Chinese has a lot of grammar, they insisted, even if it is not based on gender, declension and conjugation.

All this simply enraged my father. He could list at least 500 characters which he knew were pictures. He had begun to illustrate all these connections in the late 1940s. His work had not been helped when the Chinese government introduced simplified characters in 1956, which removed half the pictures he had carefully identified. But he had pressed on.

Since no one in Scotland seemed to be interested, he had published a first draft of the book, now called *Chinese Without Tears*, in Hong Kong with an Italian collaborator. Then, in 2010, the Scottish National Party government, keen to prove it had international links outside Britain, opened a representative office in China, accepted two pandas for Edinburgh Zoo and announced that Chinese would be taught in Scottish schools. The local secondary school offered my father a chance – aged eighty-eight – to give some lessons to their students. This he had done, and greatly enjoyed. And Edinburgh University had given him a contract for a new edition of the book. It was to be called *Cracking the Chinese Code.*

Meanwhile, he continued to write other books. There was his autobiography, *Memoir of a Roving Highlander*. There was *Smashing Terrorism in the Malayan Emergency*. There was a collection of essays on his officer training college. There was *Breaking the Panzers* – an account of the battle in which he had fought in Normandy. And there was a project on the uses of intelligence called *Why Spy?*, which grew and stretched and spewed over twenty years, without ever seeming to come close to completion, the piles of manuscript and typescript stretching across his two studies and over the billiard table. I was surprised, therefore, when he showed me the proofs, to see that he had returned to Chinese.

38

We drove together up the A6, which had been the Roman road leading from the legionary base at York to the frontier fort at Carlisle. The Carlisle street called Botchergate, by the railway station, had once been an avenue of formal tombs leading into the largest Roman settlement on the frontier. Here had once stood the headstone of Vacia, portrayed on her tombstone, aged four, holding a bunch of grapes. But while Newcastle had demolished modern houses to reveal the Roman past, Carlisle had destroyed the Roman remains in favour of new buildings. Not so much as a carved column or fragment of a wall remained above the ground. The city walls had gone, and a highway had been run between the castle and the cathedral, through the centre of the Roman fort. In the 1970s the council had replaced what remained of the Roman civilian settlement with 'the biggest shopping centre in Cumbria and the Borders'.

Archaeologists were allowed in just before the builders. They uncovered a network of Roman houses, a stone mansion, and much more, although exactly what was difficult to say, because the funding for recording the excavation ran out. The academics had moved on, leaving crates of objects and photographs and plans, and a stack of unfinished manuscripts on fish and bird bones. The dense traces of streets and houses in the Roman civilian settlement were removed to create a vast negative space: an underground car park for 650 cars. And the solemn avenue of tombs now lay under a Brazilian restaurant, Ladbrokes and the multiplex cinema.

'Do you think Romans would have felt proud of their time in Britain, in the same way that you still feel proud of the Empire?' I asked, returning to a familiar theme as we left Carlisle.

It was much easier talking in the car. He could hear and I could not be distracted. 'Well, I always thought that the Romans must have been pretty frightened and pretty cold,' he replied. 'All I knew about the Empire as a schoolboy came from watching *Sanders of the River*. Then the war was ending, I was wondering what to do next, and I saw an advertisement in the *Army Gazette*. My aunties never wanted to hear any details. I would return, sunburnt, from the Malayan Emergency, wanting to talk, and they would give me Dundee cake and talk about the other old biddies in Kirriemuir. I don't think we took it frightfully seriously,' he said and smiled.

Except I knew that he did take it seriously and his family's sense of the Empire went much deeper than *Sanders of the River*. His father had worked all his adult life in Calcutta, his grandfather worked in the West Indies. My father ate with a Russian silver spoon, inscribed by his great-great-grandfather to record his visits as a sea captain to a Baltic port in 1840. His green rug was designed by his mother in Bengal in 1924, and woven on the Afghan border.

'You must have been immersed in empire as a schoolboy – surrounded by songs, cigarette cards, pictures of cavalry charges and statues on the streets?'

After a long pause he said, 'I suppose you're probably right – I loved reading G. A. Henty of course – *With Roberts to Kabul, With Clive to India*, that sort of thing.'

'How about all the Latin you studied? Did that not bring you closer to the Romans?'

'Well, it was pretty useless to be honest. Our Latin never really became fluent – never good enough for me to want to read a Latin poem or history for pleasure. Just enough to have some "Latin tags" to tease people with – you know, "*bis dat qui cito dat*" – he gives twice who gives quickly – that sort of thing.'

'But I remember you with a Latin version of Agricola,' I said.

'I was probably just showing off.'

'So, in "the Empire" you didn't try to be Romans?'

'Good God, no. Romans? Who he?'

'What do you think it meant to be "Scottish" then? What were the particularly Scottish virtues of empire?' I asked.

'I don't know,' he said, and smiled to bring the subject to an end, 'in my day we didn't talk too much about that sort of thing.'

39

Despite his ebullience and his decisive views, my father had – with the single brief exception of music – been willing to let me do my own thing. He might have been sometimes mystified by my career choices, but he rarely judged them. He seemed to understand more clearly than me that we were different people.

When I left the Foreign Office to set up a charity in Afghanistan, he was eighty-four. He flew through the night to Kabul, came straight up to our office, laid out his sketchpad and began designing a formal Persian garden. An hour later he began an essay entitled 'You know more Persian than you think'. By supper he was standing in the kitchen, training the cooks.

I had been unable to raise any money for the charity for five months. I could not sleep. At three in the morning, I knocked on my father's bedroom door. He woke at once and patted the bed next to him for me to sit down. I held his long, dry, freckled fingers and explained that I had only three weeks' money left and I didn't know what to do.

He listened very carefully, occasionally peering at my hands and stroking them as I spoke. Then he said, 'It's not your fault, darling, you have done your best. Not your fault if the other buggers won't help. You've worked bloody hard. Call it a day, sweetheart, you can't do any more.'

The next day I flew back to London, and I somehow managed to raise the money and didn't have to close the charity, but I liked that he had not left me feeling trapped.

★

Now, crossing the Scottish border, I remembered that my mother had read me Macaulay's 'Horatius' night after night, and that my father had often asked me to recite it.

I asked, 'Didn't you ever think, when you were in a fix:

> And how can man die better
> Than facing fearful odds,
> For the ashes of his fathers,
> And the temples of his Gods?'

'That sounds more like you than me,' said my father, placing his hand on mine. 'Time for you to do some talking for a change. Tell me a story. What happened, for example, when the Romans left?'

'Well, at first I think it may have looked a little like Iraq did after the fall of Saddam – the army vanishing, wealthy families fleeing, leaving mobs to loot their villas and militias to squat in their front rooms. The Romans were in Britain for far longer than we were in Iraq – they kept tens of thousands of soldiers and officials here for almost 400 years. So they must have hoped that they had built something that would outlast them.

'But it was a complete disaster,' I continued. 'Even in Iraq, people moved *into* the cities not away from them. But in Britain after the Romans, they abandoned cities, such as London, that had been inhabited for 300 years. All repairs to roads or stone buildings and all production of coinage and ceramics ceased almost overnight. People stopped speaking Latin.

The population plummeted, fields were abandoned and became forests full of wild animals.'

'For ignoramuses like me,' asked my father, 'can we have some more detail on the departure of the legions? Did they go out as you went out from Iraq, with a parade at the Ziggurat of Ur, and bands playing? Or did they quietly creep out?'

'We don't know. There are only a very few surviving sentences that mention their departure, and they were written long after the event. The legions were probably withdrawn to defend Rome, which was under attack from the German frontier.'

'So the word "withdrawn" tells us damn all. I wonder if they crept out.' As he kept up the interrogation, I began to recognise again the distinctive quality of his speech – the sudden jumps from observations to mild obscenities, the use of different accents, of flattery, his leaps from image to image, phrase to phrase. This, I realised, was what he felt history and conversation should be like.

'You couldn't indulge us with the Roman legion – their banners blowing, and their trumpets – "clump, clump, clump"?' he asked. 'Your description of all this is terribly boring. Tell us what the locals were thinking. Were they thinking, "We've got rid of those Roman bastards at last", or' – here he put on the accent of a prim Anglican clergyman – '"Oh dear, what's going to happen now?"

'Your description is good, darling, it's fine . . .' he continued, 'but I wonder how many of the settlers went with the Romans. There's a wonderful play I heard on the radio in my caravan. Summer 1957. Just after we had handed over in Malaya. It was about the loyal Britons sitting in their villas – the horror and the terror – waiting for the barbarians to arrive, crying, "You bloody collaborators, we'll sort ye oot." Tell us what it was like.

'I take it you have read Bede?' my father concluded. He pulled a translation of the eighth-century Northumbrian monk out of his briefcase. 'When the Romans left, he makes the poor Brits out to have been standing on the wall shivering with fear – only to be grappled down by the natives and murdered. If you want I can find the piece for you. Extraordinary stuff old Bede produces.'

40

In return, I read him the description of the British monk Gildas which I had downloaded on my Kindle. Gildas was writing in the early 500s, ninety years after the Roman departure, and might – just – have known old people who had seen the Romans. This was how he described the end of British civilisation:

> all the husbandmen routed, together with their bishops, priests, and people, while the sword gleamed and the flames crackled on every side. Lamentable to behold in the midst of the streets lay the tops of lofty towers, tumbled to the ground, stones of high walls, holy altars, fragments of human bodies, covered with livid clots or coagulated blood, looking as if they had been squeezed together in a press, and with no chance of being buried, save in the ruins of the houses, or in the ravening bellies of wild beast and birds.

Much energy over two centuries had gone into discrediting Gildas. Historians emphasised that Gildas was not primarily a historian but a priest, whose account was designed to show that the British were being punished by God for their sins. They pointed out that it was difficult to tell when he was referring to ancient Israel and when to Britain. Archaeologists could find little evidence for barbarian burning and destruction. And many modern scholars were offended by the idea that a 'superior' Roman 'civilisation' had been destroyed by 'barbarians'.

Such scholars emphasised that frontiers, national differences and moral judgements were subjective and relative. They liked to emphasise signs of continuity, to describe the Roman departure from Britain as a lingering, gradual transformation from one kind of Rome to another, and to talk of 'evolution' rather than 'decline and fall'. Some suggested that the abandonment of cities reflected new cultural values; others blamed environmental factors. (I believed that Britain in AD 410 – like Afghanistan in 1991 – was too poor, and had relied too much on vast subsidies from the outside power, and therefore lacked the economy to maintain any of its infrastructure, police or army when the Romans withdrew.)

So it was difficult to reassure my father that what Gildas wrote was exactly what had happened. But Gildas was, unlike anyone else, a real living voice, preserved from the sixth century. And his rhetoric – deeply marked with classical and biblical references, analogies with the apocalypse, and a sense of being isolated at the edge of the known world – was a profound insight into his character and culture.

I loved Gildas for his deep pessimism about Britain and his painful investment in its fate, his consciousness of his own failings in a world unmoored. He spoke in ignorance, in bewilderment, in distress – writing a sermon which was also a history, as though putting it into a glass bottle and throwing it from his sinking ship, unsure if anyone would ever read it. He observes that he had tried for ten years to keep silent about the scandal that engulfed him ('Britain has rulers, and she has watchmen: why dost thou incline thyself thus uselessly to prate?') before he took on the task of a history.

He experienced Britain as a crushed, impoverished ex-colony, which had no records or sense of its own past. 'I shall not follow the writings and records of my own country, which (if there were any of them) have been consumed by the fires of the enemy, or have accompanied my exiled countrymen into distant lands, but [will instead] be guided by the relations of foreign writers, which being broken and interrupted in many place are therefore by no means clear.'

Gildas saw the Romans as alien occupiers, under whom 'Britain was no longer thought to be Britain, but a Roman island.' For Gildas the Romans had brought two things – Christianity and the wall – and it was the collapse of the wall which had led to the collapse of British civilisation. I read my father Gildas's piece which Bede had copied:

> They now built a wall across the island from one sea to the other, which being manned with a proper force, might be a terror to the foes which it was intended to repel, and a protection to their friends whom it covered . . . No sooner had they [the Romans] gone back to their land than the foul hosts of the Picts and Scots land. They seized all the northern and outlying part of the country as far as to the wall. Upon this wall stands a timorous and unwarlike garrison. The wretched citizens are pulled down

from the wall and dashed to the ground by the hooked weapons of their naked foes. What shall I add? The citizens desert the high wall and their towns, and take to a flight more desperate than before. Again the enemy pursue them, and there is a slaughter more cruel than ever.

41

At Westerkirk, fifteen miles north of the wall in Scotland, we made our one stop before Crieff. The hamlet announced itself primly with a thirty-mile-an-hour sign and a cluster of decorative cypresses. I wanted to look at the library, which had been endowed by Thomas Telford, and recently restored with a lottery grant. But it was shut. Telford was the most famous engineer, road-builder and bridge-builder of his generation, and the first president of the Society of Engineers in London. The orphan son of a shepherd, he had grown up in a single-roomed mud hut in the valley and studied at the parish school in Westerkirk with – my father reminded me – the Malcolm boys.

'You remember, of course,' said my father, guessing shrewdly that I wouldn't. 'John Malcolm, the son of a poor tenant farmer, went down from Westerkirk to London when he was eleven, having never left his parish, to sit the entry exams for the Indian Civil Service. The board of directors were on the point of failing him for being too young. Then one of them asked, "Little man, what would you do if you were to meet Tipoo Sultan in Mysore tomorrow?" "Do, sir? I'd out wi' my sword and cut off his heid," said the eleven year old. Guess who got the job.'

Each of the Malcolm boys used the opportunity provided by the British Empire to leave their inheritance of ten acres in a sodden Border valley and to become heroes. While John went off to India, his brothers Pulteney and Charles joined the British Navy, and James the Marines. His eldest brother, Robert, was already in India, where he had had seven children by his Muslim Indian mistress, all of whom were acknowledged by the Malcolm family. Pulteney sailed under the Spanish guns into Manila Bay, flying false colours, in 1798, and stole three Spanish gunboats. In 1814, his brother James was knighted for leading an amphibious assault on the American positions at Lake Ontario. And the following year Charles led a tiny party of men onto the Brittany coast at night, seized a battery and stole three armed vessels from a French port. By then John was governing a population of 10 million people in India, having combined his military victories with publishing nine non-fiction books and a volume of poetry, which established him as one of the foremost authorities on Persia in Europe. As my father observed, 'Quite different to their father's life with the sheep in Westerkirk.'

42

My father's life as an intelligence officer abroad had been about recruiting and running agents, and gathering secret intelligence. He did not give me details of these operations because of his obligation to protect the identity of those agents who had put their trust in him. But after I became a government minister, he told me that in Malaysia during the 'Konfrontasi' with Indonesia, he had been ordered to land with a miniature submarine on the Borneo coast. 'It didn't happen in the end – and I was very grateful – the submarine looked like a death trap,' he said.

He had enjoyed the operation when he had fired a laser at a window to listen to a conversation, and found that he had got the storeroom, not the conference room. He had been less proud of an operation against a Russian consulate, where they fed sleeping pills in steaks to the guard dogs. (The first dose had no impact. The second dose, the next night, knocked them out so quickly he was worried that he had killed them.)

He mocked himself as an intelligence officer, as though he was at school, for 'swotting' and 'sucking up' and making himself the 'blue-eyed boy'. 'I was not a great intellectual. I think the army ruined me – I can't really write a decent essay – but I was still "one up" on everyone else. Reading the Chinese-language papers before anyone else got up allowed me to say at the morning meeting, "Ambassador, you will I am *sure* have noticed the article on page fifteen . . ."' But he also seemed proud of displaying a certain brutality. 'I could charm the birds off the trees, but you didn't want to cross Stewart.'

He considered 'Iron fists and velvet gloves' for his motto on his coat of arms, and finally went with '*Suaviter in modo, fortiter in re*' – which meant much the same. I had only really seen this side of his character once. My father and I were walking through a crowded square by the old post office in Hong Kong, when someone came running up behind us. At the exact moment when I realised that the man was about to hit my father, my father turned his head around and delivered a back-blow with his fist to the man's nose, leaving him on the ground. 'Sorry about that, darling,' he said. 'I'm afraid he was trying to assault us.' Then he took me to a McDonald's for a hot apple pie.

When he returned to his Perthshire home, none of his foreign adventures meant much to his circle of neighbours, very few of whom had ever worked for long outside the United Kingdom. Because he was so deaf, he tended to 'trap' people after dinner, keeping them in the dining room after everyone else had gone through to the drawing room for a 'one-on-one' chat over whisky about international affairs. I learned to return to the dining room after half an hour, rub his shoulders, kiss him on the head as a cue to say to the guest, 'I think I'm being sent to bed. I'm being politely accused of monopolising you! Off we go then . . .'

His memory was filled with images – a snowy hill outside Beijing, with a sentry challenging him with a rifle; his flight to Ulan Bator with Ravasal Otgon Bayr, the Mongolian wrestler; his visits to the White Orchid Club in Vientiane – while Perthshire conversation was more likely to revolve around grouse. His neighbours mostly had a sense of what he had not been: not, for example, a regular Black Watch officer. They had no sense of what he had been: the second-most senior man in the British secret service. He thought that they wouldn't have understood, and wouldn't really have been interested if they had.

43

Twelve miles from Westerkirk, just on the other side of the border, were English parishes just as remote and poor. None of those English parishes had produced such a concentration of famous men. But many of the Scottish villages the same distance away – Ettrick, Denholm and Foulshiels – had turned shepherds' sons into famous poets, linguistic scholars and explorers. Here then was a difference between England and Scotland, apparent just north of Hadrian's Wall. But what was the explanation? For Samuel Smiles, who reflected on this miracle in the mid-nineteenth century, the secret was the Scottish education system:

> Westerkirk . . . possessed the advantage of that admirable institution, the parish school. By imparting the rudiments of knowledge to all, the parish schools of the country placed the children of the peasantry on a more equal footing with the children of the rich; and to that extent redressed the inequalities of fortune.

My father had also been to a good Scottish parish school, and he believed such schools were the secret to success for countless poor Scots. 'Take Thomas Carlyle, walking back and forth to school from his farm near Ecclefechan.' But this idea of the Scottish parish school – long precious to Scottish identity – is now rejected by academics as a 'democratic myth'. Scholars emphasise that in Thomas Telford's youth, only 15 per cent of Scottish women could read, and almost none in remote rural villages, and that there was little difference between Scottish and English primary education for boys.

My father was not pleased by this idea: 'It was not a myth that the Scottish education I knew seemed to put us ahead of our contemporaries down south. When I emerged from Auntie's class at the bottom of the Kirriemuir School, aged about seven, as far as I can remember everybody had a fair grasp of the three Rs . . . My education gave me a head start over most of the English – except their scholarship chaps.'

'The Malcolms,' observed my father, 'were the cream of the cream of the Scots, who left the countryside for the cities of the Empire. And it's no disparagement of the English to remark upon it. Take my father, leaving Dundee and establishing himself in Calcutta. But the Malcolms beggar belief.'

Whatever the explanation of their success, a striking number of these children from modest backgrounds finished their lives in heroic portraits. You could see blue eyes, red cheeks and farmers' hands and broad frames tightly wrapped in red or blue military coats. The great crosses of knighthood that had been hung around the high black stocks of four of the Malcolm brothers – winning them the name 'the Four Knights of Eskdale' – honoured prompt and unerring action, energy, decisiveness and confidence, of always knowing instantly what to do – on three continents.

Abroad, these men seemed to feel simultaneously British, Scottish and men of the Border – and to weave Scottish history into their analysis of Asia. Sir John Malcolm writes to his fellow Borderer Walter Scott of the Persians: 'Their chiefs are in some ways like our old Scottish feudal lairds.' And again, seven years later, 'I am anxious to speak to you about my Asiatic Borderers and Highlanders – for I am rich in materials to show how similarity of circumstances makes all alike.'

After a series of battles made Sir John Malcolm the ruler of Central India by 1815, he delayed retiring to Scotland. He enjoyed his anachronistic power – which echoed that of a Border lord – too much:

> I have to tempt me, complete authority, military and political, over a range as large as England and Scotland. It is my chief business to keep the Peace in this lately distracted quarter, and I have been successful beyond my most sanguine expectations. The largest tribes are quiet but the difficulty is to keep the Rob Roys under.

Finally, in an attempt to find a position at home, Malcolm left India and stood for Parliament. He established himself in a country seat, and threw himself into grand schemes of improvements for his park and garden. He combined this with trying to write two more books, but he was exhausted and ageing fast, and he never really got on top of the manuscripts. Although John Murray agreed to publish them before he died, they remained muddled and repetitive.

Parliament had no interest in his experience. He wrote to his brother:

> As to your affairs in Bombay . . . nobody cares one farthing. There is not the smallest borough in England that . . . does not excite more interest, and occupy more of the public mind, than our whole Empire in India.

And he was not a success as an MP. His biographer wrote:

> He was unaccustomed to the rather strange customs of the house, the pettifogging procedures, the shifting factional alliances. Moreover in a place and at a time when oratory was at a premium, when the ability to quote Latin tags was an admired art, his rather squeaky voice and still strong Scottish brogue were against him. 'Neither voice nor delivery were in his favour.'

He appears in contemporary diaries and letters in Scotland as a slightly absurd figure, a man too hearty at the dinner table. And although people were faintly impressed that he had once spoken good Persian and had published a Persian history, few read it. People were more aware of the discrepancies – a tenant farmer's son with the stride of a magnate, a man who purported to write oriental history who had never completed a university degree, a soldier who had never been in the regular army.

44

We had seen no mention of the Malcolm family on any monument in Westerkirk. The schoolhouse and the church which the Telfords and Malcolms attended as children had both gone. I could not have told if I had looked at a photograph of the flat fields through which we were driving whether I was in Warwickshire or Vermont.

But on the ridge line a few miles away was an obelisk or an 'Egyptian needle', a hundred feet high, dedicated to Sir John Malcolm. Thomas Telford had promoted it; Robert Stephenson's patented balance crane had swung it neatly into place. The speech at the laying of the foundation stone was made by Sir James Graham, whose family had once been Border raiders and who lived on the English side. He seemed to use the words 'England', 'Britain' and Scottish 'Eskdale' without being conscious of any significant difference:

> The history and actions of Sir John Malcolm will live in England till distant posterity . . . His history lives as one of the greatest men that Great Britain ever produced, and it may well be a proud thought that he was a native of Eskdale.

He talked as though Malcolm's monument – like Pompey's and Hadrian's monuments in Rome – might inspire people over millennia. Apparently he was wrong.

The nearby town of Langholm made much of the connection with Telford, and with the poet Hugh MacDiarmid, but I could see nothing in the tourist office or on the web about any of the Malcolms. Admiral Sir Pulteney's statue stood behind the library – it has a sunken skull-like head, the features thinned and eroded by 150 years of rain; the body has been dyed a sooty black from car exhausts, leaving only a flash of white on his chin and on his crotch, suggesting marble. But like the inheritors of a cargo cult from an incomprehensible past, the people of Langholm referred to it not as Sir Pulteney but just as the 'marble man'.

Something about the Malcolms – their exotic lives abroad perhaps, their marble obelisks, their place in the British establishment, their wars and the Empire – had not fitted them to be modern Scottish heroes. Local boys were not supposed to emulate their success. Instead, Langholm's only 'notable person' on Wikipedia was Neil Armstrong, on the grounds that his family name was a Border name. The native heroes had been forgotten in favour of an American astronaut who had visited the town for two hours in 1972.

45

Nearing Crieff, my father spotted a road sign. 'Sheriffmuir? Pretty peculiar battle. No one could work out who had won; both sides just wandered off the next morning. Wonder where it is.'

'Just up on that hill,' I said, pointing south. We were only ten miles from our house.

'Really? We should adopt it as our standard battlefield outing. Take all our guests to see it.'

Soon we were passing the Roman camp at Ardoch, and then Strathearn appeared, 200 square miles of rolling ground, round hills and solitary trees. I had known it when the mist lay in thick bands on the lower slopes; or rain lashed across a field to the east, or – on a winter evening – when the snow ridge of the Ochil mountains held the violent purple blaze of sunset.

Today, the midday light blazed on the aluminium troughs and on the desiccated stalks of old thistles. And instead of patches of mist in the dips of rolling savannah, I noticed wire fences on the verge and drainage culverts. A brand-new executive villa stood white and tall on the roadside. It seemed to have sprouted from the open fields within the previous year. A shiny black car pointed south towards an office in Edinburgh.

Our journey together along the wall had revealed something. But neither Britain nor my father had been quite what I had expected. I had hoped, for example, to show that there were no permanent differences between England and Scotland, between my cottage in Cumbria and my father's home in Scotland – that our histories and culture and soil were richly interwoven, with threads spreading far across the border. But I was more conscious now of fractures, absences and distortion. The connections between Scotland, Hadrian's Wall and Cumbria were ambiguous and often misleading. I doubted whether it was still possible to link a national identity to a soil or a historical monument.

An hour and a half earlier, for example, we had driven past Yarrow. Here, in 1804, as I explained to my father, a man, setting his plough to bring the bare moorland into cultivation, had struck a megalith six feet long and three feet wide. There were markings on it and bones underneath. A local antiquary prevented him from blowing it up. Four men were summoned to inspect it.

The men – Walter Scott, John Leyden, Mungo Park and George Scott – were all sons, or in Scott's case, the grandson, of tenant farmers in nearby valleys. Like their direct contemporaries, the Malcolm brothers, they were not going to be farmers themselves. Dr Leyden, from Hawick, had just taken a job in Bombay and was believed to be able to speak Latin, Swedish, Canarese, Greek, Icelandic, Tamil, Italian, Sanskrit, Malayalam, Spanish, Zend, Mappila, French, Pehlvi, Maldivan, German, Persian, Prakrit, Hebrew, Pushtu, Pali, Portuguese, Balochi, Jaghatai Turki, Aramaic, Hindostani, Malay, Arabic, Dakhni, Burmese, Amharic, Marathi, Rakheng, Gaelic, Gujerati, Siamese, Dutch, Bengali, Bugis, Flemish, Nuddya, Macasar, Danish-Norwegian, Telugu and Armenian.

Mungo Park, the great African explorer, was the seventh of thirteen children born to a tenant farmer at Foulshiels, eight miles away. And George Scott – the son of a tenant farmer in Ettrick – had just agreed to accompany Park back to the Gambia.

What national identity did these men feel was preserved in this chipped grey whinstone? George Scott sketched the stone and concluded that the marks were suns and moons, and that it was made by a Druid. The linguist, Dr Leyden, realised the markings were in fact letters and proposed that it was a Roman monument. Walter Scott, who enjoyed mocking the delusions of 'antiquaries', disagreed. He concluded it was the tomb of one of his relatives, 'a male ancestor of the current Lord Napier' and the hero of the ballad of the 'Dowie Dens of Yarrow', killed in 1609.

These three men with global reputations, each presented with the same stone in a Border field, saw three quite different things: Druids, Rome and Scottish Border chivalry. All were wrong.

It was a Christian monument, not druidical. The letters that gambolled across the surface were childish, and would have embarrassed Leyden's earlier Roman epigrapher, but they were a thousand years older than Sir Walter believed; and it was not 'Scottish'. The inscription on the megalith was from the sixth century: 'This is the tomb of Princes Nudd and Dyfnen of the Damnonii tribe, the sepulchre of two sons of Liberalis.' The names of the princes were not Scottish, or Gaelic, but Cumbric-Welsh. They were contemporaries of Gildas, and the princes of 'Y Hen

Ogledd', the vanished northern kingdom that once stretched from the firths of Forth and Clyde, across all of Cumbria and Northumbria, straddling the English–Scottish border.

None of these Scottish prodigies had been able to see that the Yarrow landscape contained another more ancient identity and literature, one that questioned the modern English–Scottish divide.

★

'What is this stream, Daddy?' I asked as we crossed a bridge, five minutes from home.

'Not a clue.'

'But we must have driven over it a hundred times.'

'Far more.'

'It's shocking that we don't know the name of a stream so close to our house.'

'We're shockingly ignorant actually,' he said.

It took barely two minutes to drive through Muthill, enough time to notice that scarecrows had been hung on the red sandstone houses for some festival, and to glimpse the shell of the eleventh-century church before we entered the final straight stretch, lined with lime trees, with the gates of Drummond Castle on our left and the Neolithic standing stone on our right.

Beneath the great rippling ridges and curves of the Highland hills, we swung round the former gasworks and turned down the drive, alongside the double beech hedge and the tank-traps, past the ha-ha, to the tall grey front of the house, where Torquil the lurcher was waiting for us. Torquil came to greet me first.

'Traitor,' said my father, once he had hauled himself with great effort out of the car. 'Absolutely typical. Only interested in the newcomers. Who feeds you?' He reached in the pocket of his tweed coat and pulled out first a medical inhaler and then some crumbled biscuit, which had clearly been there for months. 'Here, darling.' Torquil politely came forward, nibbled some biscuit, and then turned his back on my father and walked into the woods.

BOOK TWO

Middleland

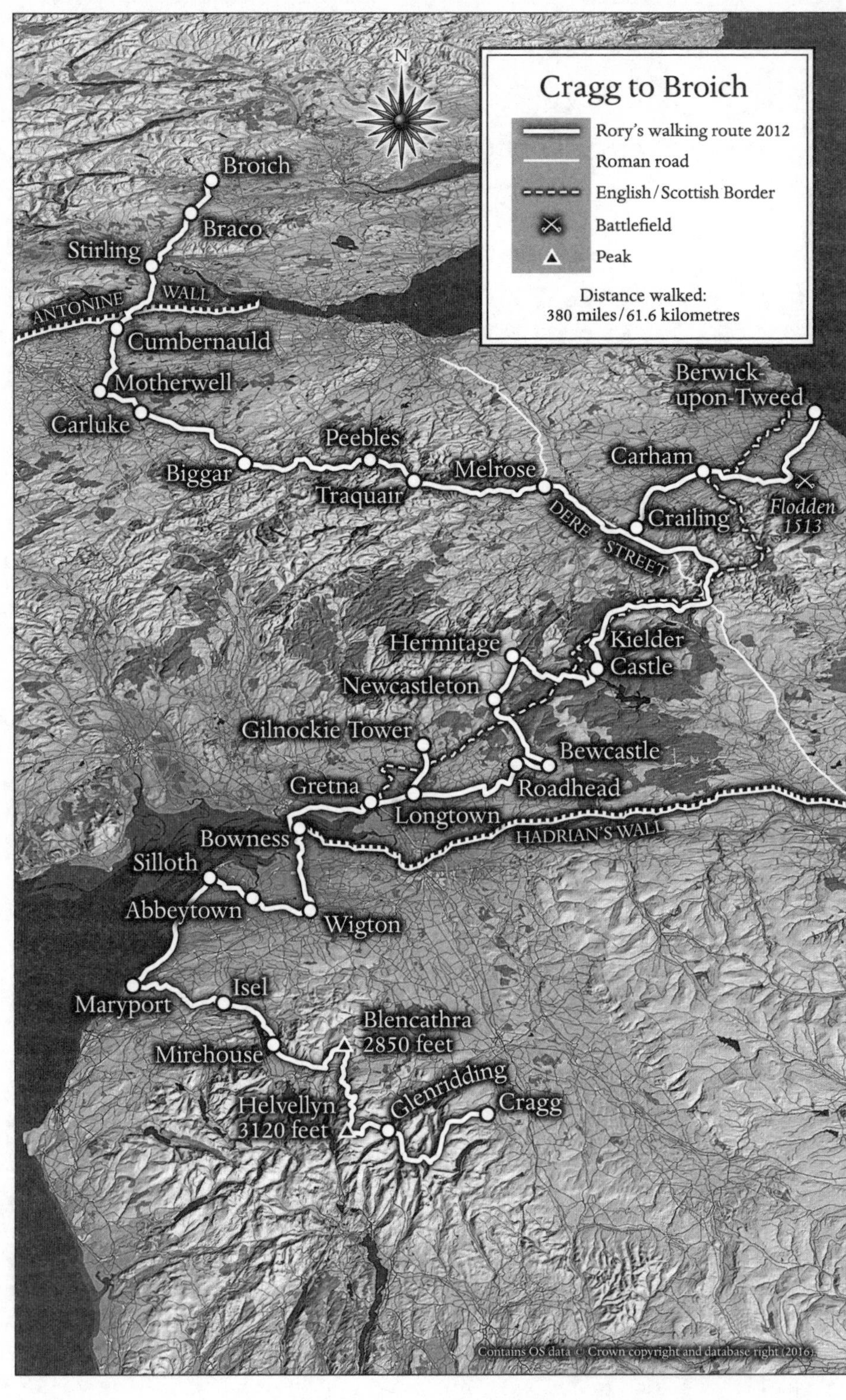

Cragg to Broich
Rory's walking route 2012
Roman road
English/Scottish Border
Battlefield
Peak
Distance walked:
380 miles/61.6 kilometres
N
Broich
Braco
Stirling
ANTONINE WALL
Cumbernauld
Motherwell
Carluke
Biggar
Peebles
Traquair
Melrose
DERE STREET
Berwick-upon-Tweed
Carham
Crailing
Flodden 1513
Hermitage
Kielder Castle
Newcastleton
Gilnockie Tower
Bewcastle
Gretna
Roadhead
Longtown
HADRIAN'S WALL
Bowness
Silloth
Abbeytown
Wigton
Maryport
Isel
Blencathra 2850 feet
Mirehouse
Glenridding
Helvellyn 3120 feet
Cragg
Contains OS data © Crown copyright and database right (2016).

46

The year after my walk with my father along Hadrian's Wall, and two years before the referendum on Scottish independence – which threatened to put my father and myself in different countries – I decided to make another walk. This time alone, from my cottage in Cumbria to my father's house in Scotland. I walked in a long curve, crossing from coast to coast, tracing the territory of the vanished nations that had existed before the invention of England and Scotland, following the full length of the modern English–Scottish border, and then turning north for the Highlands and home. The walk was to be about 400 miles in length and, unlike the four days on Hadrian's Wall, it was to take me twenty-six days.

I've never been any good at explaining why I go on long walks. The truth, I think, is I believe walks are miracles – which can let me learn, like nothing else, about a nation, or myself – helping me solve disappointments, personal and political. (My Afghan walk had, I felt, done many of those things.) And what I had glimpsed on the Hadrian's Wall walk about Scotland, our history, my father and myself had troubled me. But when I try to describe everything I hope to get out of a walk I find I embarrass myself.

Although my father didn't say anything, he probably saw that my ambitions would make much less sense in Cumbria and the Scottish Borders than they did in Afghanistan. But he still encouraged me to do the journey, and came down the night before I left to cook me a steak on his George Foreman grill. He presented me with a cassette recorder to capture conversations with people I met, and suggested that I should try to send him regular updates. Over the next few weeks, while I was walking, he borrowed books on Border warfare from the local library, tracked down friends who understood about Dark Age history, and sent me a continuous stream of 2,000-word emails, reflecting on what I had told him about the landscape and what it suggested about Britain. And he threatened – with a grin – to come and 'ambush' me frequently. I would be walking alone, but it was his journey too.

47

On 22 July 2012, I picked up my blue pack, containing my down jacket, my waterproofs and plastic water gourd. I tucked the metal-tipped *dang*, which I had carried on Hadrian's Wall, under my left arm, and knelt to tighten my boots – the same rituals with stick and boots that I had followed on 500 mornings ten years earlier as I walked across Asia. It was surprising that my boots still fitted and that my down jacket smelled all right. The pack was more stained and less heavy. Instead of having to carry $5,000 in emergency cash, I was stuffing in a BlackBerry charger, six Ordnance Survey maps and a packet of chocolate digestive biscuits. Then I stepped out of the cottage door, wondering what exactly I would see.

It was warm; a flat sheet of dark cloud lay along Knipe Scar: a gale had blown through in the night; the ash leaves were no long trembling; the cows were calm and motionless in the fields. Below the russet frame of the high fell, the facing slope was sliced into three colours by the glittering limestone walls: the brown of the ploughed fields, the olive green of the hay meadows, and the yellow-green of the enclosed sward of the sheep pasture.

If I had been looking for a symbol of my nation I might have been tempted to choose this view, this place – it was a scene as clear as a 1920s railway poster. In 1740, Thomas Gray had looked at this same Lake District landscape and been mesmerised, as I was, by the way that below the wild fells, every line in the valleys held the traces of human activity – of worship, planting, grazing, hedge-laying, cattle-breeding, building and dense-stocking of sheep. He had seen, as I saw:

> A white village with the parish church rising in the midst of it, hanging enclosures, corn-fields, & meadows green as an emerald, with their trees & hedges & cattle . . . & just opposite a large farm-house at the bottom of a steep smooth lawn embosom'd in

old woods, which climb halfway up the mountain's side, & above them a broken line of crags that crown the scene.

I squeezed through a gap in the limestone rock, reached the gate in the drystone wall and emerged onto the peat of the common fellside. This wall, mottled with verdigris and a hint of rose-pink, was the knife-edge between pasture and wilderness: at the exact line of the gate, the short grass stopped and the reeds, thistles, bracken and gorse began. It was my march wall.

Walls like this did not exist around our house in Scotland, or indeed in southern England. I was in a place that remained defiantly separate from smooth generalisations about 'a British landscape'. This wall was what the Northumbrian Angles had called *mearcað mórhopu* – the 'march of the moor'. Medieval Cumbrians called it the *ring-garth*, and modern Cumbrians the 'head-dyke'. And the different-coloured landscapes which it separated had been given different names by the separate nations of this Middleland. They had been called *ffird* and *dol* by the early Cumbrians, *mor* and *mǽd* by the Northumbrian Angles; *fjalr* and *vollr* by the Norse; and *muir* and *laigh* by later Borderers.

My father was impatient with my insistence on esoteric cultures. 'Come on, darling, you know more Northumbrian than you think, the Northumbrian words for these landscapes are simply our "moor" and "mede" for meadow, the Norse is our "fell", and "muir" is just our moor again – although I'm damned if I know what "ffird" and "dol" are.' But his modern translations – moor, meadow, fell – implied something inherent in the soil, or the altitude, the kind of contrast that existed between the Highland terrain and the lowlands near his house. In truth, the difference between the zones was a human artefact: a matter of artificial borders.

The key was that the land into which I was now stepping beyond the march wall – whether *ffird* or *mor* or *fjalr* – was not weeded, or fertilised, or protected, or walled. And it was not really 'owned'. No fence separated one flock from another. Here the farmers had a right to pasture a specific number of sheep or Fell ponies, but they did not have a right to a particular stretch of soil. The livestock wandered freely over the wet heath. This upland remained 'common land'.

Some Scottish Nationalists talk a great deal about the idea that the Highlands had once been owned in common by all the clan, not by the chief, and try to use this fact to insist that Scots are naturally more communal and egalitarian than the English. But such arrangements had not existed in Scotland for centuries; whereas here, in upland Cumbria, the ancient communal practices of early settlers had been preserved. It was still possible to walk from one end of Westmorland to the other over 129,000 acres of common land. I could walk seventeen miles from here, the top of the hill above my cottage gate, to Troutbeck in Ambleside, without leaving common land or seeing another house.

I was walking now past heather, and the electric brilliance of an emerging thistle. I brushed the tight purple tips of the long grass, and fingered wool, which hung like cotton candy on the slender stalks. A glistening star-shaped moss sank beneath my heavy boot. Then I passed another thistle, which seemed taller than me; and a white butterfly which seemed improbably smaller than my thumbnail. For the first half an hour of the climb, the march wall continued on my left, separating the green rye grass from the paler hues of the open fell.

A little higher and reed-beds began to flow in great curves across the slope, beneath bands of white, olive and rust-tinted grass. I heard the creak and whisper of my boots. Pale streamers of wind-blown fescew fluttered from thistle heads. Among the black fewmets of the Fell ponies lay the white droppings of animals who fed on limestone grassland. I picked a reed and chewed on its sharp smooth spike as I walked.

48

For the previous twelve months, since my walk with my father, I had not been in Scotland; instead I had focused on this land around my cottage in Cumbria, which stood a hundred miles south of my father's house, and thirty miles south of Hadrian's Wall. The landscapes in which we lived, either side of the border, mirrored each other. Like my father, I lived above a rich-soiled river valley, near a Neolithic standing stone, and just beyond a line of Roman forts, containing garrisons that had left traces of exotic cultures and peculiar gods (my local fort once held Pannonian cavalrymen from the Hungarian plains, who conducted elaborate rituals to bury their horses, occasionally removed the heads from the human

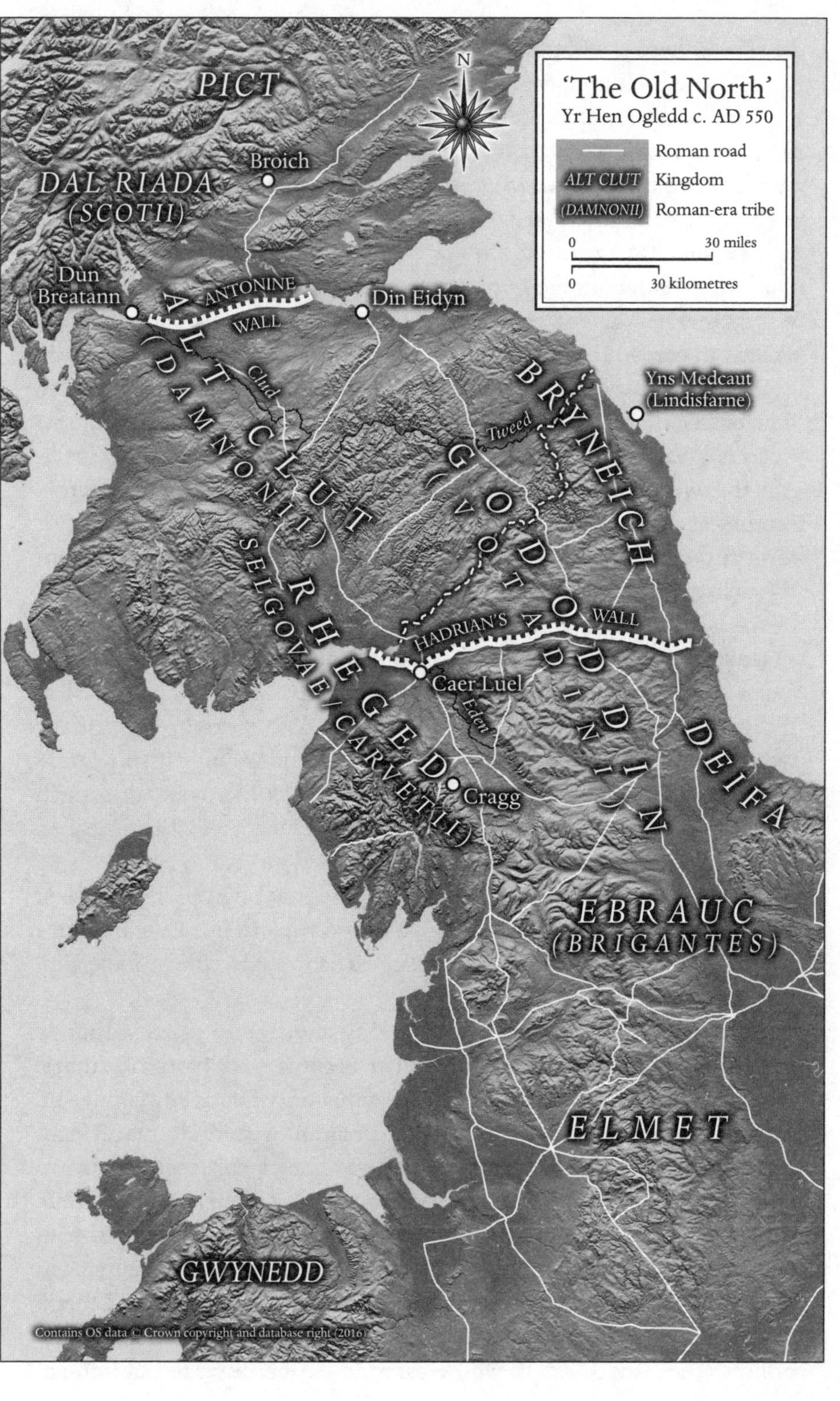

'The Old North'
Yr Hen Ogledd c. AD 550
Roman road
ALT CLUT Kingdom
(DAMNONII) Roman-era tribe
0
30 miles
0
30 kilometres
N
PICT
Broich
DAL RIADA
(SCOTII)
Dùn Breatann
ANTONINE WALL
Din Eidyn
ALT CLUT
(DAMNONII)
Clud
Yns Medcaut
(Lindisfarne)
BRYNEICH
Tweed
GODODDIN
(VOTADINI)
RHEGED
SELGOVAE/CARVETII
HADRIAN'S WALL
Caer Luel
Eden
Cragg
DEIFA
EBRAUC
(BRIGANTES)
ELMET
GWYNEDD
Contains OS data © Crown copyright and database right (2016)

dead, and kept a shrine to a god called Belatucadros, whose meaning was disputed – 'the horned one' or perhaps 'the shining one').

On both valley floors the soil was thick, the rainfall low, and you could feed a cow from an acre, or grow barley; whereas in the hills the rainfall doubled and the soil was thin, waterlogged, acidic, packed with reeds, and you would struggle to feed a cow at all. In each case, the upland hills had nurtured a quite different culture from the lowlands. Our houses stood on the line between these contrasting lands, and their very names, Cragg and Broich – meaning a bluff or cliff above the river valley – recorded the same topographical distinction.

But although the names of our houses meant the same, they came from different Gaelic dialects, different 'nations' – Cragg from the Cumbric-Celtic language of my valley, Broich from the Irish-Gaelic of the Highlands. And the two buildings were quite different. Broich was a large eighteenth-century house in a mini-park, built right below the most northerly set of forts in the whole Roman Empire – forts which were only occupied for less than a decade. It stood on the Highland Line, and had been, for most of the last two millennia, firmly in the land of the Picts and the Scots.

Cragg, on the other hand, was a low-ceilinged, medieval farm cottage, half a mile up a foot-track, in a valley which had been for 300 years at the very heart of the Roman frontier zone. The rocks by my cottage were 200 million years younger than the rocks above my father's house in Scotland, and the rainfall was lower. But my rocks were also much older than those of southern England, and the climate was much bleaker. The peculiar rocks and cultures that surrounded me had sometimes been part of Scotland, sometimes part of England, but often part of neither. And having used the walk with my father to explore our Roman past, I wanted to use this walk to explore what had happened to this 'Middleland' after the Romans left.

Sometime in the fifth century, not long after the Romans withdrew from the frontier zone, my valley had become part of the Cumbric kingdom of Rheged. These kings perpetuated what a Roman would have considered a fading half-life of civilisation, wearing Roman cloaks and worshipping the Roman Christian god, but increasingly abandoning Latin for their local Cumbric language – a Celtic relative of Welsh. They sheltered in wooden halls, unable or unwilling to repair the Roman buildings, mint coins or manufacture ceramics, and when they remained in Roman wall forts they allowed the sewers to back up around them. This was the culture of the pessimistic British monk Gildas, and of the princes Nudd and Dyfnen, whose tomb had been inspected by Mungo

Park and Walter Scott. Those in other Welsh-speaking kingdoms called it 'Y Henn Ogledd', 'the Old North'.

Very little had survived from this Cumbric culture in my valley. Whereas the soil of a site that once held a Roman camp could contain thousands of ceramic shards, shoes, letters, and dozens of rings, statues, altars, scabbards, scissors, mallets and make-up bottles, even the most prominent Cumbric-Welsh settlement has left little more than a few fragments of broken jewellery. The detritus of a single 300-yard-square Roman fort at Vindolanda was far greater than could be contained even in their large museum; whereas the remains of the 5,000 square miles of the Cumbric kingdoms between AD 400 and 600 could hardly fill a shelf. We would not even have known the name of their kingdoms if some of their poetry had not been recorded, 600 years after their fall, by a later unknown medieval monk.

And by 600, the kingdom of Rheged had vanished. The territory around my home valley had largely been conquered by a new group who spoke a Germanic dialect, worshipped not Christ but the Germanic god Woden, and who claimed to have sailed across the sea from a place called Angeln near the German–Danish border. They called themselves 'Angles' or 'North-humbrians' – meaning they had seized all the land north of the Humber River before extending their rule to the Firth of Forth in central Scotland.

Some of the old Cumbric-speaking people clearly survived, and in fact briefly took back control of the area 300 years later. But it was the Northumbrian language – Angle-isc – not the Cumbric language of Rheged, which won through and became our English; rather than any Cumbric word, it was their Woden's day that was the origin of our Wednes-day. The names of the majority of the villages in my valley, from Ask-ham to Bamp-ton, recorded the settlements not of Celtic but of Northumbrian farmers. And it was the Northumbrians who had carved the tendrils, grapes and leaves in hypnotising spirals onto a six-foot-high Christian column four miles from my home.

This was the culture of my father's favourite monk, 'the Venerable Bede'. Thanks to Bede, we know a little bit more about the Northumbrians than about the Cumbric kings. He describes their conversion to Christianity, and their renaissance, which by the late 600s made Northumbria the leading centre for theology, history, manuscript illumination and sculpture in the whole of Europe.

Then at the very end of the eighth century, a new pagan group had attacked this civilisation – first as seaborne Vikings, sailing from

Scandinavia to torch and loot the great Northumbrian monasteries; then as a 'Great heathen Army', killing the Anglian king of Northumbria and the Cumbric king of Strathclyde. ('You should remind them that they spreadeagled them, darling – tore their lungs out and arranged them spread out like eagle's wings across their chests,' remarked my father.) The Danish king Halfdan murdered and enslaved so successfully in Carlisle that 200 years later the city was still empty and had to be repopulated with people from the South.

By 915 my home and valley was probably in its third incarnation as part of the Viking kingdom of Dublin. Ten years later it was just two miles south of the new English frontier of the Saxon king Athelstan. Shortly thereafter, it was given or taken by the kings of Scotland, and then – it seems – by the English, and lost to the Vikings again. And by 1000 it was again part of an independent kingdom called Strathclyde or Cumbria, a distant descendant of the Cumbric culture of Rheged.

Cumbric, the 'indigenous' language in my valley for a thousand years, lingered now only in a few place-names: the first syllable of the farm behind my cottage, for example, 'Car-Hullan' (Hull's fort), and possibly in some numerals once used to count sheep. No one, it seemed, could speak it, or had heard it spoken in this valley for 800 years.

I only heard Cumbric when a Welsh singer gave a recitation over a meal of Spanish tapas and Herdwick lamb at my local pub, the Gate. The singer did not dress in Druidical costume or a mock Dark Ages kilt, but in a pair of slacks and a neat shirt. And he stood facing the polished dark oak bar.

'We are now,' he announced to the people at the tables, 'in the kingdom of Rheged.' (He pronounced it with a strong emphasis on the 'H' – 'Hhhegedhh.)' 'And the original language of this area in the sixth century was Welsh, so this song is in Welsh, and it praises Urien' – 'Eee-ree-ennn' – 'the ruler of Rheged.'

He spread his arms wide and began to chant:

Urien Erechwyd.
haelaf dyn bedyd
lliaws a rodyd
y dynyon eluyd.

The lines were short, so rhymes came like chopping waves against a boat in harbour – *rech-we^ed, bed-e^ed, ro-de^ed*. No one understood him.

On a table next to me a woman, hearing the Cumbrian Welsh, said, 'I thought we were Vikings?' Everyone else nodded.

When he had finished, I bought the singer a beer.

'So what do the first two words, *"Urien Erechwyd"*, mean?' I asked.

'We don't really know. Sir Ifor Williams, a great scholar for whom I have the greatest respect, thought the first words were *"Urien yr echwyd"*. But even Sir Ifor Williams is basing this on only a single syllable in a smudged manuscript. It could be ten things. But then Sir Ifor Williams is a much greater scholar than me. Who am I to disagree with Sir Ifor Williams?'

'So what did Sir Ifor Williams think *"Urien yr echwyd"* meant?'

'Well, he thought "Lord of the rip-tide". This might mean Lord of the Solway Firth. If this is right then the poem confirms that this valley where we are now was not England or Scotland, it was Urien's kingdom of Rheged.'

'And if not?'

He shrugged. 'It was somewhere nearby anyway.'

49

The singer then read me the *Gododdin*, a poem about another neighbouring Cumbric-Welsh-British kingdom of the sixth century. The inverted syntax lurched from concrete to abstract, blunt to formal, with each stroke of the battle being described:

Aryf angkynnull
Agkyman dull
Anysgoget . . .

The circumlocutions of the nineteenth-century English translation he handed me suggested a struggle to comprehend phrases so taut and pregnant with meaning:

Scattered, broken of motionless form, is the weapon
To which it was highly congenial to prostrate the horde of the
Lloegrians.
Shields were strewn in the entrance, shields in the battle of lances.

There were many double negatives: 'Without dishonour did he retaliate' instead of 'He struck back with honour'. Regret hung over the lines: 'It were wrong if I neglected to praise them.' It was difficult to tell from the translation if these were to be taken as moments of bathos, awkwardness or irony. Creating history from this kind of poem was like trying to reconstruct archaic Greek society from a reading of the *Iliad*. Worse, each section of the *Gododdin* poem is a variation on the last. Names reoccur, the same event is retold, but from a different angle and with a different outcome. Did three warriors survive, or four? The *Gododdin*'s authors did not seem to know, or chose not to reveal.

'Is the poem any good?' I asked.

'It is a part of one of the greatest literatures in the world. The problem is the translation. Because it's poetry, it is all about the word sounds, the word play, the alliteration.'

'Is that not true of all poetry?' I asked.

'No one has this alliteration and play.'

'Northumbrian? Anglo-Saxon? Norse?' I ventured.

'Primitive by comparison.'

'But is Cumbric literature all good?'

'Oh no. Parts of the *Gododdin* are terrible. Student exercises. Dreadful stuff.'

50

Now, having climbed for an hour up the hill from my cottage, the Cumbric farm 'Car-hullan' was no longer visible on my left, the thistles had become shorter, squatter, and their heads were as thick as tulip bulbs. After another

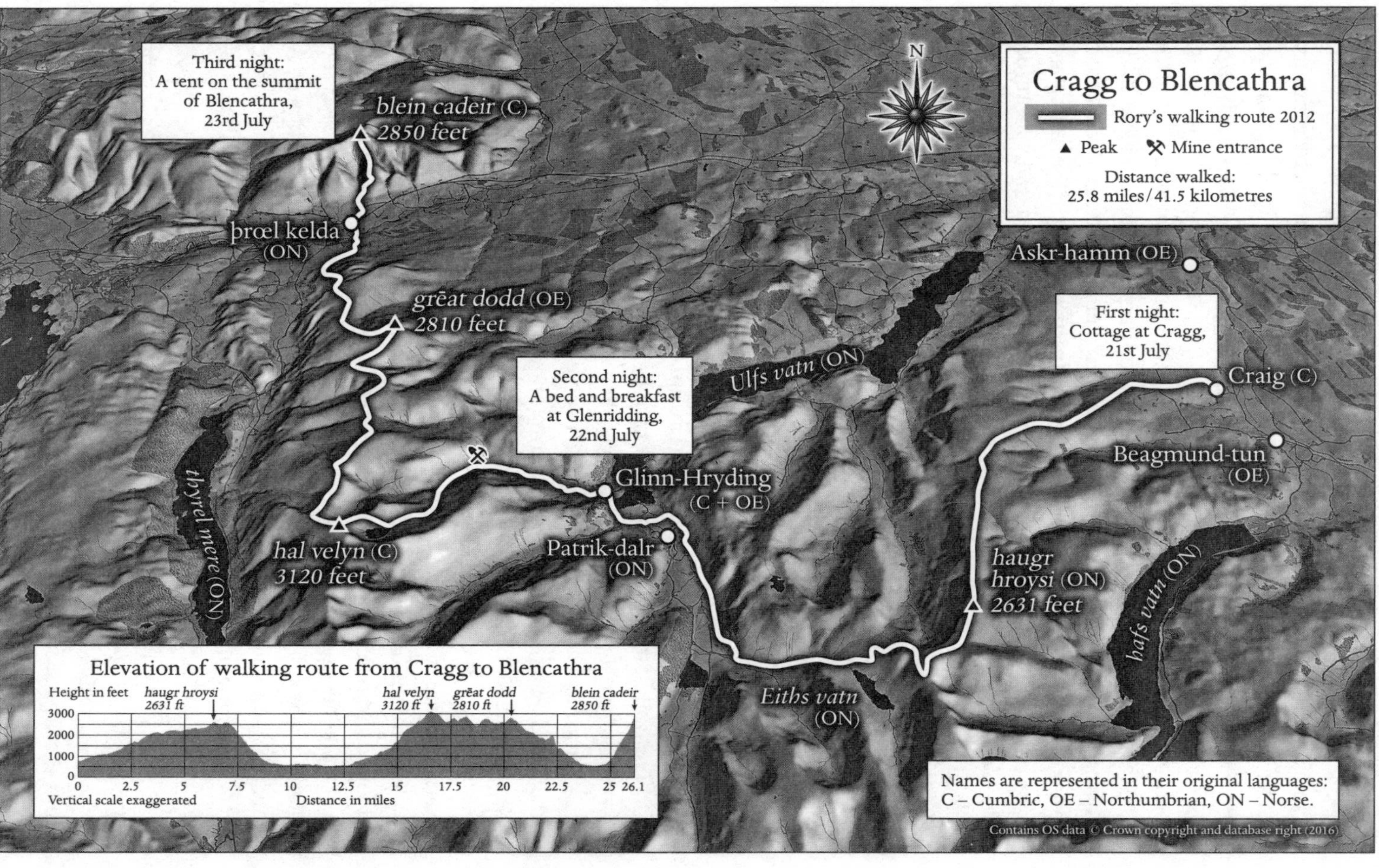

Cragg to Blencathra
Rory's walking route 2012
▲ Peak
Mine entrance
Distance walked:
25.8 miles/41.5 kilometres
N
Third night:
A tent on the summit
of Blencathra,
23rd July
blein cadeir (C)
2850 feet
þrœl kelda
(ON)
grēat dodd (OE)
2810 feet
Second night:
A bed and breakfast
at Glenridding,
22nd July
Glinn-Hryding
(C + OE)
Patrik-dalr
(ON)
hal velyn (C)
3120 feet
thyrel mere (ON)
Ulfs vatn (ON)
Askr-hamm (OE)
First night:
Cottage at Cragg,
21st July
Craig (C)
Beagmund-tun
(OE)
haugr
hroysi (ON)
2631 feet
hafs vatn (ON)
Eiths vatn
(ON)
Elevation of walking route from Cragg to Blencathra
Height in feet
haugr hroysi
2631 ft
hal velyn
3120 ft
grēat dodd
2810 ft
blein cadeir
2850 ft
3000
2000
1000
0
0
2.5
5
7.5
10
12.5
15
17.5
20
22.5
25
26.1
Vertical scale exaggerated
Distance in miles
Names are represented in their original languages:
C – Cumbric, OE – Northumbrian, ON – Norse.
Contains OS data © Crown copyright and database right (2016)

300 feet, only a few shimmering seed heads remained above the sward. On a small boulder I noticed scarlet leaves, pale moss, a black dropping, three daisies and the jawbone of a sheep. Beyond lay a ribcage and a yellow plastic ear tag numbered 01631. A plain brown bird, which the Northumbrians called an ouzel, was crying *wheesh, wheesh*, its fat body battling the wind as though it were pretending to be a hawk.

Half an hour later and the wind became sharp and cold, peeling back the pale inner stalks of the fell grass, and higher still, sweeping bands of black cloud over Loadpot Hill, so that the fractured light striped the peat hags into the pattern of a tiger's skin. I climbed steadily until I was inside the damp cloud-water and could not see beyond the cuckoo spit on a blade of grass at my boot-edge. I turned, almost in a circle, off my route.

Then the cloud frayed to reveal two white tresses on the facing slope, falling in the pattern that my father had told me the Japanese connoisseurs call a 'dragon's hair'. What was it? Water, snow, limestone? Only, I discovered when I climbed up to it, a dead Swaledale, its wool spreading from its carcass like a waterfall.

Far below me and behind me now was what the seventh-century Northumbrians who farmed the river valley at Bampton and Askham would have called the *grundweall*. I had crossed their *stangeat* at my cottage. Ground-wall. Stone-gate. Stronger pairings of noun-metaphors than our words 'mountain-base' or 'gap in rock'. The sun, which the Northumbrians called the '*heofen-candal*', the 'heaven-candle', now flickered behind cloud, and I had entered the mistcliffs, misty-moors and meres – in their epic *Beowulf*, the hell domain of the demon Grendel. This was the place of the *micle mearcstapan móras healdan*: or as my father would have it, the muckle March-steppers, moor-holding.

Two meres topped the fell, aligned on the horizon edge, like infinity pools. I had reached High Street, the Romano-British ridge-road that ran 2,000 feet above the valley floor. Another tear in the clouds revealed the black waves of Ullswater, with green ridges rolling in the distance. A middle-aged couple in bright anoraks were waiting patiently for some schoolchildren on their Duke of Edinburgh challenge. On the path beside them, I could see the tracks and treads of mountain bikes, of horses from the endurance race, and of what I thought was the quad bike that was used to lay the scent for the trail-hounds.

At the crest of this watershed I left behind the sandstone of Eden and the limestone of Lowther – valleys dominated by Northumbrian place-names. Now I scrambled down a slope of volcanic Lake District rock, past Harter Fell and Hayeswater, Boredale, Grisedale and Ullswater.

My father would have deciphered *bore-dale* as 'valley with a burgh or fort', Ullswater as Olaf's Water, and the Harter Fell (or more precisely the Norse *Hjartar*) as Hart or Deer Hill; and he would have recognised the old Scottish word 'grice' for a pig in *Grise-dale*. These were all Norse Viking words. I had left the rich soil and the Celtic and Northumbrian place-names behind and found words from the Icelandic *Book of Settlement*.

The place-names suggested that there had once been a Norse-Viking culture concentrated in the uplands of the Lake District beyond my cottage, while the Northumbrians had remained on the richer flat soil, below. Here, as near my father's house, it seemed that two different altitudes, soils and farming practices once coincided with two different languages, cultures and nations.

Once again there was very little archaeological evidence to be found in the soil for this lost Norse-Viking nation – and essentially no written sources. So a new generation of historians had come up with a dozen competing theories. They were doubtful about the neat picture of settlement suggested by the Norse place-names. ('Norse not Viking, Daddy – Viking was the word the Norse used for going on their pirate raids – and these families, whatever they had once been, were now farmer-settlers.') It was a confusing historical moment – the Norse were also fighting at about the same time on the coast of Libya and in what is today Istanbul, setting up dynasties in Kiev, and even establishing a small settlement in North America. There is no academic consensus on how or why or when they arrived in the Lake District.

The Northumbrian chroniclers of the ninth century tended to write about the arrival of the Norse in the way Gildas wrote about the arrival of the Northumbrians themselves in the fifth century. Both described a horde of blood-spattering, seaborne pagan barbarians, smashing the previous Christian civilisation. Modern historians tend to write about the arrival of both the Northumbrians and the Norse in terms of adaptation, absorption and cultural coexistence. Once again, I found the older accounts more plausible.

What struck me most strongly in the valleys into which I was climbing was that although Celtic and Northumbrian people and place-names had been here for centuries before the Norse, there was now a striking absence of Celtic or Northumbrian names. I had seen such a naming pattern before – in the military occupations of Iraq and Afghanistan, when British and American troops refused to use the local street names. Jad-e-Nadr Pushtu became Green Three, the Jade-Maiwand became Route

Idaho, and the British base in Iraq was renamed Camp Maude, after a British general of 1917.

★

In similar valleys in Iceland, the Norse had established an early democracy, reaching decisions in parliaments called 'Thing-mounts'. Such parliaments also seem to be recorded in the place-name 'Tynwald' in the Lake District. But while Norse culture may have been democratic, it was not particularly peaceable. My father's favourite story in a Norse saga comes when the eight-year-old Egil is tackled by Grim in a football game:

> Grim had now got the ball and was running away with it, and the other boys after him. Then Egil bounded upon Grim, and drove the axe into his head, so that it at once pierced his brain.

But while Norse language, attitudes and place-names swept through the central lakes, previous Cumbrian and Northumbrian communities and place-names remained in other valleys. By AD 950, the land around my cottage seems to have stood at the intersection of three distinct nations. While Hayeswater (the lake of Eithr) may have become pasture for a Norse community, speaking a Scandinavian language and following pagan customs, in the meadows of Bampton, just over the ridge line, Northumbrian Christians probably remained, speaking a Germanic language; and along the ridges to the north and south, names such as Carhullan, Yanwath and Blencathra suggested settlements of Cumbrian Celts, speaking a language related to modern Welsh.

'So it was like Syria,' suggested my father, 'with quite separate communities, religions and races living in neighbouring valleys?'

'Well, most contemporary scholars are not comfortable with the idea that there would have been a noticeable ethnic difference. They have found little archaeological evidence that these communities dressed differently. Their houses seem to have looked similar. They all would have shared in a single "heroic" culture of warriors, drinking and boasting . . .'

'But what do you think?' he insisted.

'Well, I suppose there is little proof either way, but my instinct is that people would initially have been very aware of the differences – that the cultural landscape might, as you say, have felt more like Syria. People might have been able to distinguish different ethnicities by sight. Some of the evidence from bone archaeology implies that the

Norse invaders were much taller than the Northumbrians, perhaps by as much as six inches.'

Walking through Afghanistan, I had found Hazara communities who self-identified as being descended from the Mongolian armies of Genghis Khan, and could not grow beards, whereas only a mile away there were Pushtu villages where all the men had full black beards to their chests. And walking across Irian Jaya I had found that I could recognise someone from the Yali people immediately by the shape of their face, although they had the same objects and houses as the neighbouring Dani, across the watershed.

And there were many reasons why these communities would have remained apart in the tenth-century Lake District – not least because they spoke different languages and worshipped different gods. It was not simply that the land which they prized on the lowland was called *dol* by one, *mǽd* by another and *vollr* by a third. The Northumbrian Christians in Askham would have seen the sun – the *heofen-candal* – and be reminded how God once made it halt in the sky over a Palestinian battlefield. The Norse pagans by Ullswater would have believed the sun was being dragged by demigods galloping in terror from wolves at their heels; and that the wolves would eventually catch the sun and plunge the world into darkness.

When the Northumbrians saw a rainbow they were reminded of a flood, and of a promise made on Mount Ararat. When the Norse saw a rainbow they were gazing at a bridge, at whose end lay the home of the gods. The tension between these beliefs can still be seen in Cumbrian churchyards – in the Norse 'world-serpent', apparently carved on the 'hog-backed' giant's grave in Penrith; or in the Norse god Loki carved – bound in the entrails of his children – on a stone in Kirkby Stephen church.

51

On a gravel path below Hayeswater I found Eric Weir, a broad-shouldered man in an open-necked checked shirt, examining a dead lamb. 'I haven't a clue how this happened,' shrugged Eric. 'Not a clue in this world. All I can tell you . . . they're like people, you know. You have unexplained deaths. And that would be one of them. May have been injured by another. Any number of things can happen to them.'

Eric was an upland farmer, whose family he thought had been farming in the area since about the time of the Norse. They had, he said, perfected an agriculture suited to the high rainfall, cold winters and thin, sour soil. Eric kept Swaledale sheep, tough, inquisitive, horned animals with thick white wool, and his flock was particularly tall and heavy. He bred them that way, and people paid a lot of money for Eric's tups. His cousin kept Herdwick sheep. The Herdwick have long, broad mouths, and when they meet your eyes, they seem to smile. As lambs they are black, as young adults chocolate brown, in middle age a silver grey.

The sheep lived much of the year on the open commons – land without fences or walls – and had been trained to learn the invisible boundaries on the open fellside, to prevent them wandering, mingling with neighbouring flocks or being lost. This is called 'hefting'. From that slow training, perhaps begun by an initial Norse settler, the ewes had passed on, generation to succeeding generations of lambs, a link to a particular soil so that the lambs did not need to be trained. And over the decades, the sheep had changed the nature of the surrounding ground. By grazing, they 'stayed on top' of the vegetation – eating close to the ground, preventing reeds, gorse and bracken from emerging, and opening space and providing sun for succulent tips of new grass to grow. Their droppings burned off reeds and increased the fertility of the poor soil.

Now this system of fell-flocks was being dismantled. Ecologists feel that the natural vegetation that is being suppressed through intense grazing is important, both in itself, and for the beetles and butterflies that depend on it. And the absence of vegetation means that the water can come off the hills very quickly – a critic compared it to water flowing off a Teflon pan – increasing flooding downstream. Instead, ecologists want to turn what one of them called 'the sheep desert' grazed by 'woolly maggots' into much wetter, more densely wooded ground – and use the peat and trees to store carbon, and thus slow climate change. Such arguments have more weight because European subsidies in the 1980s and 90s, paying farmers per head of sheep, had encouraged excessive numbers of sheep on the fellsides. These subsidies have now gone, but the damage remains. And since 90 per cent of the Lake District is now designated as a Site of Special Scientific Interest, and almost every small sheep farmer relies on environmental payments to survive, ecological priorities are changing the landscape.

I could see no sheep above me; the land around my feet was wet, and the vegetation was long. Eric said the National Trust, his neighbour, had chosen to stop draining the fields or dredging the river so as to make the river meander out of its existing channel and across the valley floor. They believed this was good for the environment and flood prevention, but it drowned and wrecked Eric's lowland pasture. Meanwhile, his upland pasture had been overrun by reeds and wild scrub.

An environmental scientist had come to visit Eric and assured him that laboratory tests proved the reeds would be nutritious enough. Eric's sheep apparently disagreed. 'If you get something to eat those sieves, believe me, they want a change,' Eric said. 'It may be "better for them nutritionally". But whether the sheep can break it down exactly the same way as somebody does with a test tube, I couldn't tell you.'

He pointed down again to the ground. 'That's what they call sour-docket. Nothing will eat that.' He gestured to some longer grass. 'Grass doesn't want to be much more than a couple of inches long, and they won't eat that either.' The sheep were so few that it was no longer necessary for them to touch most of the grass in the early part of the year. When they finally reached this patch, in mid-August, it was too long to be palatable. 'It's like, you know, having a heap of kids at a party: they eat all the cake first, while the sandwiches turn stale, and then they won't eat them.'

He felt that the ecologists and officials whom he met did not understand the countryside. And he suspected they didn't respect him any more than he respected them. He imagined that they left their conversations with him muttering that there was no reason why the taxpayer should subsidise farmers to destroy the environment. They probably felt his anger was simply a consequence of his age, and that a new generation of farmers would appear who would embrace these environmental schemes and move away from sheep farming.

He was determined to prove them wrong. This land had been farmed for sheep for a thousand years, since the Norse were here, he said. This was his family land. His were the stone foundations of a corn-mill, and an iron-ore mine, built by Saxons in the sixteenth century. (The last miners had left the area just after the Second World War.)

We walked down towards his hamlet, and I asked how many farmers still lived there. 'They've mostly all moved away,' Eric replied, going through the farms of his childhood. 'There's How Green and Green Farm – my father and his brother farmed them at the same time. Beckside was still farming when I was born. There were nineteen farms in this village. Now there are two. Some of them played cards for the fields. And the one that had our first farm wasn't o'er good at it. The house round the corner, they're wanting about half a million for it now. And basically all the rest's retirement homes.' We crossed a bridge across a narrow beck to a cacophony of sheepdogs.

52

In a side valley of Grisedale – the Norse name for pig pasture – five miles from Eric's house, I met Steve Allen. He was a six-foot-three sheep farmer's son, bending down in a baggy green plastic raincoat to repair the march wall. The wall ran only thirty feet above the narrow valley floor, protecting the thin strip of meadow which the Norse called the *mǽd*. The rain was steady, the mist low.

An ash tree stood near the wall. Its base was twenty feet in circumference, maybe more. The heart of the tree had died, but thin staves with fresh leaves grew forty feet into the air from the rim of the stump. I clambered gingerly into the tree, perching on the brittle wood. The ash had been pollarded, the uprights cut back every year, for sticks and fodder. It was a Norse practice – there are identical pollarded ash trees in the Norwegian fjords. Pollarded ash survive far longer than trees that have not been pollarded, because the wind is less likely to uproot the trees, and judging by the girth of this tree, it could almost have been planted by the Norse. I ran my hands along the half-rotten edge of the stump, thumped perhaps by Viking axes.

Yggdrasil, the mythical Norse tree whose branches supported the world, and whose roots reached into the underworld, was an ash. The tree was as holy as a Christian cross. In Dearham church, a ninth-century mason had carved the sacred pagan ash tree onto the base of the stone cross, to make the analogy clear.

The stone wall which Steve was repairing was almost eight feet high – unnecessarily high, I suggested. He agreed that sheep did not need a wall so high, but he implied that whoever built it must have had their reasons. He did not seem to think it polite to question the first wall-builder. As we talked, Steve worked through a large pile of stones which had fallen from the wall. The wall needed to be repaired at least every century. When had the first stones been laid? How many had been piled by the Norse-speaker who called this valley Grisedale? How many were there already in a rough wall here, when he arrived? It was impossible to answer such questions, but as at Yanwath, near my cottage, archaeologists had found a similar wall, which was more than 2,000 years old.

Steve would stop, stoop, hold a slab, bounce it in his hands to test its weight and edges, and then advance on the wall. It was not a jigsaw puzzle. He did not reassemble the stones exactly as they had been, nor spend three minutes looking for the perfect place. What mattered was the overall design and direction. He moved steadily, placing about three stones a minute on the top of the wall. He was not using everything.

I offered what I thought was a plausible stone – a neat thin rectangle.

'That's a bit too tall . . . Might go in. Will have to go in like that.' He placed it narrow side out, on its edge, so it stretched halfway through the wall. 'I don't like doing that. It's called a soldier, that one, when they're stood up straight.'

'What's wrong with them?'

'It doesn't quite look right to me, but anyway . . .' He laughed.

'How much can you build in a day?'

'A good drystone waller can build four metres in a day. A bad waller can build six.'

53

The lakeside village of Glenridding, which I reached that evening, sat at the very tip of Ullswater. Opposite the outdoor-clothing stores and gift shops lay Mrs Wear's cottage: Eric Weir's relative, although the spelling had changed over the centuries. Her father had been the huntsman of the Ullswater foxhounds for thirty years, a figure of glamour in his hunting coat and high stock. 'When the Ullswater steamboat refused to let his hounds onto the boat,' she said, 'he simply stepped on board alone, and blew his horn right across the lake, with the entire pack swimming behind him a mile and a half from Howtown to Glenridding.' Her grandparents' family, and their relatives the Lightfoots, were the oldest farming families in the area: the kind of 'Lake District statesmen' celebrated by Wordsworth, living in the land 'which they walked over and tilled . . . which had for more than 500 years been possessed by men of their name and blood'.

Many Cumbrians like the idea of such long connection and have come to embrace a Norse or Viking heritage. They have learned that the Cumbrian phrase 'Aah's gaan yem' (I'm gone home) drew on a Viking word (*yem* means home in Scandinavia, *heim* in Old Norse). Everyone appears to know that Penrith still has 'the highest concentration of Scandinavian DNA in England'. For more than a quarter of the people in Penrith, their distant male ancestor was from Norway. Just as my father's was apparently from Highland Scotland. The Cumbrian-born writer and broadcaster Melvyn Bragg goes further: 'It is that Nordic element, always building on Old English but in the North clawing more deeply into the language, which lies at the core of the fundamental separation – so often noted – between north and south.'

But whenever I looked closely at even the very oldest communities, I felt not our proximity to the past, but a startling distance. If the ancient forebear of the Cumbrian farmer Eric Weir had indeed been Norse, he might have seemed at first familiar to us: another

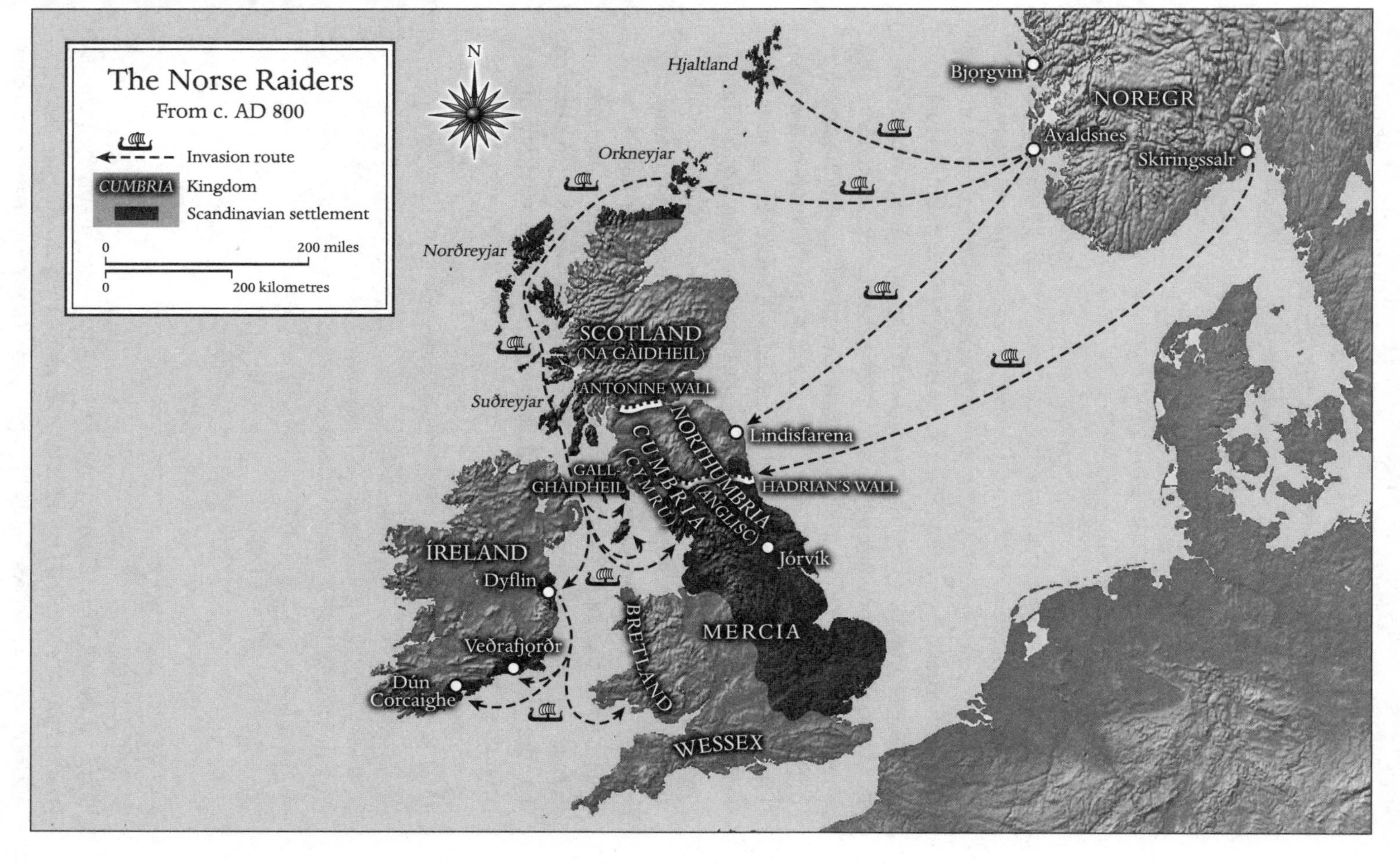
The Norse Raiders
From c. AD 800
Invasion route
CUMBRIA
Kingdom
Scandinavian settlement
0
200 miles
0
200 kilometres
N
Hjaltland
Bjǫrgvin
NOREGR
Avaldsnes
Skíringssalr
Orkneyjar
Norðreyjar
SCOTLAND
(NA GÀIDHEIL)
ANTONINE WALL
Suðreyjar
NORTHUMBRIA
(ANGLISC)
CUMBRIA
(CYMRU)
Lindisfarena
HADRIAN'S WALL
GALL-
GHÀIDHEIL
ÍRELAND
Dyflin
Jórvík
MERCIA
BRETLAND
Veðrafjǫrðr
Dún
Corcaighe
WESSEX

tall dalesman with an upland farm and a Herdwick flock behind his drystone wall. Yet the silver on his brooch could have come from Islamic coins, minted in Samarkand, his bangles would record the number of enemies he had killed, and the hammer round his neck would have been an amulet of Thor. And it would be easier for us to describe his ancestor's jewellery than his mind, or to inhabit his values, his honour and his sense of justice.

Perhaps in any case Eric's family had not been here since the Norse period. The very first parish records show a ceaseless movement of people, drifting for work, weaving cloth for cities. Phases of cultivation were separated by plague, famine, clearance and cattle murrains. Families like my father's – who for generations were born and died in the same parish – were rare. Even 400 years ago, most people in England did not live and die where they were born. I knew a family which came to Glenridding from Birmingham in the early nineteenth century, and another which saw Bonnie Prince Charlie's army advance along the ridge line in 1745. But the largest single section of the population in the Lake District seemed now to be retired professionals from northern cities. The families who first felled the trees, began the drystone walls, ploughed, built the first houses in these hamlets and turned a wilderness into a pasture – they were gone. We did not know what colour their hair was, or what language they spoke. We have inherited strangers' work. The change has been so striking that I found it difficult sometimes to remember that even 10,000 years ago the same lake was there, backed by forest and heathland, the high stone peaks always reflected in the trembling surface of the water.

54

I stayed the night in Glenridding, in what had been a cottage for lead miners, now converted into a B&B, then set off early the next morning up Helvellyn. The mist was low and settled, so I took the concrete path that ran up to the mine. Deep wheel ruts had been scoured into the cement. This, Britain's largest lead mine, was operating before Wordsworth ever saw the Lakes. After a fire which killed four men in 1952, it had been reinvented as an atomic weapons research site. Then it had closed and the last 300 jobs had gone. Looking at my map and the noticeboards, I saw that one government agency had now listed the disused mine as a scheduled monument, another as an environmental hazard.

I continued to climb up into one of the most scrutinised landscapes in the world: a patch of moorland, rock and water which by the late eighteenth century had become as famous as Venice. Like the Ming dynasty scholars in my father's scroll-paintings, contemplating the stone pillars of Yunnan, generations of writers and painters had perfected the exact image of, and reaction to, every feature of the Lakes. Below me, I could see the beach where Turner had studied the cattle; to my right was the route Coleridge took racing from Keswick to dinner in Grasmere. I was on the path Walter Scott had followed, risking his lame legs, scrabbling up behind Wordsworth. (Each composed a poem on a man who had fallen from this ridge.) It was difficult to think of a single British writer, painter or poet who had not walked where I was to walk over the next few hours. Even Hayeswater – the back-up reservoir for the Manchester supply, where I had met Eric Weir – had found its champion in Matthew Arnold.

And yet the network of small sheep farms which had entranced these writers was under threat. The distinctions between sheep lawn and moorland which Thomas Gray had admired had been eroded. I could see the black water, the native woodland and some distant white cottages, but the small farms were mostly gone, and there were no cornfields or meadows green as emerald. The heath now spread across both sides of the march wall.

Perhaps because of the mist, there were few people outside, and it was difficult for me to get a sense of what kind of people still lived in this landscape. But a few hundred yards up the path, beyond the mine, I saw a man standing with a large video camera. I walked up to talk to him. He was not a big man, and it seemed from his stiff walk that one of his legs was injured. But you could sense that he was fit. From the grey in his beard I might have guessed he was in his early fifties, but he was almost sixty. Dave lived in Alston, on the top of the Pennine ridge, not here in the river valley. I asked if I could interview him. He laughed. 'Cameramen are great behind camera, but if you interview us . . .' he said.

'What do you make of your landscape?' I asked.

'Well, looking at this view, you are very aware that Britain is a geologically very old place, rounded summits, old and worn.' And then he changed the subject, moving far away from the local scene.

'When you walk in the Himalayas, you know it is much newer. The strata are vertical, running for thousands of feet. You can see how they have been formed recently on the seabed, and twisted through ninety degrees. The Himalayas are still being formed.'

He paused. 'I remembered this morning walking in 1979 from a place called Padhum through to a Buddhist valley called Zanskar – trying to reach what I thought was the Chinese border,' he said. 'I really wanted to cross a border illegally.'

'Why?'

'I don't know,' he replied. 'A sense of adventure really, but the border there is porous and ill-defined. I got up to a col north of Leh which I thought was China – maybe it was, it depends whose map you buy: everyone seems to have the border in different places. I got stuck on this shingle plain of glacial river – I felt the last bit I crossed was the last I could with a backpack. I was going to drown. Suddenly I saw these two horsemen on the bank. One dismounted, and the other rode over with the spare horse. As he got closer I saw the bandoliers across his chest and the shotgun on his saddle. I thought here was a classic bandit, and he was going to shoot me, and the horse was for my pack. But when he reached me he pointed to his mouth – I knew what that meant. I gave him some aspirin – and he rescued me.'

I watched Dave pick up his tripod and, with the camera still attached, carry it awkwardly across to another patch of fell. He pointed it first at the lake below us, close in on the white water, and then at the branches of a tree and the sky overhead. He peered at the digital screen and said something about the daylight setting having 'too much blue tone'.

I asked him if he considered himself a local. He had only lived in Cumbria, he replied, for thirty years. But he had grown up in Chichester. Then he had moved 230 miles north and trained as a teacher and a social worker and worked with street gangs in Halifax. Then he dropped out of college and moved 200 miles south-west to Wales. 'I got a teaching certificate but not a degree. I lived on communes, did the hippie thing, lived with my girlfriend in a commune in Wales, but most of the people there had rich parents and we had fuck all, so we came up here.'

This time he moved 280 miles north again to the Roman frontier. 'I got off the train at Haltwhistle in a really bad winter, and walked all the way up the South Tyne valley, knocking on doors, camping at night until

I got to Nenthead, and got a lift with the snowplough: there was real snow in those days, every winter. Nenthead was already full of people like me – hippies – who gave me somewhere to stay. At first I lived in a caravan and cycled sixteen miles every day on the old Roman wall road from Corbridge to Newcastle to work as a social worker. I also worked in a special unit for disturbed adolescents in London. I knew I was getting burned out. I decided it was time to split and clear my head. I have always loved mountains – mountain-walking, climbing.'

Suddenly he picked up the camera and tripod and charged forward again, cradling this five-foot-long triple spike in his arms, as though he was waltzing with it. He placed it down, peered, moved it again a foot to the right. Then the sun went behind a cloud and he went back to his black plastic case, which was carefully laid on a dry stone, for another lens. Almost as soon as he had fitted the new lens, and changed the exposure, the sun came out again. He smiled and shrugged.

'I love these trees. But that is tainted for me here by the knowledge that the landowner near here has destroyed the footpath and the woodland. Still,' he reflected, 'one of our glories in Britain is mixed deciduous woodland.' He paused. 'But nowhere is trapped in the past.'

I learned that he had been involved in environmental and land-reform movements and been invited to Parliament to discuss reforming the law. I was struck by his very formal sentences – and the sudden shifts from contemporary protest to a romantic ideal of Britain, to the contemporary cliché again. And then suddenly – like other Cumbrians I knew – he left the Cumbrian landscape entirely, leaving this border again for another border.

He told me about returning to the K2 base camp – of crossing the Waga border between India and Pakistan without either an Indian or a Pakistani visa. But his favourite place was the 'magical' alpine meadow on the high plateau between Skargu and Kargil, along the Indian–Pakistani 'lines of control'. He said he had filmed a high-altitude artillery battle between the Indian and Pakistani armies, simply so that he could revisit the meadows.

The light was no longer any good for him. He dismantled his camera and tripod. I offered to carry it. He carefully removed a leaf from the spike and wiped it clean. Then he folded and reduced the legs, and wound an elastic string around them before he gave them to me. He warned me that there might be an almost invisible splinter of carbon fibre. I noticed that he had somehow managed to keep his boots clean. Mine were thick with slurry from a poorly judged short cut through a farmyard ten minutes earlier, where the thick black fermented cow manure had slopped over the top of my boots. He had also kept his lens cases out of the mud and leaves. I tried to bring him back to local people.

'In Alston,' he said, 'there are three types of people: hippies, some of whom are now third generation, off-comers like me, and the locals, many of whom are farmers. I don't think even farmers today have that real understanding of the environment in England. It's become more of a manufacturing process. I don't think they have any sense of aesthetics. When I walk onto the fells behind my house and see the rubbish and plastic bags and the plastic feed buckets for the sheep, I think the fells would look much more beautiful if they were not farmed, and were left to grow wild. The sheep do terrible damage to the wild species.'

I wondered why he did not live abroad.

'I am a great lover of the English landscape,' he said. 'I couldn't live abroad. I like the softness of it. There is a fantastic last passage in one of Bill Bryson's books – he has a line about the unutterable beauty around his house in Dorset. I made a film about Internally Displaced Peoples in Sudan. We were in the north-east, a horrendous camp, no rain for four years: people living in shelters of twigs and sacking, parched everywhere, no colour anywhere. Then I got off a plane at Newcastle in the first week in May, the whole of the Allan valley gorge was an unbelievable iridescent spring green, with the sun behind the leaves. I remember crying, the tears welling, and thinking how lucky we are to have that degree of greenness. The seasons we get here you don't get anywhere else in the world.'

Below us, we could see two people passing with more dogs. 'The fact that we have people like that in Britain,' he said, pointing to the dog-walkers, 'makes me quite emotional. The fact that we have the Ramblers Association; that people go out for walks like that; that they make the effort. The very fact that they're there with their dogs, rather than walking round a playing field, that it moves them, makes it worthwhile.'

His car, parked on the track below us, was even neater than his black lens case. Tens of thousands of pounds' worth of equipment was neatly stacked across the back seats and trunk of his new silver Mercedes estate. He took the tripod from me, wiped the black lens case one more time, and fitted it into its designated space. I asked him whether he thought it mattered to walkers that they were passing a Roman quarry, a Viking settlement or the hermitage of a Northumbrian saint.

He didn't think so. 'People come to the British landscape not for history but for peace and quiet. They want to walk and not see anything crap. In fifty years, this place is going to be awful,' he said.

'I am very depressed. It is very difficult to walk in Britain and not see ugliness. I feel we have completely lost any sense of aesthetic in our built environment and I find it very depressing. I have just been on the Isle of Harris – it must be the most beautiful coastline in the whole of Europe – and it is totally fucked by modern bungalows, plonked everywhere. I used to walk on the South Downs a lot, but I won't go there any more – you hear about all the downland being ploughed up. My home town of Chichester was a lovely historic city with a tight historic centre, but I haven't dared go back in thirty years for fear of it being totally trashed.'

'I will tell you a story, but you must promise not to write it in your book. Once when I had returned from a stupid eighteen months overseas – on the Afghan border – I went to Newcastle. It was raining and I went into a railway museum and saw all these models of beautiful buildings and this beautiful landscape – it was a model of the English landscape between 1860 and 1930. And I decided then to build model railways. Not because I know anything about trains. But for the countryside around – because I love building models of how our country used to look.'

'Why can't I write that in my book?'

'Oh you can, I suppose.' He laughed. There our conversation ended and he drove away back to Alston, and then – as he had explained – through three separate farm gates up to his once-ruined farmhouse above the Slaggyford road.

55

From the peak of Helvellyn, I could just make out the ridge I had crossed above Haweswater. Below it was a valley – called Swindale, not Grisedale, this time, although it meant the same in Norse – in which the drystone walls now functioned only as abstract sculptures on the fellside. Swindale had always been a remote parish. There was once a famous disagreement when the church bells rang about whether it was indeed

Sunday, finally resolved by the vicar's naked assertion of authority. But in 1580 there had been eighty people in the valley, a church and a school.

Now the whole valley was owned by United Utilities, the water company, which had until relatively recently been listed on the New York Stock Exchange. Their tenant was now the Royal Society for the Protection of Birds. I had been shown the land a few days earlier by officers from UU and the RSPB. Both men were in neat hiking gear: fit and smiling, I might have taken them for canoe instructors. They wanted to show me how they had managed the land, in a way that 'increased biodiversity, decreased flooding, increased carbon capture'.

'We don't believe,' the RSPB ranger said, 'that there is any contradiction between good environmental practice and farming. We believe in including farmers, and retaining sheep.'

They led me into a side valley. Rushes grew deep and tall along the bottom. On the slopes were great fields of bracken, and beyond them scrub trees, and higher still heather. Pollen samples suggest that Bronze Age people had cleared this land and kept livestock on it. The new approach seemed to be restoring a landscape which had not existed almost since the first human settlement. I could not see any sheep. They told me that they kept about one sheep for every four or five hectares. They showed me a section of 800 hectares which was being planted as forestry.

'How many sheep have you kept in this area?' I asked.

'None.'

'Are there areas in your plans, or the plans of the Lake District National Park, which have been designated to be preserved for dense sheep grazing?'

'Not as such. But we have nothing in principle against sheep farming.'

Instead of preserving tenant farms, they employed a contractor on a one-year renewable contract to look after their sheep and land. I suggested that densely cropped green sheep pasture had been – alongside the wilder fells – one of the beauties of the Lake District for Wordsworth or Beatrix Potter, and that they were removing it. A man on a one-year contract was not the same as a small family sheep farm, with generations of occupation and security of tenure. Small family farms were links to the Northumbrian and Norse past: the last traces of the indigenous population. They even formed a connection to much later people like the Romantic poets.

I suggested that if the Lake District became a wilderness reserve occupied by professionals from elsewhere, we would have lost something precious.

And, rather than bringing professionals in from other parts of Britain, they should be running training courses for local farmers to do the same job.

We talked at cross purposes. They replied by talking again about carbon budgets, flood-risk management, diffuse pollution and biodiversity. Farming for them seemed to be about subsidies and environmental impact assessments. I sensed that behind their dry language they had strong views on what they thought was right and beautiful. I guessed that they loved the idea of a much wilder landscape, more packed with wet bogs and birds, and that they felt farming and dense sheep-stocking on this land were often destructive.

But they were careful not to say these things. They did not seem comfortable engaging in a discussion about the history of the valley, about the traditions of small tenants or about the beauty of farmed land.

Swindale had always felt like a hidden miracle – a tight-necked valley opening into bright green fields by the river, with a thick tongue of land in the centre, neat and fierce as a fairy castle, and the cold waterfalls coming down from pool to pool. In the bright sun, it might appear like a corner of Jurassic Park. But on the facing slope you could see the long lines of drystone wall running almost vertically up the fellside – enclosing the mountain face in irregular geometrical slices. Each stretch was perhaps the work of a different generation: brothers dividing their patrimony and extending their grandfather's work. In the Highland glen above our house such walls survived only as broken hints, buried under a wilderness of scrub and forestry.

56

I turned at the peak of Helvellyn and continued along the sharp crest of the watershed, between the Eamont and Derwent rivers. This had been the frontier of the Cumbric kingdoms of Strathclyde or Cumbria and, much later, King David of Scotland's attempt at a frontier with England, and then – when the English moved north –

the exact border between Cumberland and Westmorland. It seemed a much more 'natural' place to divide the island of Britain than the flat land of Hadrian's Wall – a straight line, 3,000 feet high, separating the valleys of Ullswater and Thirlmere, with the nearest communities some 2,000 feet below, one to the west and one to the east.

I spent the next two hours on this gravel path, right along the spine of the ridge, the ground dropping steeply on either side. Then I met a family of four in anoraks, the Dods from Manchester. They asked me for directions to Great Dodd, which they were planning to climb for Mr Dod's fiftieth birthday.

My father had been fifty when I was born. I always talked about him – thought about him – as a Norse hero, or a warrior out of *Beowulf*, an immensely fit and strong man. But I remembered other things too. Our walks in the jungle or in the Highlands had always been in the bottom of the valleys. He had taken me skiing, just the two of us, when I was six, to a concrete hotel in an Italian resort. We read *Asterix* in French, left our cartons of chocolate milk on the windowsill in the snow, and drank them half frozen. But he announced on the second day that I was already too quick for him, and he woke me that midnight – very apologetically – to say that he had cramp, and asked me to get a pill from his washbag and to try to massage his leg. I remember his grimace and the staring eyes as I – ineffectually – rubbed his leg. I had a memory also of his getting out of a car in the Highlands, when he was about fifty-five, lifting a boulder and throwing it – not very far, it seemed to me – and saying with satisfaction, 'There you are – and people say life ends at forty!'

★

I entered the Keswick valley over the shoulder of Great Dodd. On my left were more lead mines and the cottage where W. H. Auden had stayed as a child. On my right a flood had swept gravel across the village cricket pitch. Ahead was the village of Threlkeld – another Norse place-name meaning 'the field of the slaves'. On a track leading up the hill stood a thin man in a striped polo shirt and pale blue jeans. He had broad Victorian sideburns growing along his thin cheeks. He invited me in for tea, and I saw that on the wall of his small sitting room was a framed fox-tail.

Barry Todhunter's wife had grown up on the farm a hundred yards away. They had first met and fallen in love at her gate. There was no sign of any children in the house, but there was a terrier puppy in the living room, and in an annexe fifty speckled foxhounds. Their shoulders came up almost to my waist.

'They are all descended from Briton and his couple companion, a bitch called Cruel, owned by John Peel,' Barry told me. John Peel had been Cumbria's most famous huntsman in the age of Wordsworth and Walter Scott. Barry's surname, Todhunter, meant fox hunter in Northumbrian Anglian, and through some improbable legacy, Barry was now also a fox hunter. He had been the huntsman of the Blencathra pack for almost thirty years. This was about average for the Blencathra – there have been five huntsmen in the last 150 years – but he looked as though he was good for another twenty.

The surrounding fells were not horse country. Barry's hunt followed foxes on foot. At night, they stopped in pubs to sing fell-songs. The only song that anyone knew in the rest of Britain was about the owner of Briton and Cruel ('D'ye ken John Peel with his coat so *grey*? / D'ye ken John Peel at the break of day?'). But most of the local songs were about Jim Dalton, who had become the huntsman in 1886. He was more famous even than Mrs Wear's father, who had swum the hounds across Ullswater. The songs recorded the detail of Dalton's routes over 300 square miles of country, taking in the tops of Helvellyn, Skiddaw and Blencathra. You could have sung them in place of a map:

Along Barrowside and through Ashness Ghyll,
Our huntsman he halloed both loud and shrill,
And straight to Armboth his course he did take.

There was another, much earlier, hunting song, set, it seemed, in Derwent across the valley and written in the sixth century in the Cumbric-Welsh language of the kingdom of Rheged:

Peis Dinogat, e vreith, vreith,
o grwyn | balaot ban | wreith.
Chwit, chwit, chwidogeith,
gochanwn | gochenyn | wythgeith.

When Daddy went to hunt,
Spear on his shoulder, cudgel in hand,
He called his quick dogs, 'Giff, you wretch,
Gaff, catch her, catch her, fetch, fetch!'

From a coracle he'd spear
Fish as a lion strikes a deer.
When your dad went to the crag
He brought down roebuck, boar and stag,
Speckled grouse from the mountain tall,
Fish from Derwent waterfall.

Whatever Daddy found,
Boar or *lleywn*, fox or deer,
Unless it flew, would never get clear.

There was much scholarly disagreement about the identity of the lleywn, or mini-lion, which Daddy killed. Was it a lynx? At first people thought not, since the Eurasian lynx seemed to have died out in Britain before the end of the last Ice Age, about 11,500 years ago. Then in 2006, radio-carbon dating on a femur found in a cave revealed that there had been lynxes in northern England in the fifth or sixth century. Some ecologists are now keen to reintroduce the lynx into Britain. A decade earlier, they might have argued that it was wrong to introduce pre-Ice Age fauna – alien invasive species – to the area. Now, on the basis of the femur and the hunting song, they could say they were reintroducing an 'original native of the British Isles'. The farmers were not convinced they wanted lynxes near their livestock.

★

Barry's legends focused not on lynx and Cumbric hunts, but on foxes and fox hunts. Seven years had now passed since fox hunting had been made illegal. His hunt still gathered – fully dressed – with their pack of hounds, but they were supposed to follow a laid scent rather than a fox. Their opponents claimed to have witnessed them hunting illegally, and every time now that they went out the hunt was joined by four men in balaclava masks, who filmed the proceedings, used whistles to distract the dogs and threatened criminal prosecution.

Barry's predecessor as huntsman, Johnny Richardson, had not faced these problems. Johnny had been in the Highland Light Infantry. When the Highland Division was surrounded at Saint-Valéry in 1940, he had been captured with 10,000 other men. He escaped from the prison camp and used his hunting skills to survive a year in the Apennines. After the war, he had returned to Threlkeld and continued to hunt the hounds for forty years. One cold day in 1988, running up behind the hounds, he had toppled over and died on the fell.

After supper, Barry took me to a large shed which he had filled with a model railway. Dave, the cameraman who worked in Afghanistan and South Sudan, had recreated a postcard English landscape, set about with elegant Victorian stations, for his model railway; Barry, however, had built a broad-gauge American railroad. It ran between giant water towers, across an open prairie. When he wasn't hunting in Cumbria, Barry went to the States to ride the American railways, travelling first class. He had just returned from a trip from Chicago to California.

57

By the time I left Barry the sun was setting. I climbed the gentler south side of Blencathra, quickly passing the first walls which formed the boundary of the cultivated land close to the farmhouses, known as the *inby*. Then I was into the next band of wilder pasture, still walled, which was once called the *outby*. I could hear the hounds barking in the kennels below me. And then I was climbing beyond the boundary of the march wall onto the open moorland. The night darkened, and the storm began, and I had become what the Northumbrians called a 'night-walker' – *sceadu-genga*.

In the darkness and the rain, the rocks seemed sharp and my boots slipped frequently on the surface of the wet granite. It took a careful hour and a half to come up the ridge, and once I fell down the rock, catching myself after three feet. I had begun that day at Glenridding, and I had walked over Helvellyn and Great Dodd, and I decided to end it by pitching my tent on the summit of Blencathra. At about three in the morning, it seemed for a moment that the fog was clearing, and I could make out the red lights on the submarine aerials. But from the last of the night – what the Northumbrians called the *uhta* – the fog returned. Visibility at the summit was about twenty yards. I lit my stove to make some tea and porridge.

My father would have approved of the porridge. At home, he had recently restored the Scottish tradition of making a large slab of porridge, placing it in a drawer, and then cutting off a slice every day for breakfast. He believed porridge was one of a holy trinity of healthy food along with a Szechuan soya dish called Ma Po Tofu and brown bread. He liked the porridge with salt, Ma Po Tofu with a lot of chilli, and brown bread with beer. And he had just emailed me a passage from the fourteenth-century French knight Froissart – he had the Penguin Classic on his shelf – describing how the Scottish raiders under Lord Douglas had invaded England with slabs of porridge under their saddles.

The water was boiling in the pot before I realised I had left both my mug and my spoon at Barry's house. I could eat the porridge with my fingers, using the technique my father had taught me for eating rice in the Middle East, but the blackened rim of the saucepan was too hot for drinking tea.

★

Fell. Mire. Heath. Moor. The rain did not stop. I slowed to two miles an hour and kept my eyes on the wet ground. The colours were both more muted and more vibrant than I had remembered: cherry-brown grass and yellow-brown moss blazed scarlet and chrome. The raindrops clustered in their thousands on every knot and tip of heather. The orbs of glittering light pulled slowly away from their dark centres, so that each drop stretched into a crown and pendant, like an acorn on its stalk.

This was still a place for hunting. I noticed the pile of pellets which marked the nest of the mother grouse, and the brown paste whose soft consistency seemed to suggest another part of the grouse's feeding cycle. A hundred yards further on, a hawk had left two black-feathered grouse wings, joined by a fragile skeleton. When I picked it up I felt a sudden nip on my fingers from the beak in the bare skull, swinging on its long spine. I spotted a spider on a rain-flecked web.

An hour later, what remained of a baby hare suggested that it may have been about to grow its white winter coat. I missed, and misunderstood, a lot. I glimpsed a fern in passing, and regretted I had not stopped, because I did not see another like it in the next six miles. What seemed to be a hind was only a thick tuft of yellowing grass. What seemed to be twigs were antlers. A stag rose from the hollow only sixty yards away, stepped over the heather and paused, staring straight at me, while it shook the brilliant pearls of rain from its black ruff.

Ahead of me, the fell resembled a tropical swamp seen from far above: the peat-puddles looked like lagoons; the heather, a mangrove swamp; the patches of pale dying grass, a great savannah. The peat hags on the facing slopes had the silhouettes of pot-bellied Mesopotamian gods. Nearer, it was a living reef. The lichens and ferns were coral, and the pink-brown moss like jellyfish. I pulled a piece of blackened wood from a bog. It appeared to be a piece of Scots pine, preserved in the damp soil, from a time, perhaps 3,000 years ago, when this had all been forest. It had acquired the shape of a fish.

I imagined all the scholarship that would be poured in the future into this stretch of moorland: the archaeologists who would uncover more traces of Bronze Age pasture on these slopes; the scientists who would catalogue every moss, lichen, grass and fungus; and the government policies which would protect and extend the ecosystem. But would these people – informed, intimidated, disappointed and exhilarated in ways we have not yet anticipated – continue to enter the upland ground, searching for Beowulf's demons on the fellside?

58

Next morning, in the fields below the old tuberculosis sanatorium (it was now a field study centre for geographers), stood the shepherd Willy Tyson, herding sheep. He lived on a small tenanted farm, which he had inherited from his father, at the base of Blencathra, looking over the valley towards the Neolithic Castlerigg stone circle. His old sheepdog did little more than trot and bark, 'for the memories'. The younger collie was too enthusiastic and left the ewes panting in the corners of the stone dykes.

I had seen Willy Tyson win the prize for Herdwick sheep at the Hesket Newmarket Show, beating James Rebanks. Like all the competitors, Willy dyed his sheep. He used an earthy red – although I remembered the colour as almost lavender – for shows. Willy counted sheep in the ancient Cumbric dialect of Rheged. These 'sheep-counting' numerals had been more widely used in the nineteenth century. Victorian scholars had believed that they were perhaps the last remnant of the lost aboriginal language of Cumbria, passed down through an oral tradition over forty generations. Willy could confidently count to twenty. The numbers were sounds from another world – completely alien to modern English. 'Yan, tan, tethera, methera, pimp, sethera, lethera, hovera, dovera, dick, yan-a-dick, methera, bamfit, gigot . . .' Beyond that, his numbers seemed less sure.

When Willy counted in this archaic language, he seemed a very traditional figure: white-haired, broad-shouldered, stiff-kneed, with large hands swollen from outdoor work poking from his tweed jacket – a man outside time. But he was not quite as he seemed.

For a start, he had not always been a sheep farmer. He had been a highways engineer, and then, in the early seventies, he had bought a motorbike off some New Zealand travellers he had met in the Lakes, rebuilt it with a simpler, more powerful engine, and rode it to Afghanistan. He loved Afghanistan and thought the Afghans were the friendliest people in the world.

Now that he was home, he did not really use the sheep numerals to count very often. It was mostly a party trick in the pub. 'I challenge any other local to count to twenty for a pint of beer. I've not lost in forty years.'

★

From Willy's farm, I walked west through a fine wooded country, over the shoulder of Skiddaw. At Mirehouse that night I stayed with a man whose ancestor had captured the King of Afghanistan. It was a family that believed in getting things in writing. On the wall was a signed receipt taken when delivering the prisoner into custody. It said: 'Received: One Afghan King, 1881'.

The next morning I continued along the Derwent River in step with the leader of Cockermouth Mountain Rescue. Every mile, a different geological base, or the barrier formed by a bridge, changed the flow or chemistry of the water. Here there was no limestone to provide the calcium for the shells of the white-clawed crayfish. Instead, the Borrowdale volcanic rock yielded water poor in nutrients and filled with oxygen, a feast for those flies which abhor the nutrient-rich Eden. We passed the riffles, which pleased the new-hatched fry, the pools for the parr and the runs for the adult salmon.

The Middleland
AD 900
Roman road
CUMBRIA Kingdom
0
30 miles
0
30 kilometres
N
SCOTLAND
(NA GÀIDHEIL)
Broich
Dùn Breatann
ANTONINE WALL
Din Eidyn
Clud
CUMBRIA (CYMRU)
NORTHUMBRIA
(ANGLISC)
Tweed
Lindisfarena
Bebban-burgh
Jed-burgh
HADRIAN'S WALL
GALL-GHÀIDHEIL
(ØSTMENN)
Caer Luel
Eden
Ulfs Vatn
Cragg
Ellan Vannin
DANELAW
(NORARRAENIR MEN)
Eoforwic
GWYNEDD
ENGLAND
(WESTSEAXNA)
Contains OS data © Crown copyright and database right (2016)

For my companion, this clear, clean river was a destroyer. Two years earlier, after a week of heavy rain, the water had run in a torrent down from the 3,000-foot peaks, tumbling into Bassenthwaite before reaching Cockermouth, where it gathered and boiled up, rising over the banks, pounding down the lanes and flowing freely under people's doors, then later through their windows. He and the Mountain Rescue teams had spent three days in dry-suits, clambering along roofs to rescue people from the floods. Waters rippled though kitchens and front rooms. After the flood, the town was cracked open like an egg. Interiors of houses were exposed like museums to public view. Half their contents and their occupants were in the streets. A scum of twigs and vegetation showed the high-water mark, four feet up the walls. Cockermouth had flooded only once in this way, he said, between 1905 and 2005. Since 2005 it had flooded twice.

59

That night I walked up the long drive through formal gardens to the pink-plastered medieval fighting tower that formed the corner of Isel Hall. Mary Burkett stood at the threshold. It was difficult to know how tall she had once been, but now at exactly my father's age she was tiny, wearing rubber-soled shoes and a striped skirt. Her smile revealed every tooth when she greeted me.

The house was unheated behind its rows of tiny sixteenth-century windows, and many of the rooms were unfurnished, but she had decorated the house with felts she had collected on trips around Central Asia and Afghanistan, and gifts brought from her friends – painters, civil servants, sheep farmers, archaeologists – from London or Tunis.

Mary Burkett was not originally from Cumbria, but she had become a fervent Cumbrian patriot, preserving and creating much of what is now contemporary Cumbrian culture – building a great museum, championing forgotten seventeenth-century Cumbrian painters and modern Cumbrian poets. Over dinner, she talked about trying to get an English archaeologist – who wore a watch chain and a three-piece suit – out of an Afghan jail; about Kushan jewellery; and about Lady Anne Clifford – who as a single, elderly woman had moved to Cumbria in the seventeenth century and dedicated the rest of her life to preserving and restoring Cumbrian buildings. I slept that night under six felts on a mattress, stuffed with thick lumps of horsehair.

Mary, hearing about my walk, had invited her close friend Julian, a Cumbrian painter, to guide me from Isel to Cockermouth the next morning. We climbed up into a wood. Our uneven path was broken by miniature gullies, spate-full of angry water, but the tall oaks kept off the worst of the rain. Then a fierce wind drove the clouds away, revealing the high grey ridge of Skiddaw, and the greener slopes above Dunmail Raise, the traditional boundary of the Middleland.

Here, in the early eleventh century, there had still been a King of Cumbria who claimed a territory stretching from what is now northern England into southern Scotland; further east, the man who claimed a similar cross-border territory called himself 'Earl' of Northumbria, and retained much of the aura and autonomy of the anointed kings of Northumbria. The land around was still owned by people whose names – like Dunmail's – were quite different from the names familiar in English or Scottish history. Further east, the leaders retained a mixture of Northumbrian names like Uchtred and Norse names like Siward. In this valley, in the 1060s, the lord had a Cumbric name: Cospatrick. And he called his sons Gospatric, Waltheof and Dolfin.

Similarly, the territory on both sides of the border had retained its own 'laws', land-holding structures and field patterns.

The Middleland's last hope of independence came with the tumult of the Norman Conquest. It was crushed by William the Conqueror in 1070. His armies killed more than 100,000 people north of York. His soldiers burned the villages and destroyed the ploughs and grain stores, which meant crops could not be planted in the following year. They piled the cattle on great pyres and burned them too. At first the survivors were forced to eat their horses. They then fed on cats and human flesh. At last, the only thing left moving through the deserted villages were wild dogs and wolves, feeding on the bodies of the dead. The chronicler said:

> I have often had cause to praise William. But when I think of helpless children, young men in the prime of life, and hoary greybeards perishing alike of hunger, I am so moved to pity that I would rather

lament the grief and sufferings of the wretched people than make a vain attempt to flatter the perpetrator of such infamy.

When William the Conqueror's Domesday Book was completed a decade later, entry after entry in the old Middleland reads *'hoc est vast or vasteas est'* – this is wasteland. But this ethnic cleansing was not a purely English endeavour. The Scottish king, William the Lion, followed William into the devastated lands. He rounded up survivors and took them back to Scotland as slaves. For decades afterwards it was said that every Scottish home, even the poorest, had its own slave from the Middleland.

And William the Conqueror's sons confirmed the fact that everything was now unambiguously either England or Scotland, with nothing in between, by building their frontier castles on the sites of Roman forts at Carlisle and Newcastle, and running the border between them, along the old line of Hadrian's Wall.

The Norman kings then designated almost all the land to my east and north-east – Allerdale, Thornthwaite, Inglewood, Nicol and the rest – as a royal forest. (The Scottish kings did something similar from Etterick to Cheviot.) The existing farms were confiscated, the buildings demolished, and the entire remaining population driven from their homes. For the next 400 years, it was illegal for humans to live in hundreds of square miles of Cumbria, Northumbria or the Scottish Borders. An army of government officials moved in. They drove the cattle and sheep that remained alive from the land. They prohibited peat-digging, the clearing of trees and vegetation, or the planting of crops. Much of the best farmland in the Middleland, which had been farmed for 2,000 years or more, was rewilded – including the Eden valley between Penrith and Carlisle – converted back into swamp, scrub and woodland, as a protected habitat for birds and above all for deer.

★

My walking companion Julian was a Cumbrian painter. His wife, his mother, his father, his father's father, his father's mother and his mother's mother had all been Cumbrian painters. Painting was another kind of Cumbrian tradition, reaching back not through generations of hill farmers but rather to his grandfather's friend Ruskin, and to Turner's depictions of the Lake District. Julian's father had been born in 1903, but he had painted pictures that still reflected the taste of the late eighteenth century – scenes from the Lakes where every slope carried in each furrow or drystone wall the memory of a hundred human generations in a particular place.

Julian was about sixty, I guessed, but he looked forty and moved like a fell-runner – thin in his waterproofs, with a long stride. He loved mountains and climbing in the Lakes. But when he walked he did not lift his head.

'What do you think of the view?' I asked.

'Oh, yes, the view!' He paused. 'I haven't done views. There is no need for any more of them, is there?'

The trees among which we were walking were vast-trunked, with bulging boles; moss, lichen and larvae wrapped the rain-soaked oaks. I pointed at a branch over a narrow beck, trailing dark sessile leaves, and asked if he might paint that. He shook his head. 'It's too obvious,' he said. 'I mean I can't look at that tree without thinking, "There's no point." I couldn't think of anything new to do with it.'

After five minutes of silence, he relented. He pointed at a small fungus. 'This would interest me. You'd have to paint every little bit. You couldn't be vague.'

Julian had tried to get out of Cumbria. He felt that his family's Cumbrian traditions of landscape had become exhausted. He had gone to an art school in London in the 1970s, but he hadn't felt at ease there. The conceptual artists seemed as obsessed as his forefathers with 'meaning'. 'For my father and grandfather, it would have to be "place", the geographical name: it would be meaningful, babbling becks.' He did not like 'meaning'. 'What mattered in London,' he said, 'was still what something meant: all the power lay with the people who could interpret the *meaning* of pieces.'

So he had returned to his father's gallery at Grasmere. His father did not understand Julian's paintings, and they did not sell in the gallery. But he forced Julian to look harder. 'Everything – my father told me – mind, eyes and brain, need to focus on every bit of negative rock: to understand what is physically going on.'

Even when Julian had moved to Mexico, he still felt forced to create paintings with 'meaning'. 'I painted volcanoes, and the death of the Brazilian union leader and environmentalist Chico Mendes in Amazonia. I flew to Egypt, anywhere that has a sort of political background. Not just straight landscape. Always years and years of trying to say things with people and situations in landscapes, all in the open.' When his father died, Julian was in the Himalayas. The news came by runner to his base camp. He could not return in time for the funeral.

Finally, he had settled back in Cumbria. Suddenly, after his father's death, he no longer put people or politics or places in his landscapes. Instead, he drew patterns of vegetation on blank slopes. Although he loved the outdoors, and was skilled at painting in the open, he preferred now to take a photograph with a long lens, to zoom right in on a piece of hillside. Then he would paint from the photograph.

My father also liked to paint from photographs. But the ones he chose were tourist postcards of the Highlands. In his pictures, the first slope of purple – signifying heather – was always followed by a slope of dark grey, then another of lighter grey. Green Scots pines stood on the lower slopes, above 'the Scottish loch'.

'I once went to an art class,' my father said, 'and an old lady came to look at my picture and said, "Oh, I know that loch," and I thought, "Little do you know. I've never seen your loch in my life."' My father chortled. 'That is just "THE Scottish loch".'

But while my father resisted a specific place in favour of a generic national scene, Julian resisted both place and scene.

'I want to fill the whole frame with the raw stuff,' Julian said. 'The pale yellow grass on the tops, the scree, the lusher bottoms, the angle of the sheep tracks. Behind the flat surface are the hidden forces of physics. Gravity is holding it all together.'

I asked him whether he felt that the Lake District landscape was still at the core of the British imagination – of British identity. Was this not the landscape – of sheep, drystone walls, churches and farmhouses – that British soldiers dreamt of in Afghanistan? He answered me by praising the abandoned industrial workings of the central lakes. 'Slate quarries, rotting away – fantastic things, the colours: reds, yellows coming in, the leaves and rock faces . . . I like the copper mines, full of holes and gashes.' He looked up at me through the rain, smiling. 'It's all disintegrating, isn't it?'

Then Julian left me and I was alone. Two hours earlier I had been among volcanic rocks, on the thin acidic Lake District soil. Now, beyond Cockermouth, the drystone walls were no longer grey but red sandstone, and I was walking through planted fields of maize in the shade of giant oaks. When I stopped at Bridekirk church, I looked at its 800-year-old font, carved with runes, depicting a figure like a Norse hero, a Northumbrian vine in his mouth curling like a French horn.

The following hour, walking between Bridekirk and Dearham, I crossed the invisible coal seam that ran 300 feet below ground and entered a place which had gone in my father's lifetime from prosperous coal mines to unemployment, and where life expectancy was now twenty years shorter than in the village three miles away. Before the coal was discovered this had all been a single cultural zone. When the warden unlocked Dearham church, I saw the stone carving of Yggdrasil, mother ash tree of the pagan Norse world, diplomatically supporting a Northumbrian Christian cross.

The track that I followed that afternoon to Maryport was the remains of a Roman road – interrupted by a barbed-wire fence and a railway line. I came up through the seaside town at dusk in rain, past teenagers bound for a jazz festival, and stayed the night in a Victorian villa with a family who energetically debated the industrial regeneration of the west coast of Cumbria in the late 1940s. My host ran the trust for the local Roman fort – in this case a base for Spanish cavalrymen, who appeared to have built one of the earliest Christian churches in northern Britain. A line of Roman fortifications had once stretched all the way from the fort in a continuous line along the coast from this fort to Hadrian's Wall. And across the water, I could now see the hills of Scotland.

60

I walked for twelve miles the next day, up the beach from Maryport to Silloth, passing a dead porpoise and a crumbling Roman clifftop cemetery. The line of wind turbines in the estuary had been planted along the sea-border between England and Scotland. (My father wrote to me with delight that the turbines had been made in China, and shipped at immense carbon cost to Scotland.)

At Silloth, I turned into land that was not entirely land. Ten thousand years ago, retreating glaciers had left humpbacked drumlins of coarse clay which still stood proud of the surrounding soil, untouched by either the sea or the freshwater streams. Fed only by cold acidic Border rain, domes of peat had emerged above the mounds, and then begun to sprout hairs of pallid green and coral moss, which faded above the surface of the swamp. And among the mosses were other tinctured, water-swollen growths which passed for flowers – a pink anemone (like a shrunken hyacinth) and yellow bog myrtle growing from a floating mattress of black peat. Alive, not dead; growing, not decaying.

Such ground was too wet for agriculture: crops would be drowned; an oak would not survive three days; a cow could sink into it. It was not surprising therefore that there were no place-names from Cumbrian, Northumbrian or Norse farmers in this spot. The salt-marsh-ringed peat had been almost unoccupied until, in the twelfth century, Cistercian monks had been given it as a place to pray. They built their first huts on an Ice Age relic – an island of rock – in the middle of 300 square miles of floating peat. To their east stretched 500 square miles of what had been the Middleland – now reduced to a depopulated wilderness and royal hunting forest.

They were permitted no personal possessions in their bare rooms in Holme Cultram abbey. They could eat only vegetables. They could not put on an extra gown in the winter, or a blanket on their bed. Their robes were of the roughest unbleached wool. They were locked in the monastery under a strict rule of obedience, some of them thousands of miles away from their original homes. And they were, of course, chaste. No part of their work was done for the sake of their families, for they had none: no wife, no children, no heirs.

The Cistercians all assembled at three in the morning – six hours before a Cumbrian winter dawn – to pray for two hours. They prayed again at six. And at nine. And at midday, and at three in the afternoon, six in the evening, and nine at night, and at midnight. When they cleared the land – standing in cold water, in their rough gowns, thin from their sparse diet, tired from their hard beds and the bells that never allowed them more than three hours' sleep – they did so because it was a practice that they believed strengthened their prayers. They continued, generation after generation, in this practice for 300 years.

The unintended by-product of their faith was an agricultural revolution. Working alongside lay brothers and serfs, they dug great ditches to drain the heaped glacial debris, burned some of the peat-spoil for fuel, and stacked the rest into turf walls. As the turf died, the monks planted hawthorn hedges on these banks, which allowed them to keep sheep and cattle whose grazing removed the heather, further drying the peat. The manure, rich in nitrogen, like the manure from Eric Weir's sheep and cattle, suffocated the bog plants and burned the reeds away.

Because of the monks' work, the soil on the southern, English, side of the Solway began to produce oaks of prodigious girth. (The identical soil on the northern, Scottish side, where there had been no monastic draining, remained wet, treeless and desolate for another 600 years.) A new ecosystem emerged. Caterpillars ate the oak buds, and birds ate the caterpillars and nested in the branches. Bats, which roosted in the oak holes, consumed the hundreds of insect species which fed on the trunks. Badgers lived on their acorns; beetles and mushrooms thrived in the leaf mould beneath.

Eventually, beneath the oaks, was pasture capable of supporting 20,000 sheep. Over time, the abbey had grown into a town called Abbeytown. I continued on my road to Wigton, walking for twelve miles through fields of cattle, silage and tall maize. Where there had once been wetland, thousands of lumbering Holsteins were each now steadily converting rye grass into 10,000 litres of milk a year.

61

That night I slept on a large new black leather sofa in Jackie's house on the Greenacres Estate, by the factory in Wigton. Wigton was not a wealthy area – in part because it was some way from the tourist industry of the Lakes, and from the industry of Carlisle and the west coast. More than half the people in the town worked in the factory – a great grey stack of chimneys that included Europe's last cellophane plant, and which made plastic film for banknotes for Australia, Vietnam and the Bank of England.

My hostess had a shy, engaging smile, and a shock of electric red hair. Her front room was neat, clean and well painted, backing onto a modern kitchen and a sizeable garden, but it was almost bare. In Asia, I had slept in many front rooms; they all had posters on the wall and rugs on the floor – even homes which could not afford meat. Most possessed a large black television cabinet with the manufacturer's labels left on the glass, even if they did not own a television, and instead filled the cabinet with models of mosques and tiny perfume bottles. But Jackie's front room contained no decorations, and there were no pictures on the wall. It was carpeted with squares of carpet samples. Her miniature pedigree spaniel lived upstairs. Her grey cat slept on the top of the sofa above me.

Jackie went to bed early, and I stayed up to send an email to my father describing the monks. By the time I woke up the next morning, my father had already replied in capital letters – with an email beginning, 'SUGGESTIONS. THOUGHTS, REACTIONS'. He had sent it at five in the morning. It began with six questions (I have removed the capitals):

> Cistercians. They sound particularly admirable chaps. But could our guru spare us a little time to discuss who they were – it's an odd name – and where they came from? And what was the origin of their agricultural expertise? And do we know whether their wool was special, or merely plentiful? Indeed, any idea what sort of sheep there were at that time? (You know my line that you should inform us as well as entertain us!) Could their serfs move on to better themselves if they felt inclined? What did they use for fences in those days? My school books tended to depict the monks as an idle comfortably living lot of epicures, but your Cistercians sound like a very different sort of people.
>
> Next subject.
>
> I am still suffering severely from stiff neck trouble. Infuriating, but I think it is slowly diminishing in intensity and frequency of stabbing pains. At least I can sleep with codeine [aka opium!!].
>
> All love daddy

As on Hadrian's Wall, I could answer only some of his questions. The monastic order had come originally from France; their serfs were not allowed to move; since there was little stone around they would have probably used earth dykes, or even ditches like my father's ha-ha, to fence the sheep. But most of the studies of the Cistercians seemed to focus on their beliefs, not their farming techniques. And I didn't know any historian who had really studied these things. It was a reminder. My father had never been very interested in people's motivations or their legacy. He was interested in how they got things done.

62

Thomas lived in Ellen Close, 200 yards down from Jackie. Some gardens on the estate were tidy, some houses were privately owned. The untidiest gardens seemed to be in front of the private houses. Thomas's garden was tidy. He lived at number 11. He had grown up in number 9; his mother was now in number 10, and his sister lived at number 6. As I reached Thomas's door, a large boy, wrapped in a big black bomber jacket on a warm afternoon, an oversize black baseball cap on his head, strode past, shouting, 'Mom . . . Mom . . . MOM!' in a crescendo of need. No one replied. That was Thomas's brother, Chad.

Thomas was about my age. He had a shaven head and pale thin cheeks, and his T-shirt hung very loose on his frame. His right arm was unnaturally straight. Later someone explained that he had been paralysed when he had crashed his car seven years earlier, killing a friend. He spoke in the accent of a Cumbrian farmer. But while farmers might half mock an earnest question and give little away, Thomas was talkative, using half-formal phrases, changing tense, voice, pronoun and perspective in mid-paragraph. With his permission, I recorded him. I asked what it had been like to move to the estate, aged seven. Where a Cumbrian farmer might have replied, 'Not a lot of choice about it,' Thomas said: 'At that age, it didn't really faze me in any way, until later on, when I think – well, if I'd had freedom of speech, then I probably would have chosen not to move here. I don't know. You're basically basing it on your everyday life as it is. It was the change. And leaving my real, biological father. We got on brilliantly, and we just got tore apart, really. It was because my mum wasn't happy.' Midway through these reassessments of his early move, a tall, cream-coloured lurcher entered the room. When Thomas called her, she laid her head on the arm of his chair for a moment, then she pulled away and walked back into the kitchen. Two minutes later he called her again and this time she tried to climb onto the sofa. Thomas apologised and pushed her off. She began pacing between the chair and the kitchen again. (My father would have called her 'couthy' and admired her gravity, and the slight distance she kept from her master.)

Meanwhile, Thomas was talking about his time in jail. About 20 per cent of the households on the estate had a family member in jail. 'It's not so much the problem with drugs, it's the type of drugs that are a problem, like amphetamines, that's the worst – tears families apart. There's more than there was because nowadays there's that many different ways of making that type of high, and the effect that high can give. It's not so much heroin, it's more skunk and amphetamines.' He glanced down. 'There's a couple of smackheads.'

He said that he had once been 'the main cause of a lot of the violence' on the estate but had changed completely. 'You're better off communicating . . . There's no point arguing about something, you should just talk about it. I hate confrontations and that, I don't like it . . . life's too precious.' He sounded like a therapist – perhaps his therapist. 'You've got to change around if you're not making any type of positive impact . . . You can help the next generation by learning them the ways you should have done.'

The room felt empty – a single man's house – but there were porcelain figurines and souvenir plates on the shelves. Thomas's mother had got them from 'clearing houses' and had given them to him. There was a shout outside. Through the window, we watched Thomas's mother step out of a police car.

'You have a lot of your family on the estate,' I said.

'Family's a big word, isn't it?' said Thomas.

I walked outside. His mother was waving and greeting everyone. A policewoman was standing nearby. Thomas's mother had been arrested that morning because her partner had claimed that she had assaulted him, but she had been released almost immediately. 'They're a good family,' the police officer explained to me, 'but sometimes the family needs us to step in.'

63

Wigton church, a mile from Thomas's house, had been on the edge of the monastery's possessions. Holme Cultram abbey had expanded its business from sheep farming to mining, salt factories, industrial salmon-netting along the Solway, and finally to opening a port to trade directly with Spain. By 1300 – 150 years after the monastery had been founded – the surrounding communities had long forgotten that they had once been Cumbric Celts, or Northumbrian Germans, or Norse Vikings. Instead, a single religious and knightly culture now spread across both sides of what was now the English–Scottish border. And its rulers were French-speaking.

The dominant families were the Balliols and the Bruces, descendants of French knights who had come to Britain after the Norman Conquest. Ahead of me, the low rising ground of Scottish Annandale was the land of Robert the Bruce; to the west, in Galloway, was the land of John de Balliol. But their estates also stretched deep into English Yorkshire. Robert de Brus meant 'Robert from the village of Brus' in northern France, and Jean de Ballieul meant he had come from Ballieul in Picardy (where he still owned land and where he died).

Since they held so much land between the realms of the English and Scottish kings, these French-speaking families seemed to be with both and neither. At a twelfth-century battle, Bruce, who was a friend of the Scottish king, explained that he felt forced to fight on the English side. Balliol fought for the Scots. Later, it was the other way round. This particular monastery's patron was Robert the Bruce VI, and the broken sandstone slab in the corner of the vestry was his tombstone. This father of a Scottish king was buried in England.

The monks also remained not entirely Scottish or English. Their monastery belonged to a French order. It had been established in the old Middleland of Cumbria by a Scottish king on what became English soil, so they were able, with the support of the French order, to play their monastic superior, who was in Scotland, against their diocesan bishop, who was in England, and maintain rights of free trade with both.

At the heart of this monastic Middleland was the drainage system – the channels and rivers, which meant the land could now be weeded, regulated and controlled, to support the great flocks which supplied Flanders' demand for wool. The monks – who had come to the area for wilderness, poverty, dispossession and isolation – had through their presence made those very things vanish.

Much of this wealth was poured into building the abbey itself. I had walked through its red sandstone foundations. It was an austere architecture. The abbey in Melrose in Scotland, from which these monks had originally been sent, and to which I would now be walking, was also built from red sandstone. But Melrose had two great towers, and slender stone columns – thin as bamboo – obscuring and revealing crisp, high arches; it had side chapels with rich carvings of vines, grapes and apostles. Holme Cultram was vast, squat and towerless, like a great barn. There was no decoration on the walls. The long, high nave, the thick trunks of the columns and the bare floor made it a fortress of God, in which the monks respected the old Cistercian suspicion of ornament.

The white-robed monks no longer chanted six daily services in the nave. But when its mother and daughter abbeys in Scotland had been left roofless, empty and desolate, this abbey, just on the English side of the border, had continued to function as a parish church, its vast sandstone walls continuing to echo with 800 years of worship.

Then, in 2010, a thirteen-year-old boy, angry at being unable to find the communion wine, had set the abbey alight. I walked into ruins, across the bare earth floor where Robert the Bruce VI had been laid in 1304. The timber beams, which had survived the Reformation and the Puritans, had not survived the boy. You could see the sky. A builder in a hard hat stood with me in the nave, gazing at the size of the remaining sandstone blocks, the depth of the floor space, the height at which the altar had once stood.

64

Someone had described my host in Wigton, Jackie, as a 'single mother living on benefits'. In fact, she worked sixteen hours a week as a barista in town. She explained that she had just taken the children on holiday to a fixed caravan at Great Yarmouth, and since they had liked it, she was saving £20 a month so they could go back there again. Her seventeen-year-old son was an apprentice in Carlisle. Her fourteen-year-old daughter was thinking of becoming a mental health nurse. 'I met someone who does it,' her daughter explained. 'It sounds like a good job.'

Like the rest of the crescent of council houses, Jackie's house had been built on a flat field beside the Wigton factory in the 1930s. Each was identical in design and date to the houses on the estate near my father's house in Crieff. The architecture insisted far less on its 'identity' than the Lake District villages with their uneven houses, steep lanes and rearing barns, brooding around the mass of a parish church. But it was a far more entrenched community. Jackie, her parents and her children had lived on the estate since birth, just as their ancestors had lived in the now demolished narrow tenements a mile away, behind the high street. Here there were no Lake District issues of 'affordable housing', second homes or ageing. People were out in the streets all day. Jackie could walk me round the 103 houses in the estate and tell me who lived in nearly all of them.

'You like it here?' I asked.

'I like my house very much,' said Jackie, 'but my mother is horrified that I moved here, because she thinks it's a terrible place to live and very dangerous.'

'This housing estate?'

'No, of course not,' Jackie laughed. 'She means this street.' Her mother and father lived fifty yards away and her sister lived a couple of doors from her parents.

Ellen Close, a hundred yards down the hill – where Thomas lived – was, in Jackie's opinion, a more dangerous place. She would not like to live beyond that invisible border. But she was fond of Thomas. 'He's a good lad,' she said.

'Is he?' asked her son. 'Or do you just say that because he says, "Good morning, missus" every time he sees you in the street?'

The next morning, as I was setting off, there was some argument that I couldn't follow. I barely took in the face of the woman who walked into Thomas's house.

'That's Thomas's girlfriend, who's had her daughter taken away because she's got mental health issues,' a bystander said, offering facts I hadn't asked for. 'Her son is an arsonist,' the bystander said. 'He arsoned the abbey.'

65

Walking north from Wigton the next morning, I re-entered the landscape created by the monks: the rich fields which had emerged through draining mire and salt marsh. Around me only fragments of the original wetland remained. But on a track on my right, where a field drain had been abandoned, I saw a circle of moss. It looked like dry land but it wasn't. The glaciers had left an ice plug. The ice plug had melted, the space had filled with water, and the moss had grown above the water, floating on a shaft thirty feet deep.

All around was dry. The hedges that now grew on the margins of the arable fields sheltered angelica, bettany, hemlock, Yorkshire fog and meadow buttercup. I plucked the tiny white flowers of cow parsley and crushed the leaves. When I crushed them they smelled not so much of lemon or aniseed as almond. There was bird's-foot trefoil, and tufted vetch. Yellowhammers and grey partridges nested on the bank, and in the hedges were blackbirds, chaffinches, song thrushes and dunnocks. And there were endless subspecies of dandelion. All of this, like the oaks, insects, bats and squirrels, wildlife of dry farmland, and had emerged from centuries of monastic drainage.

At Wedholme Flow I was stopped by a press of dairy cows. Here I found a thickset middle-aged man, now working for the Environment Agency, who told me that he had joined the drainage board in the 1970s, when there had been sixty people in his team laying and maintaining the agricultural drains, to keep the water off the fields. 'Little Stan was only a tiny chap, but he could keep going all day. He had a good eye. He could see the undulations in the ground and put the drainage tiles in, exactly where they needed to be. Then we would keep them in good order. You'd work down this watercourse in teams of three. One of us pulled down the willow and alder stems, the second cut them with a sickle, the third forked them out. The river bottom is wicky – it goes like quicksand. Ideally, by the time you'd finished, and the foreman came along, we had a line of grass in a nice straight tidy line along the top.'

This was the same work the monks had done – the struggle to keep the drains open through thick glacial clay, barely above sea level, lashed by some of the heaviest rain in Britain. Every year, more foliage grew, and more debris was washed down the river. Every year, men with scythes and sickles and spades cut and cleared and dredged again. Now a team of sixty men for this river alone had been reduced to six for the whole county. The vegetation was choking the drainage ditches, the water was backing up under the bridge and there was standing water at the edge of the fields. A week earlier, the water had stood two feet deep in the farmyards, lapping just below the windows of the houses, and the fields had been so wet that the dairy cows were crushing and ruining the soil.

At first, it seemed as though the problem was simply lack of manpower. But at Wedholme Flow, peat-digging had been prohibited; drainage ditches had been deliberately blocked to flood the surrounding land. The same was true at Glasson and Bowness. For a new generation of ecologists, the rich farmland, the tall trees and the hundred different plants and birds which I had noticed in the hedgerows were an abomination. They felt there had been far too much agricultural improvement, and this land was too fertile. In the place of dry fields, they wanted to recreate salt marshes, mires and nutrient-poor, waterlogged soil. Instead of hedges, moss; instead of oaks, stunted bushes of bog rosemary; instead of hedge flowers, reeds; instead of birds that nested in trees and hedges, birds that waded in mud.

I reached a nature reserve an hour later. The director explained that when his charity bought the land in 1988, it had been cow pasture. They had let the cows go, and blocked Little Stan's header drains to make the fields so wet that you could push a six-inch nail easily into the soil. 'That tells you how easy it would be for a wading bird to probe its beak in to find food,' he said.

But the land had then become too wet even for the wading birds. So they gradually began to reintroduce some agricultural practices – not for their own sake, but for the birds'. To get the right length of sward for the lapwings, the manager took on his own flock of sheep, contracted with nine different graziers, and experimented with native-breed cattle: 'light grazing' with specialist animals that needed to be housed somewhere else for the winter.

The director guided me into the marshland, explaining how in place of the old dairy pasture he was now creating and sustaining three different types of wetness for three different types of birds. He showed me the 'rushy' habitat which he had made for snipe, 'with a few dry bits to lay their eggs on'. Then the closely cropped sward he was maintaining for the lapwings – 'Drier conditions, but they do like the odd tussock dotted about that they can get tucked behind to hide; and small pools with lots of muddy edge so the chicks can get to it and feed.' And then a third area for the redshank, 'More tussocky with more clumps of rush. But not,' he added quickly, 'wall-to-wall rush.' In order to achieve this micro-variety, the grazing had to be supplemented every autumn by machine-cutting, and an artificial raising of the water level. 'If you can get the water just above the cut stems of rush, it tends to kill them off, but it's an art in itself timing it just right.'

His greatest pride was a fragment of peat bog which the monks and their successors had never managed to drain. He had tried to encourage a farmer to put cows onto the edge of this bog to graze the tops, but it was too deep. The cows almost disappeared into the water. 'When they get out about thirty yards onto the bog, it turns out they're just thrown. They start sinking up to their bellies. There was one in particular, it just wouldn't move. We had to drag it out.' The farmer had, it seemed, been reluctant to put his cattle there again. However, the director felt the bog was perfectly suitable for curlews.

We walked gingerly along a plank. 'What we're standing on here is something like 95 per cent water. Milk's got more solids than this.' Above the sodden blanket of moss, nestled among the staghorn lichen, were tiny spikes of yellow bog asphodel, white tufts of beak-sedge and dark bog rosemary. 'When I first came here and started monitoring the site I found five plants of bog rosemary in a whole day of searching. Now we've just mapped its distribution right across the bog. If I'm doing surveys at night when everything's out, I just crush that up and rub it over my face. Have a whiff,' he encouraged me. 'It keeps the insects off to a certain degree. I wouldn't say that it's as good as the juice you get in a can but it's the next best thing.'

In the place of 1,000 acres of productive land, which might have held 800 cows – producing, I guessed, enough milk for tens of thousands of people – sixty-five pairs of wading birds had emerged. The old avenue of oaks, four feet thick after 200 years of growth, stood in three feet of water. They had been drowned and their bare branches had been stiffened by death, in their final stretch for sunlight.

'When we moved here twenty-two years ago we didn't have any waders,' said the director. 'Zero to sixty-five over the years,' he said with pride. 'The numbers everywhere else in the country are going down.'

Now he wanted to extend the bogs. 'Given time, when we've reduced the nutrient levels down, and the phosphates, the sphagnum moss will come back, which enables the peat to grow, and then that'll eat up more of the nutrients, and you'll eventually get more bog flora starting to come through.' This would provide even more space for the curlews.

'Amazing. And how long do you think that will take?'

'No one really knows. I mean, a lot of what we're doing here is quite groundbreaking . . . There's been some remarkable changes in that fifteen years, but nothing suggesting we're getting much closer to creating ideal conditions for bog flora. So, fifty years, maybe?'

On the way out of the bog, he pointed out a round-leafed sundew. A large heath butterfly hovered just over the sundew. One false beat of its delicate wings and it would stick to the gluey hairs on its leaves and be slowly devoured by this carnivorous plant, which was the colour of drowned flesh.

66

At Bowness, an old Roman fort on the banks of the Solway Firth, the English–Scottish border coincided precisely with Hadrian's Wall. And the lane on which I was walking seemed to follow the old Via Principalis, from the west to the east gates of the fort. Over time, however, the road had drifted lazily off the straight line of the Roman engineers, and the council had now tarmacked it into a permanent curve. I passed a barn made of rain-darkened cubes of stone, marked with legionary chisels. Glancing into a courtyard, I saw a whitewashed eighteenth-century mansion built into the end of an older red sandstone house, whose heavy sash windows brooded over a pediment fit for a classical temple. The King's Arms, a bland white building, must have sat above the site of the *principia* or headquarters. The sacred standards of the legion would perhaps have been stowed somewhere beneath the bar.

Beyond the east gate, the grey beach of the estuary was littered with branches and leaves, swept miles down from the beech trees on the Esk and Eden. The Romans wouldn't, I thought, have seen beech this far north, their leaves would have been alder and oak, but they would have felt the same tide, which was quivering now against the outflow of the rivers, filling the channels, lifting the driftwood, and forcing me off the beach onto rocks and against the foundations of the wall itself. Across the bright water I could see the low shoreline of Scotland.

A border became necessary in the eleventh century, when the English and the Scots, having eliminated the last Cumbrian kingdom of the Middleland, became neighbours. But where exactly were they to place the new border? On the Firth of Forth, or on the Humber – like the borders of the old kingdom of Northumbria? On the Clyde or on a Lake District ridge like the last kingdom of Cumbria?

The answer for William the Conqueror's son was apparently to place the new border precisely on Hadrian's Wall: building border fortresses on the Roman wall forts at Carlisle and Newcastle in 1080 and 1092, and thereby investing the border with the antique authority of the Roman Empire. Over the following decades, the English and Scottish kings pushed the line back and forth, through a sequence of massacres, slave-raids, homages, treaties, bank loans, treasons, and finance packages for the Crusades. The Scots continued to claim and occupy much of the old kingdom of Cumbria, south of the Solway Firth and the wall, until the Scottish king David died in his palace at Carlisle in 1153. And the English claimed the old rump of Northumbria that stretched north of the wall to the Tweed.

Briefly, under Richard the Lionheart, a century after the Conqueror's son, the border seemed to return to the wall again, the Scots by then having lost English Cumbria, south of the wall, and regained Northumbria, north of the wall. But by 1230, the English had pushed the borderline much further north to the River Tweed. And this has remained the border to this day. It began in the west here on the Solway Firth, but then ran diagonally north-east and finished – some sixty miles north of Hadrian's Wall – at Berwick.

★

At eight the next morning, with a falling tide, Mark Messenger walked me into the water. Mark had a broad pink face, and he was dressed in a green plastic smock with a sack over his shoulder. He looked about fifty. In his hand he carried a pole to which was fixed a rigid net, about the size of a small dining table. Mark was the landlord of the Highland Laddie Inn on the English side of the estuary. He smiled a lot, revealing the gap in his teeth from a fight in Benidorm.

We were stepping into an estuary, a mile wide and ten miles long, heading towards the far shore and Scotland. The waves were gentle but we had to keep a steady pace, to keep our boots free of the 'wicky' sand. Mark explained that some fluke combination of the rippling outflow of the Esk and Eden and the tides of the Atlantic Ocean had just created this ford at low tide. A similar route had existed in the Middle Ages. Somewhere near our feet was the bell of Bowness church, which Scottish raiders had dropped on their way home. The current bell in Bowness had been stolen from Dornoch in revenge, and carried back across the ford.

Four other men dressed in waterproof smocks stood in the sea to our east. They were ex-factory workers from Carlisle and they were catching salmon, on the flow, in their large, rigid hand-nets. It is called 'haaf-netting' – a Norse word. They believed that people had been fishing in this way in the Solway since the Viking era. The length of their net pole was measured from a Viking oar. In the thirteenth century the monks had used fixed nets here as well. In the eighteenth century, people had speared salmon here from horseback – a difficult task from high above the water, given the refraction of the light. But whatever the technique, the challenge remained the tides. A riptide with the wind behind it would move faster than a person could run. A thousand Scottish raiders were supposed to have been drowned just here, returning from a raid on the Holme Cultram monastery.

Jim shouted, 'No one Mark has ever guided has made it back alive!' Mark bared his gums. It was perfectly safe, he explained, the secret was never to leave your feet still in the sand. If you did, the sand would disappear beneath your feet and you would be unable to pull your boots out. The other secret was to prod with your stick, to make sure there wasn't a hidden shelf.

A fleet of angry anglers, of environmental trusts and agencies had tried to stop haaf-netters from fishing in this way. The river-owners accused them of preventing the salmon from entering the Esk and the Eden, rendering salmon beats which had once generated tens of thousands of pounds worthless. But the haaf-netters felt they were being blamed for problems actually caused by climate change and sea-lice on Norwegian salmon farms. New licences had now been introduced, limiting their fishing to set numbers in daylight hours, in fixed season. Each catch needed to be tail-tagged and recorded in a book, and a plastic strip for each fish sent to the Environment Agency in Bristol. The men thought that this bureaucracy had been designed to force them to give up, but they had no intention of stopping. Only fifty people in the country, they said, continued to fish in this way.

67

I was now standing up to my waist in the water that marked the line of the final break between the kingdoms of England and Scotland. In 1286, racing to visit his mistress, the Scottish king had fallen from a cliff, leaving as his heir first a Norwegian princess, and then, when she died, a throne which was disputed between the two great border dynasties, the Balliols and the Bruces, with their loyalties to both English and Scottish kings, and their land stretching both sides of the Solway border. They were eventually challenged in turn by the English king Edward I. Robert the Bruce had led his cavalry, cantering through the Solway perhaps not far from the point at which I was standing, and to display his newly found Scottish chauvinism sacked Holme Cultram abbey in which his father was buried, bringing the roof down on his father's grave. And in 1300, the cavalry of Edward I had cantered along the Solway shoreline directly ahead of me, trailing silk and satins.

These men were killers. Bruce and Edward were both remembered as standing well over six feet tall – perhaps ten inches taller than the average man of the day. My father's favourite moment in the Battle of Bannockburn came when Bruce took on the English champion in front of the battle-line, crushing his skull with a single hammer blow. We had often enacted the moment with plastic soldiers. Edward's greatest moment had come on crusade. When an assassin had charged into Edward's tent in Damascus and stabbed him with a poisoned knife, Edward had killed him with his bare hands.

The contemporary description of Edward's ride along the Solway in 1300 was in yet another language of the medieval Middleland – not Cumbric, Norse or Northumbrian but the mother-tongue of the kings of England and of Bruce and Balliol, that is to say, French:

Meint beau penon en lance mis
Meint banier deploie
Se eftoit la noife loign oie
De heniffemens de chevaus.

As my father would have translated it ('You know more Norman French than you think'): 'Many bonny pennons in lances, many banners deployed, the noise long off of harrumphing of horses.'

The chronicle continues its account of their Solway ride with a description of knights whose minds were filled with heraldry, who used silks imported from China, enjoyed references to King Arthur and unicorns and rode with companions who included Aymer, the nephew of the Emperor of Constantinople, and a descendant of the rulers of Kiev.

But the Scottish account of the same war by John Barbour does not focus on coats of arms. Instead it uses rough Northumbrian words to describe the solitary wanderings of Bruce. And while the chroniclers and poets of the English campaign were writing in French, he – a Scot – wrote in what even today we can almost understand as English:

The kyng toward the vod is gane
Wery for-swat and vill of vane

The King towards the wood is gone
weary with sweat, and baffled in will.

'I prefer,' commented my father when I shared this with him, 'Edward's comment on toppling Balliol – *"bon bosoigne fait qy de merde se deliver"* – isn't it great to push out a turd.'

68

Mark Messenger and I stopped mid-stream. The tide was beginning to rise again now, a slow movement of brown water on grey sand, a break in the ripples of the river water. The beach began to vanish. My father and I had crossed many borders together: the Chinese, the Montenegrin, the Indo-Pakistani, but never in this way. Now, standing 200 yards off the north coast of England with salt water up to my waist, I was on the boundary between what I increasingly thought of as my land – Cumbria – and what I thought of as my father's land – Scotland. Ahead of me was thirty miles of Scottish coast, behind me twenty miles of Cumbrian coast. The English Channel would have been no wider than this 10,000 years ago.

The Solway had once been a much more fundamental divide than the Channel. The north shore and the south shore – both built up from an identical sour glacial clay, almost flat as a desert – were not originally even part of the same continent. The 'English' shore – behind me – had begun its journey 8,000 miles away, swinging up from somewhere down by the South Pole; while the 'Scottish' shore drifted east, attached to what is now America. The channel beneath my feet was the point at which they met, 200 million years ago. A great convulsion then tore a deep gap between Scotland and the rest of the American continent, and a flood separated Britain from France. Here, where I was standing, was the rough Frankenstein mend of the encounter of these two landmasses. You could not see the difference in the grass, or the trees, or the topography. But in the gravel beneath my feet, you could find the fossils of American molluscs which could not be found in the layers of the Cumbrian shore, a few hundred yards behind me.

People noted this firth long ago. Three miles away, on the waterfront, was the Lochmaben stone, a Neolithic monument; and a pre-Roman tribe, the Selgovae, had a name which echoed the Solway. Rome had reached this point in about AD 70. The Roman Empire then contained what is now most of the European Union as well as the Arab League – from North Africa to Syria – and stretched for 2 million square miles. But this narrow stretch of sea was where it ended. From the second to the early fifth century AD you could have ridden from modern Iraq through to Belgium, on fine roads, speaking a single language, in a single state, until, here in this brown water, Rome stopped and barbarians began.

Mark was not concerned by the nuclear waste that had been released along the Solway coast. He did not believe the stories that the water was still contaminated with depleted uranium from the RAF bombing exercises. He did, however, believe the photograph taken on the Solway in 1962 of a girl with a spaceman behind her head. He left me in the shallow water on the Scottish side, then turned to hurry back to England. I had left what the English called the Border and entered what the Scots called the Borders.

Climbing the far shore, no one shouted or appeared. ('It's a bit dull, isn't it?' emailed my father. 'No border guards, or barbarians. What I'd like is someone pointing a bayonet at us at least. How about a glimpse of the Scottish hills?' 'No, Daddy, not even that.') I climbed up onto a long shoreline, passing the wooden bases of collapsed jetties, and wooden pilings which I guessed once held salmon nets – the fixed kind, preferred by the monks, which annoyed the spear fishermen here in Walter Scott's novel *Redgauntlet*.

Immediately in front of me stood the foundations of a railway bridge that had once crossed the Solway, almost precisely on the route that I had walked through the water. When it was begun in 1863, it was the longest viaduct in Europe, requiring new engineering techniques to secure the foundations in the treacherous peat. Once it had been opened, Scots were able to walk – illegally and at some risk – across the bridge for a drink in Bowness, avoiding the stricter drinking laws in Scotland. But the bridge was very vulnerable to the unpredictable conditions of the Solway. The ice that formed in the estuary in 1881, for example, knocked down fifty of the bridge piers. The venture lost a colossal sum of money, and the bridge was closed in 1921, the year before my father was born.

The tide was just beginning to turn and, as I turned east, inland along the estuary, fences forced me to walk along the edge of the choppy water, over a slag heap of black, uneven boulders, glistening with algae. Fragments of broken concrete with rusting reinforcement struts jutted above the scum of bird feathers at the high tide mark. The gulls screamed. The morning was getting warm, and the inlets and the uneven beach made for slow going. Behind me I could see the great forest of aerials which marked the nuclear submarine control centre at Anthorn.

69

The Scottish side of the border looked different to the English side. Here the agricultural improvements had happened much later, the land drains had not been abandoned, and rewetting and rewilding schemes were yet to commence. Oaks loomed above long-eared grain and thoroughbred horses. Between the coast and the fields were dense thickets of briars and nettles, raspberry bushes and hints of more exotic, pink-flowered aliens – all taking advantage of the nitrogen-rich soil.

In 1914, this whole patch of mostly Scottish ground, nine miles long and three miles wide, had been fenced in by the Imperial War Office. They had expelled a dozen small family farms, breaking for ever their connection to this particular soil. The War Office replaced them with people from across the seas. First, they ordered a manager to report immediately, plucked from his civilian work in South Africa; another was posted in from British India. Then builders were shipped across the sea from Ireland. (My father loved the fact that they would pay the train driver extra to rush them to Carlisle, where 200 whiskies were laid, six deep, on the bars, waiting for their arrival.) The purpose of the site was a secret.

Finally, 30,000 women, many from the most remote Highland valleys of Scotland, were sent to live and work on this spot: stirring, squeezing, rolling, cutting and packing. The women turned yellow from the fumes. Their packages were moved by train to Dover and then shipped to Normandy, where they were revealed as cordite and fired, night and day, at the German trenches. By 1918, this patch of land was producing 800 tons of cordite a week, more than every other British dynamite factory combined. The work killed tens, perhaps hundreds of thousands of German soldiers.

After the war, the government no longer needed the munitions factories. They tried to create a new industrial park, offering the already-built factories and workers' housing to civilian buyers. One entrepreneur agreed to try sugar beet on the site, but even explosive contaminant could not make this wet, northern soil suitable for beet. So the government dismantled the facility. And like the Romans before them, they divided the military land into regular strips and settled demobilised soldiers on it. Pre-First World War farmers had gone; but the descendants of the First World War soldiers were still there.

I walked up to a heavy gate of spiked metal struts, six feet high. Past the gate and in front of some farm buildings, I saw an old man with fair skin and thin white hair. The sleeves of his shirt were neatly folded back. I wished him good morning. He nodded shyly. I passed on and then, reconsidering, introduced myself.

He told me that he was Mr White. He said this in an Ayrshire accent – the first real confirmation that I had arrived in Scotland. He asked me, twice, to confirm that I had forded the Solway. He seemed sceptical of the idea. He had lived 200 yards from it for eighty years, but he had never tried to walk to England, and did not know anyone who had. If he had ever wished to go to Bowness, he would have taken the thirty-mile trip by road. I asked him about his farm.

'My father was in the Cameron Highlanders in the First War,' said Mr White. I had seen pictures of the Camerons in the trenches. They, like the Black Watch, wore khaki covers over their kilts, heavy with mud or ice. 'He was originally from Kirkpatrick Fleming. When he returned, he bid in the army lottery, and was allocated this land – number four Clarkson – roughly fifty acres. Good land.' But the ancient characteristics of the marsh had never entirely disappeared. 'What we've got is brilliant. This other side here, though, it's quite wet. Most with this kind of weather. In fact, he can't even get his hay crop off. I mean, it's standing water.'

Then came the Second World War. Some of the old site was brought back into use as a munitions factory again, and anti-aircraft guns were placed 'beside Westhills, and beside the lock at Dornock fisheries', but the War Office did not reacquire his father's farm. The 7th of April 1941 was a hot day. His father was ploughing the fields with some horses, with the help of a friend. 'Oh hell, I can't mind his name now . . . What the hell was it? I think they called him Noble,' Mr White suggested. 'And the ploughman said, "I'm going to go into town, Willie, and get very drunk." But my father didn't drink, so he didn't go with him. And they had so much in the Masonic Hall that night that they left the door open, and the German bombers coming south saw the light.

'First we felt the house shake, and then we went to that small window, there, and my sister and I saw all the German bombers flying out across the Forth again. The headmaster at my school lost half his foot. My father's friend the ploughman was one of the twenty-eight killed. We were expecting to hear the anti-aircraft gun open fire. The bombers were only a few yards from the gun. But they didn't fire. They didn't want the Germans to know the depot was here.'

After the war, Mr White worked in the munitions factories, then he became a policeman. After that he returned to the farm in which he was born. He was now in his eighties.

I wanted to hear more such oral history. Walter Scott and Robert Louis Stevenson had insisted that what made the Scots different from the English was their deep absorption in their local tales. I felt I had grown up with the end of such stories in the Highlands. So I prompted Mr White: 'My map says that in that field was a Roman altar. But presumably a farmer found it and got rid of it . . .'

'No, that's something I cannae tell you. Never heard about a stone.' Pause. 'Never been into that.' And then he said in a more contemplative voice, 'I've never really delved into the history of things.'

I opened the map, and tried to show him the position of the altar. It was only 300 yards from his farm gate.

'There's a fellow at Longtown on the English side,' he said, emphasising the 'Long' and separating it – '*Lang-toon*' – 'who can give you all the history. Gordon Routledge. I think he's in Swan Street, I'm not quite sure. He's the best man to see about that. He'll give you all the gen about all the places.'

A row of white doves sat along the eaves, cooing. It seemed a strong emblem of something Scottish not English – the dovecot or 'doocot'. I asked how long he had kept them. 'I don't keep them, they just settled here. I'll let you see my hobby.' He fumbled with his keys beside a small tractor. A number on the machine's body suggested that it had been made in 1958. 'Terrible to have to keep everything under lock and key . . . We've had two break-ins here.' It was only later that I thought how humiliating the break-ins must have been for a man who had been a policeman.

We entered what had been his father's house. 'Watch yerself here.' We climbed a narrow staircase to a bedroom full of glass cabinets, every square inch of which was occupied by plastic models of Second World War aeroplanes, their wings overlapping. 'Just watch what you're doing here.' I took off my pack. He led me through to the other bedroom, filled again with cabinets of grey aeroplanes. I had made a dozen with my father as a child. Here were 2,000.

'Do you think you got interested in Second World War planes because of that night, seeing the bombers flying over?' I asked.

'No, not really. I had rheumatic fever when I was young. I couldn't move for many years. I took up this hobby.'

'Which were the first ones you built?'

'Oh, hell, I couldn't tell you. I've sold about 600. There's no the room. You see, the mice get onto them. They jump on them and break the wheels and propellors off.'

'And which is the kind of plane – sorry to keep coming back to this – which you saw the Germans bomb with?'

'I think most of the German planes are away . . . except here,' he pointed to a shelf with the familiar grey and black crosses, 'these are all German planes, Focke-Wulfs and Messerschmidts.' He paused. 'I think it would have been the Heinkels that bombed Gretna. There might have been Dorniers as well. A mixture of Dorniers and Heinkels, I think . . .' He settled into a long pause.

Finally I said, 'Well, thank you very much. I must be on my way.'

On the way down the stairs he showed me a framed photograph of a mid-air collision at an air show. 'I saw that. I was there for that. Fairford. Two fellows in the media were killed as well, because of no ejector seats.'

'I think I will walk along the waterfront. I'm going to walk to Redkirk Point.'

'Oh, aye.'

'And from there to the Lochmaben standing stone,' I said.

'Redkirk Point is where they used to collect the fish,' he observed.

'And then the Lochmaben standing stone . . . ?' I wanted to know what he thought of the ancient stone, so near to him. It was 4,000 years old, a sacred Neolithic stone that was still being used as a border meeting place between the English and the Scots as late as 1600 – representing almost 3,500 years of tradition and use.

There was another pause.

'Loch-may-ben – you're going the wrong way, Lochmaben's up in Dumfriesshire. It's above Lockerbie.'

'This is a different one. A standing stone on the shoreline, just half a mile from you.'

'Mmm. Mmmm. I don't know that one.'

'Thank you.'

'Nae bother. Farewell.'

I passed the neat-layed hawthorn hedge, a sign reading, 'Number 4 Clarkson', and then another, fifty acres on, 'Number 6 Clarkson'. One swift, two, three; the stately procession of a honking raven; and a great flock of small nondescript brown birds, swooping low towards Gretna.

I stumbled through mudflats, over hidden channels towards a flat horizon of smoke-smudged sands. Reeds surrounded me; geese crowded the estuary. In the winter, I had read, they had once been joined by bar-tailed and black-tailed godwits, ringed, golden and grey plovers, oystercatchers, dunlins and turnstones. But the climate was changing. The migrants no longer seemed to find the border waters cold enough, and such birds were now only found further north.

On my right, across the firth, I could see Burgh by Sands, the Roman fort where Edward I died, preparing to cross the waters again for his last invasion of Scotland. By then a decade of war – first between Edward and John de Balliol and his champion William Wallace, and later against Robert the Bruce – had torn the Middleland decisively in two. The distinctions between Scotland and England which had hardly mattered to the previous generation of monks or noble landowners assumed a terrifying significance. Edward I massacred the people of Berwick, and hung Bruce's female supporters in cages from the castle walls. Robert the Bruce raided his former estates in England, tearing up even the orchard trees. The *Lanercost Chronicle* took up a hyper-nationalist catalogue of Scottish atrocities, which describe how William Wallace flayed the skin from the English treasurer 'to make a baldrick for his sword'. The populations of the Border valleys emptied, leaving only the toughest or most desperate behind.

In the twelfth century, King David of Scotland had still seen himself as ruling a mixed people: Northumbrians, Scots, Flemings and Cumbrians. But in the Declaration of Arbroath, a document written after two decades of border war in 1324, the Scots are beginning to describe themselves as a single people – in words which might almost have appealed to a nineteenth-century nationalist:

> As long as but a hundred of us remain alive, never will we, on any conditions, be brought under English rule. It is in truth not for glory, nor riches, nor honours, that we are fighting, but for freedom – for that alone, which no honest man gives up but with life itself.

This claim of national identity – which now appears on countless tea towels and mugs – was less straightforward than it seems. It was written not in Scots or Gaelic but in Latin and the aristocrats signing it (whose families had come from half a dozen different countries within the last two centuries) claimed to all be immigrants from the Black Sea who had massacred the previous indigenous population of northern Britain. The full declaration ran: *De Maiori Scithia . . . et in Hispania . . .*

> The Scots nation journeyed from Greater Scythia . . . and dwelt for a long course of time in Spain. Thence it came, to its home in the west where it still lives today. The Britons it first drove out, the Picts it utterly destroyed, it took possession of that home.

None of this is on the tea towels or mugs. Nor is Bruce's later insistence, before he invaded Ireland, trying to establish his brother as king, that the Scots were really Irish. Meanwhile, his 'English' cousins whom he was fighting were claiming to be descended from immigrants from Troy in Asia Minor.

On the basis of such ethnic myths of exotic immigration, everything was recast into the categories of English and Scot, split exactly between two new nations. The culture of Norman knighthood or Christendom or crusading no longer held the peoples together. Nor could any memories of the vanished Middleland.

Each of the leaders of this national war died, broken into his component parts. Last to die was Robert the Bruce, already losing parts of his flesh to leprosy. He asked that his heart be cut out of his body and sent to Jerusalem. It made it no further than the dust beneath the hooves of a charging squadron of Muslim cavalry in Spain. Edward – who died of dysentery on the site of the small Roman fort I could just see across the Solway, one down the line from Bowness – is said to have asked his son not to bury him but instead to carry his eviscerated skeleton in front of the English armies.

William Wallace had been the first to die. Mel Gibson's *Braveheart* portrays Wallace as a tartan-clad, mud-spattered villager. But Wallace had been an educated man, speaking English, French, Latin and probably a Celtic language too, and was remembered for the beautiful silk clothes he wore as a young man. He had travelled abroad, and was sent as a diplomat to the royal courts of Europe, where he remained deeply loyal to the king, John Balliol. Like Bruce and Edward he was remembered as being a giant – some said six foot seven – and had trained very effectively, like all knights, to kill in single combat.

But he was – as *Braveheart* emphasises – not technically a nobleman. He came very close to throwing out all the normal rules of chivalric warfare. And his resistance seems to have become a popular insurgency, which was stirred by Scottish priests into a holy war against an infidel invader. As for his identity, his name William 'Wallace' meant William the Welshman. It implied that his family had either migrated from the Welsh borders, or were part of the indigenous Cumbric-Welsh population of the Middleland. But he became a Scottish nationalist.

When Wallace was finally captured, he was torn in two by teams of horses. His limbs were placed at the four corners of Britain, in a savage attempt by Edward to emphasise a concept of Britain, as an island, whose natural frontiers were the sea.

But by then even Edward, despite his claims to a single Britain, implicitly acquiesced through some of his legal judgements in the idea of separate nations. Nothing demonstrated the surreal distinctions of this new and brutal division more than the execution of William Wallace. His name and birthplace made him the quintessence of the old Middleland, but he was convicted in Westminster Hall as William 'the Welsh' – 'a Scot, Scot-born'.

★

After back gardens, a barbed-wire fence, and the high banks of an abandoned railway line, I reached the Sark. On a busy road above, a sign announced: GATEWAY – DUTY-FREE ZONE. This was Gretna Green. What had been a Scottish refuge for eloping English couples was now dominated by a wedding complex, including a four-storey hotel, an outlet store and a 'courtship maze'.

The trickle of the Sark was no more substantial than the stream-with-no-name by my father's house. I waded it in five steps. But the Sark had held on to a name because it had been made into the English–Scottish border: the Border Sark. The stream at my father's did not divide anyone or anything.

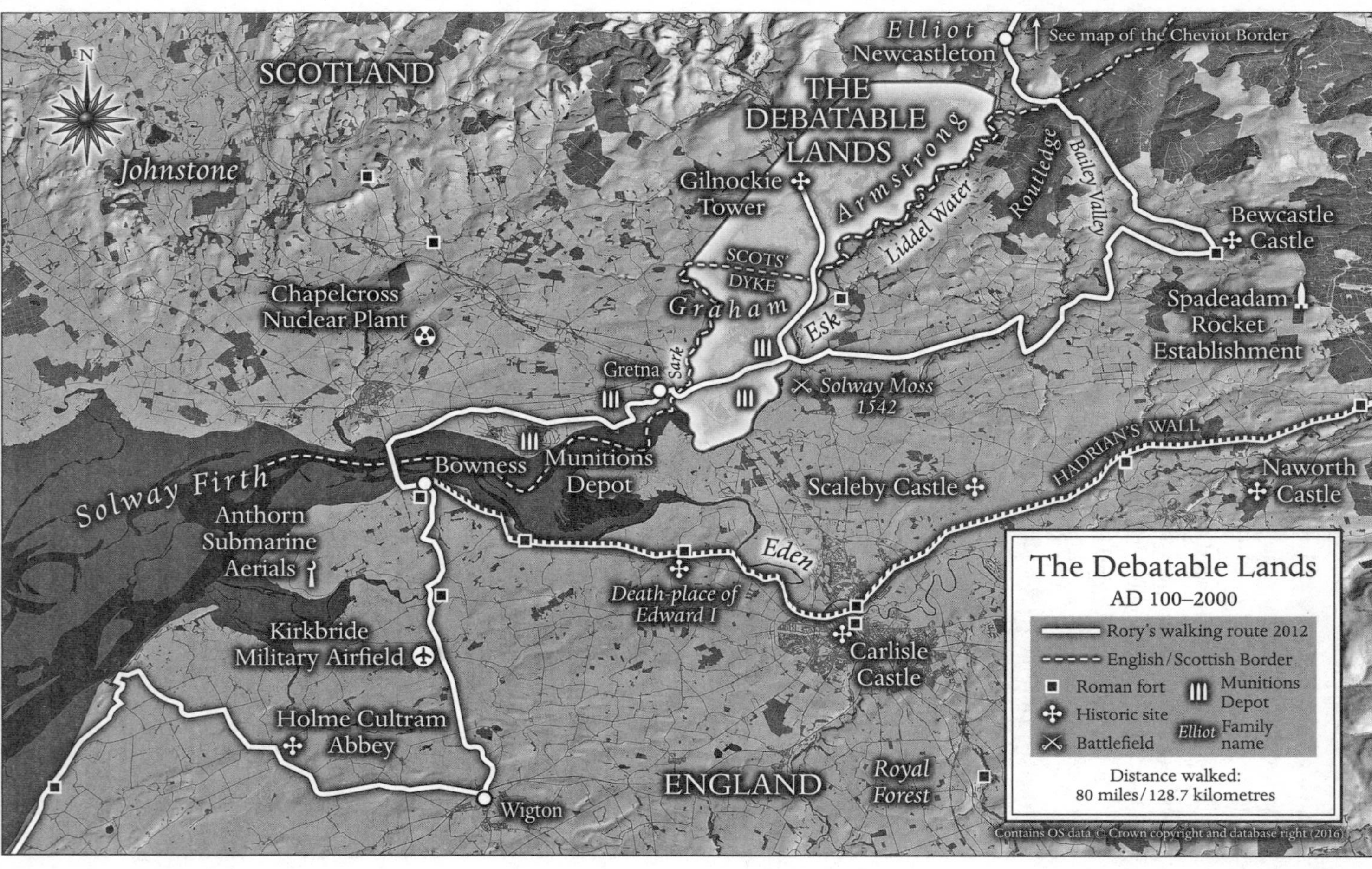
The Debatable Lands
AD 100–2000
Rory's walking route 2012
English/Scottish Border
Roman fort
Historic site
Battlefield
Munitions Depot
Elliot Family name
Distance walked:
80 miles/128.7 kilometres
Contains OS data © Crown copyright and database right (2016)
N
SCOTLAND
Johnstone
Elliot
Newcastleton
See map of the Cheviot Border
THE DEBATABLE LANDS
Armstrong
Liddel Water
Routledge
Bailey Valley
Bewcastle Castle
Gilnockie Tower
SCOTS' DYKE
Graham
Esk
Sark
Spadeadam Rocket Establishment
Chapelcross Nuclear Plant
Gretna
Solway Moss 1542
HADRIAN'S WALL
Bowness
Munitions Depot
Scaleby Castle
Naworth Castle
Solway Firth
Anthorn Submarine Aerials
Eden
Death-place of Edward I
Kirkbride Military Airfield
Carlisle Castle
Holme Cultram Abbey
ENGLAND
Royal Forest
Wigton

I climbed onto the bridge and looked east: six lanes of the motorway, a high-speed railtrack protected with razor wire and legal threats, and pylons stretched into the distance, five or six miles to my eye, with no hint of a pause, or a break in the stream of traffic and people and power flowing between the nations. Below me the Sark appeared again behind an old white house on which a large sign said, 'Last house in Scotland'. And on the other wing: 'First house in Scotland'.

71

The territory I was entering now was the third historical territory of my walk. I had begun among the Norse and Northumbrian place-names of the Cumbrian Middleland; then turned into the waterland of the medieval monks, and the frontier of Robert the Bruce, along the Solway coast and estuary. Now I was walking east, inland into the heart of the sixteenth-century Borderlands.

After an hour's walk from Gretna, I reached the Debatable Lands. It was not inspiring land for a modern walker – the ground was low and undulating, with limited horizons. For two miles I remained on a busy road, with a thick plantation of pines on my left and a tall razor-wire fence and a line of trees on my right that protected what remained of the old cross-border munitions factory. This small section still belonged to the Ministry of Defence and was now supplying ammunition to the troops in Afghanistan. Through a gap in the trees, I could occasionally glimpse a vast expanse of concrete and dozens of ammunition sheds.

When the plantation ended, I found myself at an old gravel pit, now converted into a lake, and graced by four swans. At a nearby road junction, I found signs insisting ever more vehemently on the border – Border Vets, Border Auction Marts, Border Loos. Turning up the road to Canonbie, I noticed still more First World War munition bunkers, now converted into cattle sheds.

For centuries the land into which I was now walking – bigger than five modern states in the United Nations – had been recognised in law as neither England nor Scotland. Even in the sixteenth century – 400 years after the kingdoms met on the Cheviots, and 200 years after Bannockburn – it was a no-king's-land, swelling in a seven-mile bubble of exception: an air-pocket between two borders. The kings of England and Scotland had made living here a capital offence: their subjects could kill on sight anyone found in the zone, without trial, as vermin.

But the Armstrong and Graham clans had chosen to ignore the English and the Scots, and made this their home. I was passed on the road by an 'Armstrong' truck, painted in British racing green; and saw across the Esk the fort and country house built by a Graham over another old Roman frontier camp (this one containing specialist scouts, Spanish cavalry, and the tombstone of a woman from what is now the Czech Republic). After another four miles I reached the stone tower that Johnny Armstrong had built at Gilnockie in about 1500. It was four storeys high and one room square, on a steep bank above the Esk, encircled by a car park, a bungalow and the flag of the Armstrong Heritage Society. From this stronghold, dressed more splendidly than most Renaissance monarchs in Cloth of Gold, Armstrong had treated freely in the early sixteenth century with the kings of England and Scotland. He maintained a mounted army, financed by cattle raids against his two neighbouring states. And his reign was commemorated in many of the ballads for which the Borders are still famous. French was now forgotten and the common language of Borderland was a descendant of Northumbrian English that mingled English and Scots words:

> Sum speiks of lords, sum speiks of lairds,
> And siclyke men of hie degrie;
> Of a gentleman I sing a sang,
> Sumtyme calld Laird of Gilnockie.

Scotland and England finally combined against this potentate in 1530. Johnny Armstrong was flattered into attending a meeting with the King of Scotland. He rode out followed by his troop of golden cavalry, stopping to wave their lances on the lawns at Langholm, and swept into the king's court at Carlanrigg, expecting to be offered an alliance against England. (He was simultaneously negotiating a similar deal with the English, to attack Scotland.) But James V refused to recognise him as a laird, a lord, or even a gentleman. James had Johnny Armstrong of Gilnockie and his troop hanged from a nearby tree.

This insult to the honour and culture of the Debatable Lands is preserved in three ballads, in which Johnny Armstrong defies the king. But the court document suggests that the Scottish government had a different view of his status: *'John Armestrange, "alias Blak Jok" and Thomas his brother convicted of common theft and reset of theft etc. – Hanged.'*

A generation later, a French ambassador was given the task by the English and Scottish kings of making this anomalous Debatable Land through which I was walking part of either England or Scotland. Like a Renaissance Hadrian, he drew a straight line, granting half to the English and half to the Scots, and marked the line with great sandstone blocks, stamped with the wax seals of the treaty. Most of the local Grahams were allocated to England; the Armstrongs were left on both sides of the border. Brothers and neighbours found themselves divided between the jurisdictions of different kings, courts and churches.

When I walked south again from Gilnockie Tower, and climbed up into a narrow strip of forest above the road, I found what appeared to be one of the boundary stones lying broken in a circle of nettles, birch, sticky willy and briar thorn. I thought I could see a letter on the stone. Ever since the French ambassador had divided the Debatable Land in 1552, any man – or indeed hedgehog – wandering over this earth dyke had entered another nation – a step north, and I was Scottish, a step south, English.

Back on the road, the ambassador's line had now been marked with a giant road sign saying in Scottish Gaelic 'Welcome to Scotland': *'Failte gu Alba'*. The people who lived on this spot today, like 99 per cent of Scots, spoke English. Over the last 2,000 years, people here had spoken Cumbrian Welsh, Latin, Northumbrian Norman French and Borders English, but they had never spoken Scottish Gaelic and they had never called this place Alba. If the idea was to reproduce what someone might have said in an ancient language, my father suggested the sign should read something like *'Cryso i Cymbru'*, or *'Wilcuman Norþhymbraland'*.

But this arbitrary line drawn by a French ambassador had severed and obliterated the previous linguistic and cultural history, and created a new heritage in its place. Only 58,000 people in Scotland out of 5 million spoke Scottish Gaelic in 2012; almost as many spoke Polish; and there were twice as many people in Scotland of South Asian descent; but the sign was still written in Scottish Gaelic. The Middleland had been forgotten, the Debatable Lands were gone and an invented nation had triumphed. *Failte gu Alba.*

Beside the road sign stood a scarecrow dressed in a kilt and holding a saltire flag. Behind the scarecrow stood his creator: a large man in tight shorts who had been sunbathing and burned the top of his head. His cottage, with its large conservatory, stood only ten yards on the Scottish side of this new border. Twenty yards south stood a thin woman in a black trouser suit, the owner of the Marchbank Hotel, which stood on a slope on the English side of the border.

I gestured from one of them to the other. 'Do you know each other?' I asked.

'Well, we recognise each other; we know who each other are,' she said.

'Why did you put up the scarecrow?' I asked the man in shorts.

'For the tourists,' he replied. He elongated the 'o', and over-rolled the 'r', as though to stress his Scottish accent. 'I was fed up with them stopping and taking photographs of the road sign. I thought I would give them something better to photograph. I get dozens every day.'

The man and the woman belonged to different postcodes, but they also belonged to different nations. His children's university tuition, his medical prescriptions and his eye tests were free. She paid. They were in different emergency-service zones, and the ambulances were often reluctant to cross the border. He reckoned he was in Scotland by 'about twenty yards'.

'Would you ever live in England?' I asked.

'Definitely not,' he said with a smile.

72

I once spent an hour perched between a stuffed panda and a large child seat in the back of a Toyota. In the front were two academic experts on borders, and we were driving past Tucson not far from the border with Mexico. The front-seat passenger was a young Iranian-American man in a starched white shirt.

The Arizona–Mexico border was marked by an eighteen-foot fence, almost 600 miles long. In 2005, 1,189,000 people had been apprehended trying to cross the border. I had been told that more people had died crossing that border in the last five years than American soldiers in Afghanistan. Most had died from heat and dehydration in the desert. In 2012, a sixteen year old was shot by the US border police. 'He was riddled with bullets, and was well on the Mexican side of the border. We don't know exactly what happened. It is being tried in a secret military court.'

The Iranian-American professor seemed to want to question the naturalness of borders, and to emphasise that they were 'socially constructed'.

'But,' I said, conscious that I might be sounding a little pompous, 'however artificially or cruelly imposed, they soon take on a deep, almost permanent reality.' When I was walking from Turkey into Iran, I explained, I had been moving through a single ethnic and linguistic zone. On both sides of the border were related Kurdish and Azeri peoples and I had been drinking Turkish coffee since Izmir. Then I walked through the border fence. A hundred metres into Iran, the border guard asked me what I wanted to drink. 'Coffee,' I said, and he laughed. 'We only drink tea,' he said and gave me a cup of black tea. And it was only tea for the next 800 miles.

Again, precisely at the Iranian–Afghan border – a zone of a single Farsi 'Khorasani' culture – they began to drink green tea. At the Khyber Pass – a line which Afghanistan does not even recognise, an absurd line, scratched by Sir Mortimer Durand to mark the edge of British India, running straight through the middle of a single Pushtu tribal group, who continued to trade and intermarry; they put milk and sugar in their tea.

I assumed that the Arizonan border would make my fellow passengers feel how strongly artificial borders could define national cultures, in defiance of any 'natural facts' of geography or historical ethnicity. The contrast between the Mexican settlements south of the border and life in Tucson was startling. To my eye, Tucson was far more like Columbus, Ohio, than Tijuana. Tucson and Tijuana, which had once been parts of a single desert culture, might now have been separated by 4,000 miles of ocean. It was clear from my companions' expressions, however, that they did not agree with me.

I tried to explain the English–Scottish border to them. How it had only existed in the Debatable Lands for fifty years before England and Scotland were unified under a single king, and how thereafter, for 400 years, there had not even been a border post. How there was no difference between the hummock of wet grass on one side of Scots Dyke, and one on the other. Yet how permanent and dramatic the impact of the border had been. 'Ultimately, because of a division which originated with the Roman frontier forts,' I told them, 'if you walk a hundred yards across the modern border, the dialect changes – within a hundred yards a "lord" is called a "laird", a "beck" is called a "burn"; and the accent changes completely: on the one side people speak with a Cumbrian accent, and on the other side, Scots.'

'That's not true,' interrupted the driver. Something in her tone made me feel she was irritated by what I had been saying, or the way in which I had been saying it.

'Really, it is. I live on the border. The difference is quite striking,' I said.

'You think it is. But there has been a lot of good work on this recently. There is actually no difference.'

'Well . . .' I was at a loss. I'd been contradicted, in Tucson, about my backyard, but I was also suddenly conscious of being ignorant of a whole field of research on a subject that I had wanted to make my own. I stumbled forward, defensively. 'We are, I think, very sensitive to accents in Britain. It is partly to do with—'

'I am aware of that,' said the professor, 'I am a linguist. We distinguish two things. What you and your constituents are talking about is what we call an "ideological difference". In other words, I don't doubt that you all believe there is a difference. But recent research demonstrates that there is no "objective difference".'

'I live there,' I snapped. 'When were you last there?'

'That is not the point. Two years ago, if you must know. But this is about academic research.' Then she said two things that I couldn't understand. They sounded something like 'voiceless phonation' and 'rhoticity' – socio-linguistic and phonological terms I had to hunt to find later. 'It has been established that both of these things are vanishing.'

'Look, I am prepared to accept that the Scottish accent is becoming less distinctive in general, but that is different from there being no difference at the border.'

'It is very interesting for me as an academic to meet a politician,' she said coldly.

Later, to try to work out why I had offended her, I read one of her articles. It was entitled '*Muy Macha*: gender and ideology in girl-gangs' discourse about make-up'. In it, she questioned the naturalness of gender, as a 'social construction'. But even in the car, unfamiliar with her work, I could sense she felt my view of a decisive border was politically motivated, and reactionary.

'I can send the articles to you,' she snapped back at me.

'Do please. I can't believe they claim there is no difference. But if they do, I will apologise.'

'There are no apologies in academia. Only facts. This is a fact.'

She never sent the articles.

★

It took me a day to walk from the Debatable Lands to the Bewcastle Wastes. I was still keeping Hadrian's Wall on my right and the Scottish border on my left, and thus technically walking on English soil. I walked through a strip of ancient woodland by the White Lyne. Fragments of pale light, falling through the canopy of oak leaves, danced on the black water. A dozen different miniature grasses grew from a single fallen log. I admired a fellow walker's collie, as she circled, thrusting in and out of the crevices of branches, scratching at the soil, breathing in the dank smells from the specks of red mould, the fur of the white fungi, the teeming ants.

By the middle of the morning, rain was beginning to fall hard on the canopy, and the river water was simmering and spitting around the rocks, beneath the black crags which the Cumbrians called the 'fairy-tables'. Back on the road, the rain came down at the speed of a tropical storm. The tarmac ran with a foot of water. At the stone bridge, the engorged Black Lyne had broken over the ramparts, so that viscous peat-brown waves washed over the parapet. The hoofprints of the cattle in the fields beyond were filled with dark blue, foul-smelling groundwater. The clay soil had been 'poached' by stock who had been left to graze too long, crushing the substructure. In every hamlet around I passed abandoned buildings – pubs, an auction mart, a village shop, a school.

There was still a village hall at Roadhead. I stepped in out of the rain. On the wall was a map dividing the valley into the different clan territories of the sixteenth century, and shields decorated with the coats of arms of the clans. You could see the long bubble of the Debatable Lands on the map, marked 'Armstrong' and 'Graham', then the land to the north 'Elliots, Scotts, Kerrs, Douglases', and the valley in which I was standing, the Roadhead of Bailey and Bewcastle, marked 'Routledge', and then, in smaller letters, 'Loder, Telford, Douglas, Crozier, Dodd.'

When I walked out of the village hall, Barbara Loder saw me across the street and invited me into her bungalow for a cup of tea. Barbara Loder was a small woman in her seventies with a deeply lined face and an engaging smile. I had heard a great deal about her over the last few hours of walking. Whenever I asked anyone about the Bewcastle wastes, they would say, 'You've got to see Barbara, she's the man.'

She took me to a back room, where fifteen-year-old Shaun Douglas was standing staring at her computer. His father had been from the valley, but they had moved nine miles away to Longtown, and Shaun had returned to teach Barbara how to use the computer. He seemed defeated by her old machine. While I drunk my tea, she talked rapidly about things I could only half follow: how Malcolm Dodd's mother had cleaned the hall for £5 a week; how there was a proposal to establish a Christian community nearby. She had been the head of the parish council for a long time. 'People who have only been in the village seventeen years,' she said, 'have been demanding publication of the parish minutes. I refused. It would set the village afire.

'Where are you going?' she asked.

'I'm on my way to see Trevor Telford,' I said.

'Oh, I know Trevor,' she said.

'Isn't he your cousin?' I said.

'Oh yes, he would be,' she replied.

73

Roadhead was, as the name implied, the last settlement in England before the Scottish border. And until the 1950s this was where the road ended, leaving only farm tracks beyond. Still today, there were no villages or hamlets between Roadhead and the border – only small farmsteads, each a few hundred yards apart, hidden by the deceptive undulations of the clay soil. I followed a line of unkempt hawthorn hedges, planted on banks above the drenched ground. Some of the farmers here had tried to plant new grasses: not rye – because the climate was too wet and cold, the soil too poorly drained – but hardier varieties of what seemed to be some perennial, perhaps Old Timothy. The rain, however, had ruined their planting: the 'improved' fields were now as drenched and poached, crushed and ruined as the older fields. The cattle had already been held on the land too long; soon the farmers would have to pay to move them, down to the better land by the Solway.

In one field an elderly farmer, once known for his stockmanship, had simply given up. He had made no attempt to cut, spray or manure the rushes. A scattering of thin sheep were hidden by the thick stands of reeds. Another 500 yards and I saw that a famer had cut the silage the previous year, but then had just left it in the black plastic bags through the winter, so that the bags had now burst, spilling ruined grass over the land.

Above, on rougher ground, were shielings or byres once used for summer pasture. Higher still was the wet moorland. And beyond, on the borderline, were the dense dark-green plantations that formed the edge of the Kielder Forest. There were signs – fragments of pollen preserved in the peat – that people had farmed this difficult clay soil since before the Roman occupation. But the population was falling. There had been twice as many people and farms in this valley a hundred years ago, and four times as many in the sixteenth century.

Trevor Telford met me on the lower ground of what he seemed to call 'Scuwarpadale'. As the corbie flies we were still only three miles south of the Scottish border. He was a slender forty year old with a long head and a high forehead: the sort of face which the Cumbrian writer George MacDonald Fraser claimed was typical of Border families. Trevor blushed slightly when he shook my hand. The farm on which we were standing had only been in the direct male line of his family since 1824, but his Armstrong and Forster relatives had been significant in the valley since the fifteenth century.

This land of Bewcastle in England, and the facing land across the border, Liddesdale, had become the epicentre of the Border banditry during the 300 years between Scotland effectively winning its independence at Bannockburn in 1314 and the Union of the English and Scottish Crowns in 1604. Trevor's English relatives had been granted their land by the English king (and his Scottish relatives by the Scottish king) in exchange for 'border service'. They paid their rent not in cash, but by mobilising with horse and sword to fight across the border.

On the Balkan border between Austro-Hungary and the Ottoman Empire such a zone would have been called a *krajina*. Because the farmers/fighters paid next to no rent and were able to pass their land on to their descendants, they had far more land security over the generations than tenants in other parts of Britain – and this was the reason why a network of small farms still survived in the valley – but they had had far less security of life.

Behind Trevor was a ruined medieval stone building, its entrance blocked by tall nettles. Access to the living quarters on the upper storey, he explained, had been by a ladder which was drawn up to exclude the Border raiders. The scale of your farming was limited by the problem of defence. 'You couldn't have kept more cattle than you could squeeze beneath this bastle house.'

Once the English–Scottish border was established, this frontier zone – which overlaid the old Roman frontier zone, and the old Cumbrian and Northumbrian kingdoms of the Middleland – was called the Marches. The territory was divided by the medieval kings into the West, Middle and East Marches, each governed by a 'Warden of the March', often from powerful aristocratic families such as the Scottish Douglases or the English Percys, who based themselves in a chain of fortresses. Three of these – Askerton, Naworth and Bewcastle – lay within a few miles of where Trevor and I were standing.

The wardens continued to govern the Marches through ancient tribal arrangements, based on clan vendetta, centuries after such legal systems had been abolished in the rest of England or Scotland. These codes were called the March Laws. Right up until the early seventeenth century, for example, a man of the Marches could lead his own private reprisal raid across the border to steal back any cattle and goods which had been taken from him. And it remained legal to imprison and punish someone's cousin or brother for their crime – as was the case until recently on the North-West Frontier of Pakistan.

The central pastime for the Borderers, as in traditional Cumbric-Celtic society, was cattle-raiding, typically conducted on horseback. The raiders were called 'reivers'. A daring expedition could involve a journey of forty miles, the burning of dozens of farmsteads and the theft of 1,000 'kine' or cows. The peat over which these reivers rode was cut with ditches, gullies and tunnels. In this land a cow could sink to its neck, bellowing and swinging its wicked horns in fright, a family could hide, an assassin could lurk or a horse could break its leg. They raided across lowland and upland mire, over the wet clay of the Bewcastle wastes and through the great floating beds of sphagnum in the Solway mosses.

They learned how to ride across the border at night, under a full moon, while evading the watch-posts placed on Hadrian's Wall. They learned how to attack a farm and get away before the beacons could summon assistance. They learned how to drive the cattle back using secret routes. By 1550, this particular valley had been well established as 'a common and waye as well for the theves of Tyndall, Bew Castle, and Gillesland in England as for the theves of Liddesdale in Scotland with there stollen goodes from th' one realm to th' other'.

The surrounding population was forced to live for protection in either one-room-square, tall, fortified 'pele' towers, or squatter bastle houses, or in mud huts, which could be abandoned when the reivers arrived. Certain things which were taken for granted in the south of England – villages arranged around medieval stone cottages, Elizabethan mansion houses and elegant Norman churches – simply did not exist in this landscape, then or now.

74

When the Archbishop of Glasgow issued a curse on the Border reivers in 1525, excommunicating every 'name' and their descendants as though they were a foreign nation, he did so in one of the last great displays of vernacular Scottish Catholic rhetoric, imagination and anatomical comprehensiveness:

> I curse thair heid and all the hairs of thair heid; I curse thair face, thair ene, thair mouth, thair neise, thair toung, thair teith, thair crag [neck], thair shulderis, thair breist, thair hert, thair stomok, thair bak, thair wame, thair armes, thair leggis, thair handis, thair feit, and everilk part of thair body, frae the top of thair heid to the soill of thair feit, befoir and behind, within and without.
>
> I curse thaim gangand [going], and I curse thaim rydand [riding]; I curse them standand, and I curse thaim sittand; I curse thaim etand, I curse thaim drinkand; I curse them walkand, I curse them sleepand; I curse thaim rysand, I curse thaim lyand; I curse thaim at hame; I curse thaim fra hame; I curse thaim within the house; I curse

> thaim without the house; I curse thair wiffis, thair bairns, and thair servandis participand with thaim in thair deides.

He went on to curse their corn, cattle, wool, sheep, horse, pigs, geese, hens, vegetable patches, ploughs and harrows. Trevor and the majority of people in this valley were still descended from the men cursed by the archbishop.

This curse had found a modern afterlife. First, in 2001, it had been resurrected and carved, word for word, into a round granite boulder in Carlisle's 'Millennium Gallery' – an underpass beneath the ring road which had torn up a section of the Roman fort. Then in 2006, Jim Tootle – a Liberal Democrat councillor on Carlisle city council – argued that the curse on the boulder was too dangerous and powerful, and was bringing disaster to the city again. 'As time has gone in the last five years, various things have happened. We have had floods, pestilence, a great big fire in the city.' He demanded that the boulder be destroyed. The sculptor compared the threat to the Taliban's destruction of the Bamiyan Buddhas: 'It is of that order. They want to smash it to pieces.' It stayed in the underpass.

Trevor talked me through the various families who had lived round the edges of the valley in the sixteenth century. 'At Kershopefoot,' he explained, 'controlling the Scottish border were the Forsters of Stanegarthside.' He pronounced it '*Stingerside*'. 'They are my relatives. Armstrongs definitely in about Dirtup, and Snouts and Lowtoddles; and then some Elliots from the other side of Kershopefoot. The owners of this bastle house were Crosiers.'

The Routledges, he said, were Scots who had been given land in England by the English king Richard III in exchange for their services defending the border against the Scots. But it seemed to me that it hardly made sense to describe the Routledges as either Scots or English. A court case recorded a Mrs Routledge being raided by thirty Scots, and then being raided again, a few weeks later, by the English. A document of 1491 describes the Routledges as English subjects living on the English side of the border, but paying taxes to the Scottish Crown.

'How do you know all this history?' I asked.

'The funny thing is I know more, even though I'm a younger generation, because I listened to people before they died. My mother and brother, they don't know half of what I know because they just weren't interested.'

'Did you learn any of this in school?'

'What we learned at school was more to do with Nazis.'

As we walked past a quad bike chained to a farm gate, he remarked, 'It's such a pity how times have changed. You can't leave a piece of machinery out on the road any more.' He seemed to have forgotten that he had just been describing a time when you couldn't leave your cattle out.

75

Christopher lived on the other side of the Black Lyne from Trevor. His farmhouse, like almost every farm in the area, still contained a fortified bastle house embedded in its walls. It had probably been placed to be visible from Trevor's bastle farm, for the families' mutual protection. It took me half an hour to walk from one to the other across the ford, which was only passable with a stick. In the fields were Christopher's sheep, whose diet of wet border grass made them, he said, more delicious. Farm buildings sprawled around the courtyard. A barn had been converted into a hall. At the end of the hall was a portrait of the family, just completed, showing his two sons in tricorn hats, with wooden swords in their hands.

Christopher said he had bought the farm 'because land was cheap and because no farmer believes his land is as bad as it is'. But he was not a full-time farmer. He was a barrister who specialised in planning, and spent much of the week in London, commuting on the train from Carlisle. The rough landscape entranced him; he had not prettified his yard or house. I had first met Christopher two years earlier in midwinter. I had walked twelve hours that day through snow and was soaked through. There was no heating because the boiler had broken, and the family sat indoors in coats and hats. The kitchen was crammed with dogs, children's weapons, plates, pots and what seemed to be copies of medieval manuscripts. I slept in an armchair in front of the fire. Christopher had just bought a shell of a Jacobean mansion in a flat field a few miles away, to pass on to his younger son.

On this occasion he pulled out a map of the area made in the 1590s on which tiny towers and bastle houses were drawn – in almost every case on the site of a current farmhouse. He had been reading some letters written by an English doctor in 1746, and was contrasting them with some letters from 1810 which showed the improving of the fellside by laying coal-burnt lime. 'You can still see the coal mine, and a little lime kiln across the river at Haggbeck.' But the improvements were fragile. He reckoned it would take only four years of neglect for all the land to revert to barren fellside.

'Once across Hadrian's Wall, you've left the modern world,' said Christopher. 'I can't imagine living anywhere else. It's the sense of independence, something about hidden corners. I remember, twenty years ago, I could lie in bed and mentally go around every house, and – apart from the vicar and publican – everyone was a farmer or farm worker or supplier. All were interrelated. A settled, indigenous population, which have never moved. The abiding sense,' he insisted, 'is still of the original people.'

Although he lived just across the river from Trevor, and in sight of Trevor's farm, he seemed to know his neighbour only by sight. And Christopher, whose speech was more formal, at times almost archaic, was more inclined than Trevor to emphasise how little had changed. 'The Lawsons, who still live here, built a new house here in the 1650s. Look at the Lawson twins – compare it to portraits of the Lawsons hundreds of years ago – look at their faces.' When he talked about the past, he referred not to cows but to 'kine'.

Although he was Cumbrian, he was not originally from this valley. He had grown up in Welton, forty miles away, on the rich dairy land that had emerged on the Cumberland plain. 'As a child I had no real sense of reivers, and wasn't particularly brought up with reiver tales. There wasn't the same sense of fortification.' He had developed his delight in the Marches as an adult. So, he conceded, he was not quite like Trevor Telford. But he insisted he was also not like the hippies and organic farmers who were beginning to settle further along the ridge line. He called them 'yoghurt weavers'.

★

When I had asked Trevor what he felt about living on the border, he replied, 'Well, I've never lived anywhere else so I wouldn't know, really. You do know that is Scotland and this is England, but you've got friends both sides of the border.'

I asked if his family were still conscious of having originally been Scots.

'I don't really know,' Trevor had said. 'Maybe. People say the Scots are a little bit more careful in their spending; that's something that's still said today. But we've got both Scottish and English blood. It's a bit of both really.'

I reminded him that a mutual friend's sister had complained about being abused at her work across the border 'because she was English'. I wondered what he thought about Scottish nationalism.

'I have to say that people can be patriotic. Nobody knows how it would be split, that's the thing. I suppose everybody has a different view, don't they . . .? Some might be in favour and some won't. Maybe they think all the money goes down to Westminster. There would be more comes up than goes down, I would imagine?' he asked doubtfully. 'I tell you what's been a great thing for the country,' said Trevor. 'The Olympics.'

Christopher's response had been different. 'I was born in Scotland and feel English. I wake up every day thanking God I wasn't born a foreigner.' He laughed. 'I ally myself with the Norman Conquest, the Plantagenets, the Queen, the Church of England – although I am about to become a Roman.'

I asked about his wife, who was from Perthshire. 'She feels 100 per cent Scottish. It is a purely tribal, nationalistic thing. When I read about Bannockburn there is only one side I am favouring, whereas she is favouring the other side. You just have to cross the river – Langholm is closer to us than Longtown – but it is very different, because it is in Scotland.'

Christopher didn't try to define the differences between the national characters. He thought there was 'no difference in culture, we are exactly the same: we are indistinguishable because we share the same climate and topography, but if you blew a horn, all the Scots would line up one side'.

My walk had often made me feel how modern Britain was: how bewilderingly mobile, how thin in identity, how unconcerned with history, how severed from its deeper past. But this was not how Christopher saw the land around him. Every building in the valley still suggested ancient lives and deep histories. He could deconstruct almost any Cumbrian cottage, roof beam by roof beam, speculating on the aspirations of each generation of builders.

'As you walk on through Kershopefoot,' he said, encouraging me on my way, 'look at Stanegarth Hall. It's from the 1680s. The builder had lived through civil war. He would have seen the disturbances in Scotland. It's only eighty years after the Union of the Crowns. And the end of reiving. It's a tower house, with a little courtyard in the middle, big windows. There's a crow-step gable – very Scottish-looking. You don't get those further into England. It was never roofed and glazed. If things had become good, they would have roofed. If it had got really bad, they would have bricked up the big windows. But things here have clearly never been quite good nor bad enough.'

76

Behind Christopher's romance, and Trevor's learning, behind the ballads and the heritage signs posted in the village hall, stood the figure of Walter Scott. He was born in Edinburgh in 1778, the son of a lawyer, whom Scott portrayed as an eighteenth-century pedant in a wig, cautiously shuffling between his law books. Walter Scott too became an Edinburgh lawyer. But his heart was with the sixteenth-century Border reivers – in particular, with his great-great-great-great-great-great grandfather Wat Scott of Harden.

Scott, who had been lame from childhood, forced himself to take arduous journeys on foot to recover the history of the reivers. In 1803, for example, he walked for three weeks through the Ettrick and Yarrow valleys of the border, 'in defiance of mountains, rivers, and bogs, damp and dry', feeding off a dead sheep on one mountainside. Washington Irving gives us a sense of Scott in motion:

> His dress was simple, and almost rustic. An old green shooting-coat, with a dog-whistle at the buttonhole, brown linen pantaloons, stout shoes that tied at the ankles, and a white hat that had evidently seen service. He came limping up the gravel walk, aiding himself by a stout walking-staff, but moving rapidly and with vigour.

He was often accompanied by Hamlet, a young greyhound, Finette, 'a beautiful setter, with soft, silken hair, long pendant ears, and a mild eye', a superannuated greyhound and a 'little shame-faced terrier with glass eyes' – whose names are sadly not recorded. Like my father he enjoyed talking to his dogs, and speculating at length on their pretensions. Maida, his staghound, whom he compared to 'the great gun of Constantinople', was too pompous to allow herself to be seen playing by the 'laird', but, he suspected, played when no one was looking.

On his Border walk in 1803, Scott found that the isolation and poverty of Border valleys had preserved forty-two 'Border ballads' which had never been previously recorded. They were not a 'pure' set of oral texts preserved unbroken from the Middle Ages. Some, it seemed, had been printed on broadsheets in the sixteenth century; some bore the marks of improvement by aristocratic poets in the early eighteenth century; others had been part of the repertory of travelling minstrels. But they had been passed down from generation to generation, and the people who sung them felt they were singing local songs about their local landscape.

Scott rediscovered not only the ruined fortress which had once been Blackwood Tower, but also the ballad in which it features as the home of the seven Douglas brothers, who were slain one after another by their sister's lover. He walked the patch of ground by the edge of St Mary's Loch, where in the same ballad the lover had tried to conceal the drips of blood from his mortal wound.

> Tis naething but the shadow o' my scarlet cloak
> That shines in the water sae plain.

Scott recruited a team to help collect these Border ballads, led by a poet-shepherd from Yarrow called James Hogg; and his best informant was Hogg's mother herself, who could recite many hundreds of these verses. Scott then dove into the archives in Edinburgh to find the context for these songs. He searched letters and chronicles, re-thickening the stories that shadowed the Marches and the Middleland, reviving dead men. He placed the memory of ancient oaks back onto treeless slopes. He linked rivers to struggling cavalrymen, rocks to long-forgotten ambushes, and found in sorry piles of stones the foundations of infamous pele towers.

Just as later Victorians took inspiration from the values of Rome, so Scott used the ethos of sixteenth-century 'Border chivalry' to shape his nineteenth-century life. His new house – heated and lit with the very latest technology – was built in the form of a Border castle. Its name was an exercise in medieval aspiration: Abbotsford. (The original name of the place meant 'muddy hole'.) When his publishing company collapsed shortly after he moved in, leaving him with immense debts, his sense of Border chivalry and honour encouraged him to rebuff gifts from his adoring public, including even the king. Instead he struggled for years to repay all the money in full from the proceeds of his writing. Like a modern American general adopting the mantle of a warrior-monk, Scott arranged his life on the model of a reiver from an alien society.

Scott believed so fiercely in his vision of these places, fringed them so enticingly with such 'local attachments' and oral history, that the Border landscape became irresistible to later Scottish writers. Robert Louis Stevenson put the birthplace of a hero in one of these Border valleys. John Buchan put the home of his Arabic-speaking, hard-travelling, aristocratic Scottish spy Richard Hannay in another. Scott's Borders – like Scott's Highlands – became a central component of Scottishness, often contrasted with an England that was supposed to lack such romance and local history.

The real Border culture of the sixteenth century, however, had resisted such national divisions. The differences that mattered in the Marches had not been national but tribal. English and Scottish reivers had sung the same ballads, changing only the clan names. The hero of 'Jamie Telfer of Fair Dodhead' was an Elliot in one version, an Armstrong in another and – in Sir Walter's favourite – a Scott. Far more copies of Scott's work were sold in England than in Scotland. And a new generation of nationalist writers soon saw that such attitudes to nation, soil and oral history could be applied right across Scotland, Wales, England and Ireland – and ultimately from the Balkans to Lithuania.

For a century after Scott's death, guidebooks inspired visitors to seek the presence of such legends in every ruin and valley across Europe, rooting romantic history in local soils. Tens of thousands of English monographs and parish histories took their tone from Walter Scott. The idea of local attachments became a cornerstone of the 'British' identity – an identity Scots and English alike carried to empire and war, and which partly helped to bind them together.

Scott had, however, captured the dying echoes of the Border minstrels, in a landscape which was already largely an evacuated wilderness. In 1830 the local minister, James Russell, whose father had been minister of Yarrow before him, described how the beetles had wiped out the grass pasture in Yarrow in repeated years, and how it was 200 years since there had been any trees, deer, badgers or even foxes. Most of the people had left the poor thin soil, leaving only abandoned foundations and ghost-furrows.

By 1830, when Scott visited the Yarrow valley again, this time bringing Wordsworth, nothing was left. Russell recorded in the same year that the ballads – and the superstitions – had been utterly forgotten. There was no one to point out the goblin's haunt, the knight's demise or the leaping hart. He observed: 'Local attachments had given way to general knowledge.'

Russell added that the final blow to the oral tradition had been Scott's efforts to collect and preserve the verses. Hogg's mother, who had known so many, complained:

> There was never ane o' my sangs prentit till ye prentit them yourself; and ye have spoilt them awthegither. They were made for singin' and no' for readin; but ye have broken the charm now, an' they'll never be sung mair.

77

Trevor Telford's family claimed its own Border ballad, the one about Jamie Telfer of Fair Dodhead. It described how – apparently sometime in the early 1500s – reivers had stolen kine from Jamie, and how Jamie had then tried to call all his neighbours to mount a revenge attack against Bewcastle. Many suspected the tale had been not only found but 'improved' by Walter Scott.

By 1700 the Telfords had moved from Dodhead in Scotland to the Bewcastle valley in England. They were poor people, and the land-holdings had become smaller over the years. Their fortunes had only been saved when they married well, acquiring a relative who rose to be the head of the Indian veterinary service. 'My grandfather joined the army and also went to India, and when he came back he married my grandmother Nora Foster from Mosstone. So that's how we're further down the valley,' explained Trevor.

We walked past the Presbyterian kirk that his family had built in the brief days of its prosperity, a rare sight in Anglican England, and a reminder of how Scottish they had once felt. But they had not remained Presbyterian. 'My grandfather wanted to be cremated and have his ashes spread on the farm,' he said. 'He'd seen in the army in India how everything had to do with religion. He wanted no part of religion.'

Most of the farms Trevor showed me had been Routledge farms. 'Colin Charnock's house at Cumcrook was a Routledge house. So was the house of the Kerrs. They'll all be related. That's the problem with the Routledge family, they didn't really get on with other families, so they didn't marry out of their own family. About a hundred years ago a lot of imperfections came in because they married cousins just to keep property in the family, and there aren't many Routledges left now.' I put this down, perhaps unfairly, to some long-held Telford prejudice about the challenge of marrying a Routledge heiress.

And although I learned a great deal from Trevor about the families and about reiving over the three hours we walked together, he did not convey to me, a visitor, the extent of the killing that had once defined life in this valley. The dry administrative lists, which I saw later, recorded for example attempts to exterminate entire clans.

Take the report in idiosyncratic spelling sent to London listing only some of the casualties of a raid in this valley, probably led by some of Walter Scott's ancestors, in 1583. From Comcrauke – Colin Charnock's farm at Cumcrook – to Lukknes (Low Luckens, the 'yoghurt weavers') beside Christopher's, through Todhills, Bailey Head and Sleetbeck, you could still trace most of the place-names on a map today. The phrase 'of the same' reflected the fathers, sons (Jamie and young Jamie) and brothers from a single household:

> John Rutledge of the Cructborne, slayne by the Scottish ryders. Gerrey his sonne; Andrew Rutledge of the same; Dikes Rowe Rutledge; Jeme Rutledge of the Neuk; Jeme Rutledge of the Stubbe; Jeme Rutledge called yonge Jeme; Jarre Rutledge of the Stubbe; Thome Rutledge of Todhills; Allane of the same; Dike Rutledge of the Baley heade; Thome Rutledge of the same. All theise dwell downe the water of Levne. John Ruttlidge of the Black Dobs; Nicoll Rutlidge his brother; Andrewe Rutlidge called Black stafe; Gourthe Rutledge of Sletbeke; Jeme Ruttlidge of the

> same; Will Ruttlidge of Comcrauke; Riche of the same; Johne of the same; Jeme Rutledge of the same; John Ruttlidge of Troughed; Riche Rutlidge of the same; John Rutlidge of the same; Allan Rutlidge his brother; John Dodshone, slayne by the Scottes; Willie Rutlidge of the Lukknes. And manie more that I omyt for tedyousness to your honor.

★

I took the high road, on the east side of the Bailey–Bewcastle valley, heading north towards the border. On my right, despite the torrential rain, the grass was so brown that the standard trees, standing out bare on the earth banks, seemed part of an African savannah. I passed stumps of grey, dead trees: the forest seemed to have been torched, but no attempts had been made to burn back the reeds, plant new grasses or drain.

Duncan Telford, Trevor's forty-five-year-old cousin, met me at his farm. He was wearing military trousers. There was a simple earring in his left ear.

'Do you want a beer?' Duncan asked. It was ten in the morning.

He explained he had built the standing stones – a mock Neolithic circle – as a place where he and his friend Crud (who lived in Duncan's caravan) could drink, chat and smoke 'whatever I roll'.

On a highly polished Georgian dining table inside his farmhouse he had laid out photocopies of copperplate parish records, family trees and letters, and another ballad, set in the valley. It was called 'The Fray of Suport'. Walter Scott knew four very different versions of it:

> Of all the Border ditties which have fallen into the Editor's hands, this is by far the most uncouth and savage. It is usually chaunted in a sort of wild recitative, except the burden, which swells into a long and varied howl . . . 'Fy, lads! shout a' a' a' a' a' / My gear's a' gane.'

The narrator of the ballad was a sixteenth-century English widow – probably, judging by the geographical references, a Routledge – who had lived a couple of miles from Duncan's farmhouse. A Scot, presumably her lover, from the other side of the border had been sleeping over when Scottish reivers attacked. He had been run through the thigh, trying to defend her. Her song was one long shrieking demand for every neighbour on every farm to join her in a reprisal raid.

As I read the ballad, Duncan would interrupt to discuss the names of the farms. 'Where's the Berwicken Hill? The Grahams was Berwicken Hill.'

He was particularly taken with the ambush place which the Routledge woman had chosen in response to the raid. He reckoned she had blocked every ford and crossing point (so comprehensively that I suspected the song was used as a memory aid for later ambushes):

> Ah, lads, we'll fang them a' in a net,
> For I hae a' the ford o' Liddel set:
> The Dunkin and the Door-loup,
> The Willie-ford, and the Water-slack,
> The Black-rack and the Trout-dud of Liddel.

'Yes, that's the fastest route,' said Duncan. 'If you spoke to local fellas they would know. The Boogly Holla', well, that's just another nickname of the hollow. The byres and store buildings, we still call them bow holes.'

Duncan had persuaded the pony-trekking company from the next farm at Bailey Mill to lend us two horses. His was a full two hands higher than mine. We rode up Tarras Moss. It was said that the Routledges could hide almost 300 of their family members in the gullies and the tunnels cut into the moss. I hadn't believed this until I saw the ground.

The upper slopes were still split with peat hags; again and again we had to turn the horses round to try to find a path through streams, through bog, through gullies. Rather than splash, my pony preferred to jump dramatically – clearing the stream by at least four feet. Duncan's ancestors who specialised in navigating this moss had been known as moss-troopers. But Duncan did not seem completely comfortable on his horse. He kept rolling and smoking to calm himself.

Duncan had a reiving tattoo, and had called his son Reeve. He liked the fact that they still used the old nicknames, calling people after their farms, or after other things. 'Look at the names,' said Duncan, 'Colin Charnock of Cumcrook; Buggerback; Nebless Clem.'

'What is your nickname?' I asked.

Duncan pushed his hair back from his earring, took his hands from the reins and rolled another cigarette. 'What do you think?' he asked, grinning. I had no idea.

As we rode, he sang two verses of a song about the Bewcastle reiver Hobie Noble. There were places in this peatland where even Hobie was forced to dismount:

He has guided them o'er moss and muir,
O'er hill and hope, and mony a down;
Until they came to the Foulbogshiel,
And there, brave Noble, he lighted down.

In Foulbogshiel, Duncan explained, Hobie had been ambushed by the land-serjeant of Askerton, captured and hanged at Carlisle. He made it sound like *Butch Cassidy and the Sundance Kid*.

Yet the government archives of the time implied that the essence of this lost world was not chivalry but brutality. In 1596 John Carey, a leading frontier official, had sent a raid into Scotland to punish a horse-rustler. They broke into his house and without any attempt to arrest the rustler or try him, cut him to pieces. In his defence of his actions to the queen's chief minster, Carey wrote:

> And my good lord, for your honour's better satisfaction, that it was not so barbarously nor butcherly done as you think it to be. It should seem your honour hath been wrongfully informed, in saying he was cut in many pieces after his death – for if he had been cut in many pieces, he could not have lived till the next morning, which themselves reported he did – which shows he was not cut in very many pieces.

78

Two miles from where I'd parted ways with Duncan I walked up a small grass hill. Looking west from the edge of the hill, the bleached wastes rolled, without a hamlet and with hardly a tree, to the dark green smudge of Kielder Forest on the horizon. Behind me in the empty moorland were a dozen places reinvested with human life by Walter Scott: from the ford where the widow set the trap for the reivers, to the bog where Hobie Noble was betrayed by Sim o' the Mains.

On the hill stood a church, a rectory, a farm and two houses. This was the heart of Bewcastle, home of the Routledges, of Duncan's Telford ancestors and of Hobie the reiver. Generally in Britain places get bigger over time: hamlets become cities, the stone of the old buildings is quarried for new structures, and foundations vanish beneath an underground car park. The Fleet River in London, which once welcomed ships, becomes a sewer. Or, as at my father's home in Crieff, the town expands to overrun the Neolithic cursus line, and the chieftain's mini-mansion finds itself in a suburban housing estate.

But here at Bewcastle the opposite had happened. I was standing back on the Roman fort, the shrine of Cocidius, where a Roman officer had dedicated an altar to a local god, which I had visited a year earlier with my father. Two thousand years ago Bewcastle was one of the most populated sites in the British Isles, with 2,000 soldiers crammed on the mound alone. Its location was carefully recorded in a 1,600-year-old document written in Ravenna, the capital of the western Roman Empire.

Thirteen hundred years ago the fort at Bewcastle appears to have been converted into the site of a prestigious Anglo-Saxon monastery. Five hundred years ago, it had one of the largest fortified buildings in the Marches, and was the seat of a royal captain and his garrison, appointed directly by the Crown. But by 1811, only a small population remained, spread thinly over the surrounding forty square miles. This community shrank by a further two-thirds between 1811 and 2011. It had lost its religious significance when the Northumbrians were destroyed by the Vikings; it had lost its military significance for the first time when the Roman wall was abandoned, and for the second time when the English–Scottish border ceased to be defended; and finally it had lost most of its farmers. According to the most recent census, only six people now lived on the Bewcastle mound.

Because the settlement had been reduced over the centuries, unusually in our crowded industrialised island, the ancient past here had not been quarried, reused or buried. On the almost empty plain I could still see the lines of the Roman fort, built on the sacred Celtic shrine, the towering walls of the medieval castle, and the Anglo-Saxon cross, poking above a stack of silage and the tin roof of an agricultural shed. Beyond them stood a cluster of sandstone headstones recording the names of Duncan and Trevor Telford's reiving ancestors. (In 1912, a visitor observed there were far more women than men on the headstones in Bewcastle churchyard. The sexton replied, 'What happened the men? Wey, the men were a' hangit at weary Carlisle!')

My father came down from Scotland to join me for dinner that night. I had not seen him for two weeks. 'Now I've got you to myself,' he said, 'tell me all about it.' I told him about the journey thus far, pedantically listing every night's stop, and as much as I could remember about the weather and the terrain. I talked for almost an hour and a half. And it would have been pretty dry stuff.

'At first, in the Lake District, I was mostly in cloud and fog. On the seventh day, I turned inland, past an ancient abbey, recently burned. On the eighth day, I stopped walking and stayed in a housing estate. These days were all cloudy and windy. Then I turned north towards the Solway . . .'

But through it all, he kept his eyes fixed on mine, nodding and occasionally reaching out to hold my hand, stroking his dry fingers over my knuckles. I had forgotten how good he was at listening. And at encouraging a story: 'More history, darling. The most important aspect of your walk is that it fills in a few of the gaps in our knowledge of British history – national history and identity. Tell us more about the history of Bewcastle.'

'We don't really know much,' I said. I could feel myself becoming defensive again.

'Come on, darling, a flavour will do.'

'Well, as I think I told you on Hadrian's Wall, in about AD 100 this mound was the shrine of Cocidius – the god depicted by the Romans like a cockroach in battledress. And this may then have been the territory of the Carvetii tribe. Then it became a giant Roman fort.'

'What does Carvetii mean?'

'It's guesswork, but perhaps the "Deer People".'

'Many deer round here?'

'Not any more.' I paused.

'On with the story – faster and funnier . . . The Carvetii sound pretty primitive to me . . .' said my father. 'Headhunters, I presume?'

'Archaeologists aren't keen on emphasising that – it makes the Iron Age Britons sound a little . . .'

He was smiling, but looked a little tired, and I was not sure how satisfied he was with any of these academic uncertainties. 'I'm not sure anyone is very interested in chunks of history, Daddy,' I said.

Here he put on an Irish voice. 'Don't confuse me with the facts, my mind is made up already. Onwards: then the Romans left . . .'

'Well, the Northumbrians took over this Roman fort and erected a Christian stone column on top of the pagan shrine. And they had selected perhaps the wildest, least promising and most remote location in their kingdom, but the column, or rather obelisk, they made here was the best thing they ever produced. It still stands exactly where they placed it. And – despite the never-ending rain of Bewcastle, running for centuries down the face – you can still see how sharp and exact the carving was. The south side of the Bewcastle Cross is an endless knot, intersecting whorls without an end.'

'Meaning?'

'Something like the endless chain of existence. The west side includes a chequerboard like a plaid – an acknowledgement, perhaps, of their Cumbric-Celtic neighbours. But on the east side are vine leaves, bursting around each other, which had been copied from Byzantium, 2,000 miles away. And on the north, a figure in a cloak leaning forward towards a hawk on a stand, with Christ treading the beasts of the wilderness above him. Pevsner called it the greatest piece of sculpture produced in Europe in the seventh century.'

'That's the stuff,' said my father. 'Perhaps we should say, "The Dark Ages after the Romans left were not entirely dark; there were some extraordinary flashes of light." '

'This bleak Middleland became,' said I, warming to my theme, 'the intellectual crucible of Europe in the eighth century. They built the largest library and church north of the Alps. They transformed understanding of tidal movements, refined Latin prose, produced the best histories and trained men whom popes and emperors competed to employ. No other civilisation has made such an unpromising landscape such a catalyst for seriousness.'

'Wonderful. No one knows any of this.' My father didn't like Dark Ages and he loved new intelligence.

79

The next day my father drove back to Scotland and I spent another day walking around the Bewcastle valley. I stayed the night with Steve Pattinson in his farmhouse, three miles from the Bewcastle Cross. He laid a fire for me, next to which I dried my clothes, because it had been raining hard. The next morning he took me out to his dairy parlour. What had been a pagan holy site, an imperial frontier, a centre of European sculpture and a cockpit of reivers was now a pastoral landscape of farms, few larger than a hundred acres.

Three days earlier, in Longtown, I had been on a 700-acre farm. There, a staff of five milked 1,000 cows three times a day on a twenty-four-hour cycle, producing 10 million litres of milk a year. Here in Bewcastle, Steve had a hundred acres and sixty cows. His parlour was still in a stone shed, the machinery was more than fifty years old, and he joked that he was 'welding rust' to try to keep it going. He was supplementing his income by breeding a special new type of cow, the vast-shouldered 'British Blue', and had won a prize. But the market for the breed had been smaller than he had hoped. And with wet summer after wet summer, it was difficult to see how he could get the grass to finish his cows.

Despite this impossible situation, one thing was clear: Steve and the other farmers did not intend to move. They were fixed to the soil, and they were determined to live by farming. The only question was whether the younger generation would agree to take these farms on when the time arrived. They would have to give the farms to their own sons and daughters, because no young person could afford to buy a farm – the houses were too valuable as retirement homes, and the value of even poor land had increased fivefold in the previous twenty years. The survival of these small farms depended on a slender line of succession through families.

Steve and his friends Colin Charnock and Trevor Telford were not prepared to just abandon the land or 'lightly' ranch it, and find a second income. They continued to put what savings they had into buying new fields, and borrowed to buy more. They had continued to lime the soil. They had killed the weeds, and burned the reeds, and drained, and planted better varieties of grasses. The rain had wrecked all that they had done over the previous four years, but they were going to do it all over again. After foot and mouth had wiped out all their herds ten years ago, Steve had not taken the compensation and left farming – although the government seemed to want to encourage this. Instead he had collected reconditioned computers for farmers, run IT training courses, built a website for the valley primary school and invested in more stock and better grass seed. His next ambition was to make and market a Bewcastle cheese, selling it in London.

Steve's son was ten. He seemed – it might have been his age – less physically robust than his father. Steve had given him a calf to look after, hoping that his son would fall in love with cows. On this boy depended the future, because if he did not take over, the likelihood was that the land would turn to reeds, and finally forestry.

But there were still a few men like Steve's friend Colin Charnock. Colin had moved to the area, married a farmer's daughter and embraced this life. It seemed, from the way that Steve spoke about him, that he had been embraced in turn.

'Why did Colin think of moving up here? They came up from Lancashire, didn't they?'

'The community was dying there as well, but he thinks it's great up here.'

'He prefers it?'

'It's more built to his mentality, he just fits in, he's done very well for himself . . . roaming about and doing his own thing without anybody scrutinising him. You're freer up here. Absolutely. Nobody bothers you and you can do what you want.'

While I was standing in the yard by Steve's red sandstone milking parlours, Colin drove in on his quad bike, with a child sitting on the handlebars. Colin was six foot four and weighed 250 pounds. He dwarfed the quad bike – looking as though he was riding a child's push car. He had a shock of blond hair and broad pink cheeks. You could see why Steve had named his vast muscled prize bull after him.

Colin pointed down to the fencing, and the standing water through which I'd struggled that morning. He said a government agency had spotted a rare orchid in his field so they had built an expensive fence around it, to keep the sheep away. The orchid inside the fence died, but another sprang up outside the fence. So they had built another fence around the new orchid. It too had died. Then another had sprung up in the open field alongside. The government had spent tens of thousands of pounds on fencing. It turned out that the orchid only grew if it was on land grazed by sheep. If the land was fenced off and protected, he claimed, the wild orchid died.

80

At Routledge Burn by Kershopefoot, I left England again and re-entered Scotland. This was the fifth time that I had crossed the border in a few days – once on the Solway, once at Gretna, and again, back and forth, at the Debatable Lands. This border, now open, and unmarked, had been from the thirteenth century until 1604 a closed military frontier, which could only be crossed with special permission. It was tempting to imagine, therefore, that the two sides of the border would have been much more starkly different in the late Middle Ages than they were today. But the opposite was the case. In reality, the closed military frontier had created an almost identical culture on both sides.

The English and the Scottish Crowns had pursued the same policies across the Marches. England used its Border clans to create a destabilised wasteland in Scotland, and Scotland repaid them in kind. The administrative documents are remarkably precise records of officially endorsed cross-border arson, theft and murder. One letter in 1542, for example, shows the English Warden of the Marches itemising the orders he had given to individual Border clans – including the Routledges of the Bewcastle valley – to burn specific Scottish villages.

> Details of fourteen exploits, viz., (1) Houses burnt in Jedworth by Nyxsones, 20 Oct. (2) Houses burnt in Awyke, a market town in Tevedall, by Nyxsones and Nobylls, Scots, the same night . . . (7) Fosters and Routledges burnt Cassilhyll and Reyhilles in West Tevedall.

The reivers, who raided back and forth across the same terrain for the same reasons, dressed and lived in the same way. It was almost impossible for an outsider to distinguish a reiver from one side of the border – buckskin-clad, with his lance, pony, steel bonnet and Border ballads – from a reiver on the other side of the border. Scots and English Borderers intermarried, although the government tried to prohibit them from doing so. And they collaborated in smuggling, in raids, in protection rackets, while pretending to be enemies to their governments. And over a 300-year period they created a single landscape of fortified pele towers, bastle houses and mud huts, set in a repeatedly brutalised and looted wasteland.

Throughout this period, the English and Scottish wardens claimed – like my father in Penang, or indeed my colleagues and I in Iraq and Afghanistan – to be bringing peace and security to the Marches. Different officers tried different combinations of incentive and punishment – disarming clans one moment, re-employing them as government militia the next, punishing, bribing, dividing and ruling, employing the stock tactics of counter-insurgency which would have been recognisable to their Roman predecessors, living amongst the same stones, on Hadrian's Wall.

Some of the wardens invested in learning about their subjects: living among the reivers and dressing like them, writing detailed descriptions of Border culture, and compiling encyclopaedic accounts of Border genealogies and clan strengths. They boasted how their deep knowledge and personal relations allowed them to manage the instability. But none of this energy or ingenuity made any lasting difference. Wardens came and went for 300 years – young adventurers like Carey, ancient veterans like Foster – people who kept their distance, people who 'went native'. And by 1600 the situation was if anything worse than it had been 200 years earlier.

The officers blamed the failure on the Borderers themselves. They would have claimed the Borderers were an inherently treacherous people, beyond redemption or policy, stuck in the Middle Ages, and trapped by 'centuries of ethnic hatred'. If anyone thought there was any hope – after 300 years – of pacifying the area, they would have implied that they didn't understand the Borders and they hadn't read any history. The Borders would never be peaceful because they were occupied by, in Camden's words, a 'martial kind of men'.

I had heard governments make similar claims about the people of the Balkans or Afghanistan. But, in truth, in all these places, it was not the fault of the local people. The violence was fundamentally driven by governments. And the people were victims. So long as there were two rival states, side by side, trying to undermine each other, border clans were inevitably pawns, if occasionally cheerful pawns, in proxy wars. Security was impossible because the conflict between England and Scotland took precedence over security. If a warden arrested a bandit for theft or murder, he would often be freed again on the argument that he could be useful in some other way – as a bargaining chip, or as a spy, or as a raider against the rival territory. (So too in Afghanistan it proved impossible to arrest the largest drug-dealer in the south in 2008, in part because he was being used by international intelligence agencies as a counterbalance to Pakistan, and an intelligence source on the Taliban.)

There was only one lasting solution to the problem: to bring England and Scotland into a single country and abolish the border. When the Crowns were finally unified in 1604, the violence ended rapidly. James VI convinced himself, and many later historians, that he had achieved security by hanging Grahams, Armstrongs and others in a system called Jedburgh justice: 'hang first and try later'. But brutality had been tried many times before with little effect. In truth, security suddenly became much easier because there was no longer a border, and therefore no longer two competing neighbouring states, and no longer a proxy war. These bandits clanking around with their old swords, celebrating themselves in ballads, had ceased to be useful government agents and had just become an embarrassment. James VI and I's most important policy decision was not his executions, or later deportations of the Border clans, it was his decision to turn a frontier into what he called 'the navel or umbilic of both kingdoms'. He decreed that the Marches were henceforth to be called the 'Middle Shires' of a single, unified Britain. In 1640, army recruiting sergeants were disappointed to discover that, after two generations of peace, it was very difficult to find anyone in the Borders interested in being paid to fight.

But paradoxically, at the very moment that the border ceased to be a military frontier or a barrier to movement, the two sides, which had been almost indistinguishable, began to grow apart. Now, crossing the border at Kershopefoot, I saw the landscape had changed dramatically. I had hardly seen such a stark difference since I walked from Lahore to Amritsar in half a day, through land which had been a single province – Punjab – in a single country, but was now partitioned. On the Pakistani side scrub grew from brown, dry earth; on the Indian side – thanks to generous irrigation – were brilliant green fields of crops, lined with eucalyptus trees, sucking thirstily at the water table.

Here too, within fifty yards of entering Scotland, the rough, sour ground of England, its small family farms and ruined bastle houses had been replaced by wide, open ground and fewer, newer houses. The grass was much greener. There were no reeds to be seen.

Peace and law had created differences which had not existed in war. Even after the Crowns and parliaments had been unified, the English and Scottish legal systems remained separate and this law extended precisely to the point of the old, now almost invisible, border. On the south side, English customs, contracts and laws turned the old 'Border tenancies' (rent paid through fighting) into copyhold tenancies, which could still be passed down in a family. Without a border and therefore without a need for armed men, the tenancies had little value to the landlords and many tenancies were sold to the small tenants. And the small tenants held on to them, or even divided them up between their sons, creating a patchwork of smallholdings, in which farmhouses were built on top of the old bastle houses and pele towers. Such was the origin of the landscape of Bailey and Bewcastle.

But in a peculiar combination of feudal reaction and enlightenment theory, Scottish law favoured large estates and did not support copyhold inheritance. This made it easy for the formal landowner, who no longer needed armed horsemen to defend the border, to clear the small tenant farmers and 'rationalise' their land into larger blocks. These blocks were always passed down to the eldest son of the eldest son of the landowner, who could through careful management, royal favour and marriage accumulate over 100,000 acres of land which could then be re-issued to new tenants in much larger blocks – more efficient for agricultural production.

As a result, the small farmers on the Scottish side of the border began to disappear, shortly after the Union of the Crowns in the seventeenth century, and had almost entirely vanished by the early nineteenth century. As these small farmers – called 'cotters' in Scotland – went, so too did the rough, sour ground and the ruined bastle houses, which once lay at the heart of their small farms. In their place came large, drained, improved and centrally managed agricultural businesses.

This 'clearance' of the Scottish Borders had been handled better than many similar ones in the Highlands. Here, in the Borders, a duke had built a weaving town in the 1790s, and relocated the remaining small farmers to neat stone houses in the town. These houses were larger and better built than the mud huts from which the families came; the wages were perhaps better than what they made off the land. But the clearance left a mark on the landscape more permanent than the killing of almost all the Routledges in the Bailey valley. When I crossed the border into Scotland, I had left dank soil and reeds and stepped onto a large, well-drained, bright field of grass with hardly a reed-bed or farmhouse in sight, the first of several 2,000-acre tenanted blocks of a Scottish ducal estate.

The descendants of the small Scottish 'cotter' farmers who had not left the area entirely now worked in the garages, hotels and shops of Newcastleton. In a shed half a mile down the hill into Scotland was 'Telford's Bus Company'. I got no greeting, no smile, no handshake as I approached. I explained that I had been with Telfords a mile away. But these men had Scottish accents, and did not seem to recognise or feel any kinship with the Telfords in England. They moved off, saying they had a van to wash. Then one of them turned and said, abruptly, 'You'll be knowing Duncan.'

Scottish Newcastleton, the weaving town built by the duke to house his relocated farmers, turned out to be a formal eighteenth-century town, with large squares and well-finished Georgian houses, surrounded by broad sunlit fields. Coming across the bridge, I stopped at the heritage centre, which held the giant sword of the ballad hero Hobie Noble. Inside, the posters tried to insist that little had changed. Half a dozen people busied themselves completing the last preparations for 'Scotland's best kept village' competition.

Outside, red geraniums hung in baskets from every lamp-post. The judges were about to arrive. I stood with the village committee while they waited. They told me that they didn't want independence. An older man demanded to know who would tax his army pension. Mrs Dobson wondered whether Scotland would be on a different time zone if 'Yes' prevailed.

'We've got good Berwick names,' she continued. 'We're not Scots, we're not English, we're Borderers.'

Another lady interrupted and disagreed. She said there was in fact no difference between the Borders and the rest of Britain. 'I can't even understand independence,' she said. 'Nothing changes crossing the border.'

They shared these views in distinct Scottish accents.

81

In Newcastleton, I found Duncan Telford in the pub. This was surprising. I thought he had been banned from all the pubs in the town. But he had come across from the English side of the border with his cousin Trevor, his neighbour Steve, his friend Crud who lived in Duncan's caravan, and his wife, son and daughter, to meet me for a final drink before I left the area. Big Colin Charnock, who was often with them, was absent: 'South, buying cattle.' Duncan had also brought Philip Howard with him. Philip's family had lived for forty-one consecutive generations in the English Border castle of Naworth. He was talking cheerfully to Duncan about the 'Hanging Tree', on his land, on which his ancestor had hanged some Armstrongs.

'Sixty-three in two years,' he said proudly. 'We've another tree, on which my father always assured me we hung forty-six members of the Hay family – which was another good day. We had seven separate dungeons but, sadly, that wing got burned down. We've only got one dungeon left.'

A man with a miniature bagpipe joined us. None of us had ever seen such an instrument before. Its bag was about the size of a grapefruit, and he filled it not with his lips but with a wooden bellows. The piper had a gaunt face, a goatee and a long white ponytail. He told us – in an Essex accent – that this was a 'Border' bagpipe. This man from near London was reintroducing Borderers to their own 'traditions'.

The man began with a ballad about Johnnie Armstrong, whose tower I had seen at Gilnockie, and who had been hanged in his golden clothes by the Scottish king in 1530. Duncan's son was provided with a pair of drumsticks to beat on the pub table. Rather shyly we tried to sing along. His was a different version of 'The Ballad of Johnnie Armstrong':

There dwelt a man in faire Westmerland,
Ionn Armestrong men did him call,

He had nither lands nor rents coming in,
Yet he kept eight score men in his hall.

The singer's accent when he sang was not Essex but American and the tune was unmistakably Country and Western. This, he argued, was historically correct. Many of the Border reivers had been forcibly transported to Ireland after James VI and I had unified the Crowns, and then emigrated as 'Scots-Irish' to the United States, bringing their ballads with them. Walter Scott's successors found that the oral traditions of Border ballads had survived better in the Appalachian mountains than in the Borders. They formed the foundation of the American folk music tradition.

I suspected that the singer was wrong about the Border reivers having sung in an American accent. Duncan, however, was more focused on the story told in the verses.

'The only way to sort them oot is hang 'em and hang Johnnie and all his men and all, simple as that I would think,' said Duncan.

'But who was the bigger villain?' asked the piper.

'The king . . . the government,' Duncan suggested.

Although Newcastleton was in Scotland, and Duncan lived in England, he insisted they were all still part of one reiving culture. But nothing in the pub seemed to reflect this. On a table beside us was a middle-aged couple from Melrose, and beyond them two water engineers from Edinburgh. They kept staring at Crud, who had come out in full combat fatigues. He looked very pale, and was not singing. Duncan sat Reeve on his lap and, while singing, they began to play a drum roll together, quite well. No one else in the pub joined in.

Now the singer performed the ballad of Duncan's ancestor Jamie Telfer of Fair Dodhead. This was bold, since there were four different versions, each one of which blamed a different family for betraying him. In this version, the villains were the Elliots, whose chief still lived four miles out of town. Jamie had been raided. The call to arms to rescue his flock covered every valley in a hundred square miles. In the ballad were the names of Scottish farms which were now nothing but a faint trace of stone in the reeds, and of English farms which were still farms today:

Warn Gaudilands, and Allanhaugh,
And Gilmanscleugh, and Commonside.
Ride by the gate at Priesthaughswire,
And warn the Currors o' the Lee.

Duncan liked the tradition of reiver nicknames: 'Currors o' the Lee', 'Buggerback', or his ancestors 'Jamie over the moss' and 'Jock of the corner'. He was wearing a baseball cap and a T-shirt which said 'Redneck warrior'. He was looking relaxed, so I asked him again what his nickname was. This time he told me.

'Dunk the Punk,' he replied.

82

Walking out of Newcastleton, I passed a lady who was sitting on the pavement in the sun, scraping away at her pebble-dashed wall (another hint that I had crossed the border, as it was less common for Cumbrians to put cement and pebbles on their walls). She had revealed beautiful pale yellow sandstone beneath the render, but regulations compelled her to reinstate the pebble-dash.

She said she was from Texas. Her great-uncle had traced a thirteenth cousin – an Armstrong – in Newcastleton. She had come over to visit him, and married him. 'He wouldn't leave, so I moved here twenty-four years ago.'

I turned up a road that led alongside the Hermitage Water. A mile upstream, I took off my boots and waded the clear stream, scrambling up the far bank onto a drive. I followed it, barefoot, till I passed a white house with the crest of the Elliots above the lintel.

The crest had been imported from a now abandoned Elliot castle on the Borders. Just north of the house, the flat land at the valley floor became much narrower, barely one field wide. There were no longer homes to be seen on the wet slopes. Curlew cried, corbies flew. At a narrow bridge I was forced to climb the railings, away from the swinging horns of a stampede of Dexters, black Galloways and blue-grey cattle.

This had once been a densely settled region. In 1376, the slope along which I was travelling held, according to a contemporary legal document, '157 settlements, freeholds, and other portions of land'. The surrounding valley had held as many as 5,000 people. Today there was only a bare wet hill and an excited herd of cattle. I found one pile of stones, but nothing that I could be certain was the remains of a house. Thanks to some combination of poor soil, Scottish law, Scottish landlords and a lack of income from cattle-raiding now the border was gone, almost two-thirds of the people had left by 1625.

Then, across the boulders of the fast-flowing river, a turn in the curving valley floor revealed the square block of Hermitage Castle. No roof remained above its stark, undecorated eighty-foot walls. Sir Walter Scott chose to be painted by Henry Raeburn in front of the castle in 1808, and used the image as the frontispiece for his collected works. Its medieval owner had been boiled alive. Scott wrote:

> The Castle of Hermitage, unable to support the load of iniquity which had long been accumulating within its walls, is supposed to have partly sunk beneath the ground; and its ruins are still regarded by the peasants with peculiar aversion and terror.

Now the Liddesdale valley is defined not by the presence of human memories, however horrifying, but by their absence. Most of the 'peasants' had moved away long before Scott had driven his carriage up to the Hermitage. He wouldn't have seen the 157 homes of the fourteenth century; not even a tenth of that number.

Since then, writers had become ever more manic in their refusal to acknowledge the disappearance of the traditional community and the historical connections in the valley. In the 1920s they had stepped out at the railway station, two miles away, driven in cars through a landscape which had been peaceful for 300 years, and almost empty for the last 200, and then, standing by the castle, 'felt' the living links to the past. Lacking real people who might share their oral history, the writers fell back on the magical and the supernatural. Richard Oram records one writer of 1926 who wrote about his experience of 'a magic wand of malevolence' by this 'grim relic of treachery and tragedy'. Another guidebook writer exclaimed, 'How the crimson tides of war must have roared round these walls!' In Drummond Gauld's account, published in 1933, 'Every glen is steeped in old traditions, every knoll has its legend of raid and rescue, foray and fight.'

As late as 1975, my father's favourite writer, the Cumbrian George MacDonald Fraser, tried to write as though he were a war correspondent reporting from the front line of a contemporary holocaust. He still insisted on the 'medieval nightmare . . . the guardhouse of the bloodiest valley in Britain . . . the unspeakable people who inhabit the valley. Their influence seems to hang over it still.' All these writers were heirs to Walter Scott.

I found it difficult to believe Scott's energetic example could sustain this kind of response much longer. Nothing in the scene today corresponded with what I had read. The afternoon light was rich. It brought out the brilliant sheen of the cattle. Charcoal clouds arched above the bright blaze of the ash and beech. Hermitage Castle stood four-square in a mowed field, locked tight by Scottish Heritage. The valley was not the hellish 'vast expanse of barren heath and morass' described in the guidebooks, but a narrow, flat field, leading to slopes of rough scrub, between half-broken walls, lightly grazed. It is currently under consideration as the site for a wind-farm. There was no trace of the forty pele towers and bastle houses of the warring Elliots. There was a pathos in the valley. But it no longer seemed to lie in the deeds of big men in small towers. Instead, it lay for me in the loss of the hundreds of families that had farmed it for centuries, who had been removed by Scottish agricultural policy, breaking the link to everything in the past, whether violent or peaceful.

83

That night I stayed in a farmhouse, one of the hundreds of grand farm-mansions built by the duke for his tenant farmers at the turn of the nineteenth century. My hostess was from Derbyshire, where her family had been on the same land and in the same house since 1549. She had moved 300 miles north to this valley, in a different country, thirty years ago. Her husband was from Highland Perthshire. He showed me the traces of thirty medieval stock-pens, forgotten and then rediscovered through an archaeological survey ten years earlier.

I woke at 4.15 in the morning at the top of the house, and looked out of the high window towards the castle. It was first light. East of the dark shape of the keep, a white mist hung low in the valley, hiding the hills. Most of the sky was obscured, except for a patch to the west filled with stars and a half-moon. But night after night of rain and clouded skies had confused me. I no longer knew whether the moon was waxing or waning.

After breakfast I climbed back towards the watershed of the Cheviots. Dark patches of cloud lay on the folds of the higher slopes like Highland lochs. I crossed the ridge from the Hermitage into the Liddle valley, heading for Bloody Bush, Deadwater Fell and the next ridge, which divided Cumbria from Northumbria, Scotland from England.

The Liddle valley, seen from the Hermitage ridge, had the shape and soil of a Lake District valley, but it lacked the human dimension of the Lakes. There were no churches, villages or stone barns in sight. The silage had been taken in from a vast mowed field; there was a herd of Aberdeen Angus, but no network of drystone walls. A small cluster of houses stood two miles away to my north, arranged around an abandoned railway station. A startled rabbit broke from a shed beside the embankment of the old train line.

For a moment I heard a bird, and then I could not hear it any more. The wet green meadow at the bottom of a steep slope soaked my boots and my trousers. I began to climb up towards the forestry plantation, catching the scent of pine, hearing the wind moving fast through the spruce.

At the edge of the wood I could see three different tracks. I picked the middle one: a path of soft moss peppered with reddening pine needles, and walked fast through the trees enjoying the silence, the cooler air and the dappled light. These paths were firebreaks, and when they were created it had been considered a sacred duty to keep them free of trees, so flames could not spread.

After a few minutes, my way was blocked by a fallen pine, its black, wet trunk propped up by its branches about five feet in the air. The branches were too thickly clustered to allow me to go under. I got one boot on the trunk, scraping an orange mark on the bark, fell backwards, trapped my pack, squeezed out and through, and began my climb again. After five more minutes I met another fallen tree. This time I worked my way back down the hill to the bottom edge of the wood and tried the left-hand firebreak. Again, after a short climb, I was blocked.

The trees had been planted in the 1930s over what had once been the upland pasture of small farms. It was dark in the depths of the new plantation. The ground was so soft that I had to clamber down small cliffs and through narrow becks (or perhaps burns, because I was a mile on the Scottish side of the border). After half an hour I climbed an abandoned drystone wall and then a seven-foot deer fence, and re-emerged onto the open fellside. I had spent an hour in the forest, and had barely covered half a mile. I pushed up through the long heather on the edge of the plantation and, feeling hot, crested the rise at the stone monument called the Bloody Bush.

According to the sixteenth-century English traveller Camden, the valleys I was now entering had never really become part of England: 'Tynedale and Redesdale, a country that William the Conqueror did not subdue, retaining to this day the ancient laws and customs.' All this almost independent nation had now been buried under trees by the Forestry Commission. A hundred thousand hectares – a hundred square kilometres – of Sitka spruce ran down every slope. At 2,500 trees a hectare, the forest numbered 250 million trees – storing an amount of carbon equivalent to the entire globe's weekly carbon emissions. But it was an astonishing change to a landscape of upland peat. The open moss known to the Romans and the Border reivers was now a closed canopy of Alaskan conifers.

At the summit of the hill, on the edge of plantation, I saw the first person in five hours. Dave was a broad-shouldered, cheerful middle-aged man. He was wearing a pair of tight Lycra bottoms, a sweatshirt, and a tiny pack on his back. He told me, in an accent close to Newcastle Geordie, that we were on the point where England, Scotland, Cumbria, Northumberland, Dumfries and Selkirkshire met. The nearest small town was Bellingham, eighteen miles, or a day's walk, away. I had stepped from Scotland back into England.

Dave worked in the forest as a supervisor, living in a forestry cottage. His wife was a forestry worker. His father was a forestry worker. Her father was a forestry worker. His brothers, Peter and Robin, were forestry workers too. 'My older brothers, I supervise them.' His mother's family had been here before the forest; so had his wife's family – sheep farmers in the old valley, before it became clear that all their pasture, walls and sheds would be drowned by trees.

'This was all farm before,' he said. He gestured through the dark green canopy at the route his grandmother had walked to school from her farm (it had taken her an hour and a half each way), and then at the routes over the hills which they had taken to go to dances, carrying their dance shoes with them.

The transition had begun in 1911, when 230 square kilometres of the adjoining valley of Otterburn had been turned into an army artillery range. Upper Tynedale had been taken over by the government in 1922 to plant trees for trench-posts in the event of a future war. But the peat of the valley was so deep, and the ground was so wet, that planting had seemed at first impossible. Then they tried the Sitka spruce, a tree of the fjords and snow slopes of the Pacific North-West, which seemed miraculously to flourish in these conditions. 'A hardy tree: drop them on top of the soil and it will root,' said Dave.

We were following a broad track. The first large clearing was striped with narrow ridges of soil on which stood soft, pale green tips of the spruce. Between the ridges were dense thickets of reeds. 'The rushes will die out once the canopy comes across,' he said. Then we were back into the trees again. Here, the canopy had cut out not just the reeds, but all the vegetation. The ground was a plain brown earth, scattered with pine needles.

84

If my walk with my father on Hadrian's Wall had introduced me to the beginning of the story of the Middleland here I felt I was approaching the end of its story.

The artillery range at Otterburn and these plantations at Tynedale designed for military trench fortifications were only the beginning of a twentieth-century military occupation of what had once been the Marches. In the lead-up to the Second World War, dozens of military airfields had been built across the area. In 1957, the Spadeadam valley, immediately to our south, was devoted to developing a new nuclear-missile launch system: Blue Streak. On the English Solway coast, at Windscale, the government began to produce weapons-grade plutonium-237 for nuclear bombs. On the Scottish side of the Solway the government opened another reactor, at Chapelcross, in 1959, to produce weapons-grade tritium for the Polaris and Trident nuclear weapons. (Some of the nuclear material was also used in power generation.) Facing

Chapelcross was the forest of aerials at Anthorn, which I had seen when wading the Solway. They were built over a dense web of copper wire as a control tower for nuclear submarines. (The suspended water of the bog provided insulation for the copper.)

At their peak, these industries – defence, nuclear, commercial forestry – had employed more than 100,000 people across the old Middleland. Then the projects faltered or ended. Blue Streak was cancelled. Chapelcross was closed, and its cooling towers, which could be seen from fifty miles away, were blown up. An entire industry was now engaged not in creating nuclear weapons or generating nuclear power but instead in the £20 billion task of cleaning up the nuclear waste. And the Middleland was rebranding itself as the most tranquil part of Britain, the most sparsely populated, the zone of the cleanest rivers, the darkest skies, the densest collection of National Parks, the heart of the Romantic movement, our deepest historical tradition, our most protected environment: the most outstanding of all the Areas of Outstanding Natural Beauty.

A century of change was summed up by the land I had crossed at Kirkbride, on my way to ford the Solway. There, as at Bewcastle, the Romans had built a fort on a hill in a bog, and the fort had become a church, surrounded by bog. The monks had drained the bog, and the farmers had extended their pasture into the drier fields. But in the twentieth century the dry farmland had been turned into a military airfield. In 2001, the government used the airfield as a slaughterhouse to control foot and mouth disease. Almost half a million sheep, cattle and pigs had been buried or burned on the site. Next the government had spent millions turning the mass grave into a nature reserve. There were complex contracts for ground maintenance, and a ten-year grant scheme for nature conservation. A row of wind turbines whirred noisily over a visitors' centre. In the midst of what seemed – to the naked eye – mostly scrub, a variety of species responded to varieties of human intervention. The wetland which had resisted the monks was favoured by newts; the airstrip was favoured by the wall butterfly; the military base had become a haven for foxes; and through the centre of the area, a track had been built for blind cyclists.

Here, in the Upper Tynedale, the process had been much simpler. Farm and moor had become forest, and the forest was still intact. But what was originally planted for pit-props in trenches was now used for timber in housing, and to fuel a giant biomass generator in Scotland. The high wet peat-ground was rarely planted now – the moors, which had once been used by the Dukes of Northumberland to shoot grouse, were now an expanse of ageing, long-stemmed heather, in which I saw an occasional raptor, but almost no grouse – but the lower ground was replanted with native broad-leafs, encouraging species which previously struggled under the dense canopy and amongst the acidic needles of the spruce. A military logistics site was turning into a tourist destination. The reservoir – built to power industry – was now a leisure facility for lakeside chalets. And through the trees ran mountain-bike trails and, for children, statues of the Gruffalo. Such was the context of Dave's career as a 'modern forester'.

When Dave's father-in-law had started as a forester, men still used axes to fell the trees. By the 1960s, they were using the Bowman saw. When Dave began at seventeen, he was given a chainsaw. At twenty he had rebelled, and tried to become a farmer.

'I thought I'd train up on some dairy. I was young and naive, I think. People in the North Tyne valley don't get out in the big wide world.' He smiled and trotted a few paces on ahead of me. His thin parka bounced up and down on his broad shoulders. He hadn't liked the dairy.

'I lived in a caravan; I was living off cornflakes, and my health wasn't good. I caught things like ringworm. Come the harvest, they asked us to help the tractor drivers out, but they wouldn't pay us overtime.' And then there was the cruelty. 'We shaved this young cow – she slipped and got herself caught around a metal pole. We were going to break the pole, but the manager came round, pulled her out with a rope and smashed her head. I just ignored him after that and just did my job. That was another reason to leave.'

He came back to the forest and to chainsawing, which he loved. 'Back strains, cut legs – only if it went really wrong, the odd face got the bar stuck in it. It's all technique. I was fortunate enough to be put next to one of the best chainsaw operators in the North Tyne valley: Malcolm Robinson. And at the end of the day I brashed away the branches, to prepare for the next day. Malcolm told me, "Learn how to sharpen your saw, present your wood and fell your trees: always keep it tidy and you'll make money." I go to a masseur now,' he added, 'every two months, for my back.'

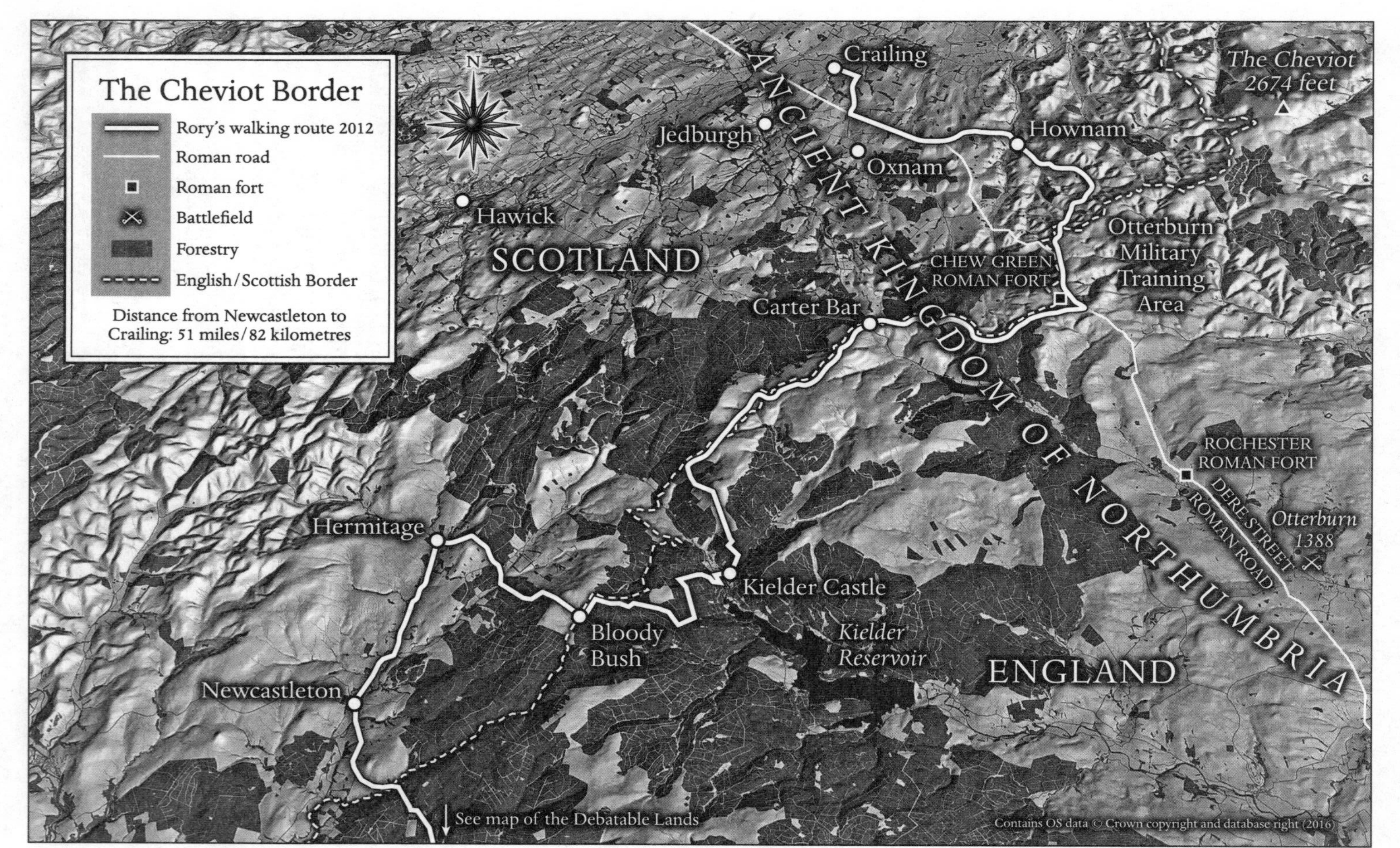
The Cheviot Border
Rory's walking route 2012
Roman road
Roman fort
Battlefield
Forestry
English/Scottish Border
Distance from Newcastleton to Crailing: 51 miles/82 kilometres
N
Crailing
The Cheviot 2674 feet
Jedburgh
Hownam
Oxnam
Hawick
SCOTLAND
ANCIENT KINGDOM OF NORTHUMBRIA
Otterburn Military Training Area
CHEW GREEN ROMAN FORT
Carter Bar
ROCHESTER ROMAN FORT
DERE STREET ROMAN ROAD
Otterburn 1388
Hermitage
Kielder Castle
Bloody Bush
Kielder Reservoir
ENGLAND
Newcastleton
See map of the Debatable Lands
Contains OS data © Crown copyright and database right (2016)

85

Further down the hill, three giant vehicles stood in a large clearing. The machine grabbing the trees was a 'harvester'. The smaller-tracked vehicle behind was the 'forwarder'. The man in the truck was Jason. And the other man, driving the harvester, was Jason's father, Olly. The Forestry Commission had grown out of the Indian Forestry Service, and still retained traces of its old colonial structure. At the bottom had been the gangers, people like Olly and Jason; above them, foremen and supervisors such as Dave, playing the role of sergeant majors; then the Foresters – an officer class of graduate trainees. But what had made sense in the 1920s, when the workforce numbered in the thousands, made less sense today, and only traces of the old attitudes remained.

The Land Rover belonged to Richard the Forester. Richard came from the south of England and had joined as a graduate. Richard waved. 'My job,' said Dave, 'is to get him whipped into shape. They're only here for a few years and then another one comes. The wife's the ecologist. He likes mountain biking, and his wife counting bats. The previous one – Ian – is now down south. He's working with animal rights groups.'

We watched Olly in the cab of his £250,000 machine, peering out through the bulletproof glass. He pushed the harvester forward, driving carefully over a carpet of branches which he had laid to keep the vehicle from sinking into the boggy ground. Then he swung the whirring blades at a hundred-foot tree, and began stripping the top branches.

Dave explained that Olly had resisted the harvesting machines when they were first introduced, believing they wouldn't be able to handle the rough branches. 'You wouldn't get anyone better than Olly with a chainsaw. He was an artist, he made it look so easy.'

Now instead of hundreds of men, they needed only ten to work the 100,000-acre forest. We watched Olly grab the tree, twist it, rip it out of the ground, and then immediately begin to cut it into sections. In the cab of the 'forwarder', Olly's son Jason measured the diameter and length with an electronic instrument, and sent the figures straight into the sawmill.

'In the old days, with a chainsaw, how long would it take?'

'He would be on his second branch now – the time we've been standing here. Now we can fell sixty, seventy trees in a day. Most operators are working two or three trees ahead, working out what they can get out of the branches. They're not very talkative of an evening because they are brain-dead, just staring at trees all day. When I was on a forwarder, I just fell asleep eating my dinner. You wake up as a log hits the cab window. Olly and Jason came at 4.40 this morning, they do an eleven-hour day. Olly's wife works late, so when he gets home he prepares the dinner.'

He pointed back. 'The danger lies in the tree coming onto the cab. All the glass is bulletproof, but if you send the tree towards it . . . My brother had his whole cab ripped out because of a computer malfunction, it – the computer – kept processing the tree into the cab.'

'What happens if the tree falls on top of Olly?' I asked.

'He gets gip off me for damaging the cab,' said Dave.

A valley which had once included hundreds of people from farming families, and hundreds of forestry workers, now had dozens. The next generation of harvesters would require even fewer people. Dave had decided his daughter needed to get out of the North Tyne valley. 'With the new forestry spending review, it's kicked on another stage again,' he said. He seemed to be spending a lot of time commissioning wooden ramps for mountain biking through the forest. I asked whether visitors were interested in the Roman or reiver history of the valley. He thought not.

'We're getting a lot of raves, people coming over and causing mayhem and leaving excrement. You go out and, say, there are twenty or so blind drunk and smoking drugs, but they'll be a hazard on the highway, so you leave them there and just notify the police.'

Finally we came down out of the trees at the base of the valley. A track led towards a village. A Victorian castle, once one of the Duke of Northumberland's shooting lodges, had become the forest centre. Around it, the Forestry Commission had built a village for the forestry workers. When Dave first moved here, every house was occupied by fellow forestry workers. Every morning, cars would assemble to pick them all up. Then the forestry housing was sold off, and now he was the only forestry worker in the village. Most of the other occupants were retired people from cities and towns in the north of England.

On weekends, Dave ran fell-races. His wife liked going to Dublin for a weekend. 'I'd rather spend the night in a tent at the top of a hilltop.

'The new people come into the village and can't understand how village life works.' At first I thought he meant newcomers were introducing unwanted innovations. But he meant the reverse – he meant that they were too conservative, and that they were blocking the new ideas and initiatives of the Forestry Commission. For him, this was a Forestry Commission village, which was supposed to support the work of the forest that surrounded it. At the moment, for instance, the commission wanted to launch a 'dark park' – a place for watching stars, taking advantage of the lack of houses, which created 'the darkest skies in Europe'. But the newcomers were opposing it, because they were worried that it would attract more tourists.

86

Starting at eight in the morning, I climbed up again through the Sitka spruce towards the next watershed of the Cheviots. To the west ran the forest which had buried Dave's mother's farm. To the south lay the reservoir which had drowned Dave's father's cottage. It took me two hours to emerge from the trees again onto the high flat watershed which formed the English–Scottish border. Above the treeline, the colours were sere, bleached – reeds now in mid-August past their best, grass grown overlong, amidst dark bracken, and the long black stems of ageing heather. I was what the *Beowulf* poet would call a heath-stepper. I saw no butterfly or bird. Even the midges seemed to have abandoned the hill.

Every few hundred yards I found a stone half hidden in the heather, carved 'D' on one side and 'P' on the other. This was the medieval march – the mark, the march-line, the *mearc* or the marches, the exact boundary between two estates, two clans – Douglas and Percy – and two nations – England and Scotland. The border stones ran through this empty moorland with no human left to embody the distinctions. I wanted to believe that these had been carved by some medieval Douglases and Percys around the time of their great battle at Otterburn in 1380 – of which Sir Philip Sidney said, 'I never Heard the old song of Percie and Douglas, that I found not my heart moved more than with a trumpet.' But I suspected they had been laid in much more peaceful times by their nostalgic descendants.

At midday, I came down from the hill onto the A68 at Carter Bar, crossing a line of parked cars, bought a burger and thin coffee from a van, and stopped for a minute with the tourists to listen to the piper on the border. Then I climbed a fence on the far side of the road, keeping my feet on the exact line of the border. Now that I had left Forestry Commission land, the ground was more densely grazed, and the slipped, soft turf allowed me to race over the ridges, past the deep shadows of Iron Age cultivation, and to turn north at the crisp outline of a Roman camp.

'Dere Street' – this Roman road along which I was now running – was older than Hadrian's Wall, built at a more optimistic time when the Roman border had been pushed right up to the Highland Line. But while in Cumbria, behind the protection of Hadrian's Wall, Roman roads had become modern tarmac roads, and the forts had become towns, here in Scotland the Roman road was only a track running through empty country, and its forts only lines of turf ramparts.

I ran each downward slope savouring the give and bounce of the turf, alive as a sprung dance floor. All of the land ahead of me and all the land behind me had become part of the kingdom of Northumbria in the sixth century. And when at evening I turned from the Roman road, which was the precise borderline, and came down from the hills to the flat land of what was now Scotland, I was passing places – Oxnam, Smailhom, Ormiston (the village of the Oxen, the small village, Orm's-settlement) – whose names were still in the Northumbrian language of a once united land.

The small hotel at Crailing where I finished my day seemed to have no connection at all to the hills which I had left behind me. It was a brick building dropped – like the model of a stationmaster's house in a train set – between evenly spaced trees on an over-mown lawn. In the centre of the lawn stood four miniature fountains, and a small rockery whose painted rocks were sprinkled with ornaments. I put my wet boots and stick carefully in one corner of the hall, afraid to muddy it.

In the dining room, I found only one other guest – a white-haired man sitting in a winged armchair, twisting a sherry glass in his left hand. He was a little out of humour, it seemed, because he had been expecting me, in the tradition of this boarding house, to join him for a drink before dinner. My eleven-hour walk was not an adequate excuse.

He had come to this B&B every summer for twenty years. His home was in England, but 'there are many good golf courses here, and they are excellent value', he gave as explanation. 'As for this hotel, it is not just the interesting type of people you meet and have a chance to get to know over drinking and dinner, there is also the food.' Over three courses, he told me stories of golfing holidays, which seemed to have become increasingly solitary as he grew older.

★

Charlie Robertson, a cheerful sixty-five-year-old Scot in a collared T-shirt which had grown a little small for him, had heard I was passing, and kindly came the following morning to show me the back-route from Crailing to Kelso. We started along an abandoned railway line. Someone had rebranded it as the 'Border Abbey Way' to make us feel we might be treading in the tracks of monks, not trains.

Charlie had had been a teacher here in the Borders for decades. But his ancestors had been shepherds in the Highlands. Like many off-comers he had developed an intense local patriotism. He loved Border rugby, and now, in his retirement, he ran the Border Union Agricultural Society – an organisation founded in 1813 by the dukes to sponsor and promote agriculture on both sides of the border.

When I asked a question about the local sheep breeds, he astonished me with the detail and confidence of his response: 'They brought the Dishley Leicester, which had been bred by Robert Bakewell, 250 miles up to the border and crossed it with the Cheviot, and that produced the Border Leicester in Hexham, and the Bluefaced Leicester is a further cross . . .' Perhaps, he winked, the differences were not as stark as the breeders suggested.

This flatland through which we were walking – Charlie's local country – was also technically part of the Borders but it felt like a completely new landscape. We were passing uniform stretches of silage, great fields of barley and hedges of young copper beech in tubes. Heavy Continental cattle, which could not have survived in the uplands, grazed turf whose green seemed particularly violent after my days in the bleached hills. The soil showed no sign of crushed damp grass, or standing water, despite five years of rain. £200,000 tractors towered over the hedges. All seemed to be municipal clipping, intensive farming or abandoned ground.

If I had seen traces of the Norse agriculture in the Lakes, of monastic drainage on the Solway and of reiver smallholdings in Bewcastle, here

I felt I had walked into the agricultural landscape of the twentieth century. This flat land was called the merse – a Northumbrian word for a march or border. Charlie said the fields around us had been wet moss like Bewcastle until the draining of the early nineteenth century. I found this difficult to believe. Could this flamboyantly fertile soil really have been a landscape of scrub trees, reeds and scrawny native cows in blue-black water? I pressed him to illustrate the draining in one of the fields through which we were walking, but his comment seemed to have been lifted from a book – something he had read as a retired teacher, rather than something he had noticed as a farmer's son.

We walked together to Mr Eliot's farm. Mr Eliot had been recommended to me as a fine example of a Scottish Border farmer, and I was sorry that he was not at home when we arrived. Instead I was greeted by his son: a twenty-five year old with muscled arms in a tight powder-blue rugby shirt. The Eliots had moved from poorer land on the high border to this rich soil.

The son took me outside to inspect a bull. To my surprise, I had met the bull before – a giant Continental Limousin, which I had seen with its breeder, Matt Ridley, twelve days previously on the English side of the border. I knew its new owner too, but apparently the £30,000 bull was too valuable to be left on Cumbrian land. It had been brought up here to the rich pasture of Scotland, to provide sperm for the laboratory and thence the international export market.

At the table of a large, well-fitted kitchen, the young Mr Eliot explained that his family was specialising in the chemical control, processing and distribution of sperm of Aberdeen Angus, a Scottish breed from 200 miles away, well north of the Highland Line. The Aberdeen Angus had a particular combination of muscle and meat, a marbling which, thanks perhaps more to a brilliant marketing campaign than anything intrinsic to the flesh, was prized for steaks in Argentina and Texas.

Our next stop was Roxburgh Castle, which stood one stone course above the ground. Only ambiguous humps in the grass suggested the medieval town and monastery which once surrounded the greatest fort in the Borders. It had been occupied by the English from 1174 till 1189, from 1290 till 1313, from 1343 till 1460 and again from 1545 till 1550. The name Rox-burgh was almost certainly the Northumbrian English for the fort of a man called Rook. But, as I showed Charlie on my BlackBerry, the Wikipedia page preferred a Scottish Gaelic nationalist etymology for the place-name – 'from the Gaelic "rosbrog"'. I suggested this was an indication that the castle was now in Scottish, not English, hands, if only by four miles.

Charlie did not find this jibe at Scottish nationalism funny. 'Roxburgh,' he said, 'has always been Scottish.'

'How about Berwick then?' I asked.

'Ah, Berwick is a different story.'

Charlie had a number of strong if paradoxical views on the identity of the Scottish Borders, the people who now lived there, and the ways in which it was changing. He was originally an outsider, and he had now retired, but he felt that the number of outsiders and retirees was driving 'a slow death of community'. He complained that the Borders was 'ultra-traditional' because the restaurants closed too early, and described the opposition to the McDonald's in Galashiels as 'terrible' conservatism. But he had also opposed the building of the supermarket in Galashiels, and had fought against the demolition of the nineteenth-century mills. 'Galashiels has sold its soul to the devil,' he concluded.

He insisted that the Borders was fundamentally a place drenched in local history. There were the different accents that still existed in the different Border towns. 'Jedburgh people don't say they come from Jedburgh, or Jedba, which is what we call it in Kelso. They say "Jera". Actually, they don't say it like *Jayd*, they say it like *Jard*. "Jara".' (I wondered whether the clearance of the countryside had created a more concentrated identity in Scottish Border towns.) He was sure there was also a difference at the national border. 'You get mushy peas in England, but never in Scotland. Haddock is the fish of choice in Scotland, it's often cod in England.'

We passed a collection of neat nineteenth-century houses, built originally for railway workers. Three separate railway companies had built lines and stations around this tiny hamlet, none of them connecting. All had been financial failures. The government had closed the last lines in the Borders in the 1960s. Now, fifty years later, the Scottish government was building a new railway line from Edinburgh. It would be immensely expensive. But Charlie thought it would transform the economy of the area: 'get people moving more'.

Charlie showed me the Victorian railway bridge, which curved at both ends. Like my father he was fascinated by how things were done. He explained how complicated the geometry of the arches had needed to be to incorporate the rail and the river. He knew a lot about it. He had tracked down the original drawings in a library.

What struck me, however, was the lost lives of the labourers who had built this bridge. The builders here 150 years ago had come from small farms in remote parts of Ireland. They were probably Irish Gaelic-speaking, and often, like my great-great-grandfather, illiterate. They had been forced to leave their country, often after famine, and live in tents in an alien place that viewed them and their Catholic religion with suspicion. Thirteen of them had been killed erecting the elegant bridge before us. The station had gone, and the line had been torn up. And now the immigrant labourers, and the folly of the project, were fading phantoms in a quiet lane.

Now no one who lived in the hamlet of Roxburgh had any connection to agriculture or the railways. That was not to say there was no interest in the make-up of the place. Someone, to my surprise, had put a sign in a shed recording the recent demographic data on the village. It seemed typical of much of rural Britain. I copied it carefully into my notebook:

> The professions are teachers, concrete fabricators, a banker, a doctor, a paramedic, an acupuncturist, a plumber, a plasterer, a chef, a colonel and an aromatherapist.

87

I slept in a B&B in Carham – a small village built apparently somewhere near the site of a battle in 1015, in which the last King of Cumbria had fought alongside the King of Scotland, allowing Scotland to extend its territory for the first time from its old boundary, north of the Firth of Forth, right down to the Tweed. Before I went to sleep, I sat down to write another email to my father. I was, although I was reluctant to admit it to myself, becoming disillusioned with how little connection I had found between modern settlements and historical landscapes. I was beginning to realise that the Middleland or the British identity I sought did not exist where I had been looking for it – neither rooted in a particular local soil, nor found in the cars that rolled relentlessly past for the supermarket or school run.

> I have been walking for twenty days through one of the most remote, sparsely populated parts of Britain, and I am yet to meet anyone who has not travelled outside the United Kingdom. Nine out of ten people had apparently not been born in the village in which they now live. But almost everyone insists on their 'local' heritage.

When I had tried to press people for more precise local history, most people claimed that I was 'just too late'. They suggested that if I had met their grandparents, I would have found a world circumscribed by the walls of a single valley, and filled with traditional tales. But I was beginning to doubt this. The Borderer Charlie had suggested his grandfather – the Highland shepherd – had seen things that were gone, but it turned out he was referring to some falls in Montana, which had since been made into a hydroelectric dam. And when a sheep farmer, whose family had lived near a Neolithic stone circle almost since the time of the Vikings, said he had some oral history from his grandmother, he could only produce a story about her having seen a leopard shot in India. In truth, I suspected the equivalents of the villages which I had seen in Afghanistan, brooding on their own distinct identities and oral histories, had disappeared from Britain many, many centuries before anyone's grandmother.

My father had – characteristically – sent me a copy of Dr Johnson's tour through the Highlands. And what I had noticed, reading it, was that the traditional world had already gone in even the most remote areas of Scotland by the time of Johnson's visit in 1773. (And it had perhaps gone in England, by the late Middle Ages.) Johnson had found that the valleys of Scotland were already largely empty and treeless, the ancient churches long destroyed, and he repeatedly recorded his disappointment at being too late for the traditions he had hoped to see and experience. At first he was told that there had been traditional Celtic bards, or *seanachaidh*, kept by Highland chieftains in living memory; later he learned that they had died out centuries earlier. Traditional Highland dress had gone. No one carried weapons any more. No one believed in the 'browny' fairy. Most Highlanders already spoke English, and many had served in the British Army or Royal Navy. The Gaelic song he heard was not an ancient ballad but an account of the 'epidemical fury of emigration' in which the Highlanders were already moving to America. Modern commerce had obliterated the old culture. He had concluded, 250 years ago:

> The clans retain little now of their original character, their ferocity of temper is softened, their military ardour is extinguished, their dignity of independence is depressed, their contempt of government subdued, and the reverence for their chiefs abated. Such is the effect of the late regulations that a longer journey than to the Highlands must be taken by him whose curiosity pants for savage virtues and barbarous grandeur.

88

Not far from Carham, along the north bank of the Tweed, I turned up a potholed drive lined with willow sweet, wild raspberry, nettles and thick-trunked beech. I heard the flap of the wings of a fat pigeon. The house at the end of the drive, Hirsel, had been the home of the 14th Earl of Home, who had been prime minister in the 1960s.

One of Lord Home's ancestors was, still to this day, accused by the people of Selkirk of running away from the Battle of Flodden in 1513. After walking up the drive, I met a loyal factor who was keen to clear up the Flodden misunderstanding: 'He had done his job, clearing the right flank. He felt that he had succeeded in his task, and so he could go home.'

I walked on, through Coldstream, in the direction of the battlefield, passing a shop selling eighteenth-century maps of the area, and a house in whose window sat a miniature stuffed gorilla with 'Kiss me' embroidered across its stomach. The bridge on which the house sat led back to England. On the other side, towering above a Doric column, was a statue to a Member of Parliament from 1833. He gazed with the haughtiness of a pharaoh down the line of the Tweed, and his plinth praised him in the grandest terms for his 'Talents, Amiable Qualities and Political Principles'. He had, it seemed, been a backbench MP for a year.

Almost exactly 500 years before my walk, the Battle of Flodden had taken place on the English side of the Coldstream bridge. The Queen of France had charmed King James IV of Scotland into crossing the English border. Her aim was to distract King Henry VIII of England, who was then campaigning in France, and she had emphasised that James need enter 'only by a yard'. He took her at her word, sitting just beyond the border. The seventy-year-old Earl of Surrey, who was 400 miles away on the south coast, pulled together a rough force and marched north to meet him three weeks later.

It took twenty minutes to walk from the bridge to the place where the two armies met. Modern wire fences ran along the edges of the battle-line, enclosing neat fields of barley. A signboard showed that the Scottish king had camped on the low ridge in front of what was now a small rectangle of forestry. Lord Home had charged down, roughly in line with the fence on the left-hand side of the field, shattering the English right wing, then cantered past the church and across the ford of the Tweed, making for his castle at Hirsel. After Home left, the rest of the Scottish army staggered into the mud, waving their brand-new pikes, and were massacred. In the words of Walter Scott, 'The Scots left on this field the King, two bishops, two mitred abbots, twelve earls, thirteen lords, and five eldest sons of peers. The number of gentlemen slain was beyond calculation – there is scarcely a family of name in Scottish history who did not lose a relative there.' Perhaps ten thousand people had died in the field; their DNA is soaked into every root of grass and grain.

Philip Howard, whom I had met in the pub at Newcastleton boasting about hanging Armstrongs, was descended from the Earl of Surrey (the English field commander), from Dacre and the younger Howard – the commanders of both the English light horse and heavy cavalry at the battle. He had a bronze relief of Flodden above his fireplace. Even 500 years was apparently not long enough for the enormity of the victory to settle in. He approached the subject as though he hardly believed he could claim anything so spectacularly delightful in his family history. It had got his ancestor a dukedom. He said that if he ever went to Scotland – which he rarely did, although he lived only ten miles from the border – he could wear a black kilt, to commemorate the massacre. He showed me their 500-year-old sword, which had been used at the battle, and his family flag, awarded by the English king for killing the Scottish king. It showed the lion of Scotland with its testicles cut off and an arrow in its throat.

Philip wasn't the only person obsessed with Flodden. It was one of my father's favourite subjects too. Like Philip, he seemed to take a positive delight in exposing the catastrophe and idiocy. 'I know how to mount a cannon – I mounted anti-tank guns for three years during the war,' he wrote,

> so I can tell you all this stuff about simply turning King James's cannons round on the ridge is absolute nonsense. They're also claiming he fortified the position in two weeks. Do they have any idea how long it takes to fortify a position? No yellow JCB diggers in those days . . . All we know about that fight is a couple of lines in a letter from the commander's son, who says, 'The Scots advance *"à l'allemand"*.' Nonsense. They had no time to train. Pikes take weeks. We shouldn't take his word for it at all. I'm not even sure they used the pikes.

A retired English engineer accompanied me down the River Twill. It was a hot day, and he was in a white short-sleeved shirt, his white hair blowing in the wind. We followed the footsteps of the advancing English army along the dark river, beneath the hawthorn bushes and oaks. The engineer came from much further south in England, but, retiring here, had embraced the battle. He had designed the signs, advised on the new website and converted a disused red public phone box in the village into a telephone-box-sized guide to Flodden.

I asked who his heroes were. Did he, like me, admire the Earl of Angus, who had tried to prevent the battle, and lost two sons on the field? Was he suspicious of Home's ride across the river? But he would not be drawn into analysis of individuals. He talked instead, like my father, about the precise design of James's cannon and how their elevation was wrong.

We followed the route along the river taken by Surrey. The written sources had convinced the engineer that King James had been completely unaware of Surrey's advance, because James had not put out scouts. When I asked how James could have been so foolish, he replied: 'Because he was a king.' He seemed to think that was all I needed to know.

But when Walter Scott had walked this path 200 years earlier, he had taken a quite different lesson from the landscape. Struck by just how narrow the gorge was, Scott had concluded that the English army of over 10,000 men would have had to clear a huge swathe through the forest to pass. Because he was Scott, he put his reconstruction of the changed landscape into poetry:

The hawthorn glade which now we see
In spring-tide bloom so lavishly
Had then from many an axe its doom
To give the marching columns room.

It would have been a noisy, dusty advance. James could not have been unaware that they were taking this route. Scott argued – more plausibly, I felt – that the problem for James was not that he was a king, but that he was indecisive.

89

The battlefield itself was owned by Lord Joicey. I had phoned him the day before, and he had agreed to meet me. He proved to be a fit man with a neat beard that made him look like a Pre-Raphaelite artist. His voice had a slight burr, which I could not place.

As a young man, he said, he had lived in the Middle East, then in Portugal, 'just as it was emerging from the dictatorship of Salazar', before setting up 'a small translation business in the south of England'. Along with the site of the battle, he had inherited from his father 16,000 acres and the Border castles of Ford and Etal. He had converted parts of the castles and estates into 'steam engines, an antiquarian bookseller, a garden centre, an architectural salvage store, cafés, bed-and-breakfasts and the rest'. He had an agreement for canoeing on his river, and had no idea, if Scotland went independent, who his agreement would be with, the English or the Scottish side. 'Is the point,' he asked me, 'that I am geographically in England, or that my waters are Scottish?'

Next year he would be hosting the 500th anniversary of Flodden. Over 400 people planned to ride from Coldstream – a mass of horseflesh, pushing across the bridge and up the narrow lanes. Philip Howard and others who were descended from the victorious English commanders would not be attending. But the event was very popular with the losing Scottish side. Thousands of Scots whose ancestors were killed at Flodden, including many of my Scottish neighbours, would be there. So would the people of Selkirk, whose town tailor, Fletcher the Soutar, had been one of the last to retreat from the disaster. Five hundred years after the fact, Selkirk still used the motto 'Up with the Soutars of Selkirk, and down with the Lords of Home'.

Lord Joicey, the custodian of this quintessentially Scottish site, was an Englishman living in England. He had no idea what his ancestors had been doing in 1513, or indeed in 1713, but they would not have been fighting here. His great-grandfather, a coal magnate from the North-East, had only bought the site in 1909. Yet Flodden had become one of the central projects of Lord Joicey's life. Aware that there were at least thirty groups interested in being involved in the anniversary, he had recruited a man from Newcastle University's Centre for Heritage Studies to help with the planning.

'I began in 2008, thinking, "What are we going to do about Flodden?" And find myself today looking at 105 different community projects, the Royal Scottish Chamber Orchestra writing a new piece, a lady from the traditional music group in Newcastle University writing a Border ballad to commemorate 500 years of Flodden, in the style of the old Border ballads.' There were groups from 'Heritage Lottery, Historic Scotland, local history groups, other churches, other parish councils, music groups, orchestra groups, BBC, rag-rugging or whatever the word is . . .'

'What's rag-rugging got to do with the Battle of Flodden?' I asked.

'Well, they want to commemorate Flodden by creating a rag rug to decorate their rather bare community hall in Coldstream. Because it's part of Coldstream's local history. Now, at the Fletcher monument at Selkirk – are you familiar with it?' he asked.

'The great Fletcher, who arrived at the river to find that Lord Home had cantered off into the sunset.'

'He stands in a rather Stalinesque pose,' said Lord Joicey. 'His statue was put up in 1813 on the 300th anniversary of Flodden, by the good people of Selkirk. But what can we do for the 500th anniversary? They've raised £135,000 themselves, and they will use it to dig up some of this ghastly tarmac that surrounds it, and we will create a mini peace garden.'

'A peace garden for the Battle of Flodden?' I asked. He did not reply.

Lord Joicey's central project was to be a website. 'Marketing is about the sizzle and not the sausage. What we are trying to do with "Flodden 500" is to raise the profile.'

The website was to be an eco-museum.

'What is an eco-museum?'

'The eco-museum of Flodden 500 links together sites so that they are all on a virtual webpage. When you go to one, your curiosity is hopefully aroused: "What's this, what's this?" And there's a website and a "zap-code for your app", and it introduces you to all the other sites that are in and around this area that are connected to Flodden,' he continued without taking a breath. 'It's a concept that is going well in Italy, Sweden and France.'

I tried to suggest that I had met almost no one who knew anything about Flodden. He interrupted: 'It's not so much what we know about the battle, and how it happened, but what it *means*. It's how the Borders is still a sort of live creature that we have to nurture and celebrate.'

'But the locals don't seem to me to have any views on Flodden—'

'They would say, "No, we don't, but by God we want to learn because it was so important."'

Lord Joicey was a great believer in the Union between England and Scotland. 'My lovely wife is a Jedburgh lass and she's just as much a Borderer as I am. When I'm asked abroad, "Where do you come from?" I often say I'm a little bit like a Saalander: I speak German, but I'm actually French. I find myself English because I pay my taxes here. But culturally I think I'm more akin to a Scot than I am to anything else. And I think most people around here would probably agree with that.'

He was somehow hoping to use the anniversary of this massacre of the Scots by the English to encourage links across the border. He talked of using it to boost the reputation of the Scottish king, James IV, who had presided over the defeat ('He was quite the equal of Henry'), while also suggesting that the Union between England and Scotland had been the right decision. He was a believer in Britain. And yet – as with unionists like my father, and indeed with many of the Scottish nationalists I had met – I became bewildered when I listened to him try to define his vision of British identity.

'Flodden makes us question what Britishness is,' he said. 'Did you ever see a play on the South Bank called *England People Very Nice*? It's set in an asylum seekers' camp outside London about five years ago, and you know that in two or three generations, those Somalis will be saying, "Hold on, we're East Enders." And if I can raise the profile of Flodden . . .'

90

My father joined me in Berwick for dinner. He was reading *The Road to Wigan Pier*, and had been struck by Orwell's description of the industrial scars and detritus that covered northern England in the 1930s.

When I told him that I was feeling increasingly disillusioned by my walk through Britain, he asked, 'The whole country has been wrecked? Too many centuries of industry? Too many people in too small an island?'

But that was not the issue. The land through which I had walked looked very different to the Britain my father had known before the war, and in many cases it had become – almost uncannily – cleaner. The lead mines, iron mines and bauxite mines of the Lake District, and the coal mines of the Cumbrian west coast – which had employed thousands in my father's youth – were all gone. So too had the munitions factories, airfields, nuclear plants and secret test sites, which had been scattered across the valleys even twenty years ago.

Only slight curves in the earth hinted at where the open-cast mines had lain. Mile after mile of new rowan, birch, oak and ash had been planted by highways, on old railway lines, and along the sides of deep ghylls. Acid rain had been removed from the air, and chemicals from the rivers. When my father was born, only 3 per cent of Britain had been covered with woodland. The figure was now closer to 12 per cent.

At the same time agriculture had changed beyond recognition. Fellside farms and lake shores, once defined by cattle, were now given over to sheep. The shorthorn cows, which filled every nineteenth-century image of the Lakes, had vanished. So had the black cattle of the Border reivers. Pale, broad-chested Continental cattle or giant Holstein dairy cows dominated the low ground. I had passed chicken sheds containing hundreds of thousands of birds; or a dairy parlour where 1,000 cows, milked three times a day by automatic machines, were producing over 10 million litres of milk a year. And instead of hay meadows and wild flowers, there were uniform fields of sprayed rye grass.

There was also much more abandoned ground: more scrub, wetland and bog, and fewer shepherds than there had been even a decade earlier. Perhaps a third of the woodland was no longer managed. Himalayan balsam and Japanese knotweed ran along almost every waterway. There were more birds of prey in the sky, more badger setts and more otter holts, but – in common with other parts of Britain – fewer farmland birds, hedgehogs, water voles and salmon. Larches and juniper were dying in their tens of thousands in Galloway. Two states now predominated – suburban and abandoned – increasingly at the expense of the alternative: a living countryside.

'And how about the Middleland, darling? Have you managed to prove that the English and the Scottish Borderers are basically the same people, with the same history, and that the border is an irrelevance?'

'Unfortunately not! I think I have found three distinct countries – the area north of the modern border, the area south of Hadrian's Wall, and the area between the border and the wall.'

★

I explained that I had been walking about fifteen miles a day for thirty days through the Middleland by the time I reached my father in Berwick. I had begun south of Hadrian's Wall, in the Lakes, walking through a landscape in which there were old villages, each with its parish church, surrounded by fields cut with neat stone walls. Small villages retained agricultural shows, and valleys communities still kept foot-packs for fox hunting. But tourism had long overtaken farming as the largest source of income. This was a terrain of Mountain Rescue teams, and of a 'visitor economy' defined not by Border ballads but by Beatrix Potter and Mrs Tiggywinkle.

Next I had reached Bewcastle, north of Hadrian's Wall, but still in modern England, an area of many smaller farms and almost no villages. There, despite a representative scattering of artists and retired city-dwellers, the valley was still dominated by farmers such as Steve and Trevor – it was they who seemed to be driving the broadband projects, collating local history and clearing the snow from the roads. They were still able to list the occupants of every building in 400 square miles, and in some cases link those buildings to reivers and Border ballads.

Crossing into Scotland, I had entered Walter Scott's Borders. He had presented it as the most traditional of areas. But it had felt the most dramatically modern place of the three. The farms were much larger, and mostly rented by very mobile tenants. I didn't meet a farmer in Roxburghshire whose family had been on the same farm for more than three generations. Many had moved there relatively recently, from Lanarkshire or the edge of Dumfries. Despite the efforts of voluble local schoolteachers and antiquarians, it was difficult for me to feel any organic links here between the modern population and the distant past.

The vernacular architecture of Roxburghshire, for example, had in the eighteenth century consisted almost entirely of medieval mud cottages with earth floors and thatched roofs. By 1963, however, they were all brick or stone, and the Royal Commission for Ancient and Historical Monuments in Scotland could not find a single example of a traditional cottage anywhere in the county. In my home valley in Cumbria it was difficult to find a cottage built after 1750; in Roxburghshire, it was almost impossible to find a cottage built before 1850.

The Cumbrians knew surprisingly little about the Scots: one forty year old described his complete bafflement at recently seeing his first Burns Night supper, although he lived only ten miles from the border. Lord Joicey, a Northumbrian, called himself 'an honorary Scot', but I never heard a Scot a mile north of the border refer to himself as 'an honorary Northumbrian'. Something, it seemed, had kept the Scottish Borders, central Cumbria and the Bewcastle valleys separate, through all the Acts of Union. And the differences could not be attributed to deep facts of geology, climate or ethnicity. In these terms they were – as my father said – all part of the Middleland.

Instead, I suggested, the differences had emerged from different legal systems and settlement patterns, which had been shaped by the arbitrary, artificial impositions – the borders themselves – drawn by foreign emperors and domestic kings. The ghosts of these two lines – the old English–Scottish Marches and its predecessor, Hadrian's Wall – still divided what should have been almost indistinguishable parts of a single island.

'But why exactly,' my father asked, 'do you say you feel bewildered?'

In part, I said, it was because I had expected to meet more people through walking – and to see more. Instead, I had only been able to note a patch of cock's-foot grass or a thick pollarded oak, stubbornly wedged on an abandoned dyke; I could think about when a particular field had been drained, and question why the ragwort was flourishing or why the bracken was turning early; I could try to decide whether a particular set of lines were from fifteenth-century ploughs or an Iron Age fort. And I could wonder what impact living in a valley – with a particular shape and history – had on people's souls. But there was rarely anyone with whom to discuss these themes, because the fields were mostly empty.

Even now in August – the peak tourist season – the national trails I followed were so deserted that it often felt as though the thousands of beautifully maintained tracks, signs and stiles were being used by almost no one except me. The footpaths between valleys, which would once have been pounded by people carrying, visiting, running errands or walking to school, were now deep in heather.

It had been different in Asia. Each orchard in Iran had seemed to contain a man on a carpet, willing to share the contents of his battered metal teapot. In Nepal, men in peaked hats and tight cotton trousers had sprinted past me with parcels for villages that stood five days from the nearest vehicle road.

In Afghanistan, each village home in which I stayed had a different set of stories of an ambush, or a lost animal, or a saint: stories from two years or two centuries ago, linked to local rocks. In Britain, the people I talked to were energetically absorbed in subjects which had little to do with the soil beneath their feet – pigeon-fancying for one (he flew his pigeons from his housing estate to France); disability legislation for another; Fair Trade bananas in the Leeward Islands for a third.

91

Reaching the hotel at Crailing again, I finally turned towards Crieff and my father's home. I had crossed and recrossed the English–Scottish border eight times – at the Solway Firth, at the Sark, at Scot's Dyke, at Kershopefoot, at the Bloody Bush, at Carter Bar, at Coldstream and at Berwick. Now I left the border. Walking to Melrose, the rain was sharp and loud on the hood of my anorak; I was distracted by the sound of a loose strap slapping against my backpack; and the wind threw me off balance. I saw a double-trunked beech, which had split down its seam, cracked like a broken bow. I passed a ruined hedge which had grown into an avenue of skinny trees, just proud of the black field water. On my left a great sycamore swung wildly above a shivering oak.

In the shadows of the early afternoon, columns of insects fought in the air. Orange mushrooms sprouted and spilled from the trunk of an ash. Then I was alongside the A68 again. In an instant the speed and noise of hurrying cars subdued all the grandeur of the previous hours' walk, trivialising, through the roar of engines, the tumult of the leaves and the spattering of the rain.

I had glimpsed the great volcanic cones behind Melrose again and again as I moved along the borderline. These were the triple mounds with Iron Age forts on their tops for which the Romans had given it the name 'Tri-montium'. It was on these slopes that Thomas the Rhymer was said to have fallen into fairyland. I came over the shoulder of the eastern mound, and through the high barley fields in the floodplain, towards the back of Melrose Abbey. There was no sprawling industrial suburb on this edge of town: the abbey rose directly from its own fields like Christ Church tower glimpsed across an Oxford meadow.

The couples in the high street moved in and out of the brasseries, delicatessens and antique shops, hand-in-hand, at the rapid pace of city-dwellers on a Christmas shopping afternoon. The manager of my boutique hotel – with its international accreditation and carefully arranged swathes of thick silk curtain – had trained abroad.

On the way out of Melrose I stopped at Walter Scott's house at Abbotsford. It was closed. A £15 million renovation was focused, it appeared, on building an underground car park and visitor centre. An artist had marked the entrance with knots of thick rope, strung from a forty-foot glass ceiling. A vast video screen showed a young fashion designer leaning out of an armchair and confiding, 'I haven't read anything by Walter Scott, but he is very important to me.'

I continued through the back of Scott's estate and came out by a small grey loch, municipally arranged with gravel and a bench. This was Cauldshiels. Scott had bought it partly to prevent the local dyers from creating an industrial reservoir and partly to protect, I was told, the habitat for the kelpy. A kelpy is a spirit-horse, which lives at the bottom of deep water, emerging to eviscerate young children, leaving their entrails on the riverbank.

In 1817 Scott told Washington Irving that the loch contained not a kelpy but a roaring lake-bull – 'a kind of amphibious bogle'. Such things, he assured the American, were 'a kind of property in Scotland that belong to the estates and go with the soil'. He added that Scotland 'was above all other countries for this wild and vivid progeny of the fancy'.

He explained how Scottish national identity had been born out of

> The nature of the scenery, the misty magnificence and vagueness of the climate, the wild and gloomy events of its history, the clannish divisions of its people, their local feelings, notions and prejudices, the individuality of their dialect, in which all kinds of odd and peculiar notions were incorporated, by the secluded lives of their mountaineers, the lonely habits of their pastoral people much of whose time was spent on the solitary hillsides, their traditional songs which clothed every rock and stream with old world stories; handed down from age to age and generation to generation.

This was how my father still enjoyed thinking about Scotland sometimes. I could imagine having similar thoughts about Afghanistan. But I had not seen this Scotland on my walk.

92

I came from Melrose to Traquair along the high ridge of the Cheviots, following in the path of the great hero of cavalier Scotland, the Marquess of Montrose, as he fled from defeat at the hands of a lowland Presbyterian army. I could see over the ridge and down to Foulshiels, which had been the home of Mungo Park, who had inspected the Yarrow stone, and who in 1795 had walked alone for 600 miles along the Niger River, posing as a wandering magician and paying his way with locks of his blond hair. On his return, he lived in his farmhouse by Yarrow with 'a black man': Sidi Omback Boubi, a Moroccan from Essaouira, who was teaching him Arabic.

We don't know what Boubi looked like. When a local Selkirk artist offered to paint him, Sidi was so outraged at the attempt to depict a human form that he tried to stab him. But there are many accounts of his quest for halal meat in Selkirk in 1805. He bought his meat live in the market, then dragged it into the square, turned the animal's head in the direction of Mecca, recited a prayer and, to the surprise of the watching crowd, cut its throat, spraying scarlet blood across the cobblestones.

Above Mungo Park's house, the grass was a pale russet-brown, the sky a pale blue; an uplands of rolling hills without rocks, or waterfalls, or wild animals. Washington Irving described looking at this landscape with Walter Scott himself:

> I could trace the scenes of those poems and romances that had, in a manner, bewitched the world. I gazed about me for a time with mute surprise, I may almost say with disappointment. I beheld a mere succession of gray waving hills, line beyond line, as far as my eye could reach; monotonous in their aspect, and so destitute of trees, that one could almost see a stout fly walking along their profile; and the far-famed Tweed appeared a naked stream, flowing between bare hills, without a tree or thicket on its banks.
>
> 'I like the very nakedness of the land,' Scott replied, 'it has something bold, and stern, and solitary about it.'

Scott's was a splendid retort, but it wasn't convincing. The steeper, bare rock slopes and deep valleys of the Highlands would have fitted 'bold' or 'stern' more easily than did these hills of the Borders. And there was nothing in Scott's own character that suggested any sympathy for nakedness, sternness or solitude as virtues. He was famous for his enjoyment of costume, his good humour and his sociability. 'He'll stand and crack and lauff wi' me, just like an auld wife,' said one contemporary.

Mungo Park had also found this scenery dismal. He had decided that he 'would rather brave Africa and all its horrors than wear out his life in long and toilsome rides over cold and lonely heaths and gloomy hills'. Scott and Mungo Park rode up to this ridge line on a foggy wet day in September 1804. As they parted, Park's horse stumbled in a ditch. Scott said, 'I am afraid, Mungo, that is a bad omen.' To which Park replied, smiling, and with a reference to an old Border ballad: 'Friets [omens] follow those that look for them.'

A year later, on a second expedition to the Niger, Mungo Park had penetrated hundreds of miles into Africa. Just as the grouse season had begun above Yarrow, Park's friend and neighbour George Scott, who had inspected the Yarrow stone with Park, Scott and Leyden, fell behind the main party. Park did not turn back to look for him, and Scott died of a fever, robbed by villagers as he died. Two months later, Park buried another Yarrow man, his brother-in-law Anderson, by the mosque at Sansanding in Mali. In his last letter, Park wrote back to the minister who was backing the expedition:

> My dear friend, Mr Anderson, and likewise Mr Scott, are both dead; but though all the Europeans who are with me should die, though I were myself half dead, I would still persevere; and if I could not succeed in the object of my journey, I would at last die on the Niger.

Mungo Park disappeared in late November, falling from a boat into rapids as he faced down a final attack. Twenty-one years later, his son mounted an expedition from Peebles to see if he could trace his father. He died of fever almost as soon as he stepped off the boat. In 1830, an explorer reached the African village where Park had last been sighted, and found a piece of stiff card. The hero's name was preserved not in the language of the *Gododdin* or of the Border ballads, but in the equally distinctive prose of a newer world:

> Mr Mungo Park
>
> Mr and Mrs Watson would be happy to have the pleasure of Mr Park's company, at dinner, on Tuesday next, at half past five o'clock.
>
> An answer is requested.
>
> STRAND, 9th November, 1804.

93

I came down off the hills, and onto the road, in the late afternoon. Ahead were the great locked gates of Traquair, which had not been opened for Montrose in his hour of need. Walter Scott suggested how the hamlet of Traquair might have looked in 1744:

> The houses seemed miserable in the extreme especially to an eye accustomed to the smiling neatness of English cottages. They stood without any respect for regularity on each side of a straggling kind of unpaved street, where children almost in a primitive state of nakedness, lay sprawling, as if to be crushed by the hooves of the first passing horse . . . a score of idle useless curs followed, snarling, barking, howling, and snapping at the horses' heels.

It had been, in Scott's description, a scene almost from the modern tropics. The naked children, however, had lived in cold rain, and in earth houses whose foundations melted beneath the snowdrifts. Now the modern houses had pebble-dashed walls. The paved streets were empty; there was no sign of children, still less of wild dogs. I felt I could stand there for hours, silent, on the real concrete pavement and see nobody, absolutely nobody. I had arranged in advance to walk up the next drive, up a long grass field, to a small stone courtyard behind an iron railing.

The house, Traquair, was an accretion of white towers, seventy feet high. Tiny windows pierced curving walls. The owner did not live in the castle itself, but in a cottage down the road, with a trampoline in the yard and two children's bicycles in the hall. I knew her husband, and she kindly cooked me lasagne. Catherine Maxwell Stuart was a Stuart descended directly from the dynasty that had owned the place since 1107. She had taken over as the '21st Lady of Traquair' when her father had died. It was, a sign explained, the oldest continuously inhabited home in Scotland, and had been visited by twenty-seven kings and queens.

Her family's history was not very different from that of the Drummonds or the Stewarts of Ardvorlich, near my father in Crieff. They were distantly related to the royal family; fought at most of the great battles; remained Catholic; lost – like almost everyone – an ancestor at the Battle of Flodden; had opposed the Campbells; had backed Montrose; then wavered a little disgracefully; been imprisoned under sentence of death; had backed the Jacobite rising; had been in exile; and experienced a brief prosperity, long past. It was a story I seemed to have heard a dozen times.

The owner had almost no land any more. She was somehow supporting the house and its treasures through selling tickets to visitors, and running a café and a brewery. The last time I had visited they had been running a festival called 'Books, Borders, and Bikes', looking at how 'landscape, identity and literature intertwined'. The logo had been a watercolour of a 1920s couple on a tandem – the man sat behind, in a trilby, holding a guidebook. There were literary walks, and opportunities to cycle from 'Walter Scott's home at Abbotsford to Traquair with Scottish storyteller John Nichol', or 'hear the Borders' landscape whisper its enchanting tales'.

But I could sense other energies animating her project. I had first met Catherine's husband, a human rights lawyer, in Afghanistan four years earlier. He had just returned from Iraq. He had stood more than once to be a Labour MP, as had she. One walk was to be led by Raja Shehadeh, whose book *Palestinian Walks* had won the Orwell Prize for political writing in 2008.

My hosts had now moved on to a larger event, to be called 'Beyond Borders', and were establishing a consultancy company with the same name. This new festival was represented in black-and-white photojournalism images. My friend Marie Colvin, the eye-patch-wearing, funny, brave war-reporter, whom I had last seen in Libya, had come not long before she was killed in Syria. So too the American poet Jorie Graham, who talked about 'her sense of place'. The idea of the festival was to

> harness Scotland's unique heritage to provide both a platform and a model to cultural leaders from around the world to exchange experiences in an effort to promote greater understanding and help reduce conflict. It uses the Scottish Borderlands – which once historically was seen as a wall of division between warring countries – as a meeting place for world cultures and leaders.

Their last event was called 'From Tahrir Square to Traquair'. They seemed generous, and global in their ambitions.

They kindly let me stay not in the cottage but in the main house. I passed the eroded, wind-warped beasts – once two bears – that stood above the great gates. The gates, like so much else, had been celebrated by Walter Scott. They were not to be opened until the Stuart dynasty returned to the throne, and, therefore, nearly 300 years later, they remained closed. Catherine showed me a picture of an ancestor: he had fair skin and high pink cheeks, and his neat beard and horizontal moustaches were cut exactly to match those of his friend and patron, King Charles I. He stood hatless in the long gold-embroidered coat of the Lord Treasurer of Scotland, one hand on his wand of office, the other on the red velvet of the privy purse. He had been for a time the most powerful figure in the kingdom of Scotland, but when the king was beheaded he was ruined.

A contemporary wrote of him:

> He was a true emblem of the vanity of the world – a very meteor. I saw him begging in the streets of Edinburgh. He was in an antique garb, and a broad old hat, short cloak, and pannier breeches . . . We gave him a noble, he standing with his hat off . . . He received the piece of money from my hand as humbly and thankfully as the poorest supplicant. It is said that at a time he had not to pay for cobbling his boots, and died in a poor cobbler's house.

I stayed in an old bedroom that was sometimes rented to guests. I remember it, perhaps incorrectly, as filled with fragile oak furniture. I have a sense of a narrow bed – was it a four-poster? – and of shutters and vast windows looking towards the river. A simple bathroom was available down the corridor. It may have been her grandmother's bedroom, that was now open to the public. My hosts had put sweet peas on the table for me.

Steep curving stone stairs led to a square library on the floor above. The 4,000 books in the library were mostly collected between 1710 and 1730. High plasterwork contained portrait heads of classical philosophers in aquatint browns and greys. The colours of the heads made Protagoras and Socrates look as though they were on their way to a meeting at Edinburgh University with an eighteenth-century political economist. For a moment I was tempted to ask to be locked in. If I could skim ten books a day for a year, I would be able to get a sense of most of what

David Hume might have read in 1730, an age when it still might just have been possible to read everything.

94

On the road out, through Innerleithen, I saw hundreds of small photographs plastering the window of the post office. They were of the 'Common Riding' – an annual event originally intended to confirm the borders of the village on horseback. It was now a local fiesta. There were photos of earnest young riders in velvet jackets, children with face paint and a brass band.

Similar traditions – of young men and women selected as champions, of a flag, bands or cavalcades on horseback round the parish boundaries – were repeated in Scottish towns across the Borders. Each event was linked to the reivers. Oddly, although the reiver culture had once spread equally across both sides across the border, there was now no equivalent in England. And although it was a Scottish tradition it was quite different from the festivals in central Scotland.

Through the online Scottish Screen Archive, I watched the images of the 1912 Bo'ness festival, in central Scotland, which had been going since the eighteenth century. Here there were no horses. In the silent film, hundreds of young women marched in column, wearing pure white knee-length dresses, with white stockings and white shoes. Their hair was long and down, signifying that they were still 'girls'. The boys followed dressed as buglers in surcoats, as Renaissance aristocrats in velvet caps with flowers, as eighteenth-century pages in knickerbockers, and as fifteenth-century knights with grieves. Two of the children were in full Japanese kimonos, embroidered with dragons. Here – a decade before my father was born – the imagery was already global. A small mining community in central Scotland in 1912 was drawing on imagery and symbols from a dozen different historical periods, and from countries 6,000 miles away.

At the time of the procession in 1912 the differences between English and Scottish institutions must have felt starker than they do today. In Scotland the state religion was Presbyterian, in England Anglican; Scottish schools, exams and universities were different – and in many ways better – than English; Scotland had a separate legal system, and there was an ancient tradition of alliance with France. Such factors, many Scots believed, had created a more egalitarian, more educated, more pro-European 'civic culture'.

But it was impossible to tell from the film whether Bo'ness was in Scotland or England. The majority of the adult men were in three-piece dark suits and stiff collars. They played with their sprawling watch chains and their pipes. Many must have gone two or three years later to fight in the First World War. The children danced round a maypole. Among all the costume and aspiration and display, the one thing that was missing was any sign of a kilt. People in Lowland Scotland in 1912 might have wished to represent themselves as Henry V, the Earl of Essex or even the Emperor of Japan, but apparently not as men in kilts.

The first kilt appeared in a film of the festival shot in 1925. It was worn by a four-year-old boy. But the camera's attention was fixed on a girl dressed as Britannia, proudly readjusting her helmet, trident and Union Jack shield. Even by 1947, Union Jacks were more numerous than the Scottish lion. By the 2008 film, however, the central parade was now dominated by pipe bands; the stewards wore kilts, and great Saltire flags were carried down the centre of the street. National institutions had changed since the time of the first film. Few of the people in the crowd went to a Presbyterian kirk, even fewer could explain what was distinctive about Scottish law, or were confident that their educational system was superior. But a kilt was no longer fancy dress, or something associated with the Highlands. There was no Union Jack to be seen. You could no longer be in England.

But there were still no kilts to be seen in the photos of the Common Riding on the wall of Innerleithen post office. Instead there was a blurred photo of my two hosts, cut off at the knees – he in a pale linen jacket, she in some form of ceremonial dress – addressing the crowd. Her family had been at Traquair since 1107, and in direct descent since 1491. It was easy to imagine they might not be there much longer. But that assumption had been made before. These Traquair Stuarts had been written off many times since the family's collapse in the 1650s. In the 1850s, the physician John Brown wrote:

> The whole place, like the family whose it has been, seems dying out – everything subdued to settled desolation. The old race, the old religion, the gaunt old house, with the small deep comfortless windows, the decaying trees, the stillness about the doors, the grass overrunning everything . . . strange and pitiful.

But another 150 years had passed, and it was Brown's essays which were forgotten. The family was still there.

95

My route had taken me on from Traquair through Peebles and Neidpath, over the hills to Broughton, Carnwath, Motherwell and Cumbernauld. I followed some of the route that Dorothy and William Wordsworth took in 1805, and I stayed in Robert Owen's vast cotton mills at New Lanark, which seemed to mark a world after Wordsworth, but which had been erected twenty years before his journey. I walked over the grass that hid the spoil-heaps of open-cast mines, and listened to a man who remembered being stoned on his way to his Irish Catholic school in the 1920s. I passed John Buchan's home at Broughton, and Hugh MacDiarmid's locked cottage at Candy Mill. (A passer-by told me that MacDiarmid smelled and was always grumpy at the bus stop.)

On the final day of the walk from Traquair – having passed the remains of the great aluminium plants, seen the space where the Glasgow tenements once stood, visited the high-rise housing and explored a 1960s 'New Town' – I reached Motherwell, where my father's great-aunt had been the hospital matron for forty years. There I stayed with a friend: a Labour MP and Irish Republican. He showed me the grotto which unemployed men had built during the Great Depression of the 1920s. It was a replica of Lourdes. He pointed out that even today you could distinguish a Catholic from a Protestant pub in Glasgow by the colour of the paint on the façade. There were invisible borders between the streets. He showed me the cathedral, where he sat every Sunday, listening to the bishop. He took me with reluctance to the Orange Lodge ('I feel like I am taking you to meet the Ku Klux Klan'). He conceded that some people thought he exaggerated the divisions between the communities – but then, he said, they didn't live here.

He also took me to meet union organisers. 'Monday to Friday, my body belongs to the trade union movement,' he said, 'Saturday, my heart to Celtic Football Club, and Sunday my soul to the Catholic Church.' He took me into the community centre where he had been married, then showed me his party office on the high street.

He had grown up in the area, and had been a steelworker in the Dalziel mill for sixteen years. He had been elected with over 60 per cent of the vote. He was in the process of sending questionnaires to every single one of his voters. I could not begin to believe that he might lose his seat to the Scottish National Party. But he did.

★

I took a detour to Bo'ness, which stands on the Roman Antonine Wall. This was the frontier line which Tacitus had preferred to Hadrian's Wall, connecting the Forth to the Clyde – 'where the sea almost makes Britain into two islands'. This 'natural line' had, for 700 years after the Roman departure, remained the boundary between the Northumbrian Angles and Cumbrian Britons on the south side, and the Scots and Picts on the north. And perhaps if the Scottish king had not won a battle at Carham in 1016, this line on the Forth might have become the border between England and Scotland.

This was the place where the festival had been filmed in 1912. Between the town of Bo'ness and the Forth there had once been clay pits, potteries, ironworks, fisheries, sawmills, ship-breaking yards, scrap-metal dealers and the oldest coal mine in Scotland. But all this industry had gone. The mine pumping station to the south of the bowling club had been made into a replica of a medieval 'doocot' or dovecot, and the mine was hidden by a neat layer of mown green grass, edged with broad sycamores. Opposite the club was a giant slab of bright yellow sandstone. I walked over, narrowly missing a Ford Fiesta full of teenagers, circling and blaring the horn. The inscription read:

> Imperator Caesar Titus Aelius Hadrianus Antoninus Augustus Pius, Pater patriae, absolvitur a legione Secunda Augusta passuum intervallo (IV)DCLV.

An adjacent sign translated the 1,900-year-old inscription:

> For the Emperor Caesar Titus Aelius Hadrianus Antoninus Augustus Pius, Father of his Country, the Second Augustan Legion completed a distance of 4655 paces.

On the right-hand side, a cow, a sheep and a pig had been carved, patiently lining up beside an altar. A band of men carried a flag which said, in case anyone was in any doubt, 'Second Augustan Legion'. It was a monument commemorating the construction of a few miles of the frontier wall of the Roman emperor Antoninus Pius, a hundred miles north of Hadrian's Wall.

The slab I was looking at was a replica, 'scientifically recreated through laser-scanning and laser-cutting'. The original, found in 1850, was in an Edinburgh museum. Online, Alan Rodger, of Development Services, Falkirk Council, said of the decision to make a replica: 'It's a very important initiative. It promotes the area in terms of tourism both at a local level, at a national level, and even an international level. It meets many of the council's objectives.' Nothing online had told me how much it had cost. There were no tourists to be seen. No people except the teenagers in the Fiesta, circling and blaring their horn for the seventh time.

On the left-hand side was another carved image. The Roman cavalryman's face was made up of four crude angles. Beneath the hooves of his prancing pony were four small naked figures, plump with passive, half-smiling, impersonal faces, like cherubs. These were the Britons, or more precisely in this area, perhaps the Votadini.

Two men walked out of the bowling club across the road, and introduced themselves as Dave and Fordie. Fordie explained that he had been a miner for twenty years, before the mines were closed. I asked them what they made of the stone. Dave observed, 'That was what the Romans were trying to convey: that anyone who wasn't Roman or part of the empire, was inferior, a bunch of savages. I don't suppose the native people were totally barbarous. But the Romans felt they were here to civilise us. I'm not sure if they succeeded.' He laughed.

The position of the limbs of the naked Britons suggested they were dancing. One had a spike through his back. Another was sitting on top of his severed head. In the original, these figures would have been brightly painted, the splashes of blood scarlet.

'No one likes us, you know,' Fordie said cheerfully, apparently reading the Roman sculpture as a piece of contemporary propaganda and seeing himself as the skewered cherub. 'The English hate the Scots, and the Welsh, but particularly the Scots. I'd like Scottish independence, but I'll not be voting for it, because I don't vote ever. Still, you can see what the English think of us in *Braveheart*.'

'*Braveheart* is nonsense,' said Dave, softly shrugging his shoulders in his tartan sweater and folding his arms. He had a gentle, confident Glasgow accent.

'Ay, weel. I suppose so,' said Fordie.

'It's nonsense,' Dave repeated.

'So how would you describe the identity of this area?' I asked Dave.

'Well, originally,' Dave said carefully, 'it was a Welsh-British kingdom, the Votadini or Gododdin. Then it was part of the English-speaking Anglian kingdom of Northumbria. It did not become part of Scotland till the Middle Ages.'

I was surprised by Dave's analysis and understanding. I had felt that we – the English and the Scots – talked a great deal about tradition and history, but that we were committed to the categories 'England' and 'Scotland'. We liked to imply the 'English' and 'Scots' were a very ancient people, organically linked to our soil. Roman history was part of our history. Even Stonehenge, and Skara Brae, 4,000 years old, were somehow 'ours'. And there was not much room in this story for Middleland kingdoms and other identities.

Some distinguished historians still like to emphasise the connection between the nations today and a very distant past. In their analysis of the Middle Ages they emphasise the kind of virtues which Scots feel they possess in the twenty-first century. I had just read one contemporary historian who wrote, 'There is evidence that medieval Scotland was a more open society, with better opportunities for social mobility [than England] . . . It would be an exaggeration to say that medieval Scotland was egalitarian or democratic, but . . .' Scotland, which retained extreme feudal practices longer than had England, was presented as a strikingly democratic and collaborative civilisation. 'The pursuit of the intellect has long been a very Scottish obsession,' wrote another about the fifteenth century.

There was little said about the alternative kingdoms, peoples and languages that had been crushed in the enterprise of forging a Scottish state. The obliteration of the Picts, the crushing of the Strathclyde Britons, the seizure of the Norse kingdoms of the Orkneys and the Gaelic kingdom of Galloway, the subjection of the Lord of the Isles, the evisceration of the Lords of Lorne and the Mormaership of Moray were all presented as part of the inevitable growth of 'Scotland'. Few ever made Scotland's status as a 'nation' seem complicated or contested. It was only other people's states – Syria or Libya, for example – which were circumscribed by 'artificial borders', that were 'not real countries'.

Dave apparently had a more complex view. His comments suggested a territory composed of many nations, which had once defied the modern borders. I assumed, therefore, that this would make him less of a Scottish nationalist. I was wrong.

'It's great,' he concluded, 'that Scotland was the point that the Romans got no further.' He continued, cheerfully, 'They didn't get beyond us. We "sent them homewards to think again", as it says in the song. At my heart I'm a nationalist.'

Dave himself had worked around Scandinavia and the Middle East, selling kitchens. He had moved to Bo'ness only because his wife was here.

'Is there a connection between your interest in history and your nationalism?'

'It's partially linked to my interest in history,' said Dave. 'I don't think you can be a nationalist unless there's a little bit of your soul that links you to the land – to where you come from.'

'And are your son and daughter nationalists?' I asked.

'Well, they are civil servants,' said Dave. 'They will vote for independence but it won't be for emotional reasons. It will be because they believe we will be better off economically.'

'What would your father have thought of your being a Scottish nationalist?' I asked.

'I don't think he'd have understood,' reflected Dave. 'He was from Birmingham. He was English, his life was in the RAF and the British Empire.'

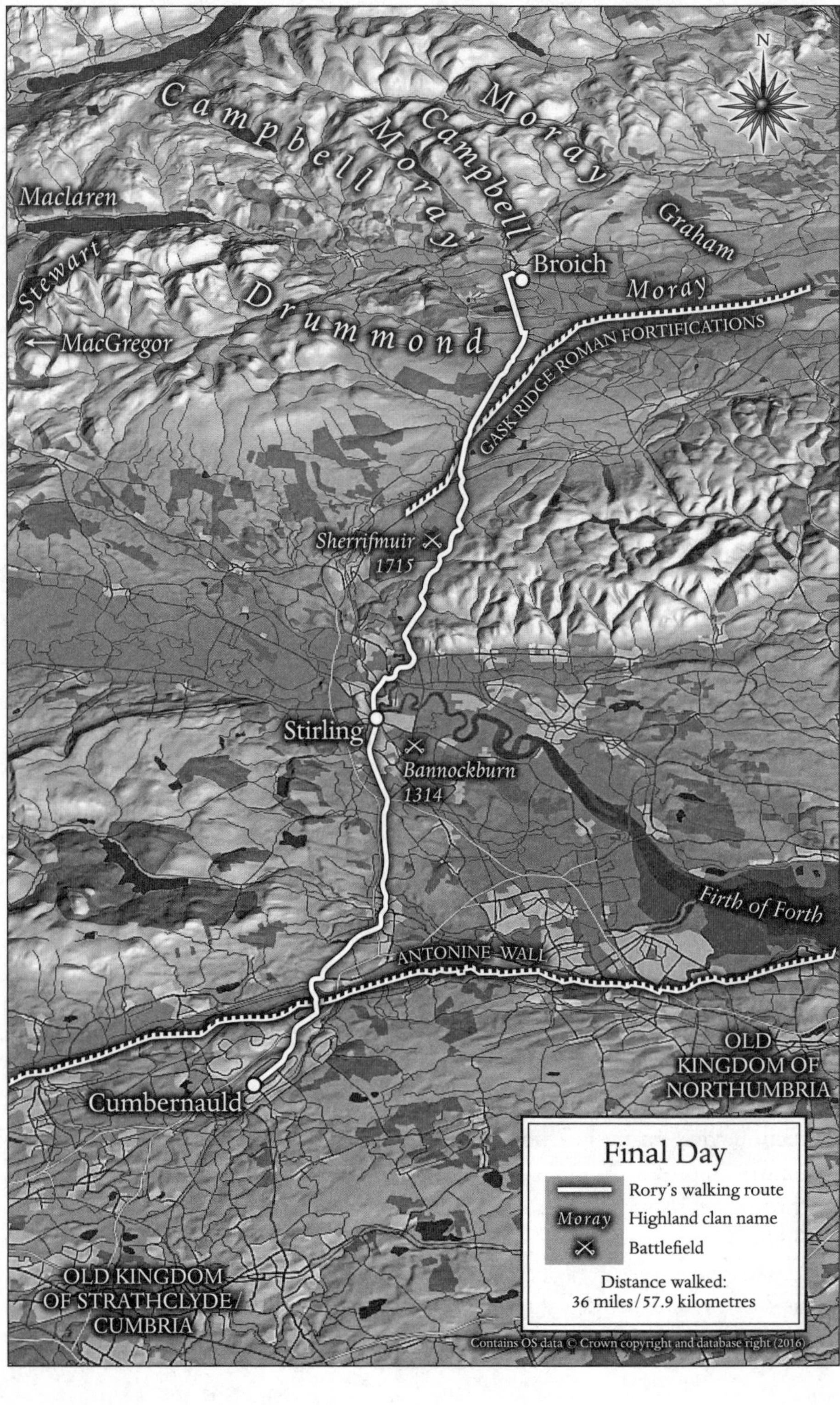

N
Campbell
Moray
Campbell
Moray
Maclaren
Graham
Stewart
Broich
Moray
Drummond
MacGregor
GASK RIDGE ROMAN FORTIFICATIONS
Sherrifmuir 1715
Stirling
Bannockburn 1314
Firth of Forth
ANTONINE WALL
OLD KINGDOM OF NORTHUMBRIA
Cumbernauld
Final Day
Rory's walking route
Moray Highland clan name
Battlefield
Distance walked: 36 miles / 57.9 kilometres
OLD KINGDOM OF STRATHCLYDE/ CUMBRIA
Contains OS data © Crown copyright and database right (2016)

96

The final day's walk from Cumbernauld back to my father's home was long. By the late afternoon, I had been walking for perhaps twelve hours, and it was raining hard. Ahead of me, thick fog billowed across Loch Turret reservoir, making Ben Chonzie stand above the cloud like a mountain above rainforest. Bands of slate grey, pale blue and cream appeared and vanished in the sky, and beside me shafts of light picked out the smooth trunks of the beech.

Returning from Asia ten years earlier, I had walked this same road, and noticed only how green it was compared to Afghanistan, and how neat the kerb had been. Now, at the end of this walk, I was more aware of the differences within the grasses: on the right, rye, and patches of intense green, where the livestock had staled; on the left, Yorkshire fog; and ahead thirty acres of land, not grazed, nor cropped for silage, but thick with dying thistles.

I was now crossing the land of the Drummonds, between the territory of a number of Scottish clans celebrated by Walter Scott. And I had learned the features of this landscape walking with friends descended from these clans. My friends could still show me the cave in which an ancestor had hid; where on the shoreline he had ambushed a raiding party; the patch on the road where he had buried nine enemies (they were dug up, constructing the A85, and consisted then of only skeletons and brass buttons). The place-names on the Ordnance Survey maps recorded the names of their family members, those who had hid, killed or mourned, in the lochans and hills. And I realised that all the way through the Borders I had been looking for, and failing to find, exactly this kind of history.

My favourite neighbour, Colonel David Rose, a Black Watch officer with a white walrus moustache, was sixty years older than me and had taught me as a child that one of his Campbell ancestors had led a revenge attack with his Drummond allies on the Murrays in 1490, burning a hundred of them alive in a church.

Later, I learned from Stewart neighbours that one of their Drummond relatives (a descendant of one of the Drummonds who had participated in the raid) caught two MacGregors poaching in the forest. He cut off their ears. In retaliation, the MacGregors beheaded him and placed his head, with oatcakes in its mouth, on the table of his brother-in-law, a Stewart. At the sight, Lady Stewart ran mad into the hills. Her son grew up to kill many MacGregors. The vendetta, which began in 1490, pulled in the MacLarens, the Campbells and ultimately the Grahams. A hundred and fifty years after the beginning of the feud one of the Grahams was stabbed in his tent by a Stewart.

This story – inevitably recounted by Walter Scott, as well as my neighbours – might have been dismissed as fantasy, except I had discovered that it was recorded chapter by chapter in the parliament and privy council papers of Scotland. Legal rulings, court investigations, sentences, incentives and pardons all demonstrated the attempts of the Scottish state to impose a bureaucratic veneer and logic on this tribal war. And then there were the artefacts in their houses. I had handled the dagger the Stewart had used to stab the Graham. This was not some distant medieval past. The killer of the Graham lived well past the Union of the Crowns, till 1680, and his life overlapped with Isaac Newton's.

Many of the feuding families still kept magical objects in their houses. In one home, a crystal; in another, a 'fairy-bolt', or arrowhead, encased in fifteenth-century silver, that was worn by the women of the family when pregnant. They had inherited secret Gaelic spells, to be spoken while stirring the objects through water. As late as the nineteenth century, farmers had come to their houses seeking cures for their cattle. Some of these treasures were perhaps part of their patrimony, as heirs to royal kingdoms. Some were inherited by marriage into families who had been in the Highlands since the Iron Age; others were jewels acquired in the Holy Land. The tradition was so old and so continuous that some of the military amulets had preceded Christianity in Scotland, and then been wielded in the Crusades.

Yet these families of lairds and Highland chieftains, who had once dominated Highland culture, were now almost invisible. The people I had grown up with felt that they were targets of the new Scottish nationalism, that they were blamed for the Clearances two centuries earlier, and that their public school accents were now considered English. So they increasingly concealed their traditions from the wider Scottish world.

And I was realising that very few people who lived in this area knew any of these traditions and stories. Instead, even those who loved to talk of the 'Celtic' past, and speak Scottish Gaelic, preferred to retell the Victorian myths about ghosts and Highland castles, which in recent decades had been reprinted in paperback and sold in newsagents across the Highlands.

97

Four miles from Crieff I reached a cottage with a bell-bottomed chimney stack bulging from the gable end, and a sign saying '*Taigh-na-Seanachaidh*'. 'The Story-Teller's Cottage' stood between a desultory avenue of middle-aged oaks, a little bent from the true, and a forty-acre field of dark chocolate soil. I must have passed it a hundred times without entering. But a friend of mine had suggested I knock on the door on the way home, so I did, and a lady with long red hair appeared around the side and led me in to her husband, Scott – the *Seanachaidh*, or, as he described himself, 'a passionate keeper and teller of the oral literature and history, folk, clan and Norse tales; historical and place tales and stories reaching back to the time of the Picts'.

Scott was warming himself by a cast-iron stove, dressed in a green kilt, army-surplus jumper, sandals and green ankle-socks. His thin auburn hair was scraped back into a plait and his goatee was streaked with white. He wore his two tiny, hairy sporrans high on his hips. I explained about my journey, and asked if he could tell me a little about his life. Scott started at the beginning. He had been born, he said, in the English Midlands, to parents originally from Glasgow. When he was five the family had returned to Loch Lomond in Scotland. They remained there for only two years before moving to Wales. 'But,' Scott said, 'that is when I gained my identity as a Scot. My brother has not retained any real attachment to Scotland. He has become very English. He lives in Manchester. It has been a long time since I spoke to him. He was born in Ireland, but he has a Luton accent.'

I asked him why, since he had grown up mostly in Wales, he didn't feel Welsh. His answer came in a flurry. 'We both learned to speak Welsh to a degree, but once we got older, they were Welsh and we were not. Anyway, we were in the north of Wales, which is like a little England . . . It was a Welsh farming community, and quite closed . . . We weren't farmers. If you're not a farmer, you don't know any farmers.' Each sentence seemed to challenge its predecessor. 'We lived surrounded by farms, and my friends were farmer's children – Eilena and Arad – Welsh-speakers.'

Scott had gone to Keele University in Staffordshire, and played the drums in six bands, what he called 'folk, blues, grungy rock'. He had tried to stay on in the area, promoting music, but things didn't work out. So he set off for Scotland on an Enfield racing bike. He ended up in the 'Pollok Free State', a demonstration camp which had been set up to fight against a motorway near Glasgow. The community had lost the battle over the motorway, but they had remained in the camp. Its leader – 'the famous Colin Macleod' – had given Scott a glass of a sixteen-year-old Lagavulin. I had imagined that this story was going to conclude with Scott's settling in Scotland, but in fact Macleod had encouraged the young man to travel to India.

Scott felt he needed to save some money for the move, so he had returned to England and spent the next five years in Daventry, driving vans and working as a council gardener. This was when he had begun to wear a kilt every day. (He opened a drawer and showed me ten kilts.) When his five years were up, he moved to Cornwall. He had heard that in the spring yachts sailed from the coast, and one of those yachts might be his first stage to India. But he arrived a bit early, in February, and the yachts were not yet sailing. He had to make other plans. 'Because I couldn't get work daffodil picking, I became a houseboy for a man who was running workshops in tantra and Eastern philosophies,' he said. 'From there, I moved to Ireland, where I was very influenced by the people.'

'By Irish people?'

'No. The people I lived with were Dutch and German. Bohemian. Organic farmers. Looking for a better life for their children. I lived with a girlfriend, Fiona, and managed a farm. Ninety acres. Thirty-odd sheep, lots of trees. Basically living off farming subsidies.'

When Fiona left him – 'Couldn't put up with him,' his wife Samantha interjected from the sofa, laughing – Scott travelled to the States. 'I studied courses in Earth Wisdom. When I came back to

Britain, I organised courses for Rainbow Hawk.' (He said 'Rainbow Hawk' as though I should have heard of him. I guessed that this was perhaps a Native American shaman.) The work hadn't been elevating. 'In the end, it comes down to parking, toilets, running water and a fire-pit.'

By then he had spent seven years preparing to go to India. 'I supported myself by repairing computers.'

In 2000 he moved to Scotland and took up selling souvenirs to tourists on the 'Jacobite' steam train, which travelled up and down a few miles of track in Glenfinnan, in the western Highlands. Finally, in 2002, he moved to Kilmartin Glen. 'I felt the freest I've ever been.'

Kilmartin Glen was, I sensed, the climax of Scott's story. It was this place that had led this man, from Wales and the English Midlands with Glaswegian parents, to say, 'I'm from Argyll. I'm from the west coast.' It was there that he had met Samantha, where he had found a home. 'It is my spiritual home. I feel different there. It was where I came to be what I am now.'

When he went to the bathroom, Samantha talked about their life in Argyll. 'It was a very insular place. The locals didn't ever accept us. We had no Scottish friends in Kilmartin Glen. All our friends were foreigners like us. They didn't like me, and they didn't like him – a man with long hair in a skirt.'

When Scott returned, I was tempted to try to explore some of the apparent contradictions in his identity. He had described himself as a *seanachaidh* 'since 1994', although it was more accurate to describe him as a gardener, truck driver and computer technician who had moved to Scotland in 2000. But I felt it would be unkind to press these points with him. That his life was somehow remarkable, even if it didn't quite add up. He was not trying to conceal incongruities or promote himself or profit by these myths. I sensed that a *seanachaidh* – a Gaelic story-teller – was what he wanted to be, and what he almost was.

He took out a lyre from a green velvet bag. 'It is the only instrument like it in the world. Unlike a dulcimer, it does not sit on the soundboard – except at the edges – which gives it a more ethereal sound. It is tuned to the white piano keys, with an added F sharp, playing D minor, with a flattened seventh to play modal music like traditional Greek modal music, the Lycian, the Phrygian . . .'

Like everything else in his life, the wood from which the lyre was made was described very carefully: Cornish yew, rosewood and lemonwood from Brazil, black ebony from a species, now extinct, that had been ballast on a ship which sank in 1830 in the English Channel. The frame had originally been made from 'birdseye maple, sustainably managed by the Algonquin'; it had since been replaced by his friend 'the luthier' and he did not know what new wood he had used. Scott had wanted twenty-one strings, but the luthier had said having twenty-four would allow him to use guitar stops, so twenty-four it had.

I liked the fact that he admitted his willingness to use more convenient guitar stops, and his ignorance of the wood that had replaced the maple in the lyre's frame. I asked what he called the instrument, half fearing he might have named it after some Celtic princess. He simply called it a 'lap-harp'.

He explained that he had been recently appointed as *seanachaidh* to a Highland chieftain, Maclean of Duart. The previous chieftain, Sir Fitzroy Maclean, an old Etonian war hero and Conservative politician, had not kept a *seanachaidh*. Indeed, it appeared *seanachaidhs* had died out long before Dr Johnson's trip of 1774, perhaps as long ago as the 1400s. But as chieftains and their clan traditions were being forgotten in Scottish culture, *seanachaidhs* seemed to be reappearing.

As a *seanachaidh*, Scott said he had assembled a large library of rare books on ballads and traditional stories. When I asked him to show it to me, he took me to a small bookcase on a landing which contained perhaps fifty books of popular history, a few modern editions of ballads, and some Victorian collections of 'Celtic myths and legends'. Among these lay an unpublished nineteenth-century Gaelic manuscript that he had photocopied in the Scottish National Archives. I asked him to read some of it to me.

He knelt down on the floor and began. It was clear that he had studied some Gaelic, but not quite enough. He could translate individual words – one came every twenty seconds or so – and he could work out some phrases, but he could not quite complete a sentence. Yet he did not give up for many minutes, not until I asked him to come down from the landing. He did not seem upset at his failure to read his Gaelic text.

Eventually we talked politics. He thought there ought to be separate governments to recognise the separate cultures of the Highlands, as well as a separate government for the Islands. The Borders, too, needed its own, because the people 'are neither English nor Scots, they are Borderers, and they wear flat caps and are forty years behind the rest of us'. Perthshire wasn't one culture, it was two, divided by the Highland Line. Perhaps Scotland should be divided by agriculture, by soil, by what people planted, he thought.

'As Ewan MacColl said, people shouldn't play the folk music of a culture they don't come from,' Scott concluded.

'But isn't your performance – Iron Age plaids, harp and folk stories – really something borrowed quite recently from Ireland? Is this kind of Celtic music really representative of Scotland?'

'Celtic music,' he pronounced, after a characteristic moment of self-reflection, 'is an incomplete truth, supported by the tourist industry, and the media and schools. We are, for example, just as much Norse. And we are equally French. Today, because of the school curriculum, there is far more Gaelic in Glasgow and Edinburgh schools, where they never spoke Gaelic in the first place. I want to say to them, "I love the fact that you speak Gaelic, but can't you celebrate who you are? Could you not speak Scots-English?"' Then he said that he was a Scottish nationalist, adding in words which did not sound like his own, 'An independent Scotland would flourish in Europe; its government would be closer to the people.'

I wanted to know what he made of the area of Scotland in which he now lived: Strathearn, in Perthshire. How did he try to weave his tales into this, his actual local landscape?

'I feel here in Perthshire that I am in a foreign country,' Scott said. 'A place of Grahams and Drummonds . . . a place where all the MPs and politicians come from. Where the Marquess of Montrose, the king's lieutenant, came from. It feels odd to me. I am quite parochial in my outlook. I feel like an interloper here.'

In Argyll, things were different. 'When I cross the Highland Line back to Argyll,' Scott said with a smile, 'I feel I own the bloody place – everyone is my friend. The physical sensation – the air is clearer, my chest opens up, I breathe a sigh of relief. I'm not at somebody else's party. I'm the host.'

Argyll was the place where, according to Samantha, he had lived only briefly, and not been liked by the locals. But as I left, I believed that there he had found a nation and a home.

98

As I continued along the last stretch to Crieff, I was approaching a heather ridge line. Beyond the ridge were what Scott had described as 'big hooses closely packed, and rich estates, and gentlemen'. But it was harsher country than he had implied, harsher perhaps than the rhododendron gardens of the town of Tarbet in Loch Lomond, where he had gained his sense of Scotland. In valleys where 400 years ago there had been crops or cattle pasture, there were now only flowers coming out to bloom from the stiff brown heather, and dark blueberries withering beneath rust-red leaves. The only traces of the huts and fields lay in the ends of broken walls, and the furrows unveiled by a setting afternoon sun. The land was wet, broken by narrow gullies. I moved from rushes and patches of burnt heath, past granite boulders, onto the spring of the heather, startling pipits. This landscape, which I loved, was largely now a half-abandoned grouse moor.

★

From the final crest above Crieff I could see two obelisks on two facing hills. One was dedicated to the Indian Army's General Baird, 'the hero of Seringapatam'. When the monuments were erected – not long before the obelisk to Sir John Malcolm above Langholm – the celebrants had imagined they addressed an imperial culture that might last, like Rome, a millennium. Perhaps my father's father would have felt this when he was in India at the time of the Delhi Durbar, admiring the mahouts and the cavalcade and the diamond-encrusted turbans, being inspected by Lord Curzon, Viceroy to Edward VII. But it had been over so fast: my grandfather had lived to see Indian independence and, after I was born, Britain's entry into the Common Market.

Colonel Rose had taught me when I was a child that General Baird was so unpopular that his family had had to pay for the monument themselves, and that when Baird – a giant – was imprisoned by Tipu Sultan, his mother remarked, 'I pity anyone chained to my Davey.' Colonel Rose also taught me – perhaps in a last trace of unbroken oral tradition from the time of its construction in 1820 – to call it simply the 'prick on the hill'.

The second obelisk was dedicated to Henry Dundas, Viscount Melville – so powerful 200 years ago that he had been known as 'King Harry'. It was he who had given thousands of Scots jobs in the Empire, making the British Empire a Scottish empire. No local person I knew had any memory of this. Even my father, for all his imperial connections and sympathies, no longer remembered Dundas.

★

Entering Crieff, it was already dark. A full moon loomed over a red bull in a field, and over the Neolithic standing stone. A sign revealed that the town had been rebranded in my absence: 'Crieff, Gateway to the Highlands', which had evolved first into 'Crieff, the Holiday Town', was now 'Crieff, the Essence of Scotland'. I walked past the site of the old gasworks, through the caravan park, between the small solar lamps on the paving stones, and climbed the barbed-wire fence into the dairy field. I continued over the drystone wall onto our drive. I was approaching our house from the back.

I could just make out the stone statue of a Hindu god that my father had brought from Bali. I could see the edge of the building that Monteath had built with his money from the Raj. And I could hear the insistent barn owl that nested in an oak planted by the Crown Commissioners after Bonnie Prince Charlie's defeat. I crossed the gathering field, to which the Highlanders brought 10,000 cattle, and where they were tried and hanged, and passed the steading of the Drummond chieftain who had joined the attack on the Morays in 1490. Above stood the Highland Line. Ahead lay the track that once connected the Roman frontier fort at Fendoch to the Roman fort at Strageath. Beyond were the Neolithic lines. And in front stood an eighteenth-century house, where an old man in tartan trews was waiting for me, a torch in his hand. I had found my father again.

BOOK THREE

The general danced at dawn

99

My father's ninety-third year was, he felt, an occasion for significant celebration. So I offered to throw a party for him in London. A few days later he emailed his instructions:

> I suggest that if anyone feels the need to explain what the party is about they could use the following formula. 'Rory is giving a party to celebrate his father's 93rd birthday; forthcoming publication of his two books, *Why Spy?* and *Breaking the Chinese Code*, his coat of arms in St Paul's, a military portrait to be hung in Clarence House, and the promise of a *Légion d'honneur* medal in honour of the fact that he fought in the campaign to liberate France in 1944.'

'But perhaps,' he added, 'no one will ask for an explanation . . .'

The previous November, he and nine other D-Day veterans had been invited to sit for portraits, which were to be hung in the Queen's Gallery in Buckingham Palace and become part of the Royal Collection.

'Should one be so thrilled?' he asked me. 'Or should one just take it as normal? I am *bouleversé*!'

As part of the commissioning, the Black Watch had asked for a brief summary of his war experiences. He produced something in the *Boy's Own* tone:

> On the night of June 30th, we were urgently summoned to an 'O' group and ordered up to take over a salient which intelligence had predicted would be attacked by a Panzer group at dawn. Intelligence was right and from dawn to dusk the battle raged. The Batallion took horrendous casualties and we lost all our guns. However we held the position and my guns claimed fifteen kills.

The portrait painter, Paul Benney, arrived at Broich in December. Paul had long grey hair and a goatee beard. He wore a denim shirt and jacket. I suspected my father expected a regimental painter to look more regimental, but his complaint was not about Paul's clothes.

My father had won a prize for painting as a schoolboy. He generally expressed his aesthetic principles by glancing at a painting and then announcing immediately, 'That's right,' 'Absolutely not,' or 'Bo-rrr-ing.' He collected Chinese calligraphic scrolls, austere Ming pen-and-ink washes of landscapes, and vividly coloured Pekinese dogs, Thai bodhisattvas, Afghan rugs and masks from Cantonese opera. His only purchase of British art was a nineteenth-century oil painting of a bug-eyed Highland stag, roaring over another dead stag, to the delight of two wet-nosed hinds.

He insisted that everyone could paint. It was a question of attitude not skill. And he painted a picture almost every day: not portraits of people – 'far too difficult'; not paintings from nature: 'unnecessary'. That was why he copied postcards of landscapes and animals, portrayed grass as an even monochrome green, and sky in a single wash of dark blue. Patches of white paper showed through the paint. At ninety-one, he had written to me: 'I am inclined to give up all except the Chinese style!!! It is strange, impressionistic, and unlike Western subjects not vulnerable to criticism Western fashion.' He added, as though trying to convince himself, 'Since it is impressionistic . . . .' The result was a collection of brightly coloured birds.

But even if he did not paint portraits, he had strong views on how he should be portrayed. He had always been considered a good-looking man, was particularly proud of his smile, and frequently asserted that you could read someone's character from the lines on their face. 'Never trust someone without laugh lines.' He thought it just and fitting that he should be portrayed as a good-looking smiling man. But that was not how Paul's portrait appeared to him:

'I hope,' he wrote to me, 'you will be less annoyed by the portrait than I am. It does not look like all the smiling photos I see around. This portrait is more likely to tell the world that I was losing it, and quizzical but melancholy. I tried to suggest tactfully more smiley. But was wasting my time. He likes quizzical and experienced.'

A month later, he wrote again in almost the same words, as though the phrases of his resentment had become fixed in his brain:

> The picture is of an old man, slightly melancholy, quizzical or puzzled. Such is life with portrait painters if they are not under

control. Of course we all have moments when our expressions are not the ones we want to see in photos. But it would be nice to be portrayed as a happy chap. I am not talking only of my own version of myself. There are plenty of photos to prove that I do not always look like a puzzled melancholy old man.

I suggested that serious faces were easier to paint. 'The truth of the matter is somewhere between the *Mona Lisa* and *The Laughing Cavalier*,' he replied. 'The family seems to like the picture of the ancient veteran looking too gloomy and perhaps even lost. No matter. But I do not like being remembered as a half-demented, melancholy, puzzled old man.'

Then, perhaps aware that he was beginning to overdo it, he shared a poem (he called it a limerick) he had written on the subject:

> There was a Black Watch Captain eclypt Brian
> His Jocks were brave as a lion
> But portrait alas is quite bad
> Not a hint of a smile; oh how sad.

100

Four days before his ninety-third birthday in April, my father had a nosebleed. A month later, he emailed me with an update on his activities:

> Gd news all round excpt for the black clud oSNP haningver S. E attended wonderful G and S screen sshow of Piraates and Penzance; ctumes no mucked abotand excellent ssinging and playing. Onl one problem here today..my node bleeding again.. I kow now eacly-thereason . . . ibuprofen whc gives my bettersleeping . . . aalas. Nomore ibuprofn itcearly tins mybloo
>
> All Love toyou three. Daddyd.

The three were me, my wife, Shoshana, and our son, Alexander Wolf. Shoshana and I had married in 2012, just after the end of my long walk along the border, and Wolf had been born in October 2014, two months after Scotland had eventually voted to remain part of the United Kingdom. When we visited for Christmas my father held the six-week-old boy on his knees and jigged him up and down while singing, in a strong vibrato, 'Ho-rro the nut-brown maiden'.

★

Sleeping was an increasing problem for my father. 'Thanks to my plumbing I have not a full night's sleep in eighteen years,' he said. Instead of rising at six, as he had for seventy-five years, he now increasingly lay in bed till eight thirty, hoping for rest. His eyes were bloodshot, itched and watered incessantly. He had acquired a steroid ointment for his eyes from a doctor in Latin America, 'but the bloody British quacks won't allow me to use it, which is why they look like poached eggs'. I realised from the fact that he was reluctant to wear socks that the skin on his feet had grown very irritable. Ibruprofen, washed down with a bottle of red wine, helped him sleep. Stopping the ibruprofen eroded his sleep and did not prevent the nosebleeds.

'There must be a cause for the nosebleeds,' I said.

'Too true,' he grinned.

'How are you feeling, Daddy?'

'Old, darling. Even the doctor has no idea how I'm supposed to feel. What's good for ninety-three? Nothing works awfully well. I think I'm just old.' His emails were increasingly signed 'Methuselah' or 'Patriarch'.

Because he was sleeping so little and didn't want to disturb my mother, he moved from their bedroom on the first floor to a single bed in his study on the ground floor. Torquil, his lurcher, four feet of sharp hips, ribcage and legs, slept with, or on, him.

It was not a big room. Without telling my mother or sisters ('No point asking them – they'd only say no'), he'd built pine cupboards across the study fireplace. They were for his tartan suits and brogues. He'd also installed a sink and loo in one corner of the room. He placed his paints in one drawer, his Chinese jade animals and tam-o'-shanters in another. His walking sticks and a sleeveless coat of snow-leopard fur hung on the back of the door. On the plain pine shelves bolted to the top of his rosewood desk went five different models of hearing-aids, bottles of pills, and angina spray. More personal things, which he now had to wear, and which we did not discuss, were stacked in another corner. And in the corner were his hanging files, filled with his monthly reviews of the financial situation of the house – each entitled 'Meeting of shadow finance committee: membership, Brian Stewart'.

101

I went up to stay with him over Easter. We had a party at home. I danced the 51 with Wolf in my arms. But for the first time, my father went to bed before the music started. On Easter Day, he gave Wolf an electric saw with a note saying 'To keep for when you are a little older'.

I thought perhaps I could stay at Broich and work on writing my book about the walk, and perhaps interview my father a little more. The following morning, we went for a walk together around the field to 'inspect the plantations'. I had Wolf strapped to my chest. My father was in a pair of green felt sheepskin-lined boots, his loose grey tweed coat and his tam-o'-shanter. He carried his ski stick in his left hand, and leaned on me with his right arm. We went at almost exactly the pace of a regimental slow march.

'So how's the writing going, darling?' asked my father as we crossed his ha-ha.

'Hmm,' I said, imitating one of his favourite sounds.

'Is there something I can do to help?'

'Well, I'm still really struggling to bring the walk "together" – make sense of it all.'

'What were you expecting to find on the walk?'

'Well, much more of a sense of local history for one thing. We know so much about these places. Every Cumbrian parish seems to have once had a clergyman or doctor who spent their time sketching monuments, conducting archaeological digs—'

'That's more like it,' he interjected.

'Yes, but the problem is that so few of the people that I met on the walk seemed to be very interested in any of this.'

'The man with the *Football Echo*, or the modern electronic equivalent, may not be much interested, but I am,' he said sonorously. 'And I think many people are whose horizons have not yet narrowed to the doings of football heroes.'

I had never liked his jibes about the '*Football Echo*'. I stopped, and looked at him. 'But I suspect no one has ever really based their identity on a deep sense of their local history. How much history, for example, did you actually learn even in the 1930s?'

'My memory,' he said slowly, looking down, 'is imperfect, but my general impression – which I cannot back with hard evidence – is that our history, our picture of Britain, dealt with little except the Roman Conquest, the Norman Conquest. Viking raiding, of course.' He waved his stick, presumably evoking a Viking blade, then looked back at me. 'The broad picture from Roman departure to 1066 was pretty empty.'

'So the point,' I suggested, 'isn't just that "the man with the *Football Echo*" doesn't know any history, you don't—'

'This is a very important point,' he said with emphasis. 'It's *not* just the man with the *Football Echo*. All Brits, including me, have always had little impression of their history.'

We walked on for a few more steps. Spotting some weeds, he began to swing vigorously with his walking stick – using it as a blunt scythe. I was worried that he was getting hot, so I took over. In return, he had an idea of how he could help me with the book. 'Perhaps I can help you prove this ignorance of history? A selection of the school history books of Victorian and recent times? I would most willingly skim a few of these books for good quotes if I knew where to find them.'

'Yes,' I said, doubtfully, 'but I'm trying to focus more on the present than the past.'

As we fed Mairi, the Highland cow, I explained how unmoored Scotland seemed – severed from small farming life as long as 200 years ago, its populations almost never in a single place for more than a couple of generations, even in the most remote places. How I had found almost no one who spoke coherently about a Scottish identity. And no one able to articulate a British identity.

'How about our Middleland?' he asked.

'Nobody seemed to have any interest in that either. I'm beginning to think Britain isn't one place, or two, or three – it's just millions of separate houses.'

In Afghanistan, I reminded him, the differences between villages were what mattered. I could cross a watershed from a Hazara village and enter a Pushtun village where everyone looked different, spoke a different language and had a different religion, and seemed to brood on their particular local history. But on this walk I had not found clear 'village identities'. Instead, the differences seemed to lie between neighbouring houses. Knocking on three doors in a typical village in Cumbria or the Scottish Borders, I would find a retired telecoms engineer who had worked in Dubai, a disabled Dutch poet, and a chef, born in the village, with a hobby of endurance horse racing. Their homes were decorated with photos of Kanchenjunga, with models of German trucks or with Buddhist thankas. Ninety per cent of people in the Borders did not live in the place in which they were born.

'I'm in a thorough muddle,' I concluded. 'Perhaps the problem is that I was walking too fast. Perhaps I should spend a few days knocking on some doors in Crieff and finding out what lies behind?'

'Good idea, darling. Onwards and upwards. Faster and funnier. See you at suppertime.'

102

That afternoon, and then every day the following week, I interviewed two or three different Crieff residents: people of different ages, with different incomes, living in different areas of the town. Everyone seemed happy to talk. Lynn, whom I met in the community centre, for example, was a woman of about sixty with punk-purple hair. She had grown up, she explained, in Dundee and moved to Crieff fifteen years ago. The red steel cherries, the size of beach-balls, which held the tourist information signs had been her design. Lynn took me to see a witch. But when we knocked on the door, the witch was not in. In the afternoons, Lynn said, the witch worked in a sandwich bar. But she was not there either. 'It is amazing,' said Lynn, 'how such ancient things survive in Crieff.' They were traces, she hinted, of a pagan past. The witch, as far as I could gather, was twenty-five.

Next, I interviewed my friend Susan. I had worked with her for five years, and she had always struck me as a typical Crieff resident, living with her family in a Victorian villa, one street back from the high street. But Susan did not seem to have much to say about Crieff. Perhaps this was because, like almost all her neighbours, she was not originally from the town. She had grown up in Livingston new town, forty miles south in central Scotland, where her father had been one of the very first occupants. She described Livingston vividly.

When Susan's family first arrived in the 1960s, the grass banks by the underpasses were still largely bare, the trees no more than tiny saplings. Residents had to cross unpaved roads, hopping between loose flagstones. But the rapid Swedish construction method was pushing up a steady 1,000 houses a year, encircled by a ring road. Underpasses connected car-parking space to Scotland's largest indoor mall. Livingston was dominated by Japanese electronics companies. It had grown from a hamlet into one of the ten largest towns in Scotland, and the centre of Scotland's silicon glen, pumping out about a third of the PCs in Europe and most of Europe's ATMs. The corporation's motto was 'Creating a future where there was only a past'. Susan had felt the absence of this past.

Although her father was an engineer, and her grandparents and great-grandparents had run a large coach business in Edinburgh, she thought of herself as working class. We had never discussed politics before. Now, however, she told me about the 1984 miners' strike: 'It is a strong word but I feel it was like the Holocaust.' And although far more miners had lost their jobs in England and Wales, she felt it was a Scottish story.

'Did you know any miners?' I asked.

'No. But I knew about them. You saw it on the news.'

In the 1990s, Susan's husband had moved their family to take up an electronics job in California. They had loved the weather. Livingston new town had been supposed to be a symbol of modern equality, where everyone had left their old communities and classes and relationships behind, and now lived in new houses, went to the same schools and stores, and worked in the same companies. But she seemed to feel that California was 'a much more equal society' than Livingston. 'No one cared who you were or where you came from. We had friends and neighbours who were millionaires – because in those days in Silicon Valley, even the admin people got shares and became millionaires.'

When they moved back to Scotland, the family had seen an advert for a house in Crieff, a place where her connection to soil or place was only tentative, and where her neighbours were commuters and retired people whose memories and interests were scattered between many other places. Crieff, she thought, was 'dismal . . . not a very friendly place. They don't greet people in the streets. And it's pretty rowdy on Saturday nights. There's no work for young people. There is nothing for them to do.'

But whatever her reservations about Livingston and Crieff, Susan was still a Scottish nationalist and still felt that both towns were categorically different from England. 'I just feel that England can't understand us. They can't even imagine what it is like here – the distances we need to drive, the rurality.' I tried to suggest northern England had equal 'rurality'. In fact, her home town of Livingston could hardly be described as rural at all. Her problem was with London, perhaps, but not England.

She did not reply. She was in any case, she said, in favour of full Scottish independence.

'And what makes you proud of Scotland?'

'Many things. The pipes. Murrayfield Stadium. "Flower of Scotland". The landscape.' She told me how much she and her husband loved the Isle of Skye. They had been holidaying in a cottage and seen a lamb stranded by the water's edge. Her husband had gone out into the storm and coaxed it inland. It did not sound like very much – the story could even have been told as comedy: this urban couple, battling a sheep – but it was precious to her, as a sign that she was linked to the Highlands. She had been disappointed next day that the farmer had not seemed more grateful.

She would never live in England. She couldn't say why. She agreed that Cumbria was not so different from Scotland. And there were jobs in England. 'But our family wouldn't dream of leaving Scotland.'

'Would your children agree?'

'No. I don't think so. My son can't wait to graduate so he can get back to California. I can't really blame them. I would much rather live in California. I think we may have made a mistake coming home.'

★

I wrote up Lynne's and Susan's stories for my father to read. And on our walk at the end of the week, I asked him what he made of them. I said I thought I would write about them in my book.

'Hmm.'

'What do you think?'

'I'm not sure we really want to read about them.' He said he found my description of Susan simultaneously irritating and 'a bore'. He hadn't liked reading them any more than he'd liked my description of Scott the *seanachaidh*. 'They really are a bit nutty. Couldn't you find someone a little more straightforward?'

'But I don't think there's such a thing as a straightforward Scot,' I said. 'I've interviewed everyone I can think of. I don't think there is an authentic, straightforward Crieff. Anyone who thinks that hasn't actually knocked on the doors.'

'Well, I am sure you're right, darling, but I don't want to hear too much about these people.'

'Who should I be interviewing then? Who? Look at all these people I've interviewed. The twenty-two-year-old marketing manager in the local hotel? The Abderdeen oil man, who worked in Nigeria? The cattle farmer? The ninety year old who had been the secretary of the local bus company in 1950? ('We offered mystery tours in Glasgow – a mystery tour then always meant Crieff.')

'That's right, darling. Time to go inside, I think,' he said. The Scottish weather, which he had always celebrated, now bothered him. Increasingly, even on a mild day, I had noticed his hands became cold, and then his breathing became laboured. We turned towards the house, arm in arm. After a minute, just as we were approaching the front steps, he added, 'I've got a pain in my chest.'

'Should I call an ambulance?' I asked.

'No, no, darling. It often happens.' He stopped, spread his legs, and pulled a spray out of the pocket of his jacket where he normally kept loose dog biscuits. 'I just roll my tongue back and spray this under my tongue.' He did so, and we continued through the front door. 'I think I'll have a bit of a rest,' he said. 'I'll be right as rain,' and closed the door of his bedroom.

An hour or so later I heard him walking down the corridor. The dining-room door opened very slowly and he peered round. I was working on my laptop. 'I'm not interrupting, am I? Just say if I am. Plenty to get on with, if you're busy,' he said.

I closed my laptop.

'I've been thinking about people for you to interview. How about Jamie the painter?' My father had known Jamie for a number of years, and often employed him to paint, or hedge-clip, or help with repairs around the house. 'I like him; he knows everyone in Crieff, is hale and hearty, and has unusually intelligent interests and views.'

103

When I arrived at Jamie's terrace house the following afternoon I noticed the ground-floor window was stacked with a pile of packet noodles and sauce bottles covered with Filipino writing. Jamie was, I guessed, about fifty. He had a shaven head, muscular shoulders and tattoos on both forearms, and because he looked like a hard man, I expected him to greet me gruffly. Instead he lowered his eyes and smiled amiably, his pale cheeks blushing, and came over to shake my hand. 'How are you? I hope you are having a good day?' His voice was higher than I expected.

Jamie had been researching his ancestry on the internet. The first trace he had found of his family in Crieff was about 150 years ago. 'We are originally from Ireland, my grandmother told me, we came to do the potato-picking in Muthill.' This was about the time when the Irish labourers had worked and died on the railway bridge at Roxburgh. But the Roxburgh workers had left no visible trace in the modern population. Jamie's family had stayed in Crieff for eight generations.

Jamie had been born in a pebble-dashed semi-detached house on a 1930s council estate, 300 yards away from where he now lived. When his parents split up, he moved in with his grandmother in another house on the same estate. Jamie said his father and uncles had been manual workers and heavy drinkers who worked their way around the six pubs of Crieff, leaving little money for food by the end of the week. The only trips Jamie remembered making from Crieff as a child were organised by the Catholic priest, to watch Celtic play football.

Many of Jamie's descriptions of his childhood sounded more like something he had read than something he had experienced.

'I remember the grocers, the shopkeepers in their aprons, the great baskets of red shining apples, the smell of fresh bread. Where have all those shops gone? It is a disgrace, what has happened to the high street.' But Jamie was only ten years older than me, and I remembered nothing like that.

He seemed more exact, however, when we began walking together through the estate. He showed me the four-storey block which they called 'Beirut', where he said the 'substance-abusers' went. People did not seem to stay in Beirut long. He showed me the field in which he and his cousins had worked as potato-pickers during the school holidays. It was exhausting, he said, following the mechanical hoe: 'The potatoes came out so fast your hands were bruised and battered. You could only do so many eight-hour days.'

At sixteen ('I was not a good student, got in a bit of trouble') he had started work in the local ceramics factory and met a girl. Her father was a Protestant, and a successful local tradesman who had not, Jamie thought, approved of her marrying a Catholic from the estate. They had two children. But 'I didn't handle it very well.' As we walked through the estate, he pointed to some young men in hoodies drinking from a bottle. 'That was me, really,' he said, 'Crieff is very, very boring for young people. There is nothing to do.'

'Do you know those kids?' I asked.

'Yes, I know a couple of them. They're mostly no trouble. One or two of them are getting into drugs a bit, but they'll be okay.'

It would be easy to turn Jamie's life into a cliché – growing up in a single-parent family on a council estate with a heavy-drinking father, part of an Irish Catholic clan, drinking, and leaving his wife and children. But the next stage of his life suggested other energies.

In the early 1990s, his wife left Crieff with his daughters ('She remarried and moved to southern England') and Jamie went to London and got a job as a painter-decorator.

'London in the 1990s was the boom-time. I took a small room in Battersea and built up a client list.' He saved money. One day, someone invited him to the Southbank Centre to hear a classical music concert. He had liked it, and had kept going back. Then he started taking tango classes. 'I went out with Latin American women.' This seemed to be the time that this man in his mid-thirties from a working-class background in Crieff, a poor student, had really begun to enjoy learning. He read history books and visited museums. It might have been a powerful demonstration of what London and the

Union offered Scotland. But on his wall, all the time, were pictures of the Highlands. 'Finally, one day, I thought, why do I have all these pictures on my wall? I must miss my home.' So he came back to the housing estate in Crieff.

A cousin told him there was a house available in Muthill. It was a wreck, 'but there is community here – everyone helps. One person brought me a fridge, someone else a set of shelves. I knew I was home again.'

Next he was caught up in another historical epoch: not the property boom in London but the great expansion of government services in Scotland. Jamie joined a social enterprise, which had bought a small Victorian villa in Perth, and delivered services for aged alcoholics. The house could accommodate six. Jamie was the caretaker, handyman and manager. On his days off, he walked in the countryside around Crieff, 'to dream of having a dog, and perhaps doing a little shooting'.

'Was the idea to wean the men off alcohol?' I asked.

'No, absolutely not. That is what the council kept asking, but the men were too old for that. They weren't going to change. No, my job was to try to bathe them, change their clothes, help them live slightly longer lives.' It seemed a modest and realistic project – perhaps too modest and realistic for government support. 'A new council contractor came in. He just didn't get it. He screwed it all up. The funding, the way it was run, all the money was wasted on bureaucracy. In the end the whole thing was shut down. A crying shame. It was such a necessary service.'

During his time working in the shelter, Jamie had been sending £20 a month to the Philippines to support orphans. He had come across the scheme online. He decided to fly to the Philippines to visit the project he was supporting. He met a woman there, and married her. They had a son. Jamie did not drink very much these days.

'I sometimes feel that some of my friends and cousins have got a bit stuck here, and when I see them I see what I might have been. I want to live in the countryside, to be honest. I love nature. I'd love a dog. I want to be among the trees. But my wife is a town person. She would be frightened by the countryside, so we live in Crieff.'

As we walked through the estate, two women with long blonde hair, pushing toddlers in buggies, saw him, stopped, laughed and then shouted in strong East European accents, 'How is Jamie?'

'Fine,' he said. 'How is Sasha?'

'Fine. You must come to eat some food with us again soon.'

There were, Jamie explained, over a hundred Poles now in Crieff. 'They can get good houses, good conditions, good jobs. They like Crieff.' In an hour's walk, we saw perhaps a hundred people, of whom about a dozen were Nepali, Bangladeshi and Thai. Jamie seemed to know each of them.

He took me home. His six-year-old son came in, staring at an iPhone. Jamie beamed and called him over. The boy sat on his knee, playing a video game. Jamie kissed him.

'I don't normally allow video games,' Jamie said to me. 'Do I, darling? Only as a particular treat . . . It's not good for the development of the mind.' But it was difficult to believe he was strict, when he seemed so obviously delighted to have his son on his lap.

Jamie was now a painter-decorator again. I wondered whether his father was proud of him. 'I don't know – fathers are odd things – not always great at talking about that sort of thing.' The cartons in the window were because his wife was running a small shop for the local Filipino community. 'In the Philippines they call it a go-down,' he said.

I asked him about Scottish nationalism and he said, 'To be honest, I really haven't got an opinion. I haven't decided. I guess I'm open-minded.'

I suggested that chapter of his life in London, where he had said 'I really became the person I am now', was an example of how the United Kingdom might work, allowing him to combine in his identity rural Scotland and tango dancing in the country's capital. He did not really seem to take up this theme.

As I left, Jamie showed me an embroidered Indian representation of Krishna, and a Victorian paperknife, both of which he had picked up in an auction. He was planning another trip to London, and one to the Philippines. He talked about a TV programme he had just seen about Iraq. 'Tell me,' he said, 'in a tribal society, how much power does a chief really have? What kind of development projects are really working in that part of the world?'

As I left, he was sitting down with his son, carefully going through the homework for the next day's school, stroking the boy's hair and saying, not too convincingly, 'No television before bed tonight, yes?'

Later, I noticed that Jamie had stuck an 'Independence' poster in one window, and covered another with a St Andrew's flag – both of them indicating that he had voted 'yes' to independence. When I got home, I described what I had seen to my father over dinner. Since my father felt intensely that nationalism would destroy everything he cared for in Britain and in Scotland, I imagined he would be disappointed with Jamie's nationalism. But in fact he seemed very impressed by what I had learned about Jamie – it seemed to make him more fond of him. 'Could we perhaps offer Jamie a plot of land at the end of the drive to build a house for himself? He loves the countryside after all.' I didn't want new buildings around, and didn't like losing the land. So I rejected the idea. But I liked the fact that where I just saw a beech wood at the end of the drive, my father had seen a house for Jamie.

104

My father wasn't slowing down, or at least not much. That January he had been with my mother to Cuba for three weeks. He had decided to increase his exercise regimen in the Crieff pool to be ready for his ninety-fourth-birthday trip to Bali. Still, I wondered whether the time was approaching for some paternal reflections on the meaning of life. He had enjoyed teaching me proofs of the existence of God when I was six, which suggested an interest in religion. And he often referred to 'Aristotle's golden mean: moderation in all things', which implied to me an interest in philosophy. But I was wrong on both counts.

'I've hated philosophy since university,' he said. 'I gave up when they asked me to prove the chair was still in the room when I wasn't there.'

I realised that the things he had praised me for as a child weren't exactly moral virtues. He did not praise me for 'truthfulness', or 'self-sacrifice', but for an 'iron constitution', 'mind over matter' and 'willpower'. 'Do as you would be done by is all very well,' he suggested, 'unless you're dealing with a sadomasochist.' He was enthusiastic about certain state institutions such as the army, and he liked reading Machiavelli, but this did not add up to a political philosophy. He often said, 'I am utilitarian: the greatest happiness of the greatest number, and the end justifies the means.' But he deployed these arguments defensively – to justify intelligence methods, for example – rather than to advocate political reform. He believed in being tough on crime, but he had no great reverence for the law. He was a great believer in 'white lies'. All this appeared to be not so much a philosophical system as the necessary mindset of a successful member of the British secret service.

Questions about religion suddenly made this extrovert and loquacious man curt and taciturn. All I ever got from him on the question of religion was that 'The church and its music has been the background of my whole life.'

'What do you think of death, Daddy?' I asked him.

'Not an awful lot.'

'Are you frightened of it?'

'Can't see the point in that.'

'What do you think of God?'

'Well . . . that's a very interesting question. I suppose I have always thought there was someone up there. But I'm not so convinced about Jesus.'

'But how about sin and atonement?'

'Not my subject.'

★

In early August 2015, I heard that my father had been taken to hospital in Dundee to have his nose 'cauterised'. My half-sister Annie sent me a photograph of him in the ward. He was smiling, and was holding a paper potty over his head, pretending it was a bowler hat. He insisted there was no reason for me to visit.

On his return to the house, he sent an email with the subject line 'Factor's report'. It described a mile-long circuit he had just made around the 'parklet'. Here it is, translated from his idiosyncratic spelling:

> So what's to tell? My main purpose was to see how the transplant, fertilising etc. had fared in this curiously uncertain but quite wet weather. The holly line is very varied in height . . . Much more impressive growth from the laurels, which seem to have in many cases 'taken off'. The main object of the inspection was to check whether we had at last managed to fill in the bald patches created by Field Marshal Sod. I think we have. The ground at Crow Wood is getting pretty jungly, but the only action I think that is necessary is a session with weedkiller against a newly appeared area of Japanese knotweed near the drive. No action required by the laird!!
>
> The morning inspection finished at the south end of the Italianate water feature, where we dug a potential swimming pool in the

spring. In view of the laird's certainty that no one will ever swim in the pool, we shall fill the hole up to near the top, leaving space for an extension of the water canal under the stone table. The water pool will finish with a wide, shallow pool. If in the fullness of time the Wolf says he wants to swim it won't be difficult or expensive to make the pool swimmable.

All Love,
Daddy

He did not mention in the note that he had asked Raul (a Filipino man who had worked for my father in Hong Kong, and was now his major partner in his earthwork projects in Scotland) to drive him 400 miles to London the next day. His objective was to surprise my mother, who was expecting to come back to Scotland alone by train. He was fine on the drive down. But on the way back with my mother, blood erupted from his nose outside a service station McDonald's.

'You can imagine the scene,' he said to me. 'The old gentleman, sitting on the bench, with the blood flowing – and all the biddies coming out' – here he put on a female Morningside accent – '"Is there anything I can do?"' He changed to a slightly exaggerated grand officer's drawl to issue his reply: '"Not an awful lot actually!" It was hardly the Normandy beaches.'

105

He had shown me his battlefield in Normandy the previous year, on the seventieth anniversary of the D-Day landings. We pulled off the narrow road that ran through flat arable fields, perhaps thirty miles south of the coast, and he led me into a cornfield. He took some time to reach the centre, stepping over the young corn in his polished brogues. About half a mile away was a small hamlet called Rauray, and in every other direction were more open, flat cornfields.

'We were dug in behind a hedge, and I'm pretty sure the hedge was here, but someone's dug it up. Look over there,' he suggested, pointing to another spot in the open, featureless field.

I walked off.

'Can you see any sign of the hedge?' he shouted.

'No.'

'Well, there was definitely a hedge. And I'm pretty sure the German tanks were coming from over there.' He shaded his eyes and looked across the road to another flat field in which heavy heads of corn quivered in the sun. The dense network of hedges – the *bocage* – which defined his whole experience of the war had been torn up by a farmer with a European agricultural grant in the 1980s, and without the hedgerows, he could no longer be certain exactly where he had fought. The site of his victorious battle was gone.

★

Before the trip, I had been through the suitcase which contained my father's and my uncle's papers. It contained hand-illustrated postcards (in 1928 George had drawn a dogfight and a naval cruiser with bullets streaming, in dotted lines, from its guns), poems (including some angry attacks by George on class and hypocrisy in Scotland) report cards, musical programmes (the boys had sung 'Bonnie Dundee') and school magazines. My father and George had been sent to the same prep school (a cold castle in the central belt) and the same public school (just four miles from our local Roman frontier fort). Then, as the local newspaper cutting preserved in the suitcase by their mother proclaimed, 'Scots triumph at Oxford': they had won scholarships to the same college. Oxford seemed to be, for both of them, about music, and a mild political radicalism. My father – who now seemed a settled conservative imperialist – had later voted for Attlee's Labour government. George had attended lectures at the Labour Club, and had taken an interest in the Indian Congress movement and Gandhi.

With the outbreak of the war, they'd both joined the Black Watch. 'We had been in the Black Watch almost since we were born,' my father said. 'The Black Watch drill hall was next to our house, our cadet unit at school was affiliated to the regiment. My father and grandfather were in the Black Watch. As far as we were concerned, it was the only regiment in the British Army.' And even in retirement, many of his closest friends and neighbours were Black Watch colonels and majors, all of whom had sons or fathers in the regiment. I had served under two officers whose fathers had commanded my uncle George.

But George was not, my father thought, 'a natural soldier'. When he was trying to find a way to describe him, he fell back on saying, 'He was a musician . . .' Although he was a year younger than George, my father had protected his brother against bullies at school, and he wanted to do the same for him in the army. But when my father tried to join George's battalion, the 5th Black Watch, in which their grandfather had served for twenty years, he found there was a policy to keep brothers apart, and that he had been posted to a different unit – the Tyneside Scottish.

My father and George spent Christmas 1941 climbing Schiehallion in Scotland. And then my father went down with his mother to watch George depart for North Africa. Twelve pipe bands marched past the king, who was wearing his Cameron Highlanders kilt, and the queen, who was wearing Black Watch. 'I don't know whether anyone can imagine the pride we all felt watching that ceremony,' recalled my father. He paused, and then he contradicted himself. 'Actually, it was awful.'

Because the Germans controlled the Mediterranean, George and the rest of the 51st Highland Division – 3,500 men – were compelled to sail for almost two months around the Cape on a ship built for 1,500. The 51st Highland Division had just been reconstituted; its predecessor, having been trapped in an impossible situation before the Battle of Dunkirk in 1940, had been forced to surrender. Two of George's fellow officers had been in that battle and escaped. His commanding officer – a prewar rugby star – did so by walking and cycling more than a thousand miles through German lines to Portugal; the second in command did so by commandeering a boat and sailing single-handed for thirty days until he reached the English coast. But the surrender had been a terrible humiliation for the division and for the Highlands, which the new general was determined to efface.

General Wimberly felt the key to victory lay in an unflinching focus on Highland identity. Although the War Office had forbidden the Black Watch to go into action in kilts in the First World War (their refusal to wear underwear left their testicles exposed to gas attack), the general insisted everyone still carried a kilt. And that officers were properly dressed – George's list of wartime equipment, taken down in blue fountain pen ink and preserved in the suitcase, included 'embossed studs, tartan trews, officers' kilt, garters and flashes, dress shirt, stiff collars, tam-o'-shanter, and Glengarry cap for blues dress'.

The general had sacked the field ambulance commander on the grounds he was English. He insisted that every morning's reveille was followed by compulsory Scottish dancing, and that every company march should be preceded by a piper, playing the company tune. The piper of George's company commander carried the coat of arms of the company commander, Hew Blair-Imrie of Lunan – the same coat of arms which was half visible on the lodge gate of his family's ruined twelfth-century castle. (The man who had been cast in the chivalric role had been for the last six years a salesman for a linen and cloth manufacturer in the market town of Brechin.)

On the voyage, George and the other officers taught regimental history to their men. They passed the spot off the African coast where the 74th Highlanders had stood to attention, ensuring that all the women and children made the boats, as HMS *Birkenhead* went down (550 of the 643 Highlanders had drowned).

The regiment made a stop at the Cape, where only forty years earlier the Highland Division had been marched in column up a hill into Boer barbed wire, trenches and machine guns, and where 700 soldiers of the Highland Division, including the general, Wauchope, had been mown down in the first five minutes of action.

My uncle's diaries show him reading Montaigne and Henry Sidgwick's *The Methods of Ethics*, and carefully noting down every classical musical concert he heard on the radio. His letter to my father from the ship did not rehearse tunes of glory:

> I was not best pleased when I heard about our destination . . . I have cleaned away a lot of half-digested pacificism . . . I suppose a horizon is always necessary because it's only dull stupid people who live contentedly for the present. Don't let all these metaphysical meanderings make you think I'm becoming difficult and introspective – I'm not – I've proved to myself that I'm happier now than before – since I joined the army.

Landing in Egypt, George focused on new techniques for preventing the giant rats stealing chocolate from his tent. His division came under the command of General Montgomery, who had never been to Scotland and claimed never to have heard of the county of Fife. Because the Scots were 'uncivilised', he said, he had decided to pair them with the Australian and New Zealand divisions in the front line of the 8th Army.

General Wimberly made the officers wear Highland Dress for the 'Orders Group' which finalised the tactics for the Battle of El Alamein – the Black Watch in tam-o'-shanters and the Gordons in glengarries. One of the central objectives of the 1st Battalion of the Black Watch was given the code-name Crieff. And the general's message had been, 'There will be no surrender for unwounded men. Any troops of the Highland Division cut off will continue to fight. Scotland for ever and Second to None.'

Sixty years later, my father found his brother's handwritten report of the Battle of El Alamein in the Public Records Office. The battalion had begun their advance at 21.40, in open formation, clad in knee-length shorts but with red flashes on their socks, red hackles in their helmets and Black Watch tartan patches on their sleeves. The A Company piper, who was playing 'Hielan' Laddie', was hit almost immediately. He clambered back to his feet to resume playing, and was killed.

George as a navigation officer led the advance through the minefield from the right, proceeding towards enemy machine-gun fire at a steady 'fifty yards a minute'. On the left flank, six navigation officers were killed or wounded in succession. George avoided being hit on the first day, and his colonel was pleased to announce that he had captured a German whom he had known in Shanghai, where they had been members of the same club.

The following night, the 5th Battalion advanced again. In the first hour, three of George's fellow officers were killed. Then George was hit by shrapnel in his ankle. By the end of that day's advance, every other officer in his company, bar one, had also been wounded or killed. George was sent to the Scottish hospital in Palestine. 'It seemed such a silly wound I almost felt scrimshanking to go back with it,' George wrote, as soon as he arrived in the hospital, 'but the redeeming feature was that I couldn't fasten my boot.'

His letter to my father from hospital describes him filling in his tax return, wondering why his pay had been cut, and listening on the Forces radio to

> most of Beethoven's 7th symphony and some clavichord solos, and Bach's quartet for cello and 2 flutes and oboe by our old friends the societé musique ancienne from France. There was a lovely simple and satisfying cello part that you would have loved to try, Brian. To finish off, a Beethoven piano concerto whose numbers I can't remember but has a skittish Rondo. Played magnificently by a very brilliant pianist and excellent orchestra from Germany.

As usual, he did not really write about the war.

After the doctors successfully reattached the flesh to his ankle, he was pushed forward to the front line again, where he rejoined the 5th Battalion, now advanced hundreds of miles further along the North African coast into modern Libya. He fought at Wadi Akarit and Sfax. Many of his fellow soldiers were buried under small white crosses beneath palm trees. The officers began to wear sunglasses.

106

Meanwhile, my father was stuck with his battalion in Shropshire. He had been put in charge of the anti-tank platoon and was determined, he told me, to create 'the best anti-tank platoon in the British Army'. By bending the rules – dismantling the gun and running straight through the assault course instead of climbing over the obstacles – his platoon broke the course record. Afterwards, he became a Battle School instructor.

'I stood screaming, "Remember Singapore!" like a demented parrot from the top of the assault course, and throwing firecrackers at the students to hurry them along' was how he summed it up. In his letters to George, he shared his experiences. A mortar exploded near him on exercise. One of his students fell to his death from a cliff. He crashed his motorcycle three times and performed musical duets with his friend Ken.

George read these letters as he fought his way across North Africa.

My father couldn't understand why his brother wouldn't put pressure on the system to let him join the 5th Battalion. He wanted to be there on the advance with him. But presumably George wanted to save my father from what he was experiencing. The advance – glossed over in George's letters – is described by the divisional commander, General Wimberly:

> The black Macadam road wound through the soft sand of the desert, pitch black in the brilliant sunshine. At intervals all down

> the road, mile after mile, the enemy had spread shovel-fulls of sand, and under every sixth heap or so, a mine had been buried, a hole having been drilled in the tarmac for it.
>
> About every quarter of a mile along the road, derelict vehicles had been pulled across it, to block it, and each vehicle was a mass of trip wires and booby traps. The very corpses of our poor dead, which we lost out on patrol, were all booby-trapped.

On 7 April, George's company led an attack up Wadi Akrit against German mortars, machine guns and Tiger tanks. In the previous day's attack, half of A Company had been hit by misplaced British artillery fire. This time, the piper was forced to stop playing halfway up the hill because shrapnel tore the pipe-bag to pieces, and he spent most of the night trying to mend it with cork and thread. After the attack, George wrote to one of his men's sisters, telling her that he had been with her brother, and had held his hand as he died.

At Sfax, he and his men wrapped towels round their waists, so that they could press the pleats of their kilts with an iron heated on a Primus stove. They marched through the Tunisian bazaar in Highland dress, led by the pipes and drums.

Meanwhile, the tiny standard-issue cards which George sent home, which even in miniature handwriting could hardly hold 400 words of description, related that he was carrying Dostoevsky, Aldous Huxley, Kingslake's *Eothen*, 'short stories of Irish country life' and a Penguin Herodotus. He described the sand dunes on which they were camped as 'rather like Carnoustie or Monifieth without the golf'.

He describes some action on 21 July, after he landed in Sicily: 'We bumped into some light tanks. Fortunately they did not realise that they were only up against a company. The next night we continued the advance and since then things have been uncomfortable.'

But Blair-Imrie of Lunan, his company commander, recorded the scene in more heroic language:

> George's platoon was pushing forward in bright moonlight after a successful attack on a German-held position, and had run into what seemed to be devastating machine-gun fire. I went forward to see what was happening, to find George and his lads taking on the German tanks with their brens and rifles, and George directing the battle and personally firing the two-inch mortar. The Germans withdrew in the face of this fusillade, although I need not tell you

that the platoon's weapons would hardly have dented the Germans' armour plate.

The temperature in Sicily in July was extreme, even for those who had spent the last six months on the edge of the Sahara Desert. George wrote to his parents from a dry riverbed. He did not explain that the Hermann Goering Panzer-Grenadiers had established outposts overlooking them from every direction; that the 5th Battalion of the Black Watch could not advance, could not be resupplied, and were not allowed to retreat; nor that they were sitting motionless in the sun, with no food and water, under continual artillery and mortar fire. Sixty men including the regimental sergeant major were killed or wounded, before George conceded in his letter home: 'We're pretty tired with long marches and heat during the day and there is a lot of enemy shell and mortar fire around.' For the first time they were experiencing a new German multi-rocket mortar that moaned and shrieked through the air. But he concluded on a more positive note. 'We had a hand-to-hand street fight in town yesterday, but finished up among figs, plums, and apple trees. I gorged myself but got away with it.' He requested some diarrhoea pills from his father in India. He finished the letter and handed it in before he was killed by one of the shells.

107

My father was informed of George's death at his battalion near Glasgow by his commanding officer at 1.15 in the afternoon, two weeks later. 'I just had time to bottle it up and get on with a lecture at 1.30,' he said. George's company commander, Blair-Imrie of Lunan, had written a letter to his mother, promising to call on her, but Blair-Imrie of Lunan was killed before he had the chance. My father had never been interested in meeting anyone who had served with George, to learn about his brother's time in the war. 'Anyway, I knew George better than anyone else,' he said dismissively. My father was able to take the afternoon off and drive up to comfort his mother. But his father was alone in Calcutta when he got the news.

'What was your father like, Daddy?' I asked my father.

'Oh, you know, a quiet, good-looking man, always reading the newspaper.'

'What was he *like*?'

'I don't really know. He never said very much.'

We sat in silence for a long time. And then, finally, he spoke.

'You see, we never really knew my father. He was in Calcutta and we were in Scotland. I saw him once as a three-year-old. He came back next on leave for a month or so when I was, oh, seven. We went to the beach at Skye for a week. It rained all the time. It was terribly boring. Poor man. Didn't know his sons, thought he would take them on holiday, but we were just fed up with the weather, and misbehaved, and he told me off. Not a great success.

'He got leave every four years, but I think the next time he was very sick, so he didn't come home. So the next time I saw him, I was fifteen. And then he was sick again. I just remember him lying in the big bed at home, and our needing to be very quiet so as not to disturb him. Then the war broke out, and I didn't see him again until I was twenty-three and turned up in India, on the way to join the invasion of Japan. By then George had been killed, and he must have been very sad, to have lost one son without really knowing him. Little wonder he didn't say much.'

★

A year after his brother had been killed in Sicily my father landed on the Normandy beaches. 'The biggest change I can think of,' my father said to me when we visited, 'is that there are now no bloated cows and horses rotting in the fields.'

My father's letters to his mother were less circumspect than his brother's: 'Yesterday, one of my platoon sergeants was writing a letter to his pregnant wife, when he was killed by a German bomb.' We passed the hamlet where on the second day of the battle one of my father's corporals decided to add petrol to a bonfire, and burned himself to death.

On the sixth day, my father watched Major MacGregor march A Company forward, 'line abreast', towards a German position. First my father heard the German snipers and machine guns, and then the scream of the multi-launch German mortars whose shrieking sounds George had heard in Sicily. About half the company was wounded or killed by the time they were a quarter of the way across the field. Finally they were allowed to retreat, led by a lone piper. My father's last glimpse of Major MacGregor was of his lying 'in a bloody mess on a stretcher'.

'I still can't understand it,' said my father. 'I never saw the Germans try to walk line abreast through an open field – they always crept along the hedge lines. What had happened to all our Battle School training? Were we trying to march back towards the Boer machine guns on the Cape? Had nothing changed since Waterloo?'

Coming towards us now through the cornfields seventy years later was Kevin Baverstock, a wiry man with a slightly anxious expression. His father had also been in the Tyneside Scottish and took part in the Battle of Rauray on 1 July 1944. He had died in 1980. 'I found an old shoulder bag at the back of a wardrobe, and learned from his army service record card that he had been a private in the intelligence section.' Kevin had visited the Black Watch museum hoping to learn more about his father's war, and the regimental archivist had encouraged him to write about the Tyneside Scottish: 'This is your duty. You owe it to your father to record the battle – they had the war, now it's your turn,' he remembered the director telling him.

Kevin had spent three years trying to describe what had happened on that single day. He had collated the personal accounts of all the surviving soldiers, and cross-referenced them with German and British records and over sixty contemporary photographs. He had drawn eleven new maps and twenty diagrams trying to make sense of the events. My father's reminiscences featured greatly in the book. Kevin had just finished collaborating with another friend on another thick book, describing in immense detail the history of his Lake District village. My father was a great admirer of Kevin's industry and his maps, but I was not sure he had read the book about the Lake District.

'I think our guns were here,' said my father, pointing vigorously to the ground with his walking stick.

'A bit more to your right, Brian,' Kevin said.

'But I'm sure there was a hedge.'

'The hedge has been removed. It was about seventy metres to the north-west.'

'My father says that he dug the anti-tank guns into position behind the hedge,' I offered.

'Well, possibly. But the aerial photograph suggests that the number four gun was forward of the hedge.'

'And that the Tiger tanks came from there?' I asked.

'Hmm,' Kevin replied.

'What?'

'Well, the 9th SS-Panzer Regiment had no Tiger tanks, only Panthers, MK IVs and StuG III assault guns. Kampfgruppe Weidinger was a Panzer-Grenadier force.'

Kevin had become very close to my father. My father thought he wanted to know someone who had fought alongside his own father. Kevin felt that they had been brought together by a shared 'pessimism, bewilderment and detachment from the modern world. I think we both live in the past. We look backwards.' This didn't seem quite right to me as a description of my father. Whatever the explanation, however, they had become good friends. He often came to stay in Scotland, and had helped my father on his books, just as my father had helped Kevin on his. He had even organised this trip to Normandy for the seventieth anniversary. My father liked Kevin very much.

'Do you ever talk to Kevin about his father?' I asked my father.

'No. That would be a little embarrassing. You see, I'm not at all sure I knew him.'

108

Although he spent four years with the battalion, my father did not seem to remember his fellow soldiers with particular fondness. Indeed, he hardly remembered them at all. 'Pretty boring people, mostly' was how he put it.

'What was Major Calderwood like?'

'He had a very good battle. Kept B Company holding that position right through the day.'

'Did you all know he was a brave officer before the battle?'

'Absolutely not,' he grinned. 'No one had ever heard of him before the battle. No one ever heard of him afterwards either.'

For many years my father had gone to a reunion in Newcastle. He had enjoyed sitting in the corner with his anti-tank section, talking to a Sergeant Swaddle and a Private Samson, but they had since died.

'Sergeant Watson was truly remarkable that day – everyone in his crew was killed or wounded and he kept operating the entire anti-tank gun himself, loading, aiming, firing. He took out five German Panzers and stopped the SS armoured advance on that flank, pretty much single-handedly.'

'What was he like?'

'Sergeant Watson? He was a butcher from Dundee.'

'And how would he have described what motivated him, what he was fighting for?'

'He would have said, "Motivation? Wassat?"'

He pointed north. 'I do remember the start of the battle, seeing these great hulks moving slowly through the mist at dawn. But from the very beginning I was too busy to really take it all in. I was running between the guns, behind the hedgerow. I had to try to collect two men who had been wounded at Sergeant Watson's gun, and get him some more ammunition, but when I was almost there, my buffoon of a company commander wanted to have a conversation, standing up in our Bren carriers in the very middle of an open field.' My father pushed his forefinger at his lower eyelid – his favourite Neapolitan insult, meaning 'so stupid he would poke his own eye out'. A German tank saw them. My father said he was lucky that the shrapnel only tore up his leg.

As I read through Kevin's careful reconstruction, I realised that my father had been wounded much earlier in the battle than I had been led to believe. Perhaps much earlier than my father himself remembered. The defence of Rauray had lasted until evening, but my father had been wounded before eight in the morning, and evacuated to the back lines. All he noticed at first was a spreading wet patch on his thigh. 'I still feel a little guilty,' he said. 'Perhaps I should have argued with the medical officer and stayed in the battle.' He paused. 'It was probably better for my mother.' He paused again. 'I was losing a lot of blood.'

By the end of the battle, every other person in his anti-tank platoon was dead or in hospital and they had destroyed, he thought, twelve Panzer tanks. The battalion had lost so many men that it was disbanded a few days later. So my father's first battle was also his last. And the first battle of the Tyneside Scottish was its last too.

He looked around the field, as I had seen him look at the battlefield at Flodden, or on a fort at Hadrian's Wall looking for ghosts, and seeing only the cornfields, which stretched in every direction.

★

That afternoon my father led the ceremonial procession up the hill of a nearby Normandy village to mark the seventieth anniversary of the landings. He marched in his Black Watch tie and red hackle, and his tartan trews, with the cross of his order on a sash around his neck. In front of him was a group of French veterans. One had been a driver for a general stationed in Saigon during the Vietnam War. My father and he exchanged views on Saigon nightclubs. I was surprised the soldier could understand my father's terrible French. Behind them was the pipe-major of a cadet unit from Northumberland. He was a thirteen-year-old boy, originally from Suzhou in central China, now living in Hexham near Hadrian's Wall. My father tried to practise his Hokkien on him, but he couldn't hear the boy's answers. The real war damage had been not to my father's thigh but to his hearing.

The quick march up a steep hill, to the tune of 'Hielan' Laddie', was too fast, and after a couple of minutes my father had to step to one side. I took him to the church to wait for the others. It was a medieval church, built for a congregation three times the size of the village. It was now only used twice a year. There was a coat of arms in the apse, but no one I met knew which local family had once presided over this village.

After dinner, my father presented the deputy mayoress with a cut-glass whisky decanter, and thanked her on behalf of the regiment for looking after them so well in 1944. 'I remember a wonderful meal in a farmhouse,' he said. 'Camembert, calvados, a farmer's daughter.' He winked at her. The deputy mayoress had not been born at the time, and her family had not lived in the village during the war. Her father was a Pole who in 1944, aged eleven, had been escaping from Danzig. But it was she who had organised the photo exhibition of the Normandy landings, and choreographed the event in tribute to my father, whom she described as her 'liberator'.

She suggested we sing Handel's 'Lascia ch'io pianga'. She did quite well, but the tune was far too difficult for me, and my father couldn't hear.

'It's funny, isn't it,' he said, 'that I seem to be the last representative of the regiment. I feel like a bit of a fraud. I wonder what all the French think of us, wandering around in our kilts? Of course they like us because we're Scottish. But do they really understand what that means?'

The deputy mayoress asked for another *'performance culturelle'*. So my father performed a sort of pas-de-basque, hopping stiffly from leg to leg. As he danced he sang:

La cucaracha, la cucaracha
Ya no puede caminar
Porque le falta, porque no tiene
Marihuana pa' fumar.

He had taught me the song when I was a child. But this was the first time I had realised it was a revolutionary song from Mexico, referring to a cannabis spliff.

109

When we returned from Normandy to Broich, my father and I went for a walk around the grounds. The sun was warm and strong. The giant dog kennel that he had built – it was five feet high, and roofed in slate – still stood under the yew tree, waiting as it had, for months, to be moved off the lawn. We examined thirty feet of cast-iron Victorian railings, with thistles along the top which resembled the thistles on his Malaysian batik and regimental crest, bought ten years earlier from some now demolished house in the Highlands. We still could not think what to do with the railings, so we laid them back, as we had on many occasions over the past decade, against the back wall.

He talked of creating a network of 'easy maintenance' paths and hedges, which I could maintain after he was gone. 'Although you never know,' he remarked, walking forward to inspect five large craters in the lawn, still waiting for their new trees, 'I may be around for some time yet – there was a man recently of 102 . . .'

'You met him?'

'No. I read about him in the paper.'

At the cattle grid that crossed his ha-ha ditch, I had to release his arm because it was only wide enough for one. My father had seen a red butterfly on a rowan that morning, which he wanted me to see, but it had moved on, so we sat on a bench and looked across the field at twenty years of work and planting. His Scots pines – bought from a garage forecourt in Perth one rushed afternoon – now stretched high into the sky, their purple trunks curved like Klimt maidens. We could see the feathery pale sweep of the deodar, the turquoise needles of the Atlantic cedar, and the soft bark of the sequoia beyond the sprawl of the hazel copse. And, as often before, we worried that in 150 years the giant sequoia would dwarf the other pines and trees, humiliating them into miniatures.

He had, as always, a number of questions about the longer term. Plans that involved my mother after his death, and then my son. The initial treehouse would need to go near the house. But when Wolf was a teenager he would need one much higher and further away, perhaps in the horse chestnut on the bank edge.

His new grandson provided a purpose for projects that had been abandoned. Torquil the lurcher had rejected the dog kennel and still lived mostly on my father's bed. The pagoda was opened only once every year or so. But now they could both become playhouses for the young boy. 'Would Shoshana and you perhaps consider building a new cottage in the field? Would people from Crieff like to create free allotments, and grow their own vegetables in the garden?'

I sat and listened and looked out at the warm sun. And then I told him about the housing development. The news had arrived on two sheets of A4 paper two weeks earlier, inviting us to a consultation. The farm that once belonged to the house had been sold in the 1950s, leaving us only with the parklet, and the cow-field. Now the son of the farmer who had bought the farm had announced he would be building an estate of 500 houses right around the house. Beyond, there would be a new campus for the primary school, and beyond that the land had been designated for a Tesco's supermarket.

Our field and trees currently stood among 400 acres of green fields above the River Earn. There were nights of full stars, we could hear the screech of the tawny owl as he flew back and forth over the stone table on the bank edge. Now, our 'parklet' would be an island in the centre of the housing estate.

'Oh dear,' said my father. 'We better start planning.'

I nodded.

'Well, the beech hedge could hide the base of the houses,' my father said. But not the roofs, I observed, which would be forty feet high.

'I'll start a line of evergreens – a triple line – and in twenty years you won't be able to see the roofs.'

Yes, I said, in summer, but in the winter, and particularly on the long winter nights, from five in the afternoon the orange glow of 500 houses and dozens of streetlights would shine through the branches of the trees. We would be enclosed in a square mile, humming with a thousand vehicles in motion. The hedges would be no longer places for birds, but a barrier for curious children. I wouldn't want to stay.

But this patch of ground and house had been the central purpose of my father's life for almost twenty years. And he had planned it with me in mind. Twenty thousand hours of work. And perhaps half a million words of emails to me had been invested in plotting, explaining or proposing new projects in the parklet. Each lochan, ha-ha, path, plantation, each improvement to the house had been announced with the phrase 'Well, I don't think you'll need to do that again for another hundred years.'

A friend had suggested that I didn't need to tell my father about the plan for the development. That he would never live to see it. But that wasn't our relationship – I couldn't have continued a charade of planning a parklet and a future which I knew to be impossible. And anyway, I don't think I had ever lied to him. But I was very worried that he would feel his work had been wasted, and that he now had nothing left to do in life.

He turned to me, smiled and shrugged, and said, 'Well then, sounds like we should just give up, move on and Get On With It. No point really. Why don't we just sell up, turn it all over to the developers, and see what they want to do with it? It's too far away for you anyway. You won't want to keep coming up and down all this way. I found it difficult finding the time to visit my parents when they were here, and you are busier than me. Perhaps we could move down, to just on the edge of Cumbria in the Scottish Borders, so we can be near you and keep some link to Scotland? Or why don't we just open our minds? Just leave Scotland entirely.'

At midnight, I lay awake and imagined him lying awake and considering the loss, the waste of all his effort. I rolled out of bed and tiptoed downstairs. Torquil was out in the hall, not on my father's bed. I opened his bedroom door. He had fallen asleep reading a manuscript on intelligence during the Jacobite rising. I took the manuscript from his hand, and the glasses from the bridge of his nose. Then he opened his eyes, grinned hugely, waved his whole arm in energetic greeting, rolled onto his side and, clutching his shoulders with great satisfaction, said, 'Night night, darling, I love you. See you in the morning. Gug gug,' and when I turned out the lights he was already asleep.

110

By April of 2015 my father was increasingly focused on establishing why exactly he had been chosen for the portrait. The answer seemed clear to me. The portrait – like his recently awarded *Légion d'honneur* – was a tribute to longevity. But he thought he might have been chosen in tribute to his platoon's performance in the Battle of Rauray.

I was right, he was wrong. My father had in fact been chosen not as an individual, but simply as a representative of the millions who had served. At ninety-three, he was now the last surviving Tyneside Scottish officer, and one of only fifteen still alive of the 5,600 men in his brigade.

In an article in the *Daily Telegraph*, the journalists and the painters emphasised the suffering, the stoicism and the introspection of their veteran subjects. The article opened: '"It changes you, the first time you see bits of blokes lying around on the beach . . ." David Burke, 90, trails off.'

One of the painters said his subject 'sat tirelessly still without complaint'. Another artist said: 'They have much in common, but perhaps the strongest is a quiet reserve about things past and their part in war.' A third: 'I have painted a quiet and contemplative portrait because that was my experience of being with Eric.'

But that is not how Paul – or the article – described my father. My father was quoted insisting: 'My five years in the army made me a different person. It made a normal, quiet chap really into an extremely confident chap. They had a bad habit of sticking snipers up trees. But I had a bad habit of shooting at snipers up trees.'

At first, I worried that my father was completely out of step. But when I looked at the words of the other veterans, I realised that many of them had also echoed his *Boy's Own* tone, talking about how many Germans they had killed, how many they had shot in close combat, what it was like to be part of an 'elite' troop, how they had escaped from a prisoner-of-war camp. They emphasised pride in their regiment and their part in a great victory. They saw themselves as victors in a heroic campaign, but that is not how the painters chose to portray them.

My father was infuriated by the article's tone:

> All the time was wasted, actually. Such is life when dealing with the media!! No mention of the battle of Rauray where my bunch of temporary soldiers saw off the famous german panzers, panthers, tigers and heavy battle tanks . . . 15 tanks knocked out by six guns!! I doubt if anyone beat that record, even if we stick to twelve victims plus three in contention!!

Nevertheless, he went to Buckingham Palace for the unveiling of the painting. I collected him from the Army Club and we travelled there in a bus. Another veteran was seated in front of him. He tapped the man on the shoulder and bellowed, 'Hey, Renouf, how are you?' When the man did not turn around (his shoulder seemed to be paralysed), my father turned to me with delight and said, 'Completely deaf, you see, deaf as a post.' Meanwhile, Renouf, whom my father could not hear, was courteously answering his question.

In the Queen's Gallery, I met Paul Benney for the first time. I joked that my father said the portrait did not make him look cheerful.

'Well, he's not a cheerful man,' Paul replied sharply. His view of my father was apparent beneath the careful language of his catalogue entry:

> The first sittings are now complete and my initial impressions of this man are a little confused. Although welcoming and cheerful, he clearly has an intractable side. On arrival I was ordered to sit down with the impatient bark of a bellicose headmaster, not a good start for a clear assessment of your sitter. Still I was willing to make allowances for this 92-year-old veteran.
>
> As the sittings progress, though, I am resigned to the fact that I am painting a man whose lifetime in the employ of the British military and secret service has, by his own admission, left him

irreconcilably disconnected from the rough fabric of civilian life. Real life for him seems to have been both his distinguished war years and subsequently a long career working undercover abroad. In addition he commanded a 2,000-strong police force in Malaya during the war against the communist insurgency.

His moving tributes and emotional recollections are performed with the rehearsed spontaneity and charm of the seasoned diplomat. The onion is firmly and resolutely left unpeeled. My aim in the remaining time will be to keep up my bonhomie in the hope of getting a glimpse of a more vulnerable human beneath the impervious outer layer. If revealed, it will guide me to a more sympathetic understanding of this fascinating and courageous man.

III

A month after we'd been to see the painting, I was in Boston. When I telephoned my parents, my mother suggested I fly straight back to Scotland. The nosebleeds had started again and she had spent the last two nights sleeping on my father's study floor, in the narrow strip between the bed and the rosewood desk. She still wasn't sure how worried to be.

I found my father in bed with dried blood on his forehead, cheeks and nose. But his green cashmere jumper was clean, and he had shaved. He smiled when I entered, then croaked that he had better lie down, and that he could only listen rather than talk. So I sat on the edge of the bed and held his hand. I felt the crisp Scottish skin, cured by fifty years of tropical sun, rendered into pink spots and brown freckles from the curved knuckles to the wrist. His long fingers gently stroked mine.

Almost as soon as I began to talk, his voice recovered, and he interrupted. 'Saw the video you sent of the little Wolf in the sea. How is he?'

'Splendid.'

He nodded. 'Well, darling. I'd better give you a summary of this bloody nose. Not, I suppose, that there's a lot of point.' He described the ambulance man who had held his head until the bleeding stopped and then left. 'As soon as he went, it started again, as I knew it would. So we had to call the ambulance again. Not very clever!' Then he described the cauterisation in Dundee. 'It's basically a plumbing issue. But burning it shut is bloody sore.'

'Slash and burn surgery.'

'That's right – you've got it. Well, they've been slashing and burning at me a fair amount. And it seems to have stopped the blood for the time being.'

'The question,' I suggested, 'is what is causing it?'

'You would have thought so, wouldn't you? But the question seems not to have occurred to the doctors. It could be caused by the drink. Friday night we had a fine party and sloshed a lot of red wine down' – here he waved his right hand, miming drinking deep – 'and it was followed by the nosebleed. But it could be that old fallacy, *post hoc* . . .' Here he paused. I thought for a moment that he was so tired that he had forgotten the rest of the Latin tag. Then he grinned and finished with relish: '*ergo propter hoc.*'

'But what do the doctors say about the cause?'

'Sweet Fanny Adams. There was a fine, big, dark-haired west Highland Scot here yesterday. I had a splendid conversation with him. He seemed to think perhaps a blood transfusion.'

'Well, you've lost a lot of blood,' I said. 'It's a bit eighteenth-century medicine . . .'

'That's right – a good bleeding and leeches!'

'That's probably why you are feeling so awful.' Although when I looked at his tanned face, with his fine nose, he looked strong and handsome. 'You're looking well,' I told him, 'but you have some blood on your face. I suppose you don't want me mucking around trying to remove it . . . .'

'Thank you so much! The ladies won't shut up about it either. I explained I have had quite enough with people mucking around with my nose.'

'Just cosmetic—'

'That's the word, "cosmetic". So leave it alone!' he growled. Then he asked, reverting to a milder voice, 'So to the hospital for a blood transfusion then?'

I suggested he could rest a little, and we could see before taking him back to hospital.

'You're right there. They're kind in the hospital, but it's pretty dull.' He paused. And then he squeezed my hand and said, 'Nothing much seems to be working. I'm not breathing very well and my heart . . . To be honest, darling, I'm not quite sure. This may be approaching the end.'

'Well, Daddy, maybe. But you are looking pretty well to me. I suspect we just need to build up your blood again.'

'So hospital then?'

'Yes, probably. But I think you should rest now.'

'Well, that's good. And you'll be going back down to London tonight?'

'No, Daddy, I'm staying tomorrow.'

'Here tomorrow? That's good, darling. It's a great relief to have you here. You'll know what to do.' He closed his eyes for the moment.

'I think you should rest, Daddy. I will read to you.' I got out Charles Dickens's *A Child's History of England.*

> If you look at a Map of the World, you will see, in the left-hand upper corner of the Eastern Hemisphere, two Islands lying in the sea. They are England and Scotland, and Ireland. England and Scotland form the greater part of these Islands . . . The little neighbouring islands, which are so small upon the Map as to be mere dots, are chiefly little bits of Scotland – broken off, I dare say, in the course of a great length of time, by the power of the restless water.
>
> In the old days, a long, long while ago, before Our Saviour was born on earth and lay asleep in a manger, these Islands were in the same place, and the stormy sea roared round them, just as it roars now . . .

I read to him for about ten minutes. He looked at me most of the time, stroking my hand. Then he said, 'Darling, I think that's enough now. It's not that you're not reading well.' His voice was soft. He squeezed my hand encouragingly. 'You read very well. It's very good stuff,' he continued, more gently. 'But I think just now I'd rather talk to you. I'd like to know what's going on in your job, with politics.'

'Well, Daddy, mostly I'm thinking about my book. I have the first part – a Romantic, child's view of Scotland and my father, played against our walk on Hadrian's Wall. And I have the second part – my solo walk – where, to be honest, I think I got in a thorough muddle, and was bewildered by the people met in the Borders, and their sense of their own country and landscape. But I haven't got the third part. I haven't got the upbeat part where I bring it all together and come to some kind of conclusion about what kind of country Britain adds up to today.'

'Yes. Yes. I see that,' he said. 'You have got the Romantic beginning and then you've got the depressing bit . . .'

'But the problem is what is the future of our people and this land? What do you think?'

'The best thing about Britain is the Empire,' he said.

'Hmm. Yes. But that's the past, isn't it? I really meant the present.'

'Well, they could start by being proud of the past in the present.'

'There's a point. But I think that might be difficult for people. The Empire feels very far away.'

'Yes. You're right, of course, quite outside their experience.' He looked at me again. 'It's taken me a long time to realise that no one understands something they haven't experienced. The young academic I was working with on *Why Spy*?, for example – I was astonished by how much I took for granted that she simply didn't know. No experience.'

'So what is it that you were proud about with the Empire?'

'I gave a talk to some American academics in Hong Kong in the 1980s and I said, "If you're expecting an apology for the British Empire, you've got five minutes to leave." They stayed. And at the end they said they couldn't believe it. None of them had learned anything about what we had achieved.'

Although we had had this conversation so often, I still didn't feel I really knew why he thought the Empire was so great. That was odd. I tried again. 'So what *exactly* was so good about the Empire?'

He paused. Suddenly, he seemed tired again, struggling to concentrate. I worried he didn't really have an answer. 'Three case studies . . .' and he paused again. I worried that he was too tired to remember the list. Then he lifted his right arm vertically in the air, squinted up at the back of his hand, as he sometimes did when yawning and stretching, and recited: 'Penang, Singapore, Hong Kong. Penang was just a little pirate kingdom. The other two were basically barren rocks.' He seemed to have regained the strength in his voice. 'Other people talk a lot about democracy and the rule of law. But I feel it was more straightforward. They were blank sheets of paper, on which we wrote. We turned them into places to rival the mother country. Perhaps better. That was our legacy.'

He paused again, swinging the subject towards what he thought interested me. 'How about the Romans?' he asked. 'I don't know anything about the Romans.' Since our Hadrian's Wall walk he had often liked to emphasise how little he knew about the Romans. 'Did they improve things here in Britain?'

'Well, they certainly built roads, cities, transformed the economy.'

'And do all scholars agree on that?'

'Yes,' I said cautiously, 'they agree on that.'

'That's good,' he said, sounding slightly disappointed, as though he would have liked to join me in laying briefly into 'bloody academics'.

'But of course it didn't last. It all collapsed when the Romans left.'

'Yes. Poor Romans. I've always felt sorry for them. The barbarians . . .'

I wanted to revert to my conclusions. 'Anyway. Despite all the depressing aspects of the walk, I think there is something to be proud of in modern Britain. After all, I chose to live here – not in America or Afghanistan. I really enjoy my job, for example.'

'You really enjoy your job . . . that's very good, darling!' He looked into my eyes again.

'Yes. And I really admire the people. The chief executives who I work with in the National Parks for example – their freedom and energy. I love visiting them.'

'You're really getting into your job. I'm so pleased.' He squeezed my hand.

'And I think there is something very splendid about all types of British people. The fact that there are millions of people who know so much about their area, who volunteer . . .'

'That's right – local historians . . .' he suggested.

'And not only history. Naturalists, ecologists, experts on water quality. Hundreds of thousands of people in every street and hamlet in Britain, volunteering, full of ideas,' I insisted, convincing myself.

'And then,' said my father, 'there's Kevin Baverstock, with his book on a Lake District village. Have you seen it?' he asked. 'Great big book. Remarkable – on a single tiny village . . . Well, darling,' he ended, 'I should probably rest for a bit.'

112

I walked outside. It was hot, and the sky was a cloudless blue, a day which would not make my father's hands cold. Hay had just been taken from the whole front field, so that it looked like a mowed ten-acre lawn. My father told me that he had just counted sixty trees from this year's planting that had already emerged above their protective sleeves. 'Your trees along the north of the parklet are doing rather well,' he told me. So I looked at them. As he had said, the oaks were growing strongly, but the avenue of wild cherries that we had planted for my wedding was doing less well. As he had warned, they were 'brown and desiccated'. There was ragwort in the sunken field and no sign of Mairi the Highland cow.

I came back to the house and had just sat on the lawn to talk to my sister Annie when my younger sister Fiona came running out, shouting, 'Action!'

My father was sitting upright on his bed, coughing, when we entered his room. He nodded but did not speak. He wanted to be sick, it seemed, so I handed him a plastic jug, and he spat up some brown liquid. Then he lay down, but something was troubling him. 'Up,' he coughed. I pulled him upright. He shook his head. 'Not comfortable. Down.' I laid him down. 'Up' again, and he struggled upright.

'He likes to lie down,' Annie said.

I helped him down.

He pulled himself up again. 'Hot,' he said, and flapped his arms. We pulled his cashmere jumper off. He lay down again.

Annie went out to call the ambulance. Now he was rubbing his chest. 'Not good,' he said. 'Not good.'

I offered him his angina spray, which he used to spray under his tongue if he had chest pains. He shook his head. I asked if he was sure. He nodded.

Then he lay down, rolled his tongue back with his fingers and said, 'Now.' But before I could spray, he closed his mouth and shook his head.

Then he opened it again, and rolled his tongue back, nodding vigorously. I sprayed twice under his tongue.

Almost immediately he took one long heaving breath. There was a six-second pause, and then, to my relief, another long breath, drawing the air deep into his lungs. His eyes were open, but his eyeballs were rolled back in his head. Everything seemed focused entirely on the breathing. Another six-second pause, another great deep breath. He sounded just as he had by the swimming pool in Malaysia, taking a last deep breath before going underwater.

'That's right, Daddy,' I said, 'well done. In. Out. Come on, Daddy.' I opened his jaw and sprayed him again under the tongue while I kept talking to him. Annie passed me the phone and an emergency operator was talking to me. She asked me how he was breathing. 'He breathes every six seconds,' I said.

'Say "in" every time he breathes.' She listened to two sequences of breaths. I had been correct. It was six seconds between each breath.

'Place him on the floor,' she instructed me.

I didn't understand this, but I pulled him out of bed, with my arms under his legs and shoulders, and laid him in the narrow space between the bed and his desk.

'Now I want you to press 160 times on his chest with the heel of your hand. Hard. One. Two.'

I cracked first his lower left rib. Then his lower right rib. I kept up the rhythmic pressure. 'Fourteen. Fifteen.'

Much sooner than I could have hoped, the ambulance team came in. His breath was still coming clearly, every six seconds. I handed him over to them. I watched as they put pads on his chest, and a mask on his mouth. Then I left the room.

My mother had been asleep, having spent the whole of the previous two nights on the floor by his bed. Now she was in the hall, with Annie, Fiona and Raul. 'What is going on?' my mother asked. I explained that I thought that he had had a heart attack. They had connected him to some machines. I suggested a cup of tea. Then I suggested my mother go out to the lawn with my sister. I waited in the hall.

I had been there twenty minutes when the ambulance team leader came out. She was a large friendly lady, with short white hair and what my father would have called 'smile-lines' on her face, who had come to see my father earlier in the week. 'What would you like to do?' she asked. I looked at her, puzzled, and she added, 'Do you want us to take him to hospital and try to connect him to the machines or . . . ?'

'Oh,' I said, 'I see. I better ask my mother and sisters.'

I walked outside.

'They have asked what we want to do,' I said.

'What does that mean?'

'I think they mean that they want us to decide whether to stop.'

'Only you can decide, darling.'

I returned inside. 'So you've not managed to get him going again?'

'It's only his pacemaker keeping him going now.'

'I see. And I suppose after a few minutes without oxygen, his brain would be damaged?'

She shrugged. This could have meant she agreed, or perhaps she didn't, that this wasn't exactly the problem. I didn't understand. Had it all been over when that first breath came? Or when I was compressing his chest? Or shortly after I handed him to the ambulance team? When?

'Well, I suppose then you had better stop.'

'Are you sure?'

'Yes.'

I walked with her back into his bedroom. She said something and a machine was switched off. She looked at her watch.

'Mark down the time of death as 4.03.'

113

I asked the ambulance team to place my father back in his bed. Different people had turned up now. The ambulance crew was joined by the police. 'Ah,' said the police sergeant, 'this is the gentleman who was a friend of Anderson the accordion player?' There was talk about which morgue he should go to – perhaps it had to be Dundee until the weekend. Andrew Gauld, the undertaker, came. My mother kept asking me what all these different people wanted. Was I sure that the undertaker was the Episcopalian, not the Church of Scotland, undertaker? 'I knew your father,' said the undertaker. 'He came to see me a few years ago, to ask whether he could be buried on his land. I said I couldn't see any problem with that.'

Finally, my mother and I went back into the room. The sheets were pulled up to my father's chin. His face was completely drained of blood. The skin was drawn very tight and thin over his cheeks. His eyes were open, and the pupils were still rolled upwards. His head was back, his mouth was open, and I could see that the yellow stubs at the back of his lower jaw were hardly teeth any more.

My mother held his right hand. I could now do what he had been reluctant to let me do, half an hour earlier, and clean the blood off his eyebrows and nose. I rubbed gently, but some of the flakes were caked in, and I didn't want to scrub too hard for fear of damaging his thin skin. When I kissed his forehead it was already a little cold, but his left hand, which I was holding under the sheets, was still warm. I stroked the freckles and the fine knuckles.

My little sister, Fiona, who has Down's syndrome, joined us. I suggested she kiss his forehead. She did so, very quickly. 'His eyes are open,' she said. I tried to close them. They closed a little, but not completely. 'How about his mouth?' When I tried to close his jaw for her, there was a noise in his throat. 'Ah ha! I think maybe he is still alive,' she said. 'His mouth is open for breathing.'

'No, darling, it is just that the muscles do this,' I tried to explain.

'I see,' she said, and after a bit she left.

My mother and I said an Our Father by his bed. And then I continued holding his hand, perhaps for an hour, patting him, and kissing his forehead again a few times. 'Poor sweet Daddy,' I said then.

'I'm not quite sure that's the right word for him,' said my mother. She was crying.

That night I shared my mother's bedroom to keep her company. I could not sleep. Despite his age, my father was not someone who had seemed likely to die. His father and mother had made it to ninety-two and eighty-seven with worse medicine, without all my father's fitness routines, diets, projects, resources and future ideas. We had been having a typical, lively conversation, only ten minutes before he died. So that was it. His last full sentence was a reference to a large book on the Lake District, which I wasn't sure he had read. His last word was 'up', or perhaps 'down'.

The ambulance had appeared within three minutes. He was still breathing when I handed him to them. They had strapped an oxygen mask to him, and pads to his chest. So I had assumed they had been in time, that it was just another near-miss, like the time I had found him, fifteen years earlier, bitten by a wasp – just as unconscious, eyes rolled back, frothing at the mouth, looking even more dead. Then he had revived after a single injection.

He had enjoyed talking about living 'three score years and ten', and it was more than twenty-three years since he had reached that point. He had always been so old that when I was at school, I had wondered whether he might die, and if so whether I could miss my exams. I had thought of writing a book about him 'after he died'. And any number of conversations over the last twenty years had seemed as though they might be our last. Which is why in part I had always focused so hard on remembering what he said. But no conversation had ever actually been our last.

I remembered our last exchange too exactly. I kept thinking through it, stage by stage, as I lay there awake, clarifying the narrative of his death. And I did not like narrating these things to myself.

How had his relationship with me – whom he called his 'very best', and sometimes, when reflecting on his friends who had been killed in the war, his 'only' friend – fared over the last few years? I felt he had begun to give me less and less advice, had stopped producing so many ideas about my job or future; had ceased to engage entirely with the topics I was working on; had resorted increasingly to answering my questions with the words 'not my subject'.

We had walked around his 'mini-park' together perhaps a hundred or two hundred times. I had probably said twenty times, as we passed the chestnuts, that they were too closely planted and needed to be thinned. At least half a dozen times, he had marked the chestnuts by cutting the bark with his hand-saw, or with a can of spray-paint that he carried in his pocket, and said they would get round to it. He never did, and I knew he never would, because he had other priorities in the garden.

When I opened my eyes, I saw an image not of my father, but of what he would have called 'the cadaver'. Not, as he feared from the portrait, looking 'melancholy, perplexed, lost', but mouth and eyes agape, looking – in death – ten years older and frailer than I had ever seen him.

He had said to me in that last conversation, 'It's a great relief to have you here. You'll know what to do.' But he had also hinted that he thought he should go to the hospital at once, and I had instead suggested we wait. He had been right, and I had been wrong. Why had he initially resisted the angina spray? Had he recently used it, and worried he would overdose? Had I hurt him with the spray? At what point exactly had he died?

Nine months earlier, I had been on a floor, balancing the phone between my head and my shoulder, while an emergency operator spoke to me. On that occasion I was delivering Wolf. The labour had come too quickly to get to hospital, or summon an ambulance team or midwife. 'Can you see the head? Okay, press it back in with the palm of your hand. Gently now. Don't let it come too quickly. Can you see the forehead? The nose? Good. Tell her to push it out, hard. Good. Check his neck for the umbilical cord, gently now – lay him on her chest.' I had felt good about myself for delivering the baby efficiently, and imagined I was good at medical emergencies. Not this time. My chest compressions had not saved my father.

Worse, when the ambulance team asked me whether they should continue, I had told them to stop.

114

I finally calmed myself about an hour before dawn by playing a recording of the meditations of the emperor Marcus Aurelius. My father was, I remembered, not interested in Marcus Aurelius. 'Give me Sun Tzu any day.' His favourite author was the Cumbrian George MacDonald Fraser. He had wanted me to write about MacDonald Fraser in this book. He adored his over-sexed, charming and unreliable imperial hero Flashman. And he particularly liked his story 'The General Danced at Dawn', in which a Highland regiment in Libya shortly after the war distracts a pompous general, who was about to fail them at their inspection, by gathering a group of passing Bedouin and bottle-washers to dance. Not an eightsome, but a hundred-and-twenty-eightsome reel. He identified with the subversive dancers.

We had discussed where he might be buried at Broich. Five years earlier, I had taken him to a spot half a mile from the house, deep in the woods – a high, flower-covered bank above the lochan that he had excavated. Dark ancient alders towered below, tall cherries climbed the slopes. I suggested we could build an ashlar-faced mausoleum, cut into the hillside, and row his coffin on a boat across the lochan. We could lay rows of empty tombs within the vault for future generations.

'Hmm, darling . . .' he said.

'A little morbid, Daddy?'

'Perhaps a little.'

We walked back through the woods. 'And it is rather a long way from the house. I'd like you all to visit me from time to time. I wouldn't mind just being cremated and having my ashes scattered.'

But perhaps to please me, he had also asked the undertaker whether it was permitted for him to be buried at Broich.

The next morning, I walked out to another spot which I thought might be suitable. It was a small clearing, really a glade, in the woods, about 300 yards from the house. He had unfortunately left a lot of stuff in the glade: four trailers (one stripped off the base of an old touring caravan), a crane, a small Italian harvesting machine, the shell of a quad bike, 200 plastic tree shelters, and about half a mile of electric fencing and barbed wire. But I thought that if we moved it all it would work well. I took my mother to see the spot, and she, loyally, pronounced it 'Lovely, darling.'

115

That afternoon, looking for a way to think about him, I remembered a morning together in Hué in Vietnam – on the same trip where we saw the honey-bear's tree, when my father was eighty-eight. We had walked outside and watched the mist drifting around the lower slopes of the green hills and above the sails of the narrow fishing boats. Teenagers were kicking shuttlecocks back and forth in the air beside the walls of the palace.

Although it was already eighty degrees, my father was wearing a blue blazer and trews in the black and green tartan of the Black Watch. His highly polished black brogues showed up the mud on my boots. In his left hand he carried a ski stick. In my right I carried a bag containing his Boots disposable camera and eight books on Vietnamese history, each of which had lines that he had energetically underlined. We crossed roads slowly, arm in arm, as some form of magical protection against the never-ceasing flow of mopeds with drivers wearing what appeared to be toy plastic helmets.

'We must look like a pretty nutty pair,' said my father.

He had already been out at first light, reading his Vietnamese dictionary over a cup of tea at a street stall. 'Vietnamese,' he observed, 'is easy if you speak Cantonese and Mandarin.' He spotted an elephant, but failed to persuade me to ride it. It had been difficult to convince him not to climb onto a motorbike.

'Boats is the answer,' he said.

But no one we met had any idea how to hire a boat.

'Sit down, darling, and give me ten minutes,' he said.

I sat on a bench by the river. He was gone a long time. And then there was the sound of a horn, and I looked down to see him waving at me from the prow of a motorboat.

That afternoon, I suggested he should rest. But while I was writing another email to the Cumberland Infirmary, he slipped out and came back two hours later, having marched the two miles back from the market in the midday heat. When I noticed his very red face, he announced, 'I don't think much of this pacemaker.'

Half an hour later, revived by a beer, he persuaded me to accompany him forty miles outside the city to see a battleground. Once there, he clambered into the Vietcong tunnel system. Then, on the basis of his experience as an anti-tank gunner in 1944, he held forth on the weak points of a ruined tank. In the evening, he discovered a toy-stall selling a battery-operated official in medieval robes, and listened to a man playing a bamboo flute. We shared a bowl of white rice by a lake.

He had last been in the country forty-three years before, as a British diplomat during the Vietnam War. He reminded me that he had been struck by the confidence of the North Vietnamese, at a time when many were arguing that they were being beaten. He had argued strongly in 1967 that the US would not win the war. And I remembered he had told me, when he came to visit me in Afghanistan, that we wouldn't win there either.

But what I learned most from him was not about international affairs. It was his approach to life: his Get On With It energy, which made him reinvent himself daily, even in his tenth decade. In the fierce heat and dust of the Imperial City, he scrabbled around with his walking stick to uncover a shard of porcelain. He no sooner arrived at a hotel than he was out again, on the streets, searching for a lost building with only a map as his guide. He tore through books, marking stories, noting new thoughts. Every evening he had a new story or connection to make between what we had seen and what we had done.

It was an attitude to life, then, and a resilience. I was only half conscious of the many ways in which he had modestly concealed how he was better than me – in singing, in his languages, in his sense of engineering or art, and in his promptitude and energy in work. In the end, I felt, his legacy was not some grand philosophical or political vision, but playfulness, and a delight in action.

We went for a swim that night in Vietnam. I don't remember learning to walk but I remember him teaching me how to swim. The freckles on his shoulders and the scar from a shrapnel wound in his thigh, which I had admired as a four year old, were still there. So were his deep breaths and slow underwater breaststroke and the way he emerged like a walrus from the water. 'It is wonderful,' he said, 'to be in water. I feel old on land. I have to walk slowly, think about my balance. But here I am weightless. I can swim as fast as I always could, travel underwater as far.'

I watched from the side while he attempted again and again to swim the whole length of the pool without breathing. He stayed in the water, till it was dark and I was cold.

116

Two days after he died I received from the local vicar a copy of the funeral instructions my father had left. He had written:

> Wonderful family. And the best wife and children I could hope for. As to my faith; it is a simple one. The Church and its music have been part of my life for as long as I can remember. For that too I thank God. Hereunder is my formal contribution to the Stewart of Broich file.
>
> 1) I have no strong views on the subject, but all things being equal, and legally possible, I should prefer to be buried with my dogs, at home.
>
> 2) If, however, Sally and Rory would prefer something different, so be it.
>
> 3) I am disinterested in whether I am cremated or not. Once again the views of Sally and my children, not mine, should prevail.
>
> Memorial or funeral service: The form is not of importance to me, but I hope that tears will be minimised and jollity will prevail.

And then, having said he had no firm views, he proceeded characteristically to lay out clear orders, for anyone inclined to follow them:

> If there is to be a formal farewell, I should like a piper to play a traditional lament, followed by a bugler to play the last post, particularly in memory of those who were killed in action in the war. The wake: plenty to drink, alcoholic and non-alcoholic, and plenty to eat (finger food, sausages, high-class sandwiches, better still, the Robbs and their spit). Perhaps we can borrow my old school for service and chapel. To sum up, gaiety, even perhaps song and dance, should be the hallmark of the exercise.

> If the weather is fine, a farewell strip the willow, 8some, a dashing white sergeant and gay gordons would not tax the young or the old.

The gardener, Natasha, who had been tasked with removing the barbed wire and trailers from the glade to create an elegant space for my father's grave, came to see me. 'I really don't want to interfere,' she said, 'but I just wondered whether your mother might not be interested in a couple of other spots, which are a little neater?' So I took my mother to the places Natasha had suggested.

One was my father's mother's garden, where her roses still grew, neatly boxed in by high walls of yew and beech. My father had been cutting the great clusters of silver birch in order to let the afternoon sun fall on the garden, and to give views of the sunset from the bench. This had made me angry. I loved those silver birch trunks – their leaves yellow in the autumn, pale trunks stretching back deep into the woods in the winter. They had taken forty years to grow to that height, yet he had cut them down. I had insisted we plant more, but they died. Every year I stubbornly bought more, and planted them as a rebuke. Every year they failed to take again. It was too dark now under the beech for them to get established. My father's clearance stayed.

In the corner of this garden were three sandstone megaliths, seven feet high and two feet wide. They looked like Neolithic standing stones, but were in fact the sandstone pillars which we had bought from the old Crieff golf club. Under them were buried his dogs. When I read in his instructions that he was interested in 'being buried with his dogs at Broich', I realised that he probably meant he wanted to go in their tombs, and had been cutting back the birch so there would be a fine evening sunlight over his grave. I agreed with my mother, however, that it seemed a 'little peculiar' to be interred in a pet cemetery.

She chose the second spot, at the south-east corner of the garden, atop the forty-foot Broich bank. Unlike the glade I had chosen deep in the woods, she said this was a place she could visit every day. She suggested we dig a double grave.

★

We oriented his grave on the Neolithic Broich cursus line which ran through the middle of our land – dug 5,000 years ago with reindeer antlers, and spotted by a Second World War plane – a monument more ancient than the Pyramids, on our land, which I had often taken him to see, and which he rarely seemed to remember was there.

His body was to be laid about 300 yards from the cursus but parallel to it, pointing across the same valley – his head in the Highlands, his feet in the Lowlands. The gravedigger was a friend of Natasha's. He was also a biker. He wore his cap in the cab of the yellow JCB – the machine my father loved best for digging up the ground. The funeral director was not impressed.

'Do you have a cover for the grave?' he asked the gravedigger.

'No.'

'How about straps to lower the coffin?'

'Well, I could get something off the truck . . .'

'The funeral is on Thursday. When were you planning to fill it in again?' asked the funeral director.

'Well, I don't know, I'm off to a wedding at the weekend. Maybe Monday?'

'Don't you think the family would prefer not to have an open grave in their back garden for four days?'

'Oh, aye. I see your point,' said the gravedigger. 'I'll ask a mate if he can come round on the night and fill it in.'

He leapt into the cab again and started digging. He was going six feet deep and three feet wide for a double grave as my mother had requested. The funeral director was worried that it was too deep, and the soil would become unstable and collapse inward. He asked whether we could put railway sleepers on the edge, so we didn't fall in when lowering the coffin. No one had any.

As the biker worked he grinned at me. 'Finders keepers right, if I turn up a Roman coin?'

He did a surprisingly neat job. And, to my relief, the earth was deep and firm and the sides held, even at a double depth. However, the area seemed unkempt after the grass had been trimmed.

Walking back to the house, I saw the cast-iron railings decorated with thistles that my father and I had bought a decade earlier, and which we had been unable to find a function for. I carried them over in pieces. They fitted exactly around the edge of the grave.

117

At two in the afternoon, the chaplain from my father's school, Glenalmond, came to consecrate the ground. Then we – my mother, my sisters, my brothers-in-law, my nephew, Shoshana, Wolf, Raul and his family – all drove up to the school. I stood outside the school chapel and watched the small groups approaching across the quadrangle in the afternoon sun. We held the funeral only five days after he had died, and I was not expecting that many would have heard, or could come. But they came: in pairs, in families, and one by one.

The school chapel was unchanged, in every detail, from the chapel in which my father had sat each morning singing the same hymns that he had asked us to sing. He had sat there on over a thousand separate occasions: bored, singing in the choir, pulling faces at his brother or perhaps genuinely moved by prayer. Now, almost exactly eighty years since he had first entered the chapel, he was there for the last time, lying in a pine coffin in front of the altar.

As we followed the coffin out, we passed a glass cabinet. It contained a book of the Glenalmond war dead. It was opened to the photograph of his brother George, in Black Watch uniform, taken when he was twenty-three. George was half turned, back at a jaunty angle, his legs crossed in his kilt, smiling, his tam-o'-shanter with its red hackle caught in sepia, just before he was killed by the German shell.

★

We drove back from the chapel and through the Highlands, past the Roman fort he had helped to excavate with his brother as a schoolboy in the 1930s. The sun was on all the slopes of the Sma' Glen. When we reached Broich, six of us lifted the coffin, and then, led by the piper and three clergy, we carried it down an avenue of rhododendrons towards his burial place, followed by a hundred mourners, the ladies sinking in their impractical heels into the deep mud.

To our left ran my father's mini-Versailles: a new canal, constructed from pieces of plywood and plastic sheeting with the slate, propped not nailed, so that the pale wood was visible beneath. Beyond the canal was a hole he had created a month earlier with his JCB. The earth had been dug out from a hill, composed of most of the demolished old wing of the house. (He had dumped it there to save money.) As my father dug, he had uncovered broken bottles, bricks, and ceramic from the kitchen sinks. These had been removed, but he had not finished the edges, which were crumbling, and Himalayan balsam had begun to cluster on the far rim in a scandal of pink.

The 'Princcipal purpose' of the hole, as he explained in the email six days before his death, was to be 'a paddling pool for the Wolf and a place for his sailboats, yachts, launches, speed boats and to play cops and robbers with radio controlled boats'. It was twelve feet long and ten feet deep. I had had to put two benches in front of it, to prevent anyone from falling in during the burial service.

Purple heather, sent from the hills of Abercairny and Monzie, had been heaped around the grave. While we lowered the coffin, a family member on each of the eight ropes, two buglers played the Last Post, not always in unison. I held the Wolf in my arms, and when the Black Watch piper played the regimental lament the Wolf's legs pumped back and forth, dancing.

An outsider might have been forgiven for thinking this was some traditional Stewart ceremony. But actually no one else would be buried in this way. A pseudo-state funeral was being enacted down a muddy path, behind the rhododendrons, the buglers and pipers could not quite work out who was to have the last note, and we were standing in a circle around his grave, not in a distant chapel, but in the garden, only thirty yards from the house. It was a 'tradition' which in fact – like his Penang dragon-boat races – was entirely invented.

But none of this seemed to rock the dignity of the regimental slow march, led by the chaplains and the military pipers. And as we marched back – under the eye of a stone Javanese lion, over a piece of plastic pond-liner that had come loose from his waterfall, past the quad bikes, ride-on mowers and rusting trailers that stood behind the thin hedge – we marched as a company of a hundred mourners, mostly in kilts, to the sound of the regimental pipe-tune – the quick marches that he had hummed on all his marches – 'Hielan' Laddie' and 'Black Bear'.

As a very old man he had seemed to me – too often – to have become a little querulous and blustering. His repeated insistence on his brief role in the Battle of Rauray had made me wonder how brave he had really been. But his last moments had rebuked me. He had known that he would die soon, and told me as much quite calmly, but didn't argue the point when I resisted it. He had laid out on his desk the papers and files in perfect order, ready for the 'handover'. And I had watched him giving calm commands throughout the final heart attack, fighting it step by step, without a hint of panic or confusion.

'Are you afraid of death, Daddy?' I'd asked on our walk along Hadrian's Wall.

'Can't really see the point in that,' he'd replied.

★

The piper led us to the top of the bank. The rich August sun fell on the leaves of the cherries – and further out it touched the deodars, which we had planted together, and the oaks which had been planted in 1746. This was the weather when he felt that what he still called the 'sheep park' was 'close to perfection'.

He would have been pleased that we had found and erected his flimsy car-park signs, and with the way the east end of the field had been converted into the car park with just enough rubber matting to stop too many cars sinking into the mud. He would have liked the way that the marquee fitted over the yew bushes, which he had just planted in front of the breeze-block ha-ha, and reassured by the sight of the Robbs and their roast suckling pig. But he wouldn't have liked everyone standing around with their plates looking gloomy.

So I asked the piper to play a dance. My father would not have been sure about this – 'Bloody difficult dancing to a piper – where's Anderson the accordion player?' But he would have enjoyed the slight horror on all the English faces – and some of the Scottish – when I asked everyone to line up for the dance. Some sat stubbornly at the tables, others took a sudden interest in the lime trees or appointed themselves officer-commanding-Torquil-the-dog.

But most of us gathered on the uneven lawn and slowly began to dance. We were dancing an eightsome reel. Or, to be precise, a fifty-sevensome. First, round in a circle. 'It's a square, darling, not a circle.' Our feet were striking back and forth on the green turf. We turned directly in front of his study window, out of which he had peered every day, pondering the shadows, the light, and the potential for more earthworks on the lawn. 'Round for eight, and then back for eight. Set. Twice.' Then off in a giant accelerating chain of hands, racing to get round and back to their partners. Sandy Stewart of Ardvorlich had, I saw, pulled his Victorian black kilt jacket out of the back of a cupboard, where it had grown more green mould around the lapels; Bill Drummond-Moray had lent me his black jacket, so was in tweed. Roderick Leslie-Melville and Thomas Steuart-Fothringham were wearing blue bonnets; Jane Willoughby wore a black bonnet over her tartan cape.

Then ladies into the middle. 'How many? It hardly matters, we're just making it up as we go along.' My little sister Fiona set to me in a leaping hop, her elbows pinned to her side, and her hands raised beside her shoulders, waving back and forth. The eightsome was my father's staple. I had photographs of him dancing it in the same kilt that I was wearing – the one made by the regimental tailor of the Calcutta Scottish – in Shanghai, and Kuala Lumpur. The eightsome was not originally Scottish at all, it was a French quadrille – a dance for four couples, arranged in a square – perfected in the court of Louis XIV. Some Scot had inserted some Highland steps – and that was how Queen Victoria was painted dancing it with her kilted children at Balmoral. And somehow, as it had faded in the rest of Europe, it had survived, here, in Scotland.

Then the men went into the middle. My nephew Gordon danced on the ground in some combination of Russian Cossack and 1980s breakdance. The Black Watch officers, who always learned the dances with men in the mess, and not women, spun each other. (The three senior officers from the Black Watch's last great action at the Hook in Korea – David Rose, Angus Rowan-Hamilton and Angus Irwin – had died before my father, but their three sons were there.) Andrew McCosh, who had made it back from the British Embassy in Turkey, twirled like a top. Felix, who was up from London, had somehow found himself in Andrew's tweed trousers. I'm not sure my father would have really approved of the way Felix swung his legs in the 'paddy-bar'.

The quadrille was an elegant dance for eight. It could be expanded with great ingenuity to a sixteensome. And my father's favourite comic story, set in Libya, had even imagined a 128-some. But we were fifty-seven. Terrain, emotion, the pipe drones and the uneven numbers meant that partners missed each other, figures of eight had to be abandoned in mid-move. The four good pipers in the set had to keep putting us right – pulling us with voice and muscle – into the next movement. But everyone instinctively saw the nature of a fifty-sevensome. Everyone grasped that what mattered was not what it meant, or exactly how the dance was supposed to work – what mattered was to get on with it.

Portrait of Brian Stewart by Paul Benney

Chronology

THE MIDDLELAND

The Middleland – a term invented by my father: The geographical centre of the island of Britain. An upland landscape, whose core is the Lake District hills, the Pennines, the Cheviots and the Scottish Borders, but whose fringes extend to the Humber in the south and the Firth of Forth and Clyde in the north. A land naturally unified by geography and culture for two thousand years, but repeatedly divided by political frontiers.

ORIGINS (before AD100)

The tribes of the Middleland in the centuries before the Roman invasion form a single cultural zone, stretching across what is now southern Scotland and northern England. Their scattered buildings and largely non-ceramic-using culture distinguish them from the ceramic/stone tower culture of Highland Scotland or the large hill forts and coinage of southern England.

MILITARY FRONTIER (AD100–400) see map p. 58

The Roman wall is laid straight through the tribal territories of the Middleland, dividing them – leaving the shrine of the Carvetii tribe god, Cocidius, north of the wall, while their population centre is south of it, and leaving most of the Votadini tribe, north, while their settlement at Corbridge is marooned south of the wall. The entire area, both sides of the wall, becomes a Roman military zone: there are none of the villas found in the civilian south of Roman Britain, instead the area is dominated for three hundred years by permanent garrisons of 15,000 soldiers, from regiments originally raised elsewhere in the Roman Empire.

CUMBRIA AND NORTHUMBRIA

THE OLD NORTH (AD400–600) see map p. 123

When the Romans leave, the frontier-line of the wall fades, and Cumbric-speaking groups reassert themselves in kingdoms, which stretch across the wall. The Roman military zone becomes a Welsh-speaking culture known as 'The Old North', known for its poetry, such as the *Gododdin*.

GOLDEN AGE OF NORTHUMBRIA (AD600–800)

By 600 almost all of the Middleland from the Humber to Edinburgh has come under the control of the kingdom of Northumbria – a Germanic-speaking culture, which becomes one of the leading civilisations in Christendom, known for its theology, sculpture, astronomy, manuscript illumination – and in particular for its historian, Bede, and its saint, Cuthbert.

NORSE INVASIONS (AD800–900) see map p. 139

The invasions of non-Christian groups by sea from Scandinavia – the 'Vikings' – inflict terrible damage on the Kingdom of Northumbria – and in particular on the monasteries which are the heart of its civilisation.

MIDDLELAND (900–1066) see map p. 155

By the middle of the tenth century, areas such as the Lake District are an ethnic patchwork of Cumbric-Welsh, Northumbrian-Germanic, and Norse-Viking communities. The core of the Middleland is dominated by the Cumbric kingdom of Strathclyde / Cumbria in the west and Northumbria in the east; these territories still stretch deep into modern Scotland and northern England, in defiance of the Roman wall. But the West Saxon kings of England are beginning to move north, and the Gaelic kings of Scotland are beginning to move south, squeezing the Middleland kingdoms between them.

THE MARCHES

NORMAN BORDERS (1066–1150)

In 1070, the final autonomy of the Middleland is crushed by William the Conqueror, and by the slave-raids of the Scottish king. A new border emerges out of the Roman Wall, and eventually runs diagonally from the wall in the west to Berwick in the east, right through the centre of the old Northumbrian/Cumbrian nations. Much of the land is now designated as 'Royal Forest' on which it is illegal to settle or farm. Vast areas are reduced to depopulated wilderness.

MONASTIC REVIVAL (1150–1300)

Recovery begins with monks, initially attracted to the wilderness as a retreat, but whose energy begins to rebuild the economy. There is now a formal border between England and Scotland. But the monastic orders and the aristocratic families still own vast estates on both sides of the border, and do not clearly define themselves as either English or Scottish – their culture is Latin and Norman-French – and they are closely tied to European Christendom.

THE MARCHES (1300–1600)

The Scottish Wars of Independence led by William Wallace and Robert the Bruce bring a final break between England and Scotland. And the border takes on a brutal reality: cross-border landholdings disappear, it becomes illegal to marry across the border, or travel across it without permission. The core of the Middleland is redesignated as the Marches – a zone of fighting and cross-border raids, financed by the English and Scottish Crowns. Driven by this proxy war, the region becomes lawless, wild and dangerous.

UNION

THE MIDDLE SHIRES (1600–1750)

The Scottish Stuart King James VI also becomes King of England, and the Union of the Crowns means the disappearance of the border, and with it the rationale for the proxy war and the border raids. Within forty years, this 'cockpit of violence' has become one of the most peaceful areas in the country. But the legal differences between England and Scotland begin to create stark differences in landholding, leading to a pattern of small traditional farms on the English side, and larger 'modern' estates on the Scottish. In 1745, Bonnie Prince Charlie, the Stuart claimant to the throne, marches through the Borders with little fighting.

ROMANTICS AND VICTORIANS (1750–1900)

For Walter Scott, the Borders landscape is now defined by its distant past, preserved in ballads and oral history. For William Wordsworth the more southerly hills represent the restorative power of nature and the pastoral world. Together these two writers make the Middleland the central landscape of the European Romantic movement.

MILITARY MARGINS (1900–2000) see map p. 188

The arrival of the First World War brings the War Office's attention to the Middleland. Suddenly its position as a sparsely-populated area, far from the capitals, makes it again an ideal location for military projects. Over the following decades, tens of thousands of acres are turned over to munitions depots, airfields, forestry for trench-props, submarine aerials, nuclear material manufacture, and rocket testing.

DARK SKIES (2000–)

By the twenty-first century, many of these industries have vanished or are shrinking. The low population and the marginal land attracts the attention of environmentalists, who see the potential of the uplands and wetlands to promote carbon-capture, and protect vulnerable species.

Acknowledgements

To Patrick Mackie, Stephen Brown and John Hatt, who read the book in many versions, with great patience, sympathy and intelligence, and who not only improved it immeasurably but also gave me the confidence to cut nearly 300 pages of the text. To Robin Dennis, who came in at the last moment and worked her way deftly through the prose. To Andy Connell and Alastair Duncan, who provided a wise and rapid review of some of my local history.

To Felix Martin and Tommy Wide, who brought the eyes of friends to the story itself.

To Catherine Anderson, who helped me plan the solo walk. To Clare Dodd, who supported all the logistics of the journey and then transcribed almost 300,000 words of interviews from tapes, and to many others who worked closely with me throughout.

I was very lucky to have Dan Franklin as my editor. His faith in the project from the beginning and throughout is what made this project possible. He read with immense care and intelligence in draft after draft. And he gave me the unique gift of time, reworking the schedule to make sure that the book in the end was 'right'. I have never worked with such a patient and understanding editor and I don't think I shall ever find another like him.

Thank you also to Clare Alexander for championing me and backing me through the last few years. And to, my father's friend, Kevin Baverstock, who having done all the maps for the book which he and my father wrote about the Battle of Rauray, with great care and generosity did all the maps for this book as well.

And finally to Shoshana, my best companion, and to my mother, two people who should have dominated the book, but who chose to remain on the sidelines, and supported it with so much love, energy and tolerance of antique obsessions and late nights throughout.

Lines from 'Lament of the Frontier Guard' by Ezra Pound are reprinted by kind permission of Faber & Faber Ltd.

Index